dig deeper

dig deeper

Seasonal, sustainable
Australian gardening

Meredith Kirton

MURDOCH BOOKS

Contents

Spring   10

Summer   130

Preface

Dig was published in 2004. Ten years later, it is a dream fulfilled to update my first book with *Dig Deeper*, which I hope lives up to its name, in so much as it offers greater insight into horticulture. Certainly on a personal front it has required a lot of sacrifice, patience and love to get the book to where it is now. Then, my preface ended with the phrase 'Remember, a garden starts but never finishes'. The same can be said about keeping information about gardening and plants up to date.

So much has happened in the last decade. Droughts, water restrictions, climate change, new discoveries in pest control and breakthroughs in plant breeding are just some of the things that have moulded *Dig Deeper*. There's a green focus to this book, and I hope that the green-tinted tips featured throughout give you some ideas on making your backyard more environmentally sustainable and that the recommended plants prove to be resilient and reliable.

In the future it will be the gardeners and farmers who will have to learn how best to manage the opportunities and challenges presented by rising temperatures and more extreme weather patterns. It's just as well that both these occupations have never shied away from adverse situations.

Many gardening techniques are like craft skills, passed down in person from one generation to the next; sadly, that means that some skills are lost over time. Within these pages you'll find many of these techniques, explained and illustrated clearly step by step, or broken down into easy-to-follow points.

Just like its precursor, *Dig Deeper* has been photographed over a year to capture the changing seasons and all the gardening world has to offer in terms of flowers, fruits, stems, nuts and so on. Many of these photographs feature in double-page spreads so that you can explore in detail a specific genus or other aspect of nature's bounty. I'm grateful to those who have shared their gardens and knowledge in making this possible, and they are named in the Acknowledgments section.

My own experience over the last decade has also shaped this book. My husband and I now own a farm with a two-acre garden called 'The Top Place', on the New South Wales mid-north coast, at Johns River. Making and maintaining this garden continues to be a great teacher for me, and in turn, I hope through this book you might glean some useful insights too.

Occasionally open to the public, 'The Top Place' will, one day I hope, draw others to come and learn the art of gardening, to design and draw, or simply to sit and enjoy the ambience of this patch of paradise with some home-grown farm fare; it's a cornucopia of delights to share.

While gardening fashions may come and go, sensible advice, great plants and good design are here to stay. All can be found within this book, I am proud to say, and it should be a very useful tool for the creation of your own Eden.

They will be like a tree planted by the water that sends out its roots by the stream. It does not fear when heat comes; its leaves are always green. It has no worries in a year of drought and never fails to bear fruit.

JEREMIAH 17:8

8

Introduction

The gardening year naturally divides into four seasons, each characterised by certain events, cycles of life and the weather. This book is likewise divided into spring, summer, autumn and winter, following nature's pattern.

Each of the four chapters begins with an overview, a synopsis of what the season has in store. The further divisions—such as 'Shrubs and trees'—are based on a plant's function and form in the garden. Delving further into these will give you a deeper understanding of the mainstays of traditional gardening, including some old favourites, and introduce you to some exciting new developments in horticulture; for example, grasses are no longer just to be mown into a turf, and have a place in the ornamental garden too.

Weather and climate

There is a worldwide agricultural zone system, which is based on minimum temperatures, as this is the greatest limiting factor when it comes to plant growth. There are, however, many factors that affect the climate of an area, including latitude, altitude, wind direction and velocity, as well as the proximity to physical features such as mountains or the sea.

Climate affects plant growth, most obviously by determining how many months per year plants can actually grow. Generally, the cooler the climate, the shorter the growth period, but extremely high temperatures or low rainfall can also be limiting factors. In addition, climate affects when seeds germinate or plants flower.

In future decades, spiking high temperatures and inhospitable low ones may create conditions incapable of supporting many of the plants we have loved and treasured traditionally. This will make clever gardening even more important, especially the manipulation of microclimates.

Microclimates are created naturally by such factors as the slope of the land, depressions creating 'frost pockets', proximity to the coast, modifying breezes and the position of the sun. Planting trees or building structures such as pergolas can also manipulate the microclimate, and thus help plants to grow in areas outside their optimum zones.

Each plant has evolved to suit its particular zone, so changing its climate can result in spectacular growth or miserable failure. Many plants have evolved with some adaptations to suit their conditions: succulent foliage or grey leaves to help cope with dry, hot conditions, or large leaves with drip points that help rainforest plants survive low light levels and high humidity. Many grey-leaved plants will therefore rot in humid areas and, likewise, rainforest plants will burn in too much sun.

Weather is the day-to-day prevailing condition. This seasonally changes, with spring and autumn characterised by milder temperatures, summer by hotter temperatures and winter by cooler ones. These seasonal changes are most noticeable away from the equator, where temperature changes little but rainfall patterns are normally grouped into wet and dry seasons.

Phenology

How do you know it's spring? Just because the calendar reads 1 September doesn't mean that spring has arrived. The answer will depend not on the date but on the weather in your area.

Australia is such a vast continent that climatic conditions vary enormously from one area to another.

Perth to Sydney and Cairns to Hobart will enjoy spring at different times, so look for nature's clues—if the birds are singing loudly, bare branches are budding, wattle is flowering and someone you know is suffering from hayfever, then spring is in the air.

These observations are known as 'phenology'. This is a field of science concerned with the influence of climate on the recurrence of biological phenomena, such as plant flowering. Some years may be cooler or warmer than others, yet the sequence of natural events is the same each year: the unfurling of leaves, the bloom of a wild flower or the appearance of a particular insect occurs in the same order.

Meteorologists measure this in degree days or number of daylight hours, and each plant has its own set number of how many of these it needs before it will react either out of dormancy or into flower.

For hundreds of years farmers and gardeners have observed that the best time to plant or harvest depends on the timing of other plants in their area. Native Americans, for example, planted corn when oak leaves had unfurled to the size of a squirrel's ear. As we reach a greater understanding of nature's signals, the better we will be able to interpret them for best management and higher yields in agriculture, and this of course will result in easier backyard gardening for us all. For the most part, I love to celebrate seasonality—the ephemeral delights of spring, for instance, with its fleeting cherry blossoms, the bite in the air when leaves start to change colour, and so on.

Author's note

The term 'bulb' refers to a modified underground bud, with a compressed stem and fleshy scale-like leaves, that stores food and water when growing conditions are unfavourable, then sends leaves upwards and roots downwards when conditions improve. For the purpose of this book, all storage organs— such as corms, tubers, certain rhizomes and true bulbs—are categorised as 'bulbs'. In a similar way, herbs are not always herbaceous—that is, dying down each winter—but are useful in some way: edible or medicinal.

Spring

Bud swell and blossom.
The warbling of magpies and
fleeting moments of delight.
Frenzy. Sniffles and sneezes. Fresh.
Fragile. Handle with care.

Overview of the season

Spring evokes a feeling of renewal and excitement in all gardeners. Novices and enthusiasts alike cannot help but be inspired by the show nature puts on.

Lime-coloured new growth bursts from tired grey twigs, flowers come to life in the most neglected beds—there is action everywhere in the garden.

If spring were to be summed up by one word, it would be 'busy'. Everything happens at once at this time of the year. New season's vegetables, herbs and annuals need planting, blossom trees burst forth with colour and a wonderful range of Australian natives come into their own. Everywhere, everything in nature is in a frenzy, with trees rocketing, weeds smothering, flowers blooming, and birds and insects all out and about breeding and feeding.

This explosion of life can leave you feeling either a little bewildered about where to start in the garden, or inspired by nature's extravagance and keen to make progress with your own patch of ground. Don't be overwhelmed: tackle each task in bite-sized chunks and the rewards will come. Make the most of glorious days in the sunshine by walking around a nursery, visiting an open garden or simply getting your hands dirty in your own backyard.

Garden spa

Why not spring clean your garden and give it the facelift it deserves? There are lots of jobs to do now. Rake up any fallen leaves still around from autumn and put them in the compost bin; the old adage 'a new broom sweeps clean' is very much the case in the garden! A dose of pelletised manure will do wonders for trees and shrubs.

Spot-spray weeds in garden beds, pathways and paved areas, then grab the hedge trimmers and get stuck into any wayward shrubs (avoid pruning late spring-flowering shrubs now, as you may be removing the flower buds). Plants are quick to recover at this time of year, and can easily be trimmed down a size or two without any harmful effect.

Once the hard work is done, it is time for a bit of fun. A trip to a local nursery during spring should inspire even the most inactive gardeners. When visiting these plant havens check the longevity of the shrubs and examine their form and foliage to gauge whether they will be good-value year-round specimens or one-day wonders.

LEFT: *The extraordinary unfurling petals of dogwood* (Cornus *sp.*).

Weatherwatch

How do you know that it's spring? The answer depends not on the date but on the weather in your area. Look for nature's clues—if the birds are singing loudly, cicadas are ringing in the trees, bare branches are budding and someone you know is suffering from hay fever, spring is in the air.

Great ideas for small gardens

If you love visiting open gardens in spring, you may return home feeling like you need another hectare or two to create a really satisfying garden, though the truth is small spaces can be just as beautiful.

Small gardens rely on dressing vertical surfaces. Here, the white-flowering Pandorea 'Snow Bells', clothes the back fence.

Confined garden spaces are becoming a fact of life for the majority of city dwellers, but the courtyard or balcony can be a big challenge on a small scale. The contained garden can be intimate, with colourful creepers, evergreen hedges and scented screens. Small spaces can be converted into green, usable extensions of a living area, becoming outdoor rooms.

With space for gardens diminishing, and the love of gardening growing, the creative use of space is becoming more and more essential. Nowhere is this more evident than in the recent trend towards vertical gardens, where plants tracking upwards have gone well beyond the traditionally used wall plants and climbing species.

These days, vertical gardens can be planted as walls, 'growing mosaics', in which plants are placed into special grid systems that also contain their root systems. The work of famous designers such as Patrick Blanc has pioneered this trend in commercial and large-scale apartment developments, but now this technology is making its way into the domestic arena too.

The various wall systems used (Helmrick is one supplier) help channel water and compartmentalise roots, meaning that they can be stacked vertically (not just laid on the ground), so long as they get structural support. A lightweight planting medium is used, with vermiculite and other expanded clay particles providing the necessary nutrition and support, together with some potting mix. Any groundcovering plants are suitable, as are climbers. Choosing a suitable mixture comes down

To own a bit of ground, to scratch it with a hoe, to plant seeds, and watch their renewal of life — this is the commonest delight of the race, the most satisfactory thing . . .

CHARLES DUDLEY WARNER

to the aspect of the site and so on. Many 'indoor' plants have been perfect for shady positions (see pages 54 and 383), while herbs such as marjoram, oregano, mint and thyme (see page 111) thrive in sunnier spots.

Espalier (growing plants like a flat pack against the wall) can also maximise the room you have for plants as this technique means they don't take up the same depth as regularly grown versions of the same plants. Traditionally shrubs or trees are espaliered, but climbers can also be trained to a similar effect. Even patterns, such as a cross-hatch, can be created to create an eye-catching pattern on the back wall. This strong focal point is a bonus and something that is often lacking in small gardens.

Spring in miniature

Why not pot up a miniature spring garden? Any container with a drainage hole will do. Wheelbarrows, wine barrels or large pieces of broken pottery can all look great once planted with a selection of spillovers, annuals and shrubs.

Choose coordinating plants with various heights to achieve a staggered planting that looks good. When selecting plants, group together those with similar cultivation and aspect requirements, such as how much sun is needed.

Espaliered fruit trees, like these apples, create a living wall.

A pretty potted display could be made from grey-foliaged plants such as *Cineraria* 'Silverdust', the mauve flowers of trailing variegated catmint and brachyscome, mixed with the white flowers of silver bush. Add some coordinating spring bulbs and you will have a garden microcosm.

WEED NOW The spring sunshine also wakes up your weeds, so one day spent weeding now saves a week of hard work later when the weeds have seeded.

Potting a miniature spring garden

1. Plant generously and make sure you have some things that 'froth over' the pot.

2. Top up with good-quality potting mix.

3. We chose rock daisy, silver bush, variegated catmint and *Cineraria* 'Silverdust'.

This mix-and-match array of terracotta pots is unified by themed planting of purple- and grey-foliaged plants.

Tips for the potted garden

🍂 Windbreaks are important for balcony gardeners. Pots and hanging baskets can dry out very quickly if they are not protected by larger plants, or by a lattice or reinforced glass panelling.

🍂 If you choose your plant material to suit the position, maintenance will be easier.

🍂 If you are unsure of your ability to mix and match, choose uniform pots made of one material, such as sandstone or terracotta.

🍂 Check weight restrictions before buying pots—plastic may be your only choice.

🍂 Rather than dot pots about aimlessly, place them in a logical order, perhaps grouped around a large central pot or other feature.

🍂 To keep your potted plants perfect, use an Australian premium standard potting mix and feed monthly with liquid fertiliser and annually with slow-release fertiliser.

🍂 Don't put gravel or crockery in the bottom of pots. This does very little, if anything, to improve drainage; in any case, it is quite unnecessary if a good-quality potting mix is used.

SMALL GARDEN TIPS

🍂 **Focal points.** Create a highlight such as a garden seat, potted urn or fountain—a focal point makes an outdoor space more inviting to explore.

🍂 **Illumination.** Lighting helps to create mood and gives a small garden depth.

🍂 **Ceilings and walls.** Plant a tree, or build a pergola or raised garden beds to help enclose an area and convert it into an outdoor room.

🍂 **Pattern and texture.** Decking and paving, unusual types of foliage and architectural shapes can add interest, definition and substance to small spaces.

🍂 **Trickery and illusion.** Mirrors, hedges, *trompe l'oeil* and manipulation of perspective can all make a space appear larger than it is.

Time-saving ideas

If you know you won't have time to work in the garden every day (or each night when you get home from work), don't plant a high-maintenance garden. Planting roses, perennials such as dahlias that need regular dividing and lifting, and very fast growers might seem like a good idea but they will make you a slave to your garden with all the pruning you'll have to do.

Choose low-maintenance plants that are drought- and wind-tolerant and that can cope with a bit of neglect. Geraniums, bougainvillea and kumquats are ideal. Other low-maintenance plants include hebes, lavender, box, most natives, daisies, citrus, olives and oleanders. Include plenty of shrubs, which generally speaking require the least amount of care. Avoid large areas of lawn, vegetables and flowers, as these plants require the most effort to cultivate and demand more of your time. Group together any demanding plants, such as fruit trees, so that feeding, spraying and watering can be done in one go.

Paving is a good alternative to lawn. It is a good surface for entertaining, relaxation and children's play, and, unlike lawn, it dries quickly after rain.

The best tip is to do a little work often. Just ten minutes a day weeding and tidying up will save hours of work in the long run.

More on low-maintenance plants

Many plants have natural mechanisms for coping with low water conditions. Called xerophytes, these plants have a range of adaptations such as succulent leaves, which store water, furry grey leaves, which create their own humidity around the pores of the leaves and repel more of the light, and leaves that are rolled and spiky, thereby hiding their vulnerable breathing holes and making them less prone to animal attack.

Of all these plant types, it's the savvy succulents with their wonderful leaf shapes, textures and colours that are most popular with gardeners.

SPRING CLEAN An easy way to make a garden look fresh is to use a high-pressure water blaster to clean paved surfaces, wooden furniture, pots and statuary. Be sure to cover and remove any fragile items, as the process can be quite vigorous.

CLOCKWISE FROM TOP LEFT: *Scented-leaf geraniums are low maintenance, though they will need the occasional prune; salvias flower for months and are trouble free; a kumquat makes a hardy pot plant that responds well to fertiliser.*

Succulents

Succulents have built-in water tanks, with the fleshy part of each leaf (and often the roots too) storing water for when tough times strike. Increasingly these plants are being appreciated, not only for their hardiness, but also for their fabulous foliage variations, often beautiful flowers, and natural resistance to disease.

Sedum 'Blue Spruce' is a beautiful groundcover with blue, pine-needle-like foliage and yellow star flowers in summer, growing to 25 cm tall and 80 cm wide. *Crassula multicava* 'Purple Dragon' is a stunner with glossy green oval leaves that have pink edges and undersides. It grows into a neat round ball 60 cm × 60 cm and is hardy enough to deal with full sun or part shade.

Aloes are another increasingly popular succulent for the garden. They are statuesque, drought-tolerant, floriferous and cope with a range of conditions, including cold, containment, heat, steep and salty terrain. Recent propagating in South Africa has resulted in longer flowering periods and a greater number of small-growing plants, making it easier to choose one for your garden. 'Topaz', for example, has gorgeous pinkish orange flowers, 'Fairy Pink' has dainty white flowers with a pink flush and 'Gemini' has pale orange blooms atop a 30 cm tall plant. Slightly taller varieties that grow about 1 m–1.5 m tall include the yellow-flowering 'Southern Cross', which looks very pretty in pots, 'Capricorn', a bicolour red and yellow form, and 'Tusker', which has ivory-coloured spires. Most aloes flower from winter onwards.

Native newcomers

Another way of achieving an easy-care garden that blends texture with wondrous colour is to look to Australian natives. Many gardeners give natives the flick because they think they're woody, scratchy, prickly and leggy. Not any more. The new Australian native garden is textural with splashes of magical colour. Thanks to plant breeding and selection, modern wildflowers are showier, bloom profusely, make excellent cut flowers and are more compact, especially with regular trimming.

The new native garden is a stylish combination of grasses, meadow flowers and colourful groundcovers, and is not afraid of mixing in the occasional exotic. Look for the *Scaevola* cultivars 'Lilac Fanfare' and 'Pink Carpet', and *Goodenia ovata* 'Gold Cover' to provide a carpet of colour. Experiment with flowering shrubs such as 'Honeybird' grevilleas, which have masses of spring flowers and attract many birds, and Federation flannel flowers, which have been bred to keep on flowering.

New breeds of natives include weeping dwarf wattles (*Acacia cognata* 'Green Mist' and 'Fettucine', *A. baileyana* 'Prostrate'), prostrate banksias called

SUMMER FEEDING Don't overfeed in hot climates and promote sappy growth that's prone to summer burn on those few spiking near 40°C days that summer can produce. In these areas, look at late summer feeding regimes instead.

CHOOSING A GOOD PLANT AT THE NURSERY
- Check that the leaves are uniformly green.
- Look for a specimen of balanced proportions, one that is not lopsided or top-heavy.
- Check for insect damage, weeds or fungus rots. Don't buy contaminated plants.
- Never buy a pot-bound plant (like the one shown at left). You can tell these from the roots growing out of the base of the pot or circling the surface. Don't hesitate to remove the pot to have a good look at the root system, but remember to replace it!
- Don't just be seduced by the flowers, ask how long these last and picture what the plant will look like when they finish.

FAR LEFT: *The dwarf river wattle* (Acacia cognata *'Fettucine')* *has flowing leaves like hair.*

LEFT: *Weeping wattles have beautiful texture. This prostrate form of Cootamundra wattle* (A. baileyana *'Prostrate') cascades from a standard.*

'Baby Banksias' that grow just 50 cm high, grafted flowering gums that cope with exotic soils, and elegant, disease-resistant kangaroo paws such as 'Pink Pearl'. These new breeds often have superior foliage to the old ones, exceptional architectural forms and a hardiness that is unparalleled. Also investigate some of the beautiful formal screening plants such as *Leionema* (syn. *Phebalium*) 'Hedger' and 'Green Screen'.

Most natives will cope with water restrictions, need little or no fertiliser, are perfect for the time-poor gardener and make stunning, simple arrangements for inside. Australia's droughts, floods, profound heat and strong winds may inspire fine poetry but they create a difficult gardening environment. It makes sense then for Australians to use more natives—plants that have evolved on this land over millions of years.

PLANTING TIPS FOR AUSTRALIAN NATIVES

- Water at least weekly from planting until the end of the first summer. This should give the plant enough time to grow roots into the surrounding soil, where they can then start to source water for themselves.
- Often rain doesn't provide enough water. Before deciding whether plants need an extra drink, check below the surface of the soil to see if water has penetrated to the root zone.
- Planting time is an ideal opportunity for adding water-storing granules. Incorporate these into the soil as you backfill around the planting hole.
- To help retain moisture, place a 'doughnut' shape of mulch around each plant, at least 10 cm thick and extending out twice as wide as the rootball.
- Although strong fertilisers should never be used at planting time, most landscapers add a little slow-release food underneath a layer of soil to provide much needed nutrients for new roots.

Sustainable garden design

Even in a dry climate it's easy to make a beautiful garden if you follow three main precepts: use clever design techniques, select the right plants and water them wisely.

CLOCKWISE FROM TOP LEFT: *A path made of a porous material allows water to drain through it; a pergola creates dappled shade; this stone swale drain acts as a dry creek bed, and looks good with or without water.*

☀ LEAF BLOWER A leaf blower that also vacuums is perfect for cleaning up gravelled paths and those areas behind furniture and pots where leaves may have accumulated.

Today, the biggest issue facing gardeners is water usage, so it's little wonder that the new buzzword in horticulture is xerophytic landscaping—using plants with low water needs and making the most of what water falls naturally.

Key steps to making a garden a waterwise success

1 Ensure that a large percentage of the ground area is made of permeable surfaces, meaning that rainfall is absorbed into the ground and water table so plants can access it directly. Think of alternatives to paving and concrete when considering non-porous materials: gravelled areas, decomposed granite, crushed roof tiles or timber decking are all useful options.

2 When designing your garden, think about ways to create shade because evaporation is reduced if plants are not exposed to hot sun all day. Plant a tree or build a pergola that can be covered in vines to create almost instant shade. The most exposed westerly face of your garden is particularly worth shading.

3 Mulch the garden heavily as this allows water down into the plants' roots, and a thick blanket layer will help reduce evaporation.

4 To capture run-off, consider adding a well-designed water feature such as a mock billabong, which will fill with water when it rains, stockpiling any excess. In drier times, the stones or feature pebbles obviate the need for topping up constantly. Many people are opting for water tanks now—just make sure it's large enough to be useful, and make sure you use it (saving it for a 'rainy day' defeats the purpose!).

5 Choose plants that are not water guzzlers. Many plant labels these days have a 'drip' labelling system with more drips indicating higher water needs. As a rule of thumb, plants with silver, furry, prickly or succulent leaves are all more water-tolerant than those with large, glossy foliage. Many

Australian natives such as bottlebrush, paperbarks and grevilleas are terrific during a dry spell and, together with other natives from similar regions around the world—such as paper daisies, drifts of penstemon, rudbeckia, echiums, euphorbias and salvias—will increasingly replace traditional, thirsty annuals.

Maintaining your waterwise approach

After you've established your sustainable garden, keep up the good work by following a few simple tips and techniques.

For a start, it's vital to water your garden wisely: do so first thing in the morning or in the cool of the evening—at other times the water will mostly evaporate before it soaks down to the plant roots. Use a water penetrant to help break down the surface area of soils and stop the run-off effect that many potting mixes and sandy soils suffer.

If you want to use pebbles for decorative effects, it's best to use them as toppings on pots or along garden bed edges where they can be seen and admired without getting in the way of maintenance. Better still, save them for pathways where you can first line the ground with weed mat (or a similar treatment) to help control weeds from popping up all the time.

Research has shown that frequent light waterings of garden plants don't really work. Plants can and need to be trained to go longer between drinks, which means deep soaks once a week to encourage deeper growing roots rather than surface roots.

Water-storing crystals, which swell like sponges to absorb water and then release it back to a plant's roots later, are an excellent way to make the most of your available water. They need to be incorporated into the soil where the roots will be before planting or laying turf. Organic matter also stores water and should be used at frequent intervals to improve the water-holding capacity of your soil.

LEFT: *Euphorbias are drought-resilient, beautiful and tough.*

BELOW LEFT: *Waterwise beauty: lamb's ears* (Stachys byzantina) *and blue-eyed grass* (Sisyrinchium *sp.*).

BELOW: *These African daisies* (Osteospermum *sp.*) *love the sun and use water sparingly.*

Mulching

1 You'll need a generous amount of mulch. It will conserve moisture and suppress weeds. **2** Spread it 10 cm thick. The mulch should be twice as wide as the rootball. Take care not to mulch up the collar or trunk of the tree or you'll end up with collar rot.

All creatures great and small

Make your garden a place everyone and everything can enjoy. It is an unexpected delight to find lizards basking on a rock or butterflies flittering about from blossom to blossom.

Birds and non-domestic animals need three essential creature comforts to make your place their home.

- **Food.** For a supply of nectar to attract bees and butterflies plant grevilleas, banksias, camellias, salvias, kniphofias; for seeds plant wattles, she-oaks, grasses, pines; and for fruit plant lilly-pillies, blueberry ash and other rainforest species such as *Pittosporum rhombifolium*.

- **Water.** Birdbaths need only be a few centimetres deep or birds can drown—place some rocks in deeper water containers so that birds have something to perch on.

- **Shelter.** Hollow logs, thickets of grevilleas and hakeas, and low-branching shrubs provide excellent shelter. Remember, dogs and cats will act as a great deterrent.

LEFT FROM TOP: *A butterfly feeds on nectar-rich native flowers; encourage birds to your garden with a birdbath; logs are the perfect protection for lizards.*

Not-so-creepy-crawlies

Encourage the good guys: nature hates any imbalance in the environment, so destroying all insects could leave your plants vulnerable to other problems. A better way is to encourage balance.

- Attract beneficial insects by dotting parsley, dill and Queen Anne's lace about, and by planting perfumed shrubs.

- Birds eat lots of grubs, but will only venture into your garden if there is water to drink and some low-growing bushes for them to perch on in safety. Growing some plants that produce seed and nectar will also encourage birds to stay.

- Lizards eat snails and slugs, but will be frightened away by dogs and cats. Rocks, hollow logs and sections of pipe will help to make them feel safe.

- Spiders and praying mantids eat insects too, so try to control the urge to kill them unless, of course, they are known to be harmful to humans, like redbacks and funnel webs.

- Plant some flowers in your vegetable garden to attract pollinators such as bees.

- The young juicy foliage of seedlings is delicious to snails and slugs. Guard seedlings with snail bait, or try putting beer in shallow containers around the garden. The slugs and snails drink up the yeasty

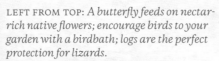

BUG WATCH—SOOTY MOULD

Spring is normally quiet on the bug front, but sometimes you will find black sooty mould on the leaves of your plants (that black substance which can be rubbed or scraped off with a little effort). You may be inclined to think it is a fungus; however, the problem is actually a secondary one related to insects such as scale (shown at right) or aphids. Wash the leaves with washing soda or soapy water (made with pure soap flakes), then spray the insects with PestOil®. It can be very difficult to treat large trees that are infested or diseased, but you can reduce the stress they undergo and help them rectify problems naturally by giving adequate water and by hosing down the foliage.

brew, which poisons them. Another alternative is to try nicotine traps, made with cigarettes, coffee, water and Vegemite, which also work really well.

- Tall new growth is attacked by aphids so be vigilant and hose them off, then spray accessible foliage with a pyrethrum-based insecticide.

- Methods of treating aphids, slugs, snails, fruit flies and caterpillars have improved dramatically over the last decade. Natrasoap®, a soap that is made up of potassium salts of fatty acids, will control organically many sap-sucking insects like aphids and mites. Along similar lines, a product called Spinosad®, derived from beneficial soil bacteria, can be used on many edible crops to control caterpillars, tomato grub, corn earworm, pear and cherry slug, light brown apple moth and that scourge of gardeners, fruit fly.

Critters!

As we try to garden more sustainably, several things that have an impact on the environment continually need our careful consideration. First are feral and domestic animals and how they affect the bigger picture of native fauna. Second is our use of chemicals to control pests and disease. These often work their way up the food chain to poison bigger predators, such as the birds that eat the caterpillars you have sprayed. Tawny frogmouths, for example, have been poisoned after eating snails and slugs contaminated by chemicals.

We also need to examine how we use our backyards to encourage wildlife. One big no-no is feeding native birds with anything other than what they find growing in your garden. Bread, sugar or any processed food increases the risk of birds developing a disease called 'runners', which makes them unable to fly and very vulnerable to predators such as cats and dogs.

Encouraging fauna and flora

Encouraging wildlife into your garden may be as simple as introducing a birdbath, but it could be something more substantial like creating a wildlife corridor. Wildlife corridors are areas where animals and birds can travel to and from larger reserves and national parks. By getting together with the neighbours and working with the local council, it is possible to plant some street trees and shrubs in your own garden where birds, possums, bats and other critters can safely travel from one park to another, increasing their chances of breeding and survival.

Remember too that different animals like different things. Cockatoos and galahs like the eucalypt knots and holes that develop once limbs fall, although perhaps installing a nesting box works better for you. Finches and wrens need prickly bushes that grow low to the ground and seeding grasses to feel safe

CLOCKWISE FROM TOP LEFT: *A bower bird's nest shows the blue trinkets it collects; a beer bottle with a few swigs left makes a great snail trap; blue-tongue lizards eat snails; ducks will forage in the garden tirelessly.*

DID YOU KNOW? Before the advent of modern pesticides, gardeners used to burn tobacco leaves to fumigate glasshouses.

and be fed adequately, and once in the garden they'll also help out by munching on spiders and small insects. The larger, showier blooms of the hybrid grevilleas, ornamental gums and bottlebrushes are great for lorikeets and rosellas.

Bees, butterflies and other beneficial insects

There is a worldwide shortage of bees, and to help them gardeners should limit their use of poisons, especially when bees are foraging. Some people might also like to consider having their own Australian native beehive, especially in frost-free areas. Native bees, which can be bought, are raised either in a hive box or hollow log; interestingly, they don't have stings, which makes them perfect for the backyard. The only catch is that they only produce a small amount of honey, so you won't be able to feed your whole community!

Beneficial insects in the garden include parasitic wasps, ladybirds, hoverflies and praying mantises. While these creatures can be encouraged by careful planting and not spraying, many today are sold as eggs to be released directly into your garden.

Companion planting

Companion planting is an environmentally friendly way to keep your garden healthy and at the same time encourage biodiversity. There are two kinds of pest-controlling plants. One type attracts beneficial insects, and includes elderberry, dill and fennel. These plants often have flowers that attract insects that prey on other destructive pests in the garden; these 'good guys' include lacewings, hoverflies, ladybird larvae and parasitic wasps.

The other category of plants repels or confuses insects with their strong scent—such as sage, oregano, lavender and basil. These pest-repellent plants work in three different ways. One group—'masking plants', such as herbs like sage, oregano and thyme—produces strong pungent oils that 'mask' other plants' perfumes, confusing pests. Sweet marjoram, for example, is sometimes planted near gardenias or roses so that its strong scent will confuse pests attracted to their flowers. Lavender (see page 113), too, with its incredibly strong scent, can be planted near whitefly-prone plants.

The second group, the 'repellent' plants, includes cotton lavender, tansy and wormwood. These plants produce a scent or taste that is so bitter or putrid it drives insects away. Pest-repellent plants can be used in the garden in various ways. You can plant tansy, for example, near doorways to repel flies—or scatter the leaves around to repel ants.

CLOCKWISE FROM RIGHT: *Bees, ladybirds and praying mantises are among the gardener's best friends.*

How doth the little busy bee
Improve each shining hour,
And gather honey all the day
From every opening flower!

ISAAC WATTS

CLOCKWISE FROM FAR LEFT: *Bronze fennel has sprays of flowers that attract beneficial insects; tansy has insect-repelling foliage; marjoram has sweet-smelling flowers and leaves that mask other plant smells; lavender flowers attract bees and the oil-rich foliage masks the smell of other plants; pungent sage (the golden tricolour form); cotton lavender has insect-repellent foliage and is useful as an edging plant in potagers.*

Finally, there are plants that contain natural toxins or 'poisons' that can be used to make sprays or washes. These include quassia chips, which can be made into a bitter tea to repel animals like possums; penny royal or fennel as a flea repellent for animals; chamomile, which can be used as an antifungal agent; and the dried flowers of pyrethrum, which can also be used as an insect spray.

Playing around with companion planting ensures a more biodiverse garden. Surely anything that promotes less emphasis on sprays and other chemical controls is worth a try.

Pets in the garden

Pets have a prominent place in many households, and their impact in the garden can be disastrous! The day a dog is brought home, for example, is the day you learn how many gaps there are in the fences and how jumpable they are. Home repairs aside, there are many ways pets affect your garden, from

SPRAY TIP Sap-suckers such as thrips, fruit fly, aphids, scale and mealy bugs can be removed easily and safely by vigorous hosing, before using an oil-based spray such as white oil.

yellow lawn patches where your dog urinates, to holes in the ground from digging, to 'wear paths' from racing around the same spots—not to mention those 'barkers' eggs'. Then there's the less obvious destruction that comes from cats' eradication of wildlife. All of this damage creates a real dilemma for the pet owner.

Digging dogs

To minimise your dog's boredom from being locked up in a yard all day, and thereby reduce destructive garden habits like digging, many vets recommend using a toy stuffed with dry food that the dog has to extract during the day, or spreading dried food around the garden (to encourage foraging). Walking your dog once or twice a day is an essential part of being a dog owner. If the animal keeps digging, moving its excrement to the dig site should deter it. Other tricks worth considering if the problem is extreme are to bury some blown-up balloons in his favourite holes, or use chicken wire spread just below the surface of the soil. If you have the space,

BELOW: *Dogs can quickly destroy your hard work when they 'help out' in the yard.*

ABOVE AND RIGHT: *Chickens love winter grass (above) and will range freely for it (and insects) if given the opportunity.*

however, consider creating a sand pit for the animal, and hiding its toys in it. That should limit the dog to digging up only one area of your backyard.

Prowling cats

Cats enjoy the entertainment of catching wildlife, as they will hunt even if well fed. Your puss should wear at least two bells to alert the wildlife in your garden, especially birds, of its approach. Lizards don't seem to be very aware of bells, however, so they should be provided with safe places in which to hide, such as rocks, pipes, hollow logs and the like. Better still, try to keep your cat inside, especially in the early morning and early evening when birds are busiest, or get them their own run.

Chooks

Many backyards are again housing chickens. Fresh eggs from your own free-ranging chooks have a taste and colour that are simply wonderful, and the average backyard is large enough for at least a couple of chickens. Chickens need water and food pellets daily and will happily scratch and forage around your garden for grubs and insects; they also love kitchen scraps, which makes them the ultimate recyclers. Weeds that you would otherwise compost such as milkweed, chicory, dandelions and chickweed are particularly tasty treats. Their coops must be cleaned out weekly and they need worming every three months. Healthy birds will live for about ten years, though they lay better when they are young. In urban residential settings, roosters are banned because of their early morning crowing, but then they don't lay eggs anyway!

Chicken coops vary widely, from a simple A-frame kit to your very own 'chickenopolis'. Whatever the design you settle on, always make sure that the coop is completely vermin proof, as foxes will dig under and climb over to get your chooks. Make sure, too, that the animals always have some shade and shelter to escape hot or wet weather.

Spring fever

With two million Australians suffering from seasonal hay fever or asthma each spring and summer, it makes sense to know more about the plants in your garden and which ones may be harmful.

Allergies are hypersensitive reactions of the body's immune system to specific substances called allergens, which include pollen. The most common allergies are those that involve skin and breathing problems. In fact, most people will suffer from some sort of allergic reaction at some time in their life, even if it is just a lump from a bee sting!

A frightening fact is that almost a quarter of the children in Australia are asthmatic, and skin allergies, including eczema and contact dermatitis, are on the increase. So it makes sense to understand how to avoid problems through careful planting and developing a low-allergen garden.

Allergy triggers

Pollen has been shown to be a major cause of allergy-related breathing problems. All flowering plants produce pollen at some time in their life, but those that rely on wind for dispersal produce so much pollen that it can easily enter our lungs and trigger a response.

The most common flowering plant in gardens, grass, causes the most damage. If you suffer from hay fever, going outside when lawns or pastures are flowering can be a nightmare. Choose a non-flowering lawn such as buffalo for your own backyard and, if you suffer from skin allergies, pick one of the soft-foliage types such as couch.

Similarly, spores from ferns, fungi and mosses float freely in the air, and can create problems. Some fragrant plants can also act as irritants, giving rise to an attack of asthma or hay fever. Common perpetrators include sweet William, honeysuckle, carnations and lilies. The pollen of plants in the daisy

ABOVE AND LEFT: *Zinnias (above) make lovely cut flowers, but unfortunately they can also trigger allergies, as can sweet William (left).*

Daylily, clematis and crab apple are all useful low-allergen flowering plants.

family, including zinnias, marigolds and chrysanthemums, can be a hazard too. The Australian native floral emblem, the wattle, has received much bad press for causing hay fever. Wattles are insect pollinated and as such have heavy pollen that normally doesn't cause allergy problems; however, the intense perfume of a grove of wattles may cause an allergic response. The fact that wattles mainly flower in spring when lawn grasses are also flowering is probably the reason for confusion.

Some plants are so toxic that if they come into contact with the skin they cause allergic responses, and not just in people with allergic tendencies. These plants, which should be excluded from all gardens, include the rhus tree (*Toxicodendron succedaneum*) and poison ivy (*Rhus radicans*). Other plants that should be avoided if you are prone to allergies include daphne, lily-of-the-valley, oleander, gloriosa lily, castor oil plant and deadly nightshade.

Planting your new, low-allergen garden

Having eliminated many plants from the garden, you'll probably want to replace them with more suitable species.

- **Annuals and biennials:** snapdragons, begonias, impatiens, forget-me-nots, petunias, salvia, pansies, phlox and love-in-a-mist.

- **Perennials:** oyster plant, agapanthus, Japanese windflower, granny's bonnet, daylily, penstemon, oriental poppy and Jacob's ladder.

- **Groundcovers:** bugle flower, lady's mantle, cranesbill, hosta, lamium, catmint and periwinkle.

- **Climbers:** ornamental grape, 'Iceberg' rose, clematis, Virginia creeper and passionfruit.

ASTHMA WEED

One weed every gardener should take care to remove is asthma weed (*Parietaria judaica*), also known as pellitory-of-the-wall or sticky weed. One square metre of this plant can produce 250,000 seeds, and it seeds year-round, with both the flowers and sticky hairs on the leaves causing allergic reactions. To remove it, wear gloves and bag it (do not compost it), or use a herbicide to poison it, roots and all.

● **Shrubs:** camellias, deutzia, banksias, escallonia, hebes, hydrangeas, viburnums, flax, weigela and photinia.

● **Trees:** bottlebrush, tupelo (*Nyssa*), Irish strawberry tree, magnolias, crab apples, ornamental pears and tulip trees.

Low-allergy plants for containers

Many plants work well in confined spaces and some won't upset the allergy sufferer. Choose from agapanthus, camellias, convolvulus, cordyline, fuchsia, hebe, hydrangea, iris, floribunda roses, salvia and petunia. You can choose virtually any container, from a plastic tub to an old chimney pot— perfect for those gardeners limited by age, ill health or lack of space.

Strategies for healthy gardening

Wearing protective clothing such as gloves, a hat, long sleeves and sunglasses is a good way of avoiding problems. The time of the year you choose to garden is also important—choose sunny days in winter, when pollen numbers are down, to do big tidy-ups in the garden.

Spring is the worst time of the year, as this is when many wind-pollinated trees such as poplars, willows, liquidambar, oaks and native pines (cypress and she-oaks) flower. Grasses also flower mainly in spring, so keep your lawn cut short and encourage the neighbours to do the same if you have hay fever or asthma. Better still, replant your lawn with low-allergy groundcovers (see opposite for suggestions).

Hot summer days seem to be worse for skin allergies and summer nights worse for fungal spores, so be mindful of this when you are outside.

Many of our gardening practices can also cause problems. Mulch, especially cypress pine flakes, can harbour fungal spores that trigger attacks. Although not the best for the garden, black plastic and gravel mulches are the easiest on allergy-sufferers' respiratory systems. Other fine organic materials such as

blood and bone can also cause problems and are best avoided if you or your neighbours react.

Once you have gone to all this trouble, don't then spoil your efforts by spraying with garden chemicals. Always try organic methods first.

Members of the daisy family, including these zinnias, should be planted with caution if you're prone to respiratory problems.

🌿 **GARDEN WARM-UPS** Do a few gentle back stretches before gardening; a few yoga cat and camel stretches on all fours and a few simple lateral stretches on a towel will help make that day in the garden trouble free.

Checklist
Jobs to do now
Annuals, perennials and bulbs

◗ With so much flowering occurring at this time of year, it is important to remove spent blossoms. This 'dead-heading' not only makes plants look fresher, it also encourages second and third flushes.

◗ Plant over yellowing bulbs with fast-growing flowers such as lobelias and sweet Alice and apply liquid fertiliser fortnightly. Never cut back or plait bulb leaves while there is any green pigment remaining as it will stop them flowering the next year.

◗ Divide water plants and lilies, and clean the pond or other water features if you're feeling energetic.

◗ Don't neglect your potted plants. All re-potting should be completed by the end of spring. Don't forget to re-pot, fertilise and re-plant hanging baskets and wall pots.

◗ Use both slow-release fertilisers—ensuring all trace elements and macronutrients are supplied—and seaweed solutions, which act like a plant 'tonic'.

◗ Not all slow-release fertilisers are the same. Read the label carefully as some release faster than others and some feed for longer.

Grasses, groundcovers and climbers

◗ Use weed-and-feed products to control weeds in lawns before they gain a foothold.

◗ Turf really takes off in spring, so treat it to a balanced, slow-release lawn food and handfuls of lime for a strong healthy carpet that will last through summer.

◗ Climbers are a lovely way to soften the look of verandah posts and pergolas, but now is the time to stop them invading your roof and gutters. Prune back long tendrils of wisteria, jasmine and climbing roses as they finish flowering.

Shrubs and trees

◗ Prune banksia roses when flowering has finished.

◗ Prune old wood out of philadelphus (mock orange).

◗ Cut back deutzia, choisya and bottlebrushes when blooms finish.

◗ Clean up scale insects and sooty mould on camellias, citrus trees, lilly-pillies and any other damaged shrubs and trees.

◗ Lightly prune native shrubs.

◗ To prevent frost damage to young plants, surround them with hessian and don't prune them until all late frosts have passed.

◗ Water gardenias regularly, fertilise with Epsom salts (1 tablespoon/10 L of water) and iron chelates (check instructions as concentrations vary), and mulch to encourage lots of summer flowers.

Remove old flowers as they fade to encourage further flushes.

Liquid fertiliser is great for greening up the garden.

It's time to re-pot indoor plants like this peace lily.

If you like the look of coppiced crepe myrtles, now is the time to shape them.

Rhododendrons, diosma, boronias, grevilleas, bottlebrush, roses, jasmine and many perennials are all in full bloom; lightly trim them after flowering has finished.

Azaleas have finished flowering now. Give them a light trim all over to remove old flowers, traces of petal blight and to encourage bushy growth.

Prune hibiscus, even if it means sacrificing a few flowers. Shorten stems by a third to promote bushy growth and encourage summer and autumn flowers.

Keep thrips, red spider mites and fungal rot at bay by misting vulnerable new growth, especially the leaves' underside where thrips and mites tend to hide.

Unless your garden consists only of acid-loving plants, spread lime on your soil to compensate for the acidifying effects of fertiliser and manure; adding mushroom compost can also lower pH.

Instead of putting out green waste for the council collection, consider buying a mulcher so you can convert prunings into mulch.

Take cuttings of frangipani. Allow the cuttings to callous (stop bleeding) and let the sap dry out for a few weeks before planting them into a sandy, well-drained soil.

Herbs, fruit and vegetables

Taste-test citrus before harvesting. Some may have coloured well already, but it can be some time before they are sweet enough to eat. A dose of fertiliser won't go astray either.

In late spring, start to regularly use white oil on citrus trees to combat pests such as leaf miner, aphids and scale insects.

Stone fruit trees, such as peaches and nectarines, should be sprayed with copper oxychloride at bud swell to counteract leaf curl.

Remove any frost protection on sensitive crops (such as tropical fruits and early tomatoes) as the weather begins to warm.

As fruit trees finish flowering, feed them with blood and bone or citrus food to produce high-quality fruit.

Prune passionfruit.

Net fruit trees to protect ripening fruit from birds, or scare them away with bits of silver paper tied onto branches or painted plastic pots (see 'Protect your harvest' on page 237).

Harvest shoots of asparagus, cutting just below the soil surface.

Pop all your prunings into the mulcher for a greener waste solution.

Use netting to protect ripening fruit crops from birds.

Citrus fertiliser should be applied twice a year.

Plant now
Annuals, perennials and bulbs

🌿 New season seedlings such as marigolds, cleomes, cosmos, dahlias and salvias.

🌿 Summer-flowering perennials such as agapanthus, canna lilies and asters.

🌿 Dahlia tubers, which are great for cut flowers until late autumn.

🌿 Annuals such as sunflowers and California poppies are easy to grow, and their cheery flowers make them perfect for children's gardens.

🌿 Perennial crowns and bulbs of red hot pokers, gerberas, *Achillea*, jockey's cap (*Tigridia* sp.) and gladioli.

🌿 Other stunning summer- and autumn-flowering bulbs besides tulips and daffodils. A mix of gladioli, vallota, nerines, crinum lilies and autumn crocus will provide picking flowers, shade, colour and foliage contrast. Liliums, eucomis and tuberoses deserve a place in every garden, and New Zealand lily is great for massed planting in shady areas.

Grasses, groundcovers and climbers

🌿 Plant warm season turf grasses, such as couch and buffalo, after all frosts have finished.

🌿 Strike cuttings of pigface, sun jewels and portulaca—great succulent, long-lasting groundcovers.

🌿 Choose wisteria and clematis in flower for variety.

🌿 Grow Spanish flag (*Mina lobata*) from seeds for vivid red and yellow flowers or plant coral vine (*Antigonon* sp.) seedlings for cerise-pink bracts in summer.

Shrubs and trees

🌿 Spring is the best time to plan and plant hedges. Look beyond the flowers and imagine what the planting will look like during the rest of the year so that you're not disappointed once spring has passed.

🌿 Spring flushes make it easy to choose potted roses for colour and perfume.

Herbs, fruit and vegetables

🌿 Salad herbs and leafy greens— including lettuce, mustard, cress, radicchio, endive and rocket.

🌿 Annual herbs such as basil, coriander, parsley and dill.

🌿 Summer berries such as raspberries, gooseberries and strawberries.

🌿 Spring vegetables such as peas, zucchini, carrots, garlic, chives, beans (dwarf or climbing), cabbage, melon, beetroot, capsicum, cucumber, pumpkin, choko, celery and eggplant.

🌿 Tomatoes—home-grown varieties are much tastier than shop-bought tomatoes and children will love them too.

🌿 The onion family, called alliums, includes chives and shallots, which look great as a decorative border because of their tufting, grass-like foliage.

🌿 Tall edibles such as sweet corn, sunflowers and Jerusalem artichoke.

African marigold 'Vanilla' and other brighter cultivars can be planted once the frosts have finished.

Cleomes, or spider flowers (see page 368), have long whiskery stamens. Their seeds can be planted now.

When all chance of frost has gone, sweet corn can be planted into well-drained and regularly watered soil.

Flowering now

Annuals, perennials and bulbs

- Annuals such as nemesia, poppies, primula, alyssum, wallflowers, lobelia, forget-me-not, nigella, penstemon, aquilegia, nepeta, campanula, dianthus, snapdragons, English daisy, petunias, phlox, portulaca, salvias and nasturtiums.

- Perennials such as Solomon's seal, bearded iris, verbascums, delphiniums, foxgloves, phlox, geraniums and pelargoniums, verbena, hollyhocks, peonies, meadow rue, red valerian, heliotrope, candytuft, red campion, violets, canna, agapanthus, gerbera, speedwell, thrift, cupid's dart, bleeding heart, rock rose and lupin.

- Bulbs such as lily-of-the-valley, anemones, ranunculus, freesias, bluebells, Dutch iris, daffodils and jonquils, tulips, hyacinths, alliums, hippeastrum, gladiolus, Cuban lily and *Tritonia*.

Grasses, groundcovers and climbers

- Flowering ornamental grasses such as greater wood rush and wide leaf sedge.

- Groundcovers such as bugle flower (*Ajuga* sp.), campanula, saxifrage, pigface, aubrieta, African daisy, cottage pinks, violets, alpine phlox, verbena, arctotis, nemesia and erigeron.

- Climbers such as the native bower vine, hardenbergia, bluebell creeper and coral pea.

- Deciduous or semi-deciduous vines such as wisteria, clematis, banksia rose, bougainvillea and chocolate vine.

CLOCKWISE FROM TOP LEFT: *The arctotis daisy closes up its flowers each night; gerberas need lots of sun to look their best; clematis (see page 80) is available in many colours and forms; the flowers of star anise; a yellow grevillea in spring splendour; the stunning white waratah.*

- Evergreen climbers such as allamanda, star jasmine, thunbergia, jasmine and honeysuckle.

- Spring-flowering climbing roses, including old-fashioned cultivars such as 'Albertine', 'Crepuscule', 'New Dawn', 'Madame Alfred Carrière' and the Australian-bred 'Lorraine Lee'.

- Groundcover roses are at their best, and continue to give colour from now into autumn.

Shrubs and trees

- Evergreen shrubs, including azaleas, rhododendrons, diosma, lavender, murraya and fuchsia.

- Native shrubs, such as boronias, grevilleas, bottlebrush and waratahs.

- Deciduous shrubs, such as roses, deutzia, viburnums and weigela.

- Trees, such as laburnum, catalpa, crab apple, bauhinia, coral trees and jacarandas and, for perfume, Bull Bay magnolia, michelia, tree gardenia and native frangipani.

Herbs, fruit and vegetables

- Lavender, rosemary, borage, feverfew, comfrey, star anise and chamomile.

- Ornamental cabbages and kale for their foliage colour; the cooler the area, the stronger the pigmentation in the coloured leaves.

- *Allium neapolitanum* (daffodil garlic) and chives in both late spring and summer.

Annuals, perennials and bulbs

Spring is certainly the time to admire your hard work in the garden. In fact, nature puts on such a wonderful display during spring that even the laziest of gardeners have something to delight in, even if it's just the good weather! Admired most are spring flowers—the bulbs, annuals and perennials that produce such a fanfare, celebrating the sunshine and this fair season.

CLOCKWISE FROM TOP LEFT: *Fairy primulas come in a range of pastel shades; violas and polyanthus in buttercup and primrose yellow; perennial nemesia and its close cousin, the buttery yellow annual type.*

Annuals

Planting annuals is the best way to revitalise a tired, lifeless garden. Annuals are cheap, take only about six weeks to flower from seedlings and come in a huge range of colours and varieties.

Paint a picture

Bedding plants, as they are also known, only live for one season (hence the name 'annual'), which means you can change colour schemes to create different effects each season.

Consider annuals in the same way you might think about changing the cushions and napery in a room rather than renovating the whole house. They truly are an excellent way of updating colour schemes, adding a fashionable foliage element or simply having cutting flowers for the house already on display outside.

Their breeding over the years has been extensive, and flowers now seem to be available in every hue with an astonishing range of growing heights and habits. You can experiment with different looks easily by changing colour schemes, staggering heights from the tallest at the back of the bed to the shortest at the front, playing with opposite colour schemes or, more ambitiously, even creating your own outdoor art displays like Floriade.

This spring, for example, you could paint a picture in your garden with pansies, primroses and poppies. For a bold and bright statement, try a mixture of flamboyant orange sweeping across plush purple using primula, nemesia and cinerarias. A mix of butter yellow and snowy white interspersed with shades of sky-blue flowers, using baby blue eyes, primroses, forget-me-nots and violas, will add springtime cheer to your garden. Alternatively, choose the exotic colours of South-East Asia, perhaps a spicy mix of cinnamon and soft rose, using pansies, snapdragons, sweet William and wallflowers.

Larkspurs are lovely upright annuals in shades of blue, pink, lavender and, as shown here, white.

A river of colour

Intense Australian light calls for the use of strong colour in the garden. Try using single, bold colours such as royal blue, dark velvety green and sunny yellow to create an impact.

For a different look, plant your seedlings in 'rivers' of colour rather than in rows. Simply prepare the soil with added compost, water crystals and a slow-release organic fertiliser. Rake this into a fine bed, then map out rivers using a stick. Transplant your raised seedlings into these swirls in thick bands. To make the effect as striking as possible use contrasting colours such as purple and orange, or even foliage colour contrast such as the green leaves of parsley mixed with red flowers. Another striking combination can be achieved by

mixing opal-leaved basil with golden yellow flowers. Choose plants of similar height, so that one variety doesn't tower over another, and limit your selection to three or four plants.

White gardens

A white garden is the essence of simplicity, yet reveals in its detail myriad possibilities and intricacies.

KEEP IT SIMPLE

Colour is a powerful element of design in the garden. As a rule, following the KISS principle (keep it simple, stupid) will pay dividends.

People from a planet without flowers would think we must be mad with joy the whole time, to have such things about us.

IRIS MURDOCH

TIPS FOR EASY ANNUALS

- Dig in manure, water-storing crystals and a wetting agent before planting.
- Buy annuals in divided cell punnets, which protect the roots of seedlings and result in quicker establishment and fewer failures. Each seedling has its own cell so there is no chance of damaging the roots of other seedlings when you remove one from the punnet.
- Pinch back young plants and prevent them from flowering until they have grown for a month or so. This will let your plants develop into larger specimens, which will ultimately last longer and flower better.
- Remove dead flowers to prolong the flower display and water with liquid fertiliser once a fortnight.
- Most annuals need sun, so turn pots to give them an even supply all round.
- After each flush of flowers feed with a complete fertiliser.

A double white cherry is so beautiful you can see why the Japanese have cherry blossom forecasts in the news.

Black gardens

Much has been written about the colour white, but rarely does its opposite get a mention. Black flowers do exist, and can be quite beautiful. Violets, tulips, scabiosa, carnations, hollyhocks, columbines, hellebores, cranesbills and iris all have black or near-black varieties.

Some of these darker flowers rely on flies to pollinate their blooms and so have unpleasant odours; an example is *Dracunculus vulgaris*. The brown-flowered chocolate cosmos (*Cosmos atrosanguineus*) doesn't fall into this category, however; it has a delicious chocolate scent.

Another interesting addition to a black garden is the globe artichoke 'Violetto', which has silver leaves and almost black edible flower heads. The black rose continues to elude breeders!

Winter blues

If you have the winter blues, these spring flowers will cheer you up! They look great planted en masse and will all grow easily from seed, so it's cheap to create a masterful sea of blue.

Try the most intense of all, the cornflower. Great for cutting stems for the house and as a bonus its silvery foliage is also lovely in the garden. Then there is *Nierembergia* or cup flower, which grows well in full sun as soon as the frosts have finished. And who could miss forget-me-nots (*Myosotis*)? They will grow easily in the sun or shade and produce masses of light blue blooms; later, their seeds, which stick to clothing, make them hard to forget! Also self-sowing is the blue pimpernel (*Anagallis monellii*), which is short and floriferous with true blue flowers. Native to the Mediterranean, it needs really good drainage to thrive. Other self-seeders include love-in-a-mist (*Nigella*), *Nemophila* and *Phacelia*.

For taller annuals try larkspur or the dainty *Delphinium* 'Blue Butterfly'. *Lithospermum diffusa* is stunning too, smothering itself in true blue blooms.

The overall effect of a white garden is fresh and pure, but a closer examination will reveal creams, soft pink centres, pale yellows and off-whites all blending with the various greens of foliage in a calm and natural harmony.

White is especially useful for night gardens, because the colour glows under moonlight, and also for small gardens as it can make a space feel larger than it really is.

DID YOU KNOW? The most popular white garden in the world is at Sissinghurst Castle in Kent, England, which was first planted in 1950 by Vita Sackville-West.

ANNUALS FOR INSTANT COLOUR

If you are after a quick fix, annuals are among the best investments you can make. They are cheap and cheery, and can be massed to fill any bare spots without great expense. Plant some annuals where they will make the most impact: a display in pots by entrance ways, in pockets in garden beds, either side of the driveway and massed in a border along the front boundary create the impression that you've spent weeks working on the garden.

Plant 'instant' colour in containers—like pots of happiness. Check out pansies, with their smiling faces, fairy primulas, nemesia and polyanthus for a splash of sunshine.

CLOCKWISE FROM TOP LEFT: *The dark tones of black hellebore; black-stemmed hydrangea;* Euphorbia *'Blackbird'; blue groundcovering* Lithospermum; *pale blue forget-me-nots; and the dark blue perennial version,* Cynoglossum amabile.

Honesty

Honesty was everywhere in the 1970s, grown mostly for the seeds, which were used as dried 'flowers'. In their day, these silvery moon-like seeds, along with statice, pampas grass and peacock feathers, were pretty much all there was for a long-lasting arrangement. In gardens today, it's about time honesty was rediscovered—not only for its delightful purple/pink spring flowers and stunning dried seeds, but also for its hardiness and ease of growing.

VITAL STATISTICS

Scientific name: *Lunaria annua*.
Family: Brassicaceae.
Climate: A Mediterranean climate is ideal, but most temperate and warm climates are suitable.
Colours: Honesty creates a shimmering effect in autumn and purple haze in spring.
Height: Grows up to about 80 cm.
Planting time: Plant from spring to early summer from offsets.
Soil: Grow in any well-drained soil.
Culture: A beautiful self-seeder, germinating by itself in sun or part shade.
Position: Plants need a full sun or semi-shaded position.
Planting spacing: Plant offsets about 50 cm apart.
Fertiliser: Not needed, though it prefers added lime.
Propagation: Grow from seed or offsets.

Feature annual

MORE SUN Turn your pots or baskets occasionally so the shaded side receives some sunshine too.

TWO BASKET PLANTS

Plan now for summer by planting one of these baskets—either orchid cactus or begonia (*Begonia fuchsioides* is shown at left). Choose a dappled shade position that is protected from hot winds. *Epiphyllum*, a spineless cactus, is ideal for hanging baskets. Many flower earlier in the season, but the spectacular 'Lady of the Night', *E. oxypetalum*, has large white nocturnal flowers that are intensely fragrant, especially on those nights when there is a full moon. The foliage is easily confused with zygocactus (formerly *Zygocactus* sp., but now known as *Schlumbergera* sp.) and flowers in winter.

The ultimate greenhouse plant, begonias are actually succulent perennials, great for growing in bare patches under camellias or azaleas, but also terrific for hanging baskets in sheltered patios. Choose from the double rose-like blooms of tuberous begonias and the stunning stained-glass leaves of Rex types.

Perennials

The emergence of the garden from winter dormancy into the full flush of spring growth is part of the magic of the season.

Using perennials

The perennials in your garden can easily be overlooked when many of them are sleeping during winter, but they in fact remain alive for a number of years. Although some perennial species have foliage that dies back, the rootstock is permanent, a bit like a bulb. Perennials, like annuals, can provide a colourful display, but they have the advantage that they do not need to be replanted each year.

Perennials can be planted among shrubs or used as a backdrop to annuals. The classic perennial border is a bed wide enough to display a range of plants, and long enough for some repetition of plantings to create a lovely flow and rhythm. Perennials vary widely in size, shape and colour, and there are plants to suit every climate, aspect and soil—not just the English countryside!

The value of the vertical

Although a sea of colour can be a spectacular sight in the garden, you could create a different look by punctuating the horizontal level with spear-like plants that spire into the sky, adding definition and accent. Flowers that give this effect in the garden include foxgloves, delphiniums, larkspur and *Acanthus*. Some, like hollyhocks, can flower 2 m skywards.

Another great spiking plant is *Verbascum*, which has a few species and is commonly called mulleins. They all tolerate dry conditions superbly, and can cope in full sun and part shade. Some can be weedy, self-seeding readily, so choose your cultivars with care. If you don't care for too tall a spike, there are also some dwarf cultivars available. One particularly attractive form is called 'Pink Kisses', and it's only 40 cm tall,

LEFT TO RIGHT: *The upright spires of delphiniums can rocket up 1 m high; hollyhocks can be the height of a tall man; oyster plants (Acanthus mollis) have slightly barbed flowers on tall stems.*

rather than 1 m. Like the larger ones, however, it still has the pretty grey-green furry leaves that form a rosette from which the flower thrusts forth.

Flowering from late spring to summer, the foxtail lily (*Eremurus* sp.) is a stunning, tall, stately plant well adapted to hot dry summers as it's native to the Middle East and Central Asia. Its strappy foliage is the backdrop for a flower spike, made up of star-like individual blooms, that rockets up to 180 cm tall, depending on the variety chosen. These perennials prefer a sunny position in well-drained soil, and once settled will grow happily for years. Plant them any time from winter to early spring. Protect the young shoots from any early frosts with some straw or mulch, and position them at the back of the garden bed so that they don't overshadow the pipsqueaks!

More grows in the garden than was sown there.

TRADITIONAL SAYING

Pride of Madeira

Looking for a bold, brave statement in the garden? Look no further than this sensational seaside-tolerant perennial that looks great year-round, attracts bees, and blows you away with its blue/purple flowers in late spring. An absolute superstar of the plant kingdom, pride of Madeira is a dramatic 'look-at-me' plant.

VITAL STATISTICS

Scientific name: *Echium candicans*.
Family: Boraginaceae.
Climate: Mediterranean.
Colour: Blue/purple flowers.
Height: 2–3 m (depending on the variety).
Planting time: Plant seedlings any time.
Soil: The soil should be free-draining; add some lime for best results.
Culture: After flowering, cut off spent flower heads.
Position: Full sun.
Planting spacing: Plant with plenty of space so that their marvellous dramatic shape can be seen to best effect.
Watering: Water regularly until established. It will then tolerate dry conditions.
Fertiliser: None needed, except for an annual application of lime.
Propagation: Propagate by layering. Peg a low branch down to the ground and scratch into the green outer layer slightly. Keep moist, and once the branch has rooted it can be separated from the mother plant.

Feature perennial

Peony

It seems unfair that we have to wait a whole year between a show of blooms, but unfortunately the peony (*Paeonia* sp.) only flowers in spring/early summer. The peony (or peony rose), a rhizome native to China, Tibet and Siberia, is the classic inclusion for a spring posy or cool-climate border. There is probably no more important or rewarding flower than the peony, which has been grown in China for 2500 years.

One great asset peonies have is a very long life—there are specimens more than 100 years old in Asian temple gardens. One reason for their long life is that they are so resistant to pests and disease—they have no natural enemies. Peonies have been a symbol of beauty through the centuries, and their forms and great range of colours are sublime.

Best suited to cooler regions, they prefer an open aspect, good light and shelter from strong winds; if they have a cool root run these plants will grow freely in most soils in sun or partial shade. Peonies sulk if grass grows too closely around them, but recover quickly when it is removed.

Plant the rhizomes 30 cm deep and 60 cm apart. Ideally, the soil should be rich, well drained, well dug, neutral to slightly alkaline, and on the heavy side. Enrich the soil with compost and well-rotted farm manure (fowl is best) as these plants are gross feeders. A handful of dolomite limestone mixed with the prepared soil will help them along (a handful of lime per square metre). Do not use peat moss or cow manure. Mix in a large bucket of pure humus or screened compost and add to this 500 g of bone meal or other general fertiliser. Water well in dry weather and generously while they are flowering.

Top dress plants annually after blooming using blood and bone or old manure, or mulch with compost or add leaf mould and bone meal. The occasional addition of a handful of wood ash is also a good idea. Propagate by division in winter.

PEONY TIPS Do not let peonies seed. While bushes are young, cut few flowers; with plants four years old and over, cut up to two-thirds of the blooms.

Peonies make beautiful cut flowers and are highly sought after by florists.

Drifts of cosmos, cornflowers and linaria create this lovely meadow.

Meadow magic

Spring lends itself to a somewhat haphazard planting style, with the plants themselves driving the design. If you are not the neat, obsessive type, then don't succumb to a clipped, manicured garden. Instead, give your creativity free rein by planting a selection of spillovers, cover-ups and wild things.

Many annuals and even some perennials have adapted perfectly to our climate. They will pop up in any little crevice, put on a show and then fade away as quickly as they came. This self-seeding process creates a delightful link with nature and can often produce chance associations that are far more effective than anything you could design. Often these little treasures are the plants that remain in old gardens. What are they, how can you obtain them and how can they be used to best advantage in your garden?

If you want to create a relaxed, cottage feeling in your garden, try to encourage plants to self-seed. This may mean putting up with some messy plants as you wait for the seed heads to form fully. It also means weeding and disturbing the soil as little as possible, as tiny plants are hard to see and can easily be damaged. Try to keep the garden moist, and wait until spring before mulching so that young seedlings are large enough to be noticed and left undisturbed.

Annual favourites include forget-me-nots with their pink or eggshell blue

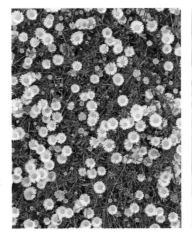

flowers, marvellous plants if kept in check; Johnny-jump-up, a self-seeding viola sometimes called heartsease; and *Aquilegia*, commonly called columbines or granny's bonnets. Other useful self-seeders include sweet Alice, primulas and cosmos. *Erigeron karvinskianus*—which goes by various names such as seaside daisy, fleabane and babies' tears—can also be a lovely groundcover, but be warned, it will overtake just about everything if given the chance.

Many perennials propagate themselves asexually, spreading into massive clumps of rhizomes or tubers. These plants can be great for stifling weeds. The Japanese windflower (*Anemone* × *hybrida*) works well under established trees, as does the arum lily. The bugle flower (*Ajuga reptans*) is another vigorous grower in difficult semi-shaded areas and comes in lovely cultivars, including variegated and large-leaved types. Don't forget that old-fashioned sweet violets can be used in these conditions as well.

CLOCKWISE FROM TOP LEFT: *Seaside daisies easily seed in crevices of rock walls; columbines pop up in shady corners; violas are adept at self-sowing and reappearing year after year.*

THE LANGUAGE OF FLOWERS

Throughout the ages, flowers have always had a special significance for us. In the flower language of Victorian times, yellow roses were associated with jealousy, while white roses were said to mean secrecy. Black flowers were regarded as bad omens, and the orchid signified good business. Forget-me-nots were symbolic of lovers being true to each other despite the separation of years, and six-petalled primroses (they normally have five petals) signified that if you were in love, your love was returned.

Different cultures sometimes view the same flower differently. In Australia, for example, chrysanthemums (shown at left) are traditional Mother's Day flowers because of their autumn flowering, yet Europeans see them as funeral flowers in the same way that we associate arum lilies with death. Today, even some Australian natives have associated meanings. Apparently, wattles are a symbol of hidden love, so consider sending a spray of wattle to your Valentine.

Asteraceae: The daisy family

There has been an explosion of breeding with daisies over the last decade or so. The humble marguerite now has multitudes of cultivars, the veldt daisy has new colours and there are African daisies that are simply 'out of Africa'! In fact, so much has gone on in the daisy world that even some botanical names have changed: what used to be *Dimorphotheca* are now *Osteospermum*, and *Argyranthemum*, as they are now called, are the marguerite daisy group.

Marguerites will cope with only light frost, and prefer full sun. They respond well to regular dead-heading and fertilising. 'Peppermint' is a striking new dark pink form that flowers in autumn, winter and spring, and grows into a neat ball about 60 cm high by 80 cm round.

Also useful garden groundcovers are African or veldt daisies. These grow easily in any well-drained, sunny position. Like treasure flowers (*Gazania*), they open their flowers each day and close them at night, and are available in a range of colours, ranging from the apricot-pink shades of 'Peach Magic' and the pale pink and musk of 'Serenity Sunset' and soft butter-cream yellow of 'Serenity Lemonade' to white with a steel-blue underside.

The *Arctotis* genus contains some other choice groundcovers in the same family. Each spring the red, orange, cherry, white and pink blooms smother their soft, felted grey leaves. They look wonderful grown in borders, along embankments to stabilise the soil and as potted plants.

An embankment is the perfect well-drained sunny spot for daisies.

CLOCKWISE FROM TOP LEFT: *Field chamomile daisy is an annual that grows by seed and looks pretty in meadow gardens; mauve* Osteospermum; Osteospermum *'Tradewinds Bronze'; veldt daisies come in double and single forms and close up at night.*

The columbines. stone blue,
    or deep night brown.
Their honey-comb like
    blossoms hanging down;
Each cottage garden's fond
    adopted child.
Though heaths still claim
    them. where they yet
    grow wild.

JOHN CLARE

Aquilegias

These enchanting spring-flowering perennials are a delightful addition to any shaded, moist spot in the garden. Although each plant lasts only a few years, aquilegias have a tendency to self-seed, creating new and interesting colour combinations and popping up where you least expect.

Aquilegias flower in spring, but their foliage is attractive for most of the year: it has a fine, delicate look to it, not unlike maidenhair or rue. For best results, divide each plant in autumn when it looks scruffy, and keep well watered in dry weather.

Many named varieties are now available. These are mostly forms of *Aquilegia × hybrida*, which have long- and short-spurred forms and vary in colour, ranging from purest white through to lemon, burgundy, blue and various bicolours.

DID YOU KNOW? Columbine, the common name of aquilegia, comes from the Latin word for dove. It refers to the flying spurs behind the flower's face.

TOP AND LEFT: *The single and double forms of aquilegia are both exquisite.*

The Ranunculaceae family

The buttercup family contains about 50 genera, including perennial herbs, such as aquilegia, meadow rue (*Thalictrum*), windflowers (*Anemone*), hellebores and buttercups; annuals such as larkspur, delphinium and love-in-a-mist; trees such as tree peonies; vines such as clematis; or bulbs such as ranunculus. Happiest in cooler temperate regions, many members of this family are poisonous when eaten.

CLOCKWISE FROM TOP LEFT: *When shown as a group, you can see the similarities between members of the buttercup family:* Anemone coronoria *(a bulb);* Anemone nemorosa *(a herbaceous perennial); the perennial hellebore; delphinium; buttercup; peony rose.*

Rose campion has soft, felt-like grey foliage and sprays of deep pink flowers.

Pretty in pink

Thrift, known botanically as *Armeria*, grows naturally on the south coast of England, particularly Cornwall. In bloom from late winter right through to spring, these impressive pompom flowers come in various shades of pink, white, salmon and mauve. Many new cultivars are now available with bigger flowers and a longer flowering period. Two of these are the 'Pink Petite' and the 'Bees' series. Thrift looks lovely massed as a border, grown in pots, between paving as an edge or in sweeps in gravel gardens in the sun and even by the seaside. Remove the spent blooms to keep them tidy and feed them with a slow-release fertiliser in spring.

Rose campion (*Lychnis coronaria*) is a dear old-fashioned perennial that deserves to be rediscovered as it blooms so generously. The botanical name refers to the Greek word *lychnos* meaning lamp, and what a bright spot in the garden it can be. It has beautiful soft, felt-like leaves, very similar to the better known *Stachys byzantina* or lamb's ears, but the flowers are a bright magenta and make a striking contrast to its silver foliage.

Rose campion is repeat flowering too, so after the first flush of these 60 cm tall blooms, cut them back and you'll get a second flowering. They also seed easily, so keep the spent flowers in check unless you want more popping up again for the following year. Being mostly biennial, they should grow for at least a few seasons.

Another species, *Lychnis flos-luculi* is also popular in England. Known there often as ragged Robin, its cultivar name is 'Jenny' and it has pretty candy-pink, fluffy, double flowers on branched stems throughout late winter and spring, and green leaves that grow in grassy mounded tufts.

L. viscaria 'Splendens Plena' is yet another *Lychnis* variety. This one has double fuchsia-pink flowers, evergreen leaves that look much the same as those of dwarf agapanthus, and is just as fast and easy to grow. Its sticky stems have given it the common name catchfly. It prefers a full sun position in well-drained soil, which makes it a perfect choice for rockeries and edging, and a gravel-style garden.

Gone to seed

All seeds have an optimum temperature range at which they germinate best. This range is mostly between 15°C and 25°C, so spring and early autumn generally make the most appropriate times to sow seeds.

A seed is a miniaturised plant, packed and stored within a protective coat, waiting for the perfect conditions that will give it its start in life. Some plants will easily self-seed, others may need collecting, treating, sowing and transplanting. Seeds from dry seed heads can be shaken or rubbed from the plant, with any debris removed. In many cases, collecting seed heads in paper bags will help contain the seed as it falls.

Seeds enclosed in fleshy fruits or berries need more vigorous treatment (see below). First mash the fruit, then place the results in a jar with water, and shake. The pulp that floats to the top can be removed, leaving behind the seeds, which can then be dried and stored in paper bags.

The seeds of certain species need to be stimulated out of dormancy before

All seeds are most interesting, whether feathered like the polished silvery shuttlecocks of the Cornflower, to whirl in the wind abroad and settle presently, point downward, into the hospitable ground; or oared like the maple, to row out upon the viewless tides of the air.

CELIA THAXTER

they will germinate. Some cold-climate plants need an artificial cool time (called stratification) for germination to occur. This is an adaptation to prevent seeds from germinating until the last of the cold weather is over, so that late frosts or snow don't harm the young seedlings. Other seeds respond to heat and smoke (which is in effect the simulation of a bushfire) or drought. Hard seed coats can prevent plants from germinating by keeping out air and water, two vital ingredients in the process, and the seeds will therefore need to be chipped or rubbed with

How to remove seeds from fleshy fruits

1. Some flax lily (*Dianella* sp.) seeds.

2. With your hands inside a large jar, mash the berries with your fingers.

3. Add some water to the jar, replace the lid and give it a good shake.

4. Remove the pulp, which should have floated to the top, and retrieve the seeds once they have settled to the bottom of the jar.

RIGHT: *The seeds of clivias (see page 372) are encased in a fleshy pod; leopard lily gets its other common name, blackberry lily, from the resemblance of its seeds to blackberries (see page 186).*

Seed treatment

Hard seeds, such as these wattle seeds, need to be scarified. Rub the seeds with abrasive paper. Alternatively, soak wattle or other native Australian seeds in smoky water: the smoke in the water mimics bushfire and stimulates the seeds to germinate.

With large seeds, such as pawpaw seeds, use a hose and your fingers to push the pulp through the holes of a colander. Dry the seeds thoroughly before planting them out.

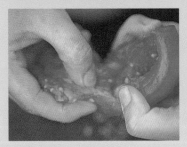

Remove the pulp and seeds from a tomato. Push the pulp through a fine mesh and then dry the tomato seeds on kitchen paper.

FUNGAL ATTACK Fungal problems are less likely if you water only the soil and not the plant, so dripper systems are ideal. You can also use a lime sulphur spray if you are prone to problems, or simply remove any diseased plants as soon as you see them.

In this vegie patch, two rills have been planted with carrot seeds, which have germinated and then been thinned out.

abrasive paper (a process called scarification) before sowing. (See 'Seed treatment', opposite.)

Once you have treated your seeds, sow them in containers. Most seeds should be sown in a seed tray initially, then pricked out and planted into larger containers as the seedling develops.

When sowing very fine seed, such as that of azalea, campanula, ferns, gloxinia, impatiens, lobelia, polyanthus, African violets and primulas, add fine dry sand to make spreading the seeds easier. Just tamp these seeds down slightly after sowing, rather than covering them over. Add sand to hairy seeds to stop them sticking.

Slightly larger seed can be sown straight from the packet or container. Draw a line (called a 'rill') with a pencil, sow the seed, then backfill slightly. Most seed can be handled like this, including seeds of asparagus, broccoli, cauliflower, chives, dianthus, eggplant, freesia, fuchsia, lettuce, onions, parsley, penstemon, phlox, salvia, tomato, verbena and violas. Even larger seed can be sown directly into clumps, while very large seed should be sown individually into pots.

Pricking out

Pricking out, or removing seedlings from trays, can be done after the first set of true leaves appears (these are the baby pair of leaves, or cotyledons) and before the third set has arrived, to minimise root damage. The more leaves a seedling grows, the more roots they also develop, and these roots might be disturbed by transplanting. Always harden plants off before planting them out.

A period of time in an open, shaded position toughens up seedlings and is particularly important if you have covered your seedling tray with glass to keep the warmth and moisture in. Try to gradually acclimatise the seedlings to cooler growing conditions, and watch that your seedlings don't dry out or get eaten by pests at this stage. (See 'Sowing seeds: Four steps to success' on page 125.)

THE PROS AND CONS OF SEEDS

The advantages of raising plants from seed are cost, access to interesting new genetic material, variation and variety, ready availability, and minimal storage and space requirements. This must be weighed against the possible loss of particular characteristics (such as flower colour) that may change in the second generation, particularly in the case of annuals and biennials.

52

Variegated clivia

Abutilon x hybridum
'Variegata'

Ctenanthe pilosa

Talinum paniculatum

Helichrysum petiolare
'Limelight'

Euonymus sp.

Variegated gold and silver foliage

Golden leaves add shimmering highlights. They can
be found in many plants and are a beautiful foil for
other colours in the garden. Silver foliage plants are
interesting because their neutral colour provides the
imaginative gardener with many creative possibilities.

Holly 'Ripley Gold'

Santolina sp.

Teucrium sp.

Flannel flower

Correa alba

Senecio cineraria

Artemisia sp.

Cyclamen hederifolium
(silver leaf group)

Plectranthus argentatus

Lamb's ears

ABOVE: *The strappy foliage of New Zealand flax is popular for its colour and ability to survive dry conditions.*

RIGHT: *New Zealand lily has sprays of lovely white flowers in summer.*

Growing foliage instead of flowers

Leaf colour is in vogue. With our increased incidence of drought, foliage is again making its mark. Smart gardeners are searching out plants prized for their sturdiness, form and—most importantly—great leaves. It's all about sensual curves, daring forms and dramatic colour and shine, with purple leaves and white variegation making the biggest impact. This makes good design sense, too: foliage makes a permanent statement.

Often the plants that make the most beautiful outlines—such as century plant (*Agave attenuata*), mother-in-law's tongue (*Sansevieria*), red cabbage palm (*Cordyline australis* 'Sundance'), ti plant (*C. fruticosa*), *Anthurium veitchii*, flax lily (*Dianella* sp.) and New Zealand flax (*Phormium* sp.)—are plant-and-forget stalwarts that cope well with abuse and neglect. New Zealand lily (*Arthropodium cirratum*) also falls into this category, though it is prone to snail attack and will need baiting.

Other eye-catching options for shady spots are large-leafed, glossy plants such as arum lily (*Zantedeschia* sp.), the fruit salad plant (*Monstera deliciosa*), taro (*Colocasia esculenta*) and the cast-iron plant (*Aspidistra*). All of these, once established, will tolerate drought. For frost-free gradens, try rex begonias. Although they need watering twice a week, it's worth the effort. It's like a stained-glass window tinted with rose, carmine, gold and pewter shades. Also, dieffenbachia (*Dieffenbachia amoena*) is striking but poisonous, and crotons (*Codiaeum variegatum* var. *pictum*) offer a dazzling combination of fiery oranges, reds and acid yellows.

Also worth considering is *Coleus*—which has many cultivars that over-winter in mild climates and add wonderfully exciting explosions of colour—beefsteak plant (*Iresine*) and Moses-in-the cradle (*Tradescantia spathacea*). They all make fabulous flower-bed borders.

CLOCKWISE FROM TOP LEFT: Iresine, *or beefsteak plant;* Cordyline *'Albertii' has marvellous form and cream-edged leaves;* Coleus *has many coloured leaf forms;* dieffenbachia *is a popular house plant but can be grown outside in frost-free regions.*

ABOVE: *Ixias decorate the front gate at this delightful cottage garden.*

BELOW LEFT TO RIGHT: *Grape hyacinth, daffodils and Dutch iris are among the most beautiful spring-flowering bulbs.*

Bulbs

Most gardeners consider bulbs an essential part of spring, and although many bulbs are happiest in cool climates there are a great number that suit warm temperate areas such as those of the greater part of coastal Australia.

Surprise packages

Bulbs are a delightful addition to a garden, make excellent container plants and are among the easiest plants to grow. Each bulb is a surprise package—it appears from previously bare ground to excite the eye, and adds a touch of spring to the garden in a way no other plant can achieve.

Bulbs have evolved to have an autumn/winter hibernation, which means they avoid severe cold climates. So if you live in a cooler climate you have the ideal growing conditions for many delightful bulbs, such as daffodils, tulips, irises and hyacinths. Bulbs are best planted out in autumn, but if you forget they can also be planted in spring once the tops are up and flowering. The

POTTED BULBS

If you forgot to plant your spring bulbs last autumn, don't despair. Most nurseries stock potted bulbs ready to flower. Plant them outside for an instant touch of spring, or bring them indoors to enjoy. Choose plants in full bud, rather than in flower, to extend the season, and put them outdoors at night so that they last longer. Once the flowers are past their prime, simply plant them outside. Crocus are shown above.

perfect spot is under the shade of a deciduous tree, but anywhere with at least half a day's sun and protection from summer winds is fine.

Feed bulbs with liquid fertiliser as the leaves start to yellow, and store cold-climate bulbs such as tulips, Dutch iris and hyacinths in net bags in a cool dry place until putting them in the crisper section of your fridge next April. Leave them in the crisper for two to four weeks.

Adaptable bulbs that can manage a more temperate climate include delightful low-growing varieties such as meadow grass, freesias and sparaxis—grassy tufts that flower in a rainbow of colours. Their low height and ease of care make them ideal for naturalising in lawn, creating a meadow garden, provided you can ease up on the mowing in early spring until they flower and die down. If you have a shadier spot and still want a meadow-like effect, consider growing some grape hyacinths, bluebells or star of Bethlehem.

CLOCKWISE FROM TOP LEFT: Babiana *is a bulb for warmer climates; bluebells work well in cool climates; watsonias cope with dry conditions; Dutch iris 'Casablanca' has yellow highlights; Triteleia 'Stars of Spring' forms a lovely clump; snowbells are very adaptable.*

1 'Phar Lap' 2 'Dolomite' 3 'Modern Art' 4 'Professor Einstein' 5 'Mopsy' 6 'Memento' 7 'Halvose'
8 'Trim' 9 'Avalon' 10 'Jenny' 11 'Flower Parade' 12 'Glenfarclas' 13 'Coppertone' 14 'Moondah'

Daffodils and jonquils

15 'Matador' 16 'Phantom' 17 'Beryl' 18 'Dolly Mollinger' 19 'Ethel Breen' 20 'Gold Sprite'
21 'Tweedle Dee' 22 'Seagull' 23 'Grand Monarch'

ABOVE: *This shady pathway is lifted with massed plantings of white nerines.*

RIGHT: *Variegated alstroemeria is easily grown. Look out for an almost pure-white leaf form called 'Rock and Roll', which is very eye-catching.*

The Amaryllidaceae family

The Amaryllidaceae family contains many perennial bulbs, corms and rhizomes such as daffodils, kaffir lilies, storm lilies, snowflakes, crinums, nerines, alstroemerias (also called Peruvian lilies or princess lilies) and spider lilies. Most of these plants are grown for ornamental use only, although it is interesting to note that flour is made from alstroemeria roots in Chile. See also pages 174-5.

The members of Amaryllidaceae are widely distributed throughout the world, with genera from the tropics and subtropics predominating. This makes many of the family perfect for bulb plantings in warmer zones, as they will flower reliably with no chill requirement.

Tulips

Tulips seem simple and serene enough. Their stunning goblet-shaped blooms are the essence of elegance and they have been used for massed displays for hundreds of years, giving delight to many. But behind that quiet, cold-climate-loving bulb lurks an uproar that created crazy 'tulipmania' in the 1630s, when a single bulb could cost as much as a horse and fortunes were made and lost trading in tulips.

There are more than 6000 cultivars today, including feathery-edged parrot types, doubles, bicolours and pointy-petalled lily-like ones to name but a few. However, some of the lesser known rockery and species types are also worth hunting for. Originally from Central Asia and Europe, these wild species multiply into small clumps and work well in pots and rockeries.

Unlike the cultivars, species tulips, such as *T. kaufmanniana*, *T. greigii* and *T. tarda*, can be left in the ground after flowering without being lifted; they will flower again the following season. Species tulips make an excellent border or rockery plant; some of them have variegated foliage.

BELOW: *Tulip petals come in many shades, but all close up each night or on a rainy day.*

Daffodils and jonquils

Daffodils and jonquils belong to the genus *Narcissus*. The home gardener generally distinguishes between the two by noting that daffodils have one flower per stem—a prominent trumpet in yellow, white, orange or pink—which is at least 30 cm high. Some have charming markings, such as the pheasant's eye daffodil (*N. poeticus* var. *recurvus*). Then there are the hoop-petticoat daffodils (*N. bulbocodium* and *N. cantabricus*) and the miniature daffodils (*N. cyclamineus*),

CLOCKWISE FROM BELOW LEFT: *The* Narcissus *genus is wonderfully diverse: the simple paper white; a clear yellow* Narcissus jonquilla; *a 'Pheasant's Eye' daffodil;* Narcissus cyclamineus.

which only grow to about 20 cm in height and have a hair-like texture.

Jonquils usually have a cluster of flowers on each stem, and include common favourites such as 'Erlicheer', 'Soleil d'Or', 'Paper White' and 'Silver Chimes'. Stems reach about 45 cm.

DID YOU KNOW? The name daffodil is a corruption of the Old English word *affodyle*, meaning 'that which comes early'.

Iris

Named after the Greek goddess of the rainbow, the iris was also the French royal family's emblem, known as the fleur-de-lis.

The majority of irises are spring flowering, and most grow from rhizomes that form clumps. Depending on the species, they grow happily in shallow ponds and other damp spots or in raised beds among roses and other perennials.

Just like a rainbow, the flowers vary from red, yellow, pink, blue, purple and orange, to near black and pure white. There are over 200 species and hundreds of hybrids and cultivars.

Louisiana iris

Bred from species native to Louisiana and Florida in the United States, these irises have a rather flat form. Hybrids available today from specialist nurseries include an amazing range of colours of astonishing depth and richness. They love moist soil and full sun. See also page 141.

Japanese iris

Although they were grown in Japan for centuries, the exact origin of these irises is obscure. They are known for their beautiful flat flowers, some having wavy or frilled margins. Many have flowers that are veined or netted in deep colours. The colour range covers many shades of blue, red and purple.

Bearded iris

The modern garden bearded irises are hybrids and come in an amazing range of single colours and bicolours. Their graceful, elegant flowers open one or two at a time on stems held well above the fans of stiff leaves. Planted en masse

The drooping petals of an iris flower are called 'falls' and the upright ones 'standards'.

Bearded irises are renowned for their wondrous range of colours. Some of the most unusual types are best sourced from online specialist nurseries.

they can be a breathtaking sight. Even a small group of these iris is worth growing. Two species of iris are grown for the production of orris, used in perfumery. They are *Iris germanica*, especially its variety 'Florentina', which is a major source of orris, and I. *pallida*. I. *germanica* is the 'fleur-de-lis' (literally 'lily flower') of French history.

*In the Spring a livelier iris changes
on the burnish'd dove;
In the Spring a young man's fancy
lightly turns to thoughts of love.*

ALFRED, LORD TENNYSON

BELOW AND RIGHT:
*Dutch iris like a cool
to cold climate, but
will tolerate warmer
conditions.*

Siberian iris

This is a moisture-loving group of irises that multiply well if they're grown in the right conditions. The foliage is narrower than that of some other groups and the colour range is confined mainly to white and shades of blue or purple, although new varieties are heading towards pinks and reds.

Dutch iris

This bulb iris dies back after flowering in spring. The stately blooms are borne singly. Available in white, blue, purple and yellow, Dutch iris make elegant cut flowers. To encourage a Dutch iris to reflower from one season to another, you may need to lift the bulbs and give them a 'cold store' period in the fridge crisper, especially in warmer zones.

Walking stick iris

Bearing iris-like flowers, this is also called the apostle plant, because it is thought to bloom best when it has at least 12 leaves, the number of the apostles of Jesus. Native to Brazil, it grows naturally as an understorey plant in forests, which makes it perfect for shadier parts of the garden such as beneath trees.

VITAL STATISTICS

Scientific name: *Neomarica* sp.
Family: Iridaceae.
Climate: Subtropical and tropical; elsewhere, provide protection of some kind.
Colours: White and blue, and yellow.
Height: Grows to about 45 cm.
Soil: It can cope in wet soils, but prefers a slightly acid loam.
Culture: Great for massed plantings under trees.
Position: Grow in part shade for best results.
Fertiliser: Add rotted leaf mould annually.
Pests/diseases: None.
Propagation: Division of rhizomes.

Feature bulb

Daylilies

Daylilies (*Hemerocallis*) are among the easiest of all bulbs to grow, are almost pest and disease free and will live happily in most parts of Australia. Their crowns can be purchased online year-round, which makes them one of the few plants whose cultivar list remains extensive all year, with good value.

These lilies can be deciduous, dying right down over winter, or evergreen, depending on the cultivar. Flowers range in shade from clear pale yellow, through rusts, browns, oranges, reds, peach, pumpkin and white tones, with many bicolours too. Some are fragrant. Their foliage is a mid-green, medium width and strappy, growing to about 50 cm or so in height and about the same width. Smaller types are available and marketed in a series called 'Echo', which includes 'Aztec Gold', 'Bright Copper', 'Grape Ripple', 'Lemon Yellow', 'Marcia Faye' (a mid-pink hue), 'Red Rum' and 'Wilson's Yellow'.

For the best results, when planting choose an open sunny spot. Dig in some rotted manure to improve and feed the soil. Once they are established, they are extremely tough and will withstand drought, water inundation and neglect, but try and give them a head start with regular water at first. Feed with manure pellets in spring and then late summer to improve blooms and vigour. After four years, divide up your clump, enrich the soil, and you're off and away again.

DID YOU KNOW? You can eat daylily flowers. Sauté the flower buds in butter and season to taste. The same can be done for the tubers too.

CLOCKWISE FROM TOP: *'Her Majesty's Wizard' is a sought-after plum-coloured, cultivar; 'Ed Brown' is an all-time favourite, with its faint yellow centre and ruffled edge; this type of marking is known as an 'eye'.*

Grasses, groundcovers and climbers

If a garden is like an outdoor room, then grasses, groundcovers and climbers are the sort of furnishings that add a finishing touch. A sweeping expanse of lawn, a wall with spillover plants cascading gently, a lovely groundcover or an arbour draped in fragrant climbers—it looks as beautiful as it sounds. These elements are charming in their own right, but also help to link buildings to their surrounds and soften hard landscaping features such as paths.

The softness of the combination of pillared roses and self-seeding groundcovers adds charm to this colonnade.

Grasses

With the arrival of warm weather your grass has a surge of energy and makes new growth. Spring is therefore an ideal time to smother weeds and repair bare patches.

Lightly fork over worn areas and mossy patches in the lawn, then give the whole area a vigorous raking over. An application of a 'weed and feed' product that clicks onto your hose will work wonders. Finally, sow some lawn seed or plant runners in any bare areas—and the job is done.

Greener pastures

Most lawns look a little tired after winter. To have a really good spring lawn, the type that reminds you of a billiards table or makes you want to set up a picnic, you need to put in more work than simply remembering to mow it when you can't get to the letterbox any more.

A lovely lawn sets off most gardens. The amount of time and care you give a lawn depends on the type of grass you choose and the degree to which it becomes an obsession. No plant grows as relentlessly as grass, and the time spent behind a lawnmower is torture for some and relaxing therapy for others.

Cutting a lawn too short weakens the grass, which gradually becomes thinner. Weeds soon take over, worn patches develop, and the ground becomes compacted before hardening in the heat of summer. You should set the mower higher, so that the grass stems are left at least 2.5 cm long. When grass is left longer it will grow vigorously to form a thick healthy turf. This in turn will allow the grass to grow much stronger as the roots will penetrate deeper into the soil.

When you mow it is best to dispose of most of the clippings into the compost bin, leaving just a small amount for use as mulch. Piles of dead grass can create fungus problems. Once a year, usually in late winter, it is a good idea to thoroughly rake the entire lawn to remove dead grass (a process known as dethatching; see page 288). This helps to rejuvenate the lawn and should be done before weed control and fertilising are carried out.

Lawn maintenance

Nothing disfigures a lawn more than bare patches, especially at gateways and other entrance ways. To fix this problem you can use either a hollow-tined roller or a strong fork to work lots of holes deep into the soil to allow air and water to penetrate. You might also find aerating shoes at your local hardware store or garden centre (see page 289).

Areas of lawn that experience heavy use should be aerated several times a year. Whichever method you use, be sure to scatter coarse, dry sand over the surface before watering—this will flow into the holes to provide long-lasting drainage plugs.

There are two types of gardener: those who feed their gardens regularly and neglect the lawn, and those who feed their lawn so much that fertiliser washes away.

Hungry, impoverished lawns quickly become infested with weeds. It is good to feed your lawn at least four times a year, at the beginning of each season. The trick is to use a specially formulated, slow-acting lawn food that will sink down past shallow roots, inducing the roots to grow downwards after the food. If you have big trees growing in your

lawn, the grass will need more fertiliser, as the trees will be constantly robbing nutrients from the ground around them. Never apply fertiliser to dry soil as this can severely burn the grass. Instead, feed your lawn immediately after rain or a good watering.

In hot areas it is wise to sprinkle your lawn with a soil-wetting agent once at the beginning of summer to help moisture penetrate. It works wonders on any type of soil and is possibly the best thing you can do for your lawn. If a lawn

The mown path through this long lawn adds not only whimsy but also a sense of journey.

TO LAWN OR NOT TO LAWN?

The pros and cons of having a lawn have been debated hotly over the last decade. Over that time many gardeners have ditched lawns in favour of paving, but don't assume that just because a green lawn requires water, food and maintenance to keep it looking good that it's bad for the environment. Grass also plays an important role in carbon sequestration, helps divert water from stormwater, can recover quickly after drought and keeps the ground and atmosphere cooler in our cities, thus reducing air-conditioning needs. Perhaps all the rooftops should have their own ovals for community use and climate modification?

is watered too frequently there is no need for the grass to make good long roots—this means that shallow roots will be cooked in very hot weather and the turf will further deteriorate.

When weeds appear, use a small-pronged tool called a flat-weeder to remove them. If that sounds too hard, cheat with 'lawn sand', which is simply one part dry sand mixed with one part of sulphate of ammonia. Scatter over weed-infested areas and within days weeds will bolt out into growth, then turn black and die.

You fight dandelions all weekend, and late Monday afternoon there they are, pert as all get out, in full and gorgeous bloom, pretty as can be, thriving as only dandelions can in the face of adversity.

HAL BORLAND

Types of grass

There are many different turf grasses available in Australia now, virtually all of which originated overseas. These can be roughly divided into cool season and warm season grasses. Cool season grasses grow in autumn and winter, and slow down or stop growing in hot weather, while warm season grasses do the opposite, growing in spring and summer. Sometimes it is necessary to combine grasses in order to have even green coverage throughout the year.

The major warm season grasses include these varieties: common or green couch, Kikuyu grass, Durban grass, buffalo grass, Queensland blue couch and carpet grass. Warm season grasses are all better suited to areas that enjoy a warm temperate climate.

The major cool season grasses include bent, Kentucky bluegrass, rye grass and fescues. In humid subtropical zones they are most often sown as blends, and can be used as an oversow to green up other grasses such as couch throughout the cooler months.

For many years researchers have been trying to develop a great Australian native lawn, experimenting with both weeping grass and Zoysia turf. 'Empire' is an early successful cultivar of the latter, but the one likely to outperform it is 'Nara', a truly fabulous Australian native turf grass that can be bought in rolls. It has a lovely fine texture, softness

This well-kept lawn resembles a river of green sweeping past the colourful flower beds.

and a stunning glaucus blue colour, and also tolerates salt, drought and cold. And for those gardeners who don't like the rough texture of buffalo, try the fine-leaf form known as 'Sapphire'.

Starting afresh

Springtime is great for establishing new lawns. The longer days are perfect for lots of leaf growth, and coolish nights help roots to establish before the onset of summer heat. Laying a lawn is a once-only job, so it is a good idea to prepare the soil bed well before you start. It is extremely expensive and difficult to improve soil quality, drainage or levels after you have laid the lawn. Follow the steps outlined over the page when preparing the site.

TOP TO BOTTOM: *Blue couch, buffalo, carpet grass, common couch, creeping bent, Kentucky blue, Kikuyu, rye grass and tall fescue.*

TOP LAWN TIPS

- Always water well before feeding.
- Mowing close to ground level increases the risk of weed invasion.
- Mow frequently, not severely—try raising the height of the mower blades.
- Areas of lawn that experience heavy use, such as gateways and the track to the clothesline, should be aerated each year.
- Top dressing can introduce weeds and is best done only if your lawn is uneven.
- If your lawn has been incorrectly fed over the years, it may have become quite acid. A pH test (kits are available from your local nursery) could help you diagnose this, and the problem can be rectified by an application of lime (see page 291).

RUNNERS Many grasses can be grown from runners pulled up from an existing lawn and transplanted into a well-raked area. As long as they are partially bedded and kept well watered they will put down roots and start filling up the gaps between them.

Rolls of turf should be laid immediately after delivery.

1 If drainage is poor, lay agricultural pipes.

2 Remove debris and old grass and eradicate weeds (use a weedicide for serious weeds, such as onion weed).

3 Once the weeds are dead, rotary hoe the soil bed, rake the surface smooth, even out any hollows and remove lumps.

4 The top 2 cm of soil should be especially well cultivated and fine textured. You may need some top-quality loam for this.

5 Rake in a lawn starter fertiliser, specially formulated for accelerating growth.

Growing grass

You can grow a lawn by sowing seed or by laying turf—ready-grown grass which comes in rolls that can be laid over a well-prepared soil bed. Which method you choose depends on your budget—sowing is by far the cheaper option.

Sowing seed

Spring is a great time to grow a new lawn from seed. Spread the lawn seed evenly over the prepared soil surface. Firm the seed into the soil with a lawn roller or tamp it down with the back of a metal rake—or just walk gently over the area in flat-soled shoes.

Keep the seeds just damp, not too wet, from the time of sowing until they germinate. Continue to water carefully: too much water and the seedlings will rot, too little water and they will dry out. Make sure you give the lawn deep watering until it is established so the roots will grow deeply.

Mow your grass once it reaches a height of 8-10 cm, and don't shave it too close. Place the mower on its highest setting and mow frequently to stimulate root growth.

Laying turf

Once your turf rolls are delivered they must be laid immediately or they will quickly dry out and deteriorate.

Lay the turf in lines, butting the edges together. Using secateurs, cut the turf to fit the required shape. Push the edges down with the back of a metal rake so that they make good contact with the prepared soil bed, then water the turf until it is soaking.

Don't allow pedestrians on the new lawn for two days. If you're laying turf over a large area that will be subject to a lot of pedestrian traffic, lay down some boards to spread the load across turves.

Keep the lawn moist as it establishes roots in the soil, and water new turf regularly for the first few months.

Laying turf

First, remove all the old turf, weeds and debris from the site. Make sure there are no runners under the surface of the soil.

Level the site by eye. Rake washed river sand over the site and re-level.

Compact the sand by tamping it down with a levelling or flat board. Apply starter fertiliser.

Rolls of turf, in this case soft-leaf buffalo, as they are delivered by the supplier. Lay the rolls of turf and be careful to leave no gaps. Water in.

FAKING IT

The quality of synthetic turf has improved hugely, and for many homeowners with little or no sun, constant traffic from pets and children, or no time to mow and care for a lawn, the idea of faking it has become more and more popular. The short, bright green stubble of AstroTurf has given way to more realistic options that have deeper greens and thicker, longer blades that fall naturally. The process of laying fake turf is very similar to laying rolls of turf, only the rolls are much wider; usually 1.8 m. Before laying, take care to create a level, well-prepared 'bed' and ensure extra drainage requirements have been addressed.

How to beat lawn weeds

Weeds are best dealt with in spring before they set seed over summer. So, to have a luscious green lawn underfoot that not only looks and feels great but also sets off the appearance of your house and garden, get out the gear and start work.

These days weeds spread into lawns mostly from mowers. In the days when everybody mowed their own grass, this wasn't as big a problem but now, if you do have a lawnmower 'man', it's worth requesting that the mower blades be rinsed before coming onto your property.

Some weeds, of course, actually come on the wind. If your neighbours, for example, have dandelions and don't cut their grass before they flower, then chances are your lawn will have them.

If your soil has very bad weeds and is infected with their seeds, it may be worth considering soil sterilisation. For solar soil sterilisation simply cover areas with black plastic and let the heat of summer kill off everything. Uncover, water and allow seeds to germinate. Repeat the process a few times to kill off all remaining seeds.

GANGSTER GRASS Many lawns can themselves easily become weeds. Couch and Kikuyu are particularly difficult to control if they get into a garden bed, so care with edging is essential to make sure rhizomes can't spread into your garden.

TEN COMMON LAWN WEEDS AND THEIR MANAGEMENT

- **Clover** (spring and summer). Clover can be controlled with extra dollops of sulphate of ammonia, which burns the clover away.
- **Bindii** (spring and summer). Bindii needs to be treated in winter when the seed heads start to appear. Controlling it depends on the grass you have, as many buffalo lawns are killed off by traditional selective herbicides such as Dicamba.
- **Creeping oxalis** (perennial weed, flowering spring to autumn, seeding summer and autumn). This needs to be sprayed with Glyphosate, a non-selective weedicide that will kill everything it touches, including your lawn. Apply it with meticulous care.
- **Onion weed** (bulbous plant, flowering spring, seeding summer). This needs to be sprayed with Glyphosate, a non-selective weedicide that will kill everything it touches, including your lawn. Apply it with meticulous care.
- **Onion grass** (bulbous plant, flowering spring, seeding summer). This needs to be sprayed with Glyphosate, a non-selective weedicide that will kill everything it touches, including your lawn. Apply it with meticulous care.
- **Paspalum** (perennial grass, flowering spring, seeding summer). This can be killed off in lawn using a herbicide combination of DSMA and MCPA. Although this can be used on buffalo and Kikuyu lawns, it does affect them too so is best spot-sprayed.
- **Winter grass** (annual) can be killed off in lawn using a herbicide combination of DSMA and MCPA. Although this can be used on buffalo and Kikuyu lawns, it does affect them too so is best spot-sprayed.
- **Summer grass** (annual) can be killed off in lawn using a herbicide combination of DSMA and MCPA. Although this can be used on buffalo and Kikuyu lawns, it does affect them too so is best spot-sprayed.
- **Dandelion** (perennial herb, flowering spring and summer). A handful of sulphate of ammonia, or Dicamba (unless your lawn is buffalo) or a herbicide combination of DSMA and MCPA will kill dandelion in your lawn. Although this can be used on buffalo and Kikuyu lawns, it does affect them too so is best spot-sprayed.
- **Kidney weed** (perennial groundcover). This native is often used as a grass substitute in lawns that have shade. It is easily killed off with Dicamba in lawns other than buffalo.

ABOVE: *The seed heads of flowering zebra grass look beautiful in every dancing breeze.*

RIGHT: *Purple fountain grass starts to become tired over winter and needs to have an annual cut back at this time. New spring growth emerges quickly.*

Ornamental grasses

Don't restrict grass to the lawn. Create interesting textures and accents in the garden with a group of plants that is as versatile as any shrub.

Ornamental grasses have greatly increased in popularity in recent years and are great for massed plantings, as a foil for perennials, or as accent plants. The new spring growth of ornamental grasses is often overlooked with so much else in flower, but they have a beauty all their own.

Grasses are a way of introducing some textural interest into a garden, with their soft strap leaves contrasting with the round form of shrubs.

For something a little different, grow the fabulous red Japanese blood grass (*Imperata cylindrica* 'Rubra'), which has sensational red leaf blades, the brilliant colour lasting from spring to late autumn. It is a slow-growing rhizomatous plant and makes a beautiful garden accent, especially in a shaded woodland location. Growing to about 45 cm, it looks particularly handsome in contrast with black mondo grass, *Acorus* and zebra grass, or planted with red-tinged shrubs, such as dwarf nandina. It can also be used in pots and, like most grasses, copes better than many other plants with neglect—perfect for the absent-minded gardener!

Although not strictly speaking grasses, members of the lily family such as the white variegated iris, striped mondo, *Liriope* 'Variegata' and the white-edged dwarf agapanthus called 'Tinkerbell' are worthy additions to your garden and give the same design effect. As well as being aesthetically appealing, ornamental grasses require very little in the way of maintenance. They don't require staking, spraying or dead-heading, and most grasses grow in a variety of climates and look good throughout the year.

Always check with a horticulturist first to make sure your selection won't seed readily and become invasive, particularly if you live near bushland.

Bamboo

More interesting than watching grass grow, is watching bamboo grow: the speed with which bamboo grows has made it a perfect source of renewal timber in Asia, where it's also a food source for both pandas and people.

In the garden bamboo can be used as an elegant feature plant, border plant or screen, depending on the variety chosen. And while bamboo does make a useful screen, growing as it does quite tall in a narrow space, it is also a plant that can run amok if you are not careful.

The trick is to choose your bamboo carefully. There are two major groups, clumping, or non-invasive bamboo, and its cousin, the running bamboo, which naturally is the real problem type. The physiology of each is different, with clumping bamboos only ever developing very short rhizomes, from which the culm shoots and new growth occurs. Running bamboo, on the other hand, has extremely long rhizomes and therefore spreads huge distances.

With the exception of the much sought-after black bamboo, most running types are inferior in grace and beauty; their one sole advantage is that they are much more tolerant of cold weather extremes. Black bamboo is, however, available as a clumping type as well as a runner.

If you are determined to plant a running variety, do ensure that its roots are suitably restrained in an escape-proof planter. To do this in the ground, use a tough, flexible plastic (like HDPE) that can be bent into curves and circular shapes as needed. Bury this in the ground nearly 1 m deep, but leave at least 5–10 cm above ground so that the rhizomes can't escape. Check this barrier periodically to make sure that rhizomes haven't 'jumped' their cage, and trim back if necessary.

Bambusa multiplex 'Alphonse Karr' is tremendous for hedging, and can grow up to 10 m but is normally around 4 m tall. It has attractive golden stems striped with green.

Perfect for hedges and screens is 'Shiroshima' (a cultivar of Hibanobambusa tranquillans), *a clumping bamboo with thin yellow strips to the leaf edge.*

Blue bamboo grows fairly upright, to about 4 m high, with long narrow leaves on arching stems. It's a non-invasive bamboo that makes a wonderful garden feature or privacy screen.

With Buddha's belly types, each segment tightens at its end, which creates an unusual bulging aspect to each stem.

If space is tight, try sasa. This is the Japanese classification for small bamboo, akin to knee-high grass.

KIDNEY WEED

Although kidney weed (*Dichondra repens*) may not sound like a plant you have to have, it is. Available in seed or plugs, it is a fabulous alternative to grass found naturally in the bush along the east coast. A recently bred silver form, called 'Silver Falls' has luminous grey leaves that cascade beautifully from urns and baskets, but it will also grow in dry shade with root competition from large trees.

project

Potted grass garden

Grass gardens can be fun additions to the smallest spaces. Dabble with your own miniature grass garden. A shallow bowl with pebble mulch and contrasting grasses makes a sensational feature.

1 Gently tease out the rootball and separate the clump slightly. This is ribbon grass (*Phalaris arundinacea* var. *picta*).

2 Remove any weed seedlings and mound up the potting mix to cover the roots.

3 Mulch with decorative gravel.

Blue-eyed grass

Although its foliage resembles grass, this perennial is in fact a member of the iris family. Native to Missouri in the United States, it naturalises in open woodlands, cottage gardens and rock gardens, and can be used as a border or path edge.

VITAL STATISTICS

Scientific name: *Sisyrinchium angustifolium*.
Family: Iridaceae.
Climate: Grows in cool-temperate to warm-temperate areas.
Colours: Bright blue flowers. Other species, such as *S. striatum*, have butter-yellow flowers, as well as soft grey iris-like foliage.
Soil and culture: Soils should be well drained. Water regularly. Divide every 2–3 years to encourage new clumps and vigorous flowering.
Height: Grows 30–45 cm, quite upright.
Planting time: Autumn.
Position: Grow in partial shade to full sun.
Planting spacing: Plant 50 cm apart for a striking massed effect or naturalised look.
Fertiliser: Feed in spring with well-rotted manure.
Pests/diseases: No significant pests or diseases.
Cutting: Prune back when the plant is looking tired.
Propagation: Propagate by division of rhizomes or after flowering to prevent self-seeding.

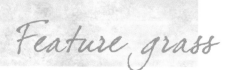

Feature grass

Groundcovers

Are your weekends spent slaving away maintaining the lawn and weeding garden beds? If you don't need a putting green, why not replant your lawn with an easier alternative? Once the warm spring weather arrives, plant groundcovers, the plants that lie low and let you lie in.

The benefits of groundcovers

Groundcovers are, as the name suggests, plants that carpet the ground. This carpeting effect has many benefits.

Groundcovers squeeze out the weeds, cover bare soil so that weed seeds can't find space to germinate and are less demanding than lawn in terms of water, fertiliser and labour requirements. They provide the seasonal interest, flowers or coloured foliage that turf lacks. If you plant in spring, these carpet-like plants will be well established by the time summer comes around, so that your garden will need very little attention next year. This type of garden is so much more restful than one that requires a great deal of labour for its upkeep.

Good preparation is the key for establishing a groundcover. Weeds need to be dealt with thoroughly before planting can begin, so solar sterilisation or weedicide sprays may be necessary. Also, if the area is likely to receive a lot of foot traffic, it's worth putting in specially designed plastic cells that can support extra compaction (even from cars) and still allow for roots to grow.

I, for one, prefer the type of garden where as much permanent groundcover as possible clothes the earth; wherein, when it is once established, a spade rarely appears.

EDNA WALLING

Hiding in the dark

Gardens that have a lot of shade don't have to miss out on groundcovers. The variegated rock cress (*Arabis caucasica* 'Variegata') looks great in a protected spot, as does the extremely vigorous *Nepeta hederacea* 'Variegata'. If you want more colour, try some of the different bugle flowers such as *Ajuga*

A true cottage garden like this one has so many plants covering the ground that pathways are almost swallowed up.

CLOCKWISE FROM ABOVE: *The long flower stems of Japanese windflower wave above their groundcovering foliage; blue bugle or carpet weed* (Ajuga) *in spring flower; a variegated form of greater periwinkle* (Vinca major *'Variegata'); yellow archangel* (Lamium galeobdolon) *is a rampant-growing groundcover.*

'Burgundy Lace', a pretty pink and plum variegated form, or golden moneywort.

Many of the campanulas make excellent groundcovers. One of them, which has an impossible name for such a charming and useful groundcover (*Campanula poscharskyana*), is vigorous, spreading and covered with gorgeous violet-blue bell flowers from late spring right through summer. This plant is very adaptable and with its vigorous runners is easily propagated.

Possibly the most difficult place for plants to thrive is dry shade under large trees where there are masses of roots. Japanese windflower (*Anemone × hybrida*) is tough enough to cope with these harsh conditions and has no trouble with the root competition. It features mid-green, lobed leaves for most of the year and in autumn produces a display of delicate flowers in soft pink and white, on tall stems that sway delightfully in the breeze.

In impoverished soils, bugle flower (*Ajuga reptans*) is a tough, obliging groundcover with deep blue flowers. It is indispensable for its ability to grow in impossible places—though be warned, in rich soils it will romp away at such an alarming rate you will have trouble keeping up with it. In addition to 'Burgundy Lace', there is a white-edged form called 'Alaska' and a large purple-leaved cultivar known as 'Catlin's Giant'. Alongside the grey-green chamomile (*Anthemis*) with its soft-textured leaves, and the vanilla-scented, blue-flowered cherry pie (also called heliotrope), it makes a charming picture.

Few silver plants cope with the shade, but members of the *Lamium* genus are made for it. Their foliage is a real highlight in dark corners of the garden, where they seem to light up a shady corner. Look out for *L. maculatum* 'Ghost', which has silver foliage and purple flowers, 'Marshmallow', which predictably has pink flowers, and 'Sensation', that has striped silver and green leaves and a deeper pink bloom. All flower in spring, grow about 15 cm tall and 50 cm wide, and make good choices for hanging baskets too.

Snow-in-summer, with its dainty white flowers, cascades softly over walls.

Sunlovers

Another foliage contrast is provided by the groundcover lamb's ears (*Stachys byzantina*), which will grow anywhere as long as the soil is well drained. Lamb's ears needs a sunny spot to keep its leaves attractive and silvery. Divide the clumps any time through spring to multiply your supply.

Another useful grey groundcover is snow-in-summer (*Cerastium tomentosum*). Its charm is provided by its silver-grey carpet of leaves, but white flowers are a bonus in summer. Use it cascading over walls like grey froth.

Lighten up an expanse of green groundcovers with touches of white. Sunny areas look great planted with trailing geraniums, and you can mix in the striking foliage varieties such as *Pelargonium peltatum* 'Ekva', which has clotted cream markings and red flowers. An attractive pink-tipped groundcover worth hunting out is *Trachelospermum jasminoides* 'Tricolour'. This technique can be used equally well in native gardens—for example, by growing the variegated *Grevillea* 'Sunkissed Waters'. You can also give your herb garden a lift with a new form of white-edged oregano called 'Cottage Cream'.

Mild traffic areas in the garden, such as side passageways, need particularly robust groundcovers. Good choices for these locations include *Vinca minor*, thyme, creeping boobialla, mints, mazus, ground-hugging grevilleas and dichondra.

Rose of Sharon (*Hypericum calycinum*) is an old-fashioned groundcover with large clear yellow flowers that are in bloom from around mid-summer to mid-autumn, each flower featuring a fluffy mass of stamens. Rose of Sharon is tough enough to grow under trees.

TOP TEN SPRING-FLOWERING GROUNDCOVERS
- Snow-in-summer
- Thrift
- Bellflower
- Aurora daisy
- Pinks
- Cranesbill
- Catmint
- Alpine phlox (shown)
- Viola
- *Erigeron*

Canberra grass

This groundcover looks so like AstroTurf that it is sometimes called Australian AstroTurf, and it has the same feel and texture to it—without the heat and petrochemicals! Native to Australia and New Zealand (the Maori name is *kohukohu*), it is perfect for rockeries, between pavers and so on.

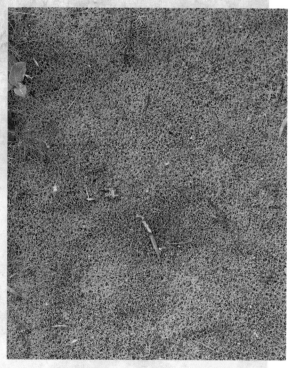

Feature grass

VITAL STATISTICS

Scientific name: *Scleranthus biflorus*.
Family: Caryophyllaceae.
Climate: Anywhere from cool to semi-tropical regions.
Height: About 10 cm high.
Planting time: Plant runners (stolons) at any time.
Soil: Tolerates a wide range of soils, though good drainage is essential.
Position: Prefers full shade, partial sun. Protect from hard frost and wet winters.
Planting spacing: Every 50 cm to 1 m.
Fertiliser: Not needed.
Watering: Keep watered till established.
Flowering time: Flowers in spring (flowers are tiny and inconspicuous).
Pruning: Remove from unwanted areas.

Another sunloving groundcover is babies' tears (*Erigeron*). It was this plant that Australian garden designer Edna Walling loved so much and used 'to take charge in some spots . . . Much better than dust and weed'. Indeed it became her signature, left in all her gardens, where she used it as a good companion to Italian lavender (*Lavandula stoechas*) and bugle flower (*Ajuga*) because all three flower simultaneously, 'and grow happily where few other plants will thrive'.

CHOOK FOOD If you are trying to get rid of the weed wandering Jew, try using chickens. They love it and will dig it all up and eat it.

NATIVE WANDERING JEW

Commelina cyanea, the native wandering Jew, is often confused with the weedy plant *Tradescantia fluminensis*, which has white flowers. This version, however, has bright blue flowers in the warm months that attract the native stingless blue-banded bee, and its leaves also provide great habitat for lizards and frogs. And if that isn't sufficient reason to let it thrive, you can also blanch the new shoots and eat them!

Lawn impersonators

There are many plants that will smother the ground admirably. Before selecting a groundcover, mentally divide your garden into low, mild and high traffic zones. Low traffic areas, such as garden beds where weed seeds rather than trampling feet are likely to be a problem, can look great with the addition of bugle flower, campanula, lamb's ear, snow-in-summer, verbena, arabis, dianthus, bergenia, windflowers, lamium and catmint. All are beautiful, and will thrive depending on the position.

High traffic zones, such as those where children play, call for tough plants. In these difficult areas only the toughest plants will survive. Choose from hardy selections such as lippia or mini mondo grass, native grasses such as *Dryandra* and *Sporobolus*, native violet and babies' tears.

For a green lawn look try these great alternatives to grass:

- **Hot, dry areas:** lippia (*Phyla nodiflora*), *Coprosma* × *kirkii*, creeping boobialla (*Myoporum parvifolium*), gazania.

- **Under trees:** clivia, turf lily (*Liriope*), mondo grass, spider plant (*Chlorophytum*), bugle flower (*Ajuga reptans*), catmint (*Nepeta hederacea*).

- **Sunny spot groundcovers:** Canberra grass (*Scleranthus biflorus*), *Grevillea poorinda* 'Royal mantle', veldt or aurora daisy (*Arctotis* sp.).

- **Shady spot groundcovers:** native violet (*Viola hederacea*), ivy (*Hedera helix*), kidney weed (*Dichondra repens*), isotoma, pratia, *Vinca minor*.

TOP: *English ivy can climb and cause grief to trees, but as a groundcover it's fantastic.*

RIGHT: *Clivias look wonderful massed under trees in the shade. The usual colour is orange; this is the rarer yellow cultivar.*

Climbers

Many climbers are so closely associated with spring that a spring garden would be incomplete without them. Wisteria, clematis, jasmine and honeysuckle herald this season as much as daffodils and bursting new leaves.

LEFT: *Chinese star jasmine bursts into bloom during spring and summer.*

Spring-flowering climbers

Spring is a feast for fragrant climbers. The heady perfume of jasmine, wisteria, climbing roses and honeysuckle scents the air. It's also worth learning more about lesser known spring-flowering climbers such as the Australian native dusky coral pea (*Kennedia*), the wonga wonga vine (*Pandorea jasminoides*) and bluebell creeper (*Sollya heterophylla*).

Chinese star jasmine

Useful because it grows in deep shade as well as full sun, *Trachelospermum jasminoides* won't disappoint with its fragrant display of white lace-like flowers in spring and summer. The glossy green foliage looks good all year round, and for different foliage effects there are also two variegated forms, one called 'Variegata', which has creamy yellow margins, and the other 'Tricolour', which has gorgeous pink-tipped new growth that fades to a clotted cream shade.

Clematis

All clematis are beautiful spring plants, but *Clematis montana* with its simple four-petalled flowers in white or pink is perhaps the most dainty of spring climbers. The *C. orientalis* hybrids are much showier, with double, ruffled, striped and splashed petals that flower later in spring, summer and autumn in shades of burgundy, pink, lilac, velvety purple and snow white.

LEFT: *This collection of various clematis (including the* C. orientalis *hybrids and evergreen types) reveals just how varied this genus can be.*

Gelsemium

Carolina jasmine is an attractive climber that doesn't become too vigorous. Bell-shaped, sunny yellow flowers appear twice a year, first in late winter and spring and then again in autumn. It has green glossy foliage and suits all climates.

Honeysuckle

Called 'woodbine' in Shakespearean times, this vigorous twiner (*Lonicera* spp.) has sweetly scented flowers in creamy white, pink, yellow or red, depending on the species. There is also a giant Burmese form with yellow/orange flowers called *L. hildebrandiana*.

Some species of honeysuckle grow as a shrub rather than as a climber. *L. nitida* has become extremely popular for hedging, while *L. fragrantissima* is great for winter perfume.

You should prune honeysuckle after flowering as it can grow out of control in warm-temperate climates.

I will wind thee in my
arms.
So doth the woodbine, the
sweet honeysuckle,
Gently entwist.

WILLIAM SHAKESPEARE

ABOVE: *Honeysuckle has honey-rich blooms from which many children have sucked the nectar. Shown here is the 'Firecracker' cultivar.*

LEFT: *The double form, 'Flora Plena', of Carolina jasmine is particularly pretty and also perfumed.*

Jasmine

The rosy pink buds and starry white flowers of jasmine are an integral part of the springtime experience. The most commonly grown species, *Jasminum polyanthum*, can become invasive—it's best to grow it in a pot to control the suckering roots.

Other jasmine species are probably better choices for the garden. For fragrance, the poet's jasmine (*J. officinale* 'Grandiflorum') is hard to beat— although it flowers later in the year, in summer. Oil is extracted from this species to make perfume. Biblical jasmine (*J. sambac*), has sweet rosebud-like blossoms that start off pale pink and open creamy white, and is somewhat gentler and more suited to growing on a trellis. The later summer- and autumn-flowering Azores jasmine (*J. azoricum*) has glossy green leaves and starry white flowers that sweeten the air indoors when used as cut flowers. *J. suavissimum*, or sweet jasmine, is an attractive Australian native species that flowers from late winter to late summer and tolerates dryness.

Wisteria

This plant evokes the magic of spring. Its long racemes of pea-shaped flowers hang like fragrant decorations, then the plant bursts into a mass of shading green foliage. This display is followed by a subtler autumn show of golden leaves and pendulous pods, which finally fall to reveal twisted, gnarled stems of great character and strength.

Wisteria originates from either Asia or North America, depending on the species. The Japanese (*Wisteria japonica*) has the longest flowers, with racemes hanging down to 1.5 m. The Chinese wisteria (*W. sinensis*) is the most commonly grown in Australia. Like the American species (*W. frutescens*) the Chinese wisteria has shorter, plumper flowers than the Japanese species, but is equally beautiful.

The easiest way for the amateur to tell the species apart is by looking at how they climb, with the Japanese growing up clockwise and the American and Chinese growing anticlockwise.

There has been plenty of cross-breeding and cultivation of these

BELOW: *Biblical jasmine is pretty, pure and perfumed. Divine!*

BELOW RIGHT: *It has a lovely scent, but* Jasminum polyanthum *can be unruly in the garden.*

species. Well worth hunting out are *W. floribunda* cultivars 'Violacea Plena' (for its double flowers of violet colour), and 'Honbeni' (which has long, pendulous rose-red blooms). 'Honbeni' is not to be confused with 'Rosea', which has paler pink flowers.

W. brachybotrys 'Shiro Kapitan', sometimes called white silky wisteria, is probably the most pure, sparkling white.

Be sure to prune back wayward tendrils as they grow. Otherwise, wisteria can quickly get out of hand and cause damage to roofs, guttering and woodwork.

Wisteria lookalikes

If you have no room for a vigorous climber, there are other plants with features similar to wisteria that may be more suitable. For example, if a small-growing clumping shrub would suit your garden, try summer wisteria, or *Indigofera*. This semi-deciduous plant has pink flowers in short racemes like wisteria, and suckers to form a clump. There is also an Australian native wisteria, *Millettia megasperma*, which has showy purple pea flowers in summer and autumn, but this vine needs a strong support on which to grow.

CLOCKWISE FROM LEFT: *The drooping racemes of Chinese wisteria are unmistakeable; the Japanese wisteria is prolific in growth and flower; summer wisteria is not even in the* Wisteria *genus, but its flowers look similar.*

Bushland beauties

Spring is a time when many Australian native climbers come into their own. There are some fabulous cultivars of false sarsaparilla or happy wanderer (*Hardenbergia violacea*) out now that not only vary from the standard purple, but also have shades of violet, pink and white. The beautiful pea-shaped flowers appear in sprays, and the gum-leaf-shaped leaves make them a lovely addition to the garden, either as a groundcover or climber.

Another interesting native climber is the wonga-wonga vine (*Pandorea jasminoides*). It has a number of interesting cultivars: 'Lady Di' has a large-trumpeted pure white flower; 'Snowbells' has clusters of tiny white flowers; 'Golden Showers' has yellowy orange blooms; and 'Bower of Beauty' has large flowers with violet throats. All have glossy green foliage that is evergreen and attractive year-round, although there is also a variegated leaf form called 'Charisma' worth finding.

Clematis also has an Australian native member known variously as old man's beard or traveller's joy, and botanically as *Clematis aristata*. It likes

Banksia rose

Banksia rose is one of the toughest plants you can get; originally, many roses were grafted onto it for this very reason. Thornless, vigorous and charming, it can be trained easily along walls, and on arbours and pergolas. Sadly, its short flowering time means you have to be quick to enjoy its blooms.

VITAL STATISTICS

Scientific name: *Rosa banksiae* 'Lutea' (yellow) or 'Alba' (white).
Family: Rosaceae.
Climate: This rose will quickly cover a wall, fence, shed or arbour. It's tolerant of just about anything, and is evergreen, unlike other roses.
Culture: Shelter from strong winds during flowering to maintain blooms. Remove straggly growth after flowering and cut back stems to within bounds.
Colours: Flowers are white and yellow.
Height: Plants grow as climbers to about 9 m high by 5 m wide.
Soil: Free-draining soil.
Position: Plants require a sunny position.
Fertiliser: Mulch around the stems in spring with well-rotted manure.
Pests/diseases: Plants are not commonly affected by black spot or other rose problems.

Feature climber

a cool, deep soil, and will cope well in shade. Its white, star-like flowers appear in spring and are followed by the curvy feathery seeds that give rise to its common name. It's easily trained along a fence or can be left to sprawl across the ground.

Snake vine (*Hibbertia scandens*) is another climber that can be used as a groundcover if preferred. Its 10 cm broad, sunny yellow flowers look like happiness itself, and the plant is terrific for erosion control in poor soils and on difficult slopes. It even grows and flowers in heavy shade. Another vine with the same common name is *Adenandra uniflora*, which seems to be just as tough and adaptable. It looks very much like Chinese star jasmine, with similarly glossy leaves and masses of tiny greenish white flowers in spring.

Another genus that can be used as a groundcover or climber is *Kennedia*, which has pea-shaped flowers. One of the more commonly grown species is black coral pea (*K. nigricans*), an extremely vigorous plant with black and yellow flowers in spring. It will cope with light frosts, drought and shade. The dusky coral pea (*K. rubicunda*) is a great choice for a waterwise garden, and its orange-red flowers can be used to great effect on trellising. More gardeners should plant this easy-to-grow show-off.

ABOVE LEFT: *The purple pea flowers of* Hardenbergia *are prolific in spring.*

ABOVE: *The white miniature flowered form of wonga-wonga vine shown here is* 'Snowbells'.

Every mountain top is within reach if you just keep climbing.

BARRY FINDLAY

Shrubs and trees

Spring is a time of renewal. Many trees and shrubs blossom now and all have a flurry of growth that will transform your garden with translucent green leaves and delicate blooms. Spring is quite a good season to plant, as the weather isn't too hot, so feel free to succumb to the odd temptation at the nursery; after all, it will probably be snapped up by autumn.

This beautiful spring scene uses the captivating pink dogwoods to charming effect.

Shrubs

Shrubs give a garden its strength, with the colour, form and flowers creating a distinctive character. Shrubs can screen out an unwanted view, provide privacy and even perfume an outdoor living area. A garden can be created entirely out of carefully planted contrasting shrubs, and be a beautiful place every month of the year.

Bare beauties

Most gardeners are aware of spring-flowering trees—apples, peaches and cherries to name a few (see page 103). Not everyone thinks about including deciduous flowering shrubs in their garden, and therefore miss out on some of the most delightful and fragrant blossoms of all.

Among noteworthy inclusions are the buttercup-yellow forsythia, the underrated spiraea (also known as may bush), hardy weigela (available in red-, pink- or white-flowered forms), deutzia with its dainty white bell-like blooms, and philadelphus, or mock orange,

CLOCKWISE FROM TOP LEFT: *Weigela has dainty bell-like flowers; blooms of the double may bush look like tiny cauliflowers; Weigela florida 'White Knight' has pure white flowers that stand out against the dark green foliage; forsythia is a golden spring delight; pearl bush (Exochorda racemosa) is a truly beautiful shrub to about 2 m; philadelphus has a perfume similar to that of orange blossom.*

which has strongly scented flowers that look like snowflakes.

Many of these spring-flowering beauties have the added bonus of coloured foliage, which extends their usefulness throughout summer and autumn. There are stunning golden-leafed mays, philadelphus and viburnums, and variegated forms of weigela and deutzia, which have pretty gold or white leaf margins.

One beautiful plant worth hunting down and including in your garden is white forsythia (*Abeliophyllum distichum*), which looks just like a white version of forsythia but grows like an abelia with gracefully arching branches. The blooms, which appear in late winter and early spring, are wonderfully fragrant, and last well indoors where the scent can be easily appreciated. It is happy in any spot as long as the summers aren't too hot and dry, as it prefers a cool-temperate climate.

Viburnum

For showy flowers, heavenly perfume, bright berries and colourful autumn leaves, the various species of viburnum cover almost every aspect you could desire in an ornamental plant. Some of them—such as *Viburnum odoratissimum*, *V. tinus* and *V. japonicum*—are evergreen and make great screens or formal hedges. Other deciduous types such as the snowball tree or Guelder rose (*V. opulus*) and Japanese snowball (*V. plicatum*) have sensational spring blossom: the former looks like snowballs and the latter like snowflakes.

CLOCKWISE FROM BELOW: Viburnum plicatum; V. × burkwoodii; *and* V. opulus *'Sterile'.*

He told of the magnolia spread
High as a cloud, high overhead.

WILLIAM WORDSWORTH

Azaleas and rhododendrons

A flowering azalea is a sight to behold, with blooms so plentiful that they almost mask the foliage.

Azaleas come from mountainous regions where they occur naturally among rock crevices and on the sides of ravines, so they are very shallow rooting and need good drainage. They are understorey plants, happiest in broken sunlight and mulched heavily by leaves that have fallen from the canopy. This makes them ideal for growing in broad shallow pots and in rockery pockets.

Today they are equally at home in garden beds of improved, rich soil with an acid pH, and breeding has extended their vigour and toughness.

Botanists used to distinguish azaleas from rhododendrons by classifying those with five stamens as azaleas and those with ten as rhododendrons. Azaleas are now classified in the *Rhododendron* genus. Few plants make such a sea of colour, ranging from pink and white through to lilac, red, orange and yellow. They belong to the family Ericaceae, which includes the heathers (see page 404), kalmias and blueberries.

Few of our evergreen garden azaleas are fragrant. The tall-growing, single-flowered varieties are the exception—for example, 'Alba magnifica' and 'Alphonse Anderson' have a delicate sweet fragrance. These make excellent screens to fence height and are tough, hardy old-fashioned varieties. Once established, these are almost indestructible and even cope with full sun.

The Kurume azaleas have simple, small flowers like tiny bells, and small foliage that is great for hedging. There are hundreds of modern hybrids with ruffled edges, double flowers and even variegated foliage, and these come in a multitude of colours.

Deciduous azaleas occur naturally in parts of Europe and North America, as well as in Asia. They mainly flower in shades of yellow and orange, and quite a few are fragrant, particularly the Ghent, Mollis and Occidentale hybrids.

ABOVE: *In contrast to azaleas, the flowers of rhododendrons are grouped in trusses and the foliage is usually large and leathery. Flowers range enormously in colour.*

RIGHT: *These two deciduous azaleas have delightful perfumes and flower on bare stems, making them quite spectacular.*

The various forms of Rhododendron spp. whose blooms are shown here include large-leaf types, and deciduous and evergreen azaleas.

The larger growers, commonly called rhododendrons, mostly have large trusses of flowers in spring, and some have blossoms in pretty lilac shades. These grow well in cool climates and tolerate light frosts. Rhododendrons are also frequently sold as potted plants. The shallow root system allows smaller species and azalea types to adapt easily to tub culture.

If you live in a frost-free region, the tropical rhododendrons (commonly called vireyas) may suit your garden better. Vireyas flower off and on through the year, with a major flush in late winter. See page 421.

Silk rose

For some reason, the silk rose (*Rhodoleia* sp.) is not as popular as *Rhododendron* sp., which it resembles. This beautiful shrub has thick, shining green leaves and pendulous flower clusters of rose red. Native to South-East Asia, it likes woodland conditions in frost-free areas. If you can find it, it is a worthwhile addition to the temperate garden. Grow it in full sun or part shade, sheltered from the wind.

Tropical, or vireya, rhododendrons have glossy foliage and cannot tolerate frost. They flower spasmodically throughout the year.

OUTLAW In some areas the common rhododendron (*R. ponticum*) has become a weed and should not be planted.

RIGHT: *Orange jessamine is an evergreen and flowers as a response to rain, usually around three times a year.*

Spring scents

Each spring we are tempted by a vast array of perfumed plants, such as lilac, viburnum and jasmine. These plants have developed this property in order to attract pollinating insects; unlike the blooms of bird-pollinated plants, the colour and size of the flowers are not very important. Perfumed plants can revive old memories, soothe the soul and uplift the spirit.

Some scents are at their strongest first thing in the morning and others at night. Many perfumes in a garden cannot be detected near the plant; in these cases the scent is dispersed and only develops into a full heady fragrance when it is 100 m away.

Orange jessamine

This evergreen has glossy foliage and a strong orange-blossom-like fragrance. White flowers appear at least three times a year from spring through to early autumn, and it makes a terrific screen, formal hedge or container specimen. *Murraya paniculata* grows to about 4 m high with a 3 m spread, in both full sun and shade. It requires well-drained soil and responds well to an application of citrus food in spring.

Philadelphus

One of the plants given the commmon name 'mock orange' is *Philadelphus*. These mostly deciduous shrubs flower in spring once the fresh green leaves have appeared. The strongly scented flowers smell as sweet as orange blossom, hence its common name. *Philadelphus* forms an erect multi-stemmed shrub and is best pruned annually to encourage new flowering canes. The blossoms are either single or double, and foliage can be golden or dark green depending on the variety.

ABOVE: Philadelphus *has pleated foliage and single or double, scented white flowers.*

ABOVE: *Cut leaf lilac* (Syringa laciniata) *has dainty foliage and masses of smaller lilac flowers.*

RIGHT: *These two beautiful cultivars of* S. × hyacinthiflora *are the rose-tinged* 'Charles Joly' *and the white-flowered* 'Mount Baker'.

Lilac blossom

Lilac (*Syringa*), a 2.5 m upright suckering shrub, is best known for its fragrance, and is often sold as a cut flower in spring. (It should not be confused with the California lilac, *Ceanothus*, which produces intensely blue flowers in early spring; see opposite.)

These plants, with their trusses of spring blooms comprising tiny flowers in dense cylindrical spikes, are an excellent choice for small gardens, and come in white, purple, pink, mauve and bicolour forms. Only suited to cool-temperate areas and requiring cool nights in order to flower properly in spring, they are tolerant of frosts and extreme cold. Lilacs grow well in many types of soil, including chalky ones.

Plant care

Lilacs are at their best in deep, friable loams with regular rainfall and full sun exposure, but must be protected from strong winds. Encourage watershoots from above any graft as new flowering wood, and lightly trim spent flowers in late spring for a vigorous balanced plant.

Lilac lookalikes and namesakes

The California lilacs (*Ceanothus*) are native to the US and Mexico, and known best for their showy blue flowers (although they also come in pink and white). Some hybrids are semi-prostrate, but most grow to about 4 m and flower in late spring. They prefer light, freely drained coarse soils in a mild climate with an open sunny position.

The New Zealand lilac (also known as speedwell, hebe and veronica) is a genus mainly native to New Zealand. It has a raceme of flowers similar to northern hemisphere lilacs. Most are small rounded shrubs to about a metre or so, and make fabulous flowering plants, growing in any open, sunny, well-drained position, even coping with strong salt-laden winds and temperatures down to –5°C. Flowering time varies depending on the species, but most are at their best from late winter to late spring. They benefit from a light trim after each flush of blooms.

Other lilac lookalikes include chaste tree (*Vitex* sp.) and butterfly bushes (*Buddleia* sp.), which both have flower spikes in the lilac, lavender, pink and white colour range. These are useful replacements if your climate differs from the cool-temperate zones preferred by *Syringa* species.

How slowly through the lilac-scented air Descends the tranquil moon!

HENRY WADSWORTH LONGFELLOW

CLOCKWISE FROM ABOVE: Ceanothus *flowers en masse in spring; buddleias grow quickly into tall shrubs with masses of flowers; hebes grow into neat, well-rounded shrubs and have sprays of lilac-like flowers.*

THE OLEACEAE FAMILY

The olive family contains some of the most ancient cultivated plants, including olives, which date back to 2000 BC as a food source in Egypt, and jasmine, which has been prized for its fragrance and oil for many hundreds of years by the Chinese.

Many genera are highly ornamental: lilacs, osmanthus, fringe tree (*Chionanthus*), forsythia and white forsythia (*Abeliophyllum*) are a few of the flowering plants, while ash are beautiful autumn foliage trees, and some (for example, privet) have become weeds in warm-temperate zones across Australia. Some genera are of considerable economic importance for food (olives and oil), timber (ash for lumber) and perfumery (jasmine oil), and as a cut flower (lilac).

Roses

Spring is the time when your rose bushes will be laden with blooms. Don't be afraid to pick bunches of them for the house and for friends—the more you pick vase-length stems, the more you encourage further flowering. For blooms that will last indoors a week or more, pick flowers first thing in the morning and plunge the stems immediately into a bucket of water.

In Australia, more than a million roses are sold each year, a statistic that makes it the most popular plant in the country. This is a plant that commands respect, and it is almost sacrilege not to have at least one rose in your garden. The trick is to ascertain what rose is right for your garden, and how to make the most of your selection.

Planning and planting

Roses are prickly creatures, and care needs to be taken when finding a home for them. For example, don't plant roses beside a path where the thorns could be dangerous. Find a spot that provides the rose with plenty of room to spread, lots of air circulation to minimise fungal disease and preferably eight hours of sunshine a day.

The rose is a hardy and forgiving plant. It can tolerate some neglect but the more care you give the better it will respond. Growing gorgeous roses is quite simple if you start with tough, robust varieties and keep the plants well watered and well fed. For best results, pay careful attention to pest control, pruning and general care.

You must plant roses in well-prepared soil. That means digging in compost or another type of soil conditioner prior to planting. Roses can be planted in early and mid-winter as bare-rooted specimens or any time of the year if they have been grown in pots. Spring and autumn are ideal times for planting container specimens as the plants still have flowers to select from, while the weather isn't too hot for their roots. Dig in plenty of rotted animal

CLOCKWISE FROM TOP: *Whatever the colour, roses make wonderful cut flowers; 'Peach Blossom', a David Austin rose; this tall rambling rose is adorned with pink cup blooms throughout late spring; 'Troilus', another David Austin rose, grows into a medium-sized bush.*

THE BASICS OF ROSE CARE

- Keep roses moist at all times but never allow the roots to sit in water.
- Feed your plants generously and frequently.
- Keep pests to a minimum (this is usually not a problem if you start with a strong variety and keep it well watered and fed).
- Prune back heavily once a year in winter (see page 412).
- Keep the area weed-free and ensure 6–8 hours of sun per day during summer.

manure, incorporate water-storing granules and add some fresh soil if you are planting in a spot where roses have grown previously.

Grafted onto hardy disease-resistant understock, roses will grow anywhere as long as there is lots of sunshine. When planting be careful not to bury the graft union below soil level. Determine which shoots grow from above the graft (desirable watershoots) and which shoots grow from below the graft, and must be removed (undesirable suckers).

Feeding and mulching

Don't fertilise roses until they are established. Wait six weeks from the time of planting and then feed either this autumn or the next spring. You should also sprinkle on a handful of pelletised manure or rose food each month during the growing season. Roses are heavy feeders and require two or three feeds during the growing season. Apply the first in spring before the leaves are fully open and then feed again in early and mid-summer, following the recommended dosage on the packet.

Do not feed roses in early autumn, because the plants should be hardening for winter at that time and should not produce soft new growth that is cold-sensitive. In frost-prone areas, do not fertilise after the end of spring.

Mulch roses with nitrogen-rich organic matter such as lucerne hay, pea straw or sugar cane mulch. Roses love mulch. A 5-7 cm layer of compost or straw stops weeds and evaporation of water and helps to keep the roots cool.

Watering

Roses are drought-tolerant but they will not thrive in very dry conditions. For best results, keep the soil moist at all times: if you were to dig down a few centimetres into the soil, the deeper soil should still be slightly moist. Ideally, you should water by slowly soaking the bed quite thoroughly to 10-15 cm deep. Sprinklers are acceptable if the top 15 cm of soil receives enough water and if the foliage has enough time to dry before nightfall. If the foliage remains wet overnight (especially in the cooler weather of spring and autumn), the plants will become stressed and will be much more susceptible to diseases.

Pruning

Don't be put off by the mystery and rigmarole that some so-called experts peddle about rose pruning. True, it can be done incorrectly, but even a bad trim is better than no pruning at all. There is no need to waste the cuttings: a 15 cm pruning can be planted into three parts sand and one part peat moss and kept moist until the new growth appears. (If you see a rose you like in someone's garden, ask for a cutting. Roses are so hardy they strike at almost any time of the year and most gardeners love to share the spoils of their toil!) Prune roses in mid-winter, except for 'spring-only' varieties, which are pruned after flowering. (See 'Rose pruning', page 412.)

Prune off the old flowers as if you were cutting stems for a vase. Angle the secateurs, cutting on a diagonal above an outward-facing leaf bud.

LEFT TO RIGHT:
'Sexy Rexy' has salmon-pink blooms with a light perfume; 'Julia's Rose' is excellent for cut flowers; 'Crepuscule' has apricot-yellow flowers for many months of the year.

Types of roses

Roses come in the form of shrubs, pillars, climbers and ramblers, ground-covers and smaller varieties suitable for containers. There are old-fashioned roses, modern roses, cluster-flowered and landscape roses. Many varieties are delightfully fragrant and these should be planted in a position where their perfume can be readily enjoyed. A variety called 'Shady Lady' will cope with less sun, and many old-fashioned roses will tolerate light shade.

BELOW: *'Zéphirine Drouhin' is a thornless climbing rose with marvellous perfumed flowers in profusion.*

- Modern roses are among the best flowering of all plants. They grow in all Australian climates from the tropics to the snow line, in reasonable garden soil.

- Bush roses are the most popular. These develop several stems at ground level and grow into a shrub that should be pruned hard in mid-winter. Plant them in a flower border with other garden shrubs, annuals, bulbs and perennials.

- Climbing roses can be trained up walls and fences. They produce masses of blooms and give a fine flower display. Plant climbing roses to disguise an unsightly outhouse, shed or garage.

- Pillar roses are slender climbers; they are not too vigorous, and so are useful for training around a decorative pillar, post or verandah railing. Make sure that the thorns will not be in the way of passersby.

- Hedge roses are usually scramblers, meaning they need plenty of space. They can be grown as an informal hedge—old-fashioned rugosa roses, for example, have a dense habit that makes them excellent hedging specimens. They are hardy, disease free and drought-tolerant, and flower for an extensive period. Light pruning after each flush of flowers keeps them in shape.

- Old garden roses are frequently seen these days, no doubt because of their simplicity

LEFT TO RIGHT: *A white, high-centred tea rose; pink* Rosa rugosa; R. rugosa *'Alba' makes an excellent hedge; 'Pierre de Ronsard' is a vigorous climber with large blooms.*

and perfume. Many types such as bourbons, China, hybrid musks and rugosas have a fascinating history.

🌹 David Austin roses are a newish type, with the charm and scent of old-fashioned roses but with the colours and free-flowering qualities of the modern rose. This result was achieved by breeding from two distinctive parents.

🌹 'Landscape' rose is a term that has been given to the almost evergreen-style floribunda varieties such as 'Iceberg' (white), 'Simplicity' (pink), 'Freesia' (yellow), 'Seduction' (bicolour), the 'Flower Carpet' range and 'Meidiland' range of roses. They respond well to pruning with hedging shears and produce flush after flush of flowers from spring until autumn.

RIGHT: *This red-flowering carpet rose is prolific, blooming for nine months of the year.*

Life is bristling with thorns, and I know no other remedy than to cultivate one's garden.

VOLTAIRE

ROSE POTPOURRI
Make a rose potpourri with this easy recipe. Combine the following ingredients, then leave in an airtight container for a few weeks to blend the scents.
4 cups dried roses
4 cups dried geranium leaves
1 cinammon stick
12 whole cloves
1 heaped teaspoon orris root chips
5 drops rose geranium oil
10 drops rose oil

...the nodding violet grows
Quite over-canopied with luscious woodbine,
With sweet musk-roses, and with eglantine...

WILLIAM SHAKESPEARE

Rose selection

What type of rose you choose should come down to why you want it. Roses for a vase do not necessarily make the best-looking plant in the garden.

Cutting roses

Why buy a bunch of roses from the florist when you can grow your own? The long-stemmed roses 'Adolph Hortsmann' or 'Catherine McCauley' are beautiful yellows, 'Eiffel Tower' or 'Peter Frankenfeld' superb pinks, 'Mr Lincoln' an intense deep red and 'Pascali' the purest of whites. Though not as strong in colour, 'Just Joey' and 'Julia's Rose' have fabulous bronze tones. To extend their lives as cut flowers, re-cut the stems under water before placing them in a vase.

Perfumed roses

It is hard to go past old-fashioned roses when it comes to scent. They are also easy to maintain and resistant to disease. Many people consider that among the best are 'Constance Spry', with its huge, clear pink cabbage-like blooms; 'Souvenir de la Malmaison', a blush-pink bourbon rose which flowers even in winter; and the hybrid musk 'Penelope', which has a pink bud opening to cream. Most of the English rose breeder David Austin's selections are also highly perfumed. The best modern cultivars for fragrance include 'Double Delight' (with crimson and ivory blooms) and 'Blue Moon' (pale lilac).

Hedging and groundcover roses

Roses can easily be grown into a bushy, repeat-flowering hedge. For a tall screen try the yellow-apricot 'Buff Beauty', delicate pink 'Celestial', 'Felicia' with its mix of coral and apricot blooms, or soft yellow 'Mountbatten', while pink 'Seduction', white 'Iceberg', pink 'China Doll' and bright scarlet 'Satchmo' make good hedges to around 1 m. Many modern hybrids such as the carpet roses have been bred with the intention of creating a ground-smothering mass. These respond well to being pinned down along the ground, which can be done with bobby-pin-like hooks made from old coat hangers. Indeed, this will force side branching, which tends to increase flowers.

Roses for containers

Any rose can be grown in a pot, as long as it has adequate fertiliser, water and a rich soil, but some roses have been bred with dwarf root systems, making them ideal for containers. Look for these patio roses at your local nursery.

Mini roses are easily grown in tubs and look beautiful in posies. White 'Popcorn', a soft lime called 'Green Ice', a ginger called 'Teddy Bear' and lolly pink 'China Doll' are tiny and delightful roses.

BELOW: *'Just Joey' is one of the most popular cut flower roses due to its soft apricot shading.*

BELOW RIGHT: *For perfume, 'Double Delight' is hard to go past. Its scent is rich and full.*

Roses for arbours and arches

Roses can be breathtaking when they are grown to sprawl over arbours, trained flat on a sunny wall, grown in rose cradles or as pillars. If you have space for a colonnade, you can smother it with roses. Masonry columns and timber rafters are the basic elements of a colonnade—plant a climbing rose at the base of each column and in no time it will be onto the rafters. You can place a piece of garden art (such as an urn or a statue) as a focal point at the end of the colonnade with a background of dark green foliage behind it, against which both the chosen ornament and the rose blooms will stand out.

To cover garden structures, try growing the climbing roses 'Monsieur Tillier', which has a coppery purple lustre; 'Blackboy', which has velvety red blooms; 'Altissimo', with its single blood red but scentless blooms; and 'Crepuscule', an apricot rose that never stops flowering.

A relatively new rose that looks like an old-fashioned variety, 'Pierre de Ronsard', has crimson edges on soft pink, double, cup-shaped blooms, and it makes a stunning climber.

Rosa rubiginosa (syn. R. eglanteria)

The 'sweet briar' or 'eglantine rose' made famous by Shakespeare is distinguished by the exquisite apple scent of its foliage, especially noticeable after rain or when the leaves are crushed. The bush grows to around 2 m, is very thorny and makes a great hedge plant if clipped into shape. It is very hardy and adaptable. Delicate rose-pink, single-cupped flowers about 2.5 cm across with showy yellow stamens are produced in spring. These are followed by glistening red hips, which last for months and have a high vitamin C content.

ROSE PROBLEMS AND TREATMENT

Aphids Prevalent in spring, these very small green or black insects are usually found on the underside of leaves and on new growth. Thoroughly hose aphids off the foliage. You can also apply insecticidal soaps in spray form to control aphids. Ensure you apply these sprays to both the upper and lower surfaces of the foliage.

Black spot Leaves develop black spots and eventually fall off. This is a problem mainly in summer. Pick off isolated leaves; control with spray or dust. Provide good air circulation and allow foliage to dry out (refrain from overhead watering) before nightfall.

Caterpillars and leaf miners The foliage becomes badly damaged and filled with holes, before the leaves are rolled up by the insects (which pupate inside the rolled-up leaves). Prevalent in summer. Remove all damaged foliage by hand or ask your local nursery for a solution to caterpillars and leaf miners.

Chlorosis Leaves pale and can turn yellow in between the veins. Usually not a serious problem, it can be caused by a lack of iron, nitrogen, manganese or magnesium. It might also indicate a salt build-up. Add chelated iron to the soil, or in severe cases spray iron sulphate on the foliage. Apply a solution of Epsom salts and water (1 tablespoon of Epsom salts to 10 L of water) to the soil every 2–3 weeks in spring and summer.

Dieback Rose canes turn dark brown or black and die off progressively down the stem. Occurs mainly in winter. Always remove any damaged part of the cane, then follow with a regular fungicidal spray/dust program. Avoid damaging the healthy canes and seal the wounds after making the cuts.

Mildew Leaves are distorted and covered with fine white fungus growth. Follow a regular spray or dust program that controls both mildew and leafspot disease.

Thrips Buds turn brown and do not open, or are distorted. Thrips feed on the plant's juices. Control with a dust or spray, following the manufacturer's directions. Spray directly into opening buds.

Two-spotted mites Leaves turn yellow, dry out and in severe cases fall off the plant. You will see tiny webs on the underside of the leaves. Hose the underside of the leaves with water for three days in a row to break the breeding cycle or ask your local nursery for a miticide. Ensure you coat the underside of the leaves.

Yellow leaves Leaves turn yellow and may fall off. Could be caused by poor drainage. Bad weather can slow chlorophyll production, so wait and see. You might need to add some sand to the soil to improve drainage.

Rock rose

This species gets its common name from its resemblance to the single white briar or rugosa rose. The two are not even related, but they do share a love of sunshine, are free flowering and tough, being able to cope with a wide range of conditions.

VITAL STATISTICS

Scientific name: *Cistus* sp.
Family: Cistaceae.
Climate: Easily grown in conditions ranging from mild to cool. Most species are moderately frost hardy.
Culture: Moderate pruning after flowering.
Colours: Plants produce purple, pink or white flowers, some with a maroon dot on each petal.
Height: About 1.5 m.
Planting time: Plant any time from pots.
Soil: Any fertile, well-drained soil.
Position: Grow in full sun. Tolerates drought once established.
Fertiliser: Mulch the surrounding area to help retain moisture over summer.
Pests/diseases: None.
Propagation: Propagate from cuttings (semi-hardwood in autumn).

Feature shrub

Troubleshooting roses

Strong rose varieties that are well cared for are generally free of problems. 'Clever' watering will also help your roses to stay healthy.

Ideally, water roses at their base so that the foliage does not remain wet; this leaves the plant vulnerable to disease. If you are using a sprinkler, ensure you water early enough to allow the foliage to dry before nightfall. This is especially important during spring and autumn, when cool nights and wet foliage encourage foliar diseases. Dry climates with cool nights can encourage mildew. Coastal and warm areas inevitably succumb to black spot each summer. To combat this, try to keep low-growing shrubs away from your roses to increase air circulation, and prune rose bushes into an open vase shape.

Many fungicides are registered for the control of black spot on roses. Spraying roses after pruning with lime sulphur will delay the inevitable attack and kill off any scale insects. This will minimise disease and insect attack during the growing season, although later on in the year it may be worth trying the American Rose Society's home brew (see tip at left), based on baking soda and horticultural oil.

The box on page 99 lists a formidable number of rose problems that may arise. However, the choice of whether or not to apply a solution is yours. You may choose to ignore the problem and accept that some of the blooms will not be pristine. You will also find that many of these pests and diseases will come and go along with changes in the weather.

ROSE SPRAY For an environmentally friendly alternative to chemical sprays, mix the following together: 3 teaspoons of baking soda, 4 tablespoons of PestOil® and 4 L of water. Shake the mixture well and spray the foliage thoroughly.

Proteas, leucodendrons and leucospermums

Australian native plants have a lot in common with their South African cousins in the Proteaceae—the protea family—which as well as proteas also includes waratahs, grevilleas and macadamia nuts. They both have proteoid roots, which have tight, densely packed hairy rootlets that are extremely efficient in extracting phosphorus and can therefore survive in low-nutrient soils. Proteas' flower display, from winter to spring, is spectacular and attracts many birds. They are great for picking and drying, and many smaller ones are now suitable for pots, which means you're bound to have a spot somewhere in your garden for one of these magnificent blooms.

Of all the proteas, the King protea is arguably the most popular. The flower heads are the largest of the genus and can be the size of a dinner plate. It appears in either a white or pink form, and there are also dwarf types suitable for tubs called 'Little Prince' and 'Mini King'. Another newly released protea called 'Nana' is available in a planter; it's grafted onto a hardy rootstock and has a miniature flower.

Leucospermums, commonly called pincushions, are another stunning plant from the Cape. They thrive naturally in coastal positions but will grow anywhere the soil drains well and the sunshine is plentiful. Their spiky flowers full of nectar will attract birds into your garden throughout spring. There are several different species and many different hybrids and cultivars, ranging in colour from yellow to orange, red and bicolour forms. Like proteas, many are suitable for pots, and some of the finer foliage types, such as So™ 'Successful' *L. lineare* hybrid, look great as low hedges.

Members of the *Leucodendron* genus have fairly unremarkable flowers and look best in autumn and winter when the cold air changes their foliage from beautiful to breathtaking, with reds, orange and citrus shades illuminating

their new growth in particular. Good for pots are *L. salignum* 'Yellow Devil', which has golden leaves, *L. saligna × laureolum* 'Katies Blush', which has striking red and green variegated leaves, and *L. saligna hybrid* 'Cream Delight', which has soft cream and apricot shades. *L. modestum* 'Strawberry Fair' is unusual in that it has pink tips to its green leaves and is smothered in bright pink cones. For garden shrubbery, 'Devils Blush' has red tips, and *L. gandogeri × spissifolium* 'Corringle Gold' has iridescent yellow and green variegated leaves. For cut flowers, try *L. laureolum* 'Winter Gold' and the hybrid × *strobilinum* 'Summer Sun', which has poached-egg-like flowers with rusty centres, but the classic red *L. stelligerum* 'Safari Magic' is the pick of the bunch!

Among the various leucodendrons and leucospermums shown here are 'Deacon Red', 'Hullabaloo', 'Red Countess', 'Harvest', 'Bronze Haze', 'Jester' and 'Safari Sunset'.

QUICKSILVER

The silver tree (*Leucodendron argenteum*) has spectacular foliage year-round and grows quickly to a height of 10 m. It is similar in appearance to the silver wattle (*Acacia holosericea*). This fast-growing species creates 'instant' shade and foliage contrast for your garden. And it tolerates drought, too, the fine silky hairs on the leaves trapping humidity and making the most of any rainfall.

Serruria is another unusual genus in this group. Its members grow very well in a container and have small flowers in either white, *S. florida* 'Blushing Bride' or pink *S. florida* 'Pretty in Pink'. Their flowers are dainty and long lasting, are popular in bride bouquets and generally as cut flowers.

Waratahs

New South Wales' floral emblem could be considered the crowning glory of the protea family, and its recent breeding, especially at the National Botanic Gardens in Canberra, has resulted in some new and improved red forms, and even white, pink and yellow cultivars. There are several different species of waratah, the most common being *Telopea speciosissima* × *oreades*, the New South Wales waratah.

Flowering each spring, waratahs shine brightly in the Australian bush against the grey-green backdrop of bush foliage and really can, as the name *Telopea* translates, 'be seen from afar'. Aboriginal legend has it that all waratahs were once white, and a wonga pigeon, injured and looking for his mate, flew from plant to plant, bleeding along the way and transforming the flowers to blood red. Luckily he must have missed a few, as white waratahs were discovered a few decades back, and the breeding process between this plant, and the other species, *T. truncata*, *T. oreades* and *T. mongaensis*, began in earnest.

Another waratah, the Queensland or Dorrigo tree waratah (*Alloxylon pinnatum*), is also worth planting. Flowering for a long season, from mid-spring through to early autumn in ideal conditions, this plant has lots of scope to be used more ornamentally and can even grow in colder climes provided it is protected. The handsome foliage and neat dense canopy are the perfect foil for these stunning red and sometimes pink blooms.

BELOW: *A full-sized New South Wales waratah like this can be 3–4 m tall and covered with many flowers; they usually don't live long enough to reach that size.*

BELOW RIGHT: *Surrounding each New South Wales waratah bloom are deep red bracts.*

Trees

Chosen carefully, trees can provide the essential elements of colour, seasonal interest and longevity in the garden. Their new growth is part of the magic of spring—acid yellow gleditsias, elms and robinia, purple splashes from many maples and the lettuce green of magnolias in young, tender growth all form part of the spell.

These blooms from spring-flowering trees announce their season like no other group of plants.

Spring blossom trees

Nothing signals the end of winter more than spring blossom. Bursting from bare grey branches, the buds swell and then open to fill the air with fragrance and a white or pink haze of colour.

All blossom trees are deciduous. Most flower on bare branches before the leaves appear, some as early as mid-winter. Many of these smaller deciduous trees are ideal for the home garden.

The majority of species tolerate a range of climates, although cherries and crab apples do perform better in areas with cold winters.

If you live in a warm coastal area and still want the beauty of spring blossom, stick with flowering peaches, which are suitable even for seaside gardens provided they are sheltered from salt-laden winds.

Soil and climate

All flowering fruit trees are adaptable to most soil types, but they benefit from regular feeding, summer watering and a heavy application of leaf mulch.

When the root is deep, there is no reason to fear the wind.

CHINESE PROVERB

Selection guide

Flowering apricots

Flowering apricots (*Prunus armeniaca*) have a delicate profusion of flowers, more so than other blossoms. Varieties include white and pink, in either single or double forms, all of which are fragrant. These trees have a broad, spreading shape and grow to about 4 m high with a 4 m spread.

Flowering cherries

One of the first of the blossom trees to flower is the weeping cherry *Prunus subhirtella* 'Winter Sun', which grows best in cool-climate gardens. The Taiwan cherry, *Prunus campanulata*, prefers warmer conditions and has pendulous, bell-shaped, deep pink blossoms throughout winter.

Different cherries have different requirements for cold temperatures; basically, without cold winters they won't flower or set fruit. The Taiwan

LEFT: *White flowering apricot are among the earliest of blossoms.*

BELOW LEFT TO RIGHT: *Cherry blossom in bud;* P. subhirtella *'Alba' is one of the simplest of cherry blossoms; the showy pink double flowers of 'Mt Kanzan' cherry.*

cherry has the lowest chill requirement of all the cherries, which means it can tolerate warmer climates and is one of the first to flower, usually in the middle of winter. The single, bell-shaped flowers are a deep cyclamen red and hang in pendulous clusters. This tree's mature dimensions of 4 × 3 m, with an upright, narrow habit, make it ideally suited to a small garden.

Other species, more suitable for cooler regions, include the Japanese and Chinese cherries, which are usually grown as standards, creating a broad umbrella effect. They can also be grafted low and used as spillover plants down an embankment. Most cherries have the bonus of a brilliant autumn show of foliage, with colours ranging from yellows to brilliant reds.

Flowering peaches

The winter-flowering peaches, reliable small flowering trees, reach about 4 m at maturity. These magnificent blossom trees grow well in warm-temperate areas. Prune them immediately after flowering to prevent fruit formation and to encourage vigorous new growth for next season's flowers.

Spring-flowering varieties such as *Prunus* 'Clara Meyer' and 'Harbinger' follow in early spring. Tending to flower mid-season, the crimson *Prunus persica* 'Magnifica' makes a strong splash of colour, while 'Versicolor' is an unusual specimen with multicoloured blooms that range from almost white to candy-striped and deep pink. The white-flowered 'Alboplena' is always popular, with its large white double flowers.

Flowering pears

If you're struggling to find the right tree to cope with pollution, poor drainage, heavy clay soils and even the odd dry spell, then think about ornamental pears (*Pyrus*) as an option. They're among the hardiest and easiest to grow of all garden trees, and have excellent foliage, bright autumn colours and white spring blossom.

Recently developed ornamental pears come in many shapes and sizes too, from the *P. calleryana* narrow cultivar called 'Capital' to the stunning 'Chanticleer', which has a dense canopy that screens beautifully before changing to gold, plum and then burgundy prior to leaf drop.

There is a silver-foliage weeping type called *P. salicifolia* 'Pendula' and a pretty snow pear (*P. nivalis*) that has grey-green leaves.

DID YOU KNOW? 'Sakura' is the name Japanese give to cherry blossoms.

The snow pear (far left) has tiny white blossoms (left).

ABOVE: *Two plums:* Prunus × blireana *(left) and* P. glandulosa *(right), also known as suckering plum.*

BELOW: *An avenue of crab apples flowering in mid-spring.*

BELOW RIGHT: Malus × purpurea *'Eleyi Spring'.*

Flowering plums

Well suited to warm gardens, the flowering plums are the hardiest of all blossoms, tolerating a wide range of climatic conditions (down to -10°C) and soil types. Foliage is one of their principal features, and the flowers, which appear in early spring, range from white through to pink in both single and double forms. Blossoms are followed by dark black-red foliage, which provides a strong contrast.

The purple-leaved cherry plum (*Prunus cerasifera* 'Nigra') has delicately perfumed, shell-pink flowers followed by deep purple foliage. *P. × blireana* is a cross between flowering plum and flowering apricot, with deeper pink double blossoms and reddish purple leaves. Flowering plums can grow to about 4 m high by 3 m wide.

Crab apples

Crab apples flower later in spring, with the blossoms appearing after the foliage. Closely related to eating apples, they have small, edible and often decorative fruit. Their moderate size and shapely spreading form make them ideal shade trees in small gardens. Once established, a crab apple flowers and fruits better if left undisturbed.

There are many varieties of crab apple, ranging from pink single-flowered trees, such as the Japanese crab apple (*Malus floribunda*), to spectacular double forms such as Bechtel's crab apple (*M. ioensis* 'Plena').

SEAWEED HELP Help newly planted trees to take root quickly by watering them with a seaweed-based liquid fertiliser, which will stimulate this area.

Dogwood

In really cold areas, why not plant a dogwood? A North American native, the dogwood (*Cornus* sp.) is a delightful tree. The simple flower head consists of an inconspicuous flower surrounded by showy white or rosy pink bracts. Its foliage is richly coloured in autumn, and its spring growth is sometimes flushed pink, depending on the variety. This is a great small tree, growing to about 5 m in height, and requires little in the way of pruning or feeding.

TOP LEFT AND ABOVE: *In spring, this variety of dogwood (Cornus florida 'Rubra') becomes covered in flower-like bracts that open up pink.*

The Oak is called the king of trees,
The Aspen quivers in the breeze,
The Poplar grows up straight and tall,
The Peach tree spreads along the wall,
The Sycamore gives pleasant shade,
The Willow droops in watery glade,
The Fir tree useful timber gives,
The Beech amid the forest lives.

SARA COLERIDGE

LEFT TO RIGHT: *The flowers of golden rain tree* (Koelreuteria sp.) *develop into bladder-like pods; the golden foliage of* Gleditsia triacanthos *'Sunburst';* Robinia pseudoacacia *in full bloom.*

Other flowering deciduous trees

If you have room, consider planting a deciduous tree. It will let in valuable winter sun and also provide some important summer shade.

The pink wisteria tree, *Robinia* × *slavinii* 'Hillieri' and *R.* × *ambigua* 'Decaisneana', grows quickly to 10 m and is smothered in flowers in tones of apple blossom, purple or white in spring, just

He that plants trees loves others beside himself.

TRADITIONAL

before the foliage emerges. A similar beauty is the *Laburnum*, or golden rain tree, which is popular in cool-temperate zones for the curtain formed by its gold spring flowers when it is trained over archways. This golden shower effect can be created in warmer climates in late spring with either a *Koelreuteria* or a *Cassia* (see page 218), both of which are also commonly referred to as a golden rain tree. Crepe myrtles have an eye-catching late spring flower display.

Many deciduous trees have stunning foliage. For a splash of lime, choose between the golden robinia (*Robinia pseudoacacia* 'Frisia'), which has an upright habit, or the more graceful,

THINK PINK AND PURPLE

It's always a classy touch to vary the lime and green growth with the red, pink and purple foliage some plants produce each spring. To think pink, look at many syzygiums, the native rainforest plant also known as lilly-pilly, *Cedrela sinensis* 'Flamingo' (shown at left), from the cedar family, and confetti plant (*Breynia disticha*). Purple hues on *Gleditsia* 'Ruby Lace', *Prunus cerasifera* 'Nigra', *P.* × *bliriana*, both ornamental plums, and the 'Forest Pansy' cultivar of *Cercis* (shown at right), all make a beautiful show.

Powton tree

This species of *Paulownia*, also called empress tree, is one of the fastest growing plants you could put in for instant shade, and it also makes a great timber tree. Its darker purple, bell-like blooms are held on spikes above the huge heart-shaped leaves and come into season at a similar time to jacarandas (see page 223).

VITAL STATISTICS

Scientific name: *Paulownia tomentosa*.
Family: Scrophulariaceae.
Climate: Prefers cool, moist climates.
Culture: Great tree for a range of climates, requiring little pruning; can also be used for timber.
Colours: Produces grey-white to lavender flowers.
Height: About 20 m.
Planting time: Plant in autumn and winter.
Soil: Requires well-drained soil. Soils with a pH above 5.5 and enriched with organic matter will get better results.
Position: Grow in full sun with shelter from strong winds.
Fertiliser: Young trees can be fed with slow-release fertiliser in early spring and again in autumn.
Pests/diseases: Caterpillars can eat new growth. Stock can too—*Paulownia* is reasonably high in protein and makes good drought fodder.

Feature tree

weeping look of *Gleditsia triacanthos* 'Sunburst'. Another *Gleditsia*, which has bronze-claret new growth and can be a good contrast specimen, is G. 'Rubylace'.

An impressive deciduous tree is the catalpa, or Indian bean tree (*Catalpa*

DID YOU KNOW? The Indian bean tree is from North America, not India. The name is a reference to Native Americans, who called this tree *catawba*, which was misheard as 'catalpa', now the genus name.

bignonioides), which flowers in profusion in summer with white flowers, stained yellow and purple. Some cultivars such as 'Aurea' also have sensational large heart-shaped leaves.

Each October in many warm-temperate areas, a purple cloud hangs below the canopy of some special trees. The palest lavender, almost smoke-like blooms, appear first on the white cedar tree (*Melia azedarach*), which is a very hardy plant in most climates, coping well with drought and tropics alike.

Every square inch in this suburban backyard is being used for production, including the clothesline as a grape arbour.

Herbs, fruit and vegetables

The delicate flavours of spring finally make it to the dinner table: young lamb seasoned with fresh mint, early berries and the first stone fruit, 'petit pois' (young peas), new potatoes and mesclun leaves for salads.

Grow your own

There is a lot of concern these days about pesticides and genetically modified food, and many experts are advancing the case for chemical-free produce. This is more than just a trend, and there is no better way to get on the right track than to grow your own food.

Indeed, there are already many people who are quiet participants in a backyard revolution, growing their own herbs, fruit and vegetables.

The possibilities, it seems, are endless: a patch of taste-laden, vine-ripened tomatoes; an old-fashioned strawberry patch with its promise of succulent, sweet berries; freshly dug heirloom potatoes with a flavour all their own; the simple pleasure to be had from picking some parsley growing in a pot at your back door.

No matter what your level of commitment, the idea of consuming produce that you have grown yourself has undeniable appeal. The dreary routine of waiting in supermarket queues in order to buy wilted lettuce and tasteless, waxy produce can, with a little planning and labour, become a thing of the past.

Herbs

Spring is the perfect time to revive tired herbs, or pot up fresh supplies for your windowsill or verandah. Growth is fast, which means they taste tender and sweet.

Planting fresh crops of herbs in spring will ensure a summer harvest of annuals such as coriander and basil. Herb gardens can range in size from a garden dedicated to herb growing to a few groundcover herbs in a rockery. In a small backyard or townhouse you can even keep your herb garden in pots on the back step, or hanging in a basket on a sunny verandah. If you live in a flat, herbs can be grown on a sunny windowsill. The more accessible the herbs are, the easier it becomes to make use of them in the kitchen.

Top ten herbs

1 **Parsley.** The mostly widely grown herb, growing to 45 cm from a thick taproot. Rich in iron and vitamins A, B and C, it is great in salads, soups, stuffing and garnishes. Legend has it that you have to be wicked to be able to grow parsley successfully. Both flat leaf and curly parsley are the same species, with the same characteristics, although the flat leaf version has a slightly more intense flavour. Replace on a regular basis as this plant has a disconcerting habit of disappearing from the garden just when you think it is established for good.

2 **Chives.** A perennial herb with fine, hollow leaves, it adds onion flavour to food and can be used as a companion plant for roses.

3 **Rosemary.** A woody shrub that loves full sun and dry conditions. It is perfect with lamb.

4 **Thyme.** A symbol of courage and vitality. This herb is used for flavouring egg and cheese dishes. It is mostly grown as an aromatic groundcover for a sunny spot.

Flowering sage takes centre stage in this herb garden.

5 **Dill.** This herb is great for use in pickling, with fish and in soups. It has attractive fine foliage and needs to be forced with lots of nitrogen fertilisers.

6 **Mint.** A herb that grows well in cool, moist areas, even shade, although it can become a pest if it likes the conditions too much. It can be used in drinks and salads and for flavouring that traditional favourite, roast lamb.

7 **Marjoram and oregano.** These closely related, strongly flavoured herbs are excellent for flavouring soups and pasta. They make a great groundcover in a sunny spot.

8 **Sage.** A close relative of ornamental salvia, with grey leaves useful for stuffing, and for flavouring soups, veal and poultry.

What was Paradise but a garden? An orchard of trees and herbs, full of pleasure, and nothing there but delights.

W. LAWSON

ABOVE LEFT TO RIGHT: *Curly parsley; flowering onion chives (all parts are edible); flowering rosemary (the flowers are edible too); flowering thyme (again, you can also use the flowers).*

9 Basil. An extremely popular cooking herb for use in soups, tomato dishes and pasta. This herb is a summer-growing annual so it needs replanting each spring. It is also an effective companion plant for tomatoes, as it repels whitefly and other pests.

10 Coriander. Also called Chinese parsley, coriander is a delicious, fresh-flavoured, lemony-like herb that is great for Thai food, Asian salads and pesto with a kick.

Indoor growing tips

Herbs really grow best in full sun, so while temporarily growing them indoors is an option, don't expect them to last forever.

- Select a pot with plenty of drainage holes.

- Use a well-drained potting mix suitable for shrubs.

- Incorporate a slow-release fertiliser at the highest rate.

- Water with liquid fertiliser regularly if growth is slow.

- Try for as much direct sunlight as possible to build in flavour.

- Try rotating your herbs with the same group outside.

- Choose herbs that cope with some shade, such as mint and 5-in-1 herb (*Coleus amboinicus*), also known as Spanish thyme or Indian borage.

TIPS FOR GROWING HERBS

- Herbs grow naturally in many different soils and climates. Some thrive in extremely dry areas, others in tropical rainforests and temperate woodlands, so if you choose the appropriate herbs for the prevailing conditions you cannot go wrong.
- Most herbs prefer full sun and free-draining soil.
- Don't pick more than one third of a young plant or more than half of a mature specimen at the one time. The more often you pick, the bushier and healthier herbs become.
- Don't overfertilise—there will be too much soft leafy growth at the expense of essential oils.
- Many herbs grow better when planted next to other herbs, but some will struggle in the wrong combinations. For example, mint hates growing near parsley. If your herbs aren't doing well, and they are growing in the right conditions, maybe they are in with the wrong crowd.
- Snails and insects like herbs too. Be vigilant and pick off grubs by hand, and trap snails with small saucers of beer.
- Have you ever wondered what the difference is between a herb and a spice? Herbs are the leaves of plants, spices are produced from the other parts, such as flowers, seeds and roots.
- To develop full flavour, most herbs should have at least 5 hours of sunlight a day or 16 hours under fluorescent lights (placed 5–10 cm above the plants).

HERB HOTHOUSE Raise herb seedlings in old strawberry punnets using the fitted lid like a glasshouse. Just make sure there are drainage holes at the bottom.

Lavender

Lavender (*Lavandula* spp.) is universally recognised as a valuable herb and ornamental shrub. With its perfume, flowers and silver foliage, it has something to offer everyone.

Caring for lavender

Lavender will cope with exposed, sunny, open positions. The best-looking plants are usually those growing in the most inhospitable conditions.

Good drainage is essential. The other critical factor in successfully growing lavender is to add lime or dolomite to your soil to raise the pH, making it alkaline. An acidic soil is a common problem for these plants both in the garden proper and in pots; it will weaken the plant and make it prone to rot and fungal attack. Mulching around the root system will help to maintain even moisture levels in the soil, and will improve the organic content.

Lavender requires two good prunings each year, in late spring and autumn, and more if the plant is being hedged. Wait until it has flowered, then cut back half the current season's growth; without this, plants become woody. Avoid cutting into older woody growth, and ensure there is green wood below the cutting line, otherwise the lavender may not reshoot.

Apply an organic fertiliser, such as blood and bone, straight after pruning.

There are 28 original species of lavender. They can all be classified into four groups.

True or English lavender

Used for oil production in the perfume industry, this is the most popular type for drying and for potpourris. All English lavenders cope with cold and frost, and have narrow, pointed, smooth grey leaves and long thin spikes of mauve to purple-coloured flowers that appear in summer.

You might buy English lavender with any of these names: *Lavandula spica*, *L. angustifolia*, *L. 'Munstead', L. 'Hidcote'*

CLOCKWISE FROM TOP: *Italian (or Spanish) lavender, with its characteristic wings atop each flower; this version of Italian lavender has pale wings; English lavender, which is used for essential oil production.*

Spanish or Italian lavender flowers for many months.

and L. 'Alba'. Cultivars range in size from 20 cm to 1 m, and the colours vary from pink, purple and lavender to white.

Spanish or Italian lavender

The winged bracts at the top of each short flower spike distinguish this group. Botanically known as *L. stoechas*, it has grey-green leaves, and flowers throughout winter and early spring. This hardy type grows between 50 cm and 90 cm tall and has white, green, pink or plum flowers, depending on the cultivar.

Culantro or spiky coriander

The annual coriander (*Coriandrum sativum*) is much loved by many cooks and often the bane of gardeners due to its propensity to bolt and die. But a much lesser known plant in the same family is a perennial, has a similar flavour and copes with the heat. Also known as Mexican coriander, culantro is native to Mexico, South America and the West Indies, and is used in Caribbean, Latin American and South-East Asian cooking.

VITAL STATISTICS

Scientific name: *Eryngium foetidum.*
Family: Apiaceae.
Height: 30 cm.
Climate: Warm, tropical and frost free.
Planting time: Spring.
Soil: Moist, well-drained, sandy loams high in organic matter are best.
Position: Full sun to part shade.
Planting: Sow seeds direct onto raked ground. In warm weather, seeds germinate in 2–3 weeks.
Fertiliser: Use a slow-release fertiliser.
Pests/diseases: Leaf spot can be a problem occasionally; treat with neem oil.
Uses: Use in the same way as for coriander; in the Caribbean, it's used to make chutneys.

Feature herb

French lavender

French lavender (*L. dentata*) is easily recognised by the toothed margin of the leaves. It copes with a wide range of climatic conditions and flowers from spring to autumn. From 80 cm to 1 m tall, it is grown mainly for its pleasant foliage and its long flowering season in the right climate. French lavender likes an open sunny spot in the garden and has light grey foliage on upright stems, which carry slightly perfumed flower heads up to 5 cm long.

Spiked or winged lavender

With its fern-like foliage and flowers shaped like pitchforks, *L. latifolia* makes an interesting addition to any garden. A popular member of this group is 'Sidonie' lavender, which is sold as the first Australian (bred) lavender. It produces sapphire-blue flowers all year-round, is frost tender, feeds heavily and grows to 1.3 m in height.

Cotton lavender

Grown for its distinctive aromatic foliage, cotton lavender (*Santolina chamaecyparissus*) is a low, shrubby perennial from the Mediterranean with golden blooms like tiny pompoms in summer. The foliage, which looks rather like a feather duster, grows into a compact bush that will stand above most other border plants and fill a corner of a rockery, making it a good feature plant. Many gardeners clip it into a round shape, discouraging flowering. Cotton lavender also looks great woven through a parterre or edging a herb garden.

This plant prefers mild winters and warm dry summers, but it can tolerate a light frost. Plant it in a light sandy soil in full sun.

ABOVE LEFT: *French lavender has plump flower buds that are popular with bees.*

ABOVE RIGHT: *This silver form of cotton lavender also repels insect pests.*

1 *Lavandula stoechas* 'Lavender Lace' 2 *L. stoechas* 'Bee Brilliant' 3 *L. stoechas* subsp. *pendunculata* 'Avonview'
4 *L. stoechas* 'Helmsdale' 5 *L. stoechas* 'Tickled Pink' 6 *L. stoechas* 'Fairy Wings'

Lavender

7 *L. stoechas* 'Willow Bridge White' **8** *L. stoechas* **9** *L. stoechas* 'Kew Red' **10** *L.* 'Bee Pretty'
11 *L.* 'Sidonie' **12** *L. dentata* **13** *L. × allardii*

Fruit

Most of us live in a predominantly temperate climate so we are able to grow a large range of fruit trees—from citrus, apples, pears, stone fruit and berries to tropical delicacies and even nut trees.

Elderberry's dark fruit is perfect for jams, cordials and syrup, but not so great raw.

Position is everything when it comes to fruit. Avoid low-lying patches, which will encourage root rot and collar rot, and improve drainage either by adding manure and gypsum to your soil or by mounding the soil to elevate the bed.

Of all our fruits, the apple is perhaps the most useful, and is appreciated by birds and beasts as well as by man. My bullfinch loves his slice of apple, my horse thanks me by many little signs for the gift of an apple and my cows delight to be offered one.

19TH-CENTURY GARDENING BOOK

Elderberry

Elderberry (*Sambucus nigra*) dates back to ancient Greek times, and is shrouded in mystery and folklore. It is said that Christ's cross was made of elderwood, and that elder would only grow where blood had been spilt!

In fact, elderberry grows happily in any temperate climate in sun or shade and, once established, will cope with frosts. There are a few species of *Sambucus*, but if you intend to make elderberry wine, sorbet or jelly, be sure to plant the edible *S. nigra* rather than the others, which are poisonous. This species bears large sprays of tiny white flowers in spring, followed by clusters of purple-black berries.

A few highly ornamental cultivars are available, including the purple-leafed 'Guincho Purple', golden-leafed 'Aurea' and the white variegated form.

HOW TO MAKE ELDER CORDIAL
- Collect the elderberries early in the morning or late in the afternoon when they are plump, and remove the berries from the stems.
- In a saucepan, cover the elderberries in water (just enough to cover them). Bring to a simmer and let cook for 20 minutes. Strain the elderberries through a muslin cloth.
- For each 2 cups of juice, add 2 cups of demerara sugar, 2 cinnamon sticks or a few cloves, and the juice from half a lemon.
- Pour the juice mixture back into the empty saucepan and bring the mixture to the boil for 15 minutes, stirring often (to ensure all the sugar is dissolved). Remove the cinnamon sticks or cloves.
- Pour into clean, sterilised bottles, tightly closing the cap and store in the fridge for longevity. It will keep for months, but is unlikely to last that long!

CLOCKWISE FROM TOP LEFT: *Keep young* Rubus *plants 'heeled in' until you're ready to plant them; a healthy young* Rubus *plant showing the green stem and roots; protecting strawberries from birds by slipping a glass over the ripening fruit; strawberry crowns.*

Beautiful berry fruits

Judicious planting of berries can supply fruit from spring through to late autumn, with a glut mid-summer for scrumptious pavlovas, fruit salads, jams and jellies. Berries are absolutely delicious when eaten fresh straight from the bush, or cooked in a little sugar and water and poured over ice-cream, or meringue and cream.

The smallish nature of many types makes them perfect for the backyard orchard. They can be broadly separated into two groups: those with an upright bushy habit, and those that ramble and trail. The two exceptions of course are strawberries and mulberries.

Bush fruits

Bush fruits include currants, blueberries and gooseberries. The most ornamental and adaptable of these is the blueberry, which ripens in mid-summer and has a piquant and unique taste. The blueberry bush has ball-shaped flowers that develop into green berries which gradually turn blue. The leaves change into vibrant autumn shades before falling, although in warmer climates the blueberry is not deciduous. It can be a very attractive addition to any garden. Growing to a height of up to 2 m, blueberries require moist cool conditions. They should be planted in a sheltered position where they can receive morning sun and afternoon shade.

The English gooseberry—unrelated to the Chinese gooseberry, better known as the kiwifruit—and currants have a high chilling requirement that makes them suitable only for cool-temperate regions. It's also advisable to shelter them from strong winds. They ripen in early summer.

Cape gooseberries, quite ornamental shrubs growing to 1 m—and with edible fruit—are not related to the English gooseberry, and are actually more closely related to tomatoes. The red or yellow globe-shaped fruits of the English gooseberry are held within papery husks, and ripen in summer. Treated as an annual in cool climates, they are in fact perennial shrubs lasting three or four years in warm districts.

Rambling and trailing fruits

Trailing berries and brambles include blackberries (yes, some varieties don't sucker and become invasive), boysenberries, loganberries and youngberries. Raspberries, the latest berries to ripen, crop right into late autumn. Blackberries, boysenberries and youngberries will grow in both cool and warm areas, but loganberries and raspberries like it cold and crisp.

DID YOU KNOW? According to medieval superstition, blackberries picked after Michaelmas Day were contaminated by the devil.

CARE TIPS

- All berries should be picked when well coloured. They store in the fridge for up to three weeks, or you can freeze them for later. Well-grown berries will fruit for up to 20 years and produce 5 kg of berries each year.
- In general, fruit is produced on year-old wood, so carefully prune and remove older unproductive stems to ensure cropping from one year to the next, and a plant that can be harvested with ease.
- Prepare the soil before planting by adding organic matter and humus. Generous amounts of well-made compost will provide the plants with excellent nutrition. Do not add lime.
- It's best to plant out young trees during the winter months when the bushes are dormant.
- When well established, mulch generously with leaves, woodchips or sawdust to a depth of 10 cm to provide protection and moisture for the surface roots. Thick mulch will also suppress weeds.
- Berries should appear in the second or third year. Fertilise each tree in spring with compost or rotted manure, and foliar spray with seaweed fertiliser during the flowering period to assist with fruit set and to supply necessary trace elements.

project

Potted strawberries

Strawberries can be grown in garden beds or in containers, such as large terracotta strawberry pots specially designed for the purpose.

1 To plant a strawberry pot, half fill it with a premium quality potting mix to just below the level of the first holes. Add water-storing granules to the mix and make sure it drains well, as strawberries hate waterlogged soil.

2 Remove the plants from their containers so that you don't damage the roots. Gently push each plant through a hole in the sides of the pot.

3 Cover the roots with more potting mix as you go, then fill the pot almost to the rim before planting another few strawberries in the top.

4 Top up with potting mix and water the plants. Water regularly during spring and summer to encourage good quality fruit. Place the pot in any sunny spot, keep it well watered and you'll have an ornamental feature for your garden, as well as a source of delicious fruit.

Rosella

Apart from being called rosella (risking confusion with the colourful birds of the same name), the fruit of this edible hibiscus is also known as the Queensland jam plant, though it is actually native to West Africa, and sometimes sorrel, as the foliage is also edible. The tea made from the fruits contains high levels of vitamin C.

VITAL STATISTICS

Scientific name: *Hibiscus sabdariffa*.

Family: Malvaceae.

Climate: Tropical climates are ideal, but most temperate and warm climates are suitable if there is 5 months free of frost. If sown after the last frost, it will flower and fruit within 3–4 months, taking about a month to ripen.

Soil: Grow in well-drained soil with added organic matter and mulch.

Culture: Makes a useful and edible windbreak in the vegie patch.

Colours: Green foliage tinged purple in its new growth producing yellow hibiscus-like flowers and dark red fruits.

Height: About 2 m.

Planting time: Fom mid-spring to early summer.

Position: Grow in full sun.

Planting depth and spacing: Sow seed 3 cm deep, and 1 m apart.

Fertiliser: Use a liquid manure every 3 weeks.

Harvest: Regularly pick calyxes when they are coloured red. Plants in warm areas can produce for 9 months of the year. Leaves can also be eaten when young if steamed or stir-fried.

Propagation: Grow from seed.

Storage: Fruits can be stored fresh, dried or frozen for later jam making, or preserved in syrup and jams. Wine can also be made. The most common use is probably as tea.

Feature fruit

Mulberries

Mulberries are often overlooked these days as a summer fruit for the home garden. Maybe the memories of stained fingers and clothing have banished them from modern backyards, but this preoccupation with cleanliness is a sad loss to children everywhere. After all, what other tree could possibly be as much fun? They are great to climb, produce fruit all summer, and grow absolutely anywhere with ease. They are also the favourite diet for silkworms, which brings children all the delights of keeping silkworms and watching the process of metamorphosis.

In a smaller garden, you can plant a weeping standard mulberry, which make a beautiful specimen tree, and if you're still worried about the stains, remember you can either use green fruits to remove stubborn marks, or choose the white, very sweet 'Shahtoot' variety.

Ripe mulberry fruits are a favourite with kids. Stains on skin can be removed by rubbing with unripe fruits.

Vegetables

Spring is the time to start your vegie patch or rejuvenate a forgotten plot. Many delicious favourites are planted right now—from tomatoes to sweet corn, cucumbers and capsicum.

Start a patch

It is quite simple to start your own vegie patch. It can be big enough to feed the family or as small as an old packing case. Start by selecting a sunny, sheltered spot. Clear away any unwanted grass and weeds, then add lots of organically rich anything to your soil—it can be home-made compost, spent mushroom compost, animal manure or worm castings. Next, apply some complete plant food and pelletised manure to ensure that your vegetables have plenty to eat. Vegetables are hungry plants and the faster they grow, the sweeter they'll taste.

Now you're ready for planting. You can sow many larger seeds, such as beans and marrows, directly into the ground, but for other types you will need to raise them first in seedling trays then plant them out as you need them. Whichever method you try, stagger your plantings by a couple of weeks so that you have a continuous supply rather than a glut at one time.

Water young plants regularly and watch out for sap-sucking insects like aphids and whitefly as well as hungry caterpillars, which like tender young greens as much as we do. Be vigilant in patrolling for pests. Hand culling at dusk is an efficient method of controlling many grubs, while yellow sticky paper or petroleum jelly on pieces of plastic is a good way of trapping the sapsuckers.

Space and conditions

The size of vegetable beds should be tailored to each family's requirements. If you eat lots of vegetables, have a big backyard and want to save money, go for broke with a large vegetable garden. An area of 80–100 square metres can feed a family of four all year.

Peas growing on a trellis fill the backdrop of this garden. Other late winter and early spring crops such as broccoli, cabbage and beets fill the remaining space.

Where to locate your vegetable patch

The first step is to select the warmest and sunniest spot in the garden. The site should also have good drainage: pick a gently sloping area if you are on really heavy clay soils and raise the beds by adding lots of compost and manure to the soil.

Keep the beds accessible for planting, weeding and harvesting; many fruits, vegetables and herbs are highly decorative, so even if you don't have room to devote a whole patch to them, grow them in borders with your ornamental garden plants.

Space-saving plants

A small vegetable patch that is lovingly cared for will be more productive than a larger neglected patch. A wide variety of dwarf cultivars are now available. Perfect for pots, these establish themselves quickly and can be grown outside the conventional vegetable-planting seasons if they are placed in protected positions. Lettuce, cabbage, oriental vegetables and tomatoes are all ideal.

If you've got a spare plot or large pot, why not add some extra flavour with easy-to-grow vegies such as carrots, radishes, beetroots and spring onions? You can buy them in seed tapes with the seeds impregnated along a bio-degradable ribbon, which makes them ridiculously easy to germinate in perfect rows. These are also fantastic 'catch crops', which means they can be planted between other seasonal vegetables as a fast-to-reap treat.

Potted instead of plotted vegies

Many vegies now come as small-growing plants that are perfect for pots. Tomatoes, for example, have patio, or intermediate forms that grow easily in tubs and don't need staking. There are even multi-grafted types that have potatoes as the understock and tomatoes above, really giving you more bang for your buck! Others to consider in tubs include eggplant, capsicum, chillies,

salad greens and winter greens such as chard, cabbages and peas.

Room to go up?

If space is a real problem, why not grow your salad vertically? Plant a cucumber vine on a trellis or plant beans on a tripod now. It's also tomato time, so think about putting in a vine of cherry tomatoes for your salads, such as 'Small Fry', 'Tiny Tim' or 'Yellow Pear'. In winter, try peas on the tripod.

Simple steps to vegie success: this paper strip (left) is impregnated with carrot seeds allowing easy and straight lines and regular spacing of seeds. Water in well after planting it.

No space at all?

Time to think of micro vegies—the latest taste sensation in the best restaurants. These are simply 'just-germinated' leaves that are plucked while still young. You can grow them in a seedling tray and harvest a fortnight later. Think mesclun-lettuce mix, pea sprouts, radish shoots, celery, baby spinach and mini radicchio.

Alternative vegetables

Heirloom vegetables

These old-fashioned types often have the best flavour. You can obtain low-acid, yellow-striped tomatoes, red-skinned eggplant and rainbow chard (silverbeet) to brighten up your dinner plate. Many other types are available, and seed-swapping or gardening clubs offer great selections.

Perpetual vegetables

Most vegetables are annuals and need replacing each season. Look for perpetual varieties of beans, beets and lettuce to save the effort of replanting.

Asian vegetables

Specialised regional cuisine has developed around the wide varieties of vegetables grown in Asia. Chinese broccoli, cabbage, radish, turnips and lettuce-like greens such as tatsoi and mizuna are all delicious additions to stir-fries and salads.

Edible flowers

Appearance is an integral part of the enjoyment of food. Borage, calendula, elderflower, heartsease, nasturtium and sage flowers don't just have pretty faces, they also taste great. See page 331 for some ideas on how to use them.

CLOCKWISE FROM TOP LEFT: *Rainbow chard gleams like a stained-glass window; heirloom tomatoes; edible flowers including calendula and borage; heirloom eggplants; Asian perilla, chive stems and shallots.*

An iceberg lettuce needs to be fed well to keep it from going to seed or becoming bitter.

Growing greens

Growing fresh salad greens is so easy that everyone should have a salad ready for picking. Salad greens come in many colours and flavours, from the sweet crispness of icebergs to the nutty taste of rocket, the lemony tang of sorrel or the bitterness of endive. What many people don't realise is just how simple and fast it is to grow your own.

Leafy greens need plenty of water and regular feeding, without which they can become bitter. They also want free-draining soil (or Australian premium standard potting mix) and loads of organic matter, which can be home-made compost, worm manure from your worm farm, rotted or pelletised manure, or even well-composted grass clippings that can be dug through. This helps build up the water-holding capacity and nutrients of the soil.

The next thing is to consider the frequency of your plantings and the varieties you wish to eat and that suit your climate and the season. Most lettuce types grow well in spring, autumn and winter, but they can run to seed in summer. It's possible then that extra shadecloth is needed for protection or you should plant specially bred heat-resistant types like 'Great

Sowing seeds: Four steps to success

Jump-start spring by planting cold-sensitive crops into peat pots that can be planted straight into the ground once the frosty weather finishes.

1 Fill the container (peat pot or seed tray) with a good-quality seed-raising mix to about 1 cm below the top of the container. Level the mix. You could plant vegies such as tomatoes, eggplants, capsicums or chillies. For this step-by-step sequence, we planted tomato seeds.
2 Sow two seeds in each pot. This will allow for any losses.
3 Sow seed to a depth that is roughly equivalent to the seed diameter. Lightly cover with seed-raising mix and press the seed gently into the surface.
4 Water in gently using a soft rose on the watering can. If it is winter or early spring, place the container in a warm, sunny position; in the summer months, place it in a shaded position.

Lakes'. Conversely, for those who get really cold winters, try growing bitter greens like endive, chicory and sorrel, which are fabulous for coping with frosts. And for the lazy gardener, the fabulous peppery rocket is dead easy, and it self-seeds.

DID YOU KNOW? Pak choi, also known as bok choi, literally means 'white vegetable'.

The pea variety 'Purple Podded' not only has purple pods but also mauve flowers.

Life is like eating artichokes, you have got to go through so much to get so little.

THOMAS A. DORGAN

Peas and asparagus, artichoke

Peas and asparagus are the voices of spring in the vegetable garden, but did you know that many of them have a dark secret? There certainly are some lovely purple-podded peas, as well as a 'Sweet Purple' variety of asparagus. Other purple cultivars include the famous black-eyed peas, black-stemmed sugar cane, the black artichoke and, of course, broad beans have a black-eyed flower.

Garden legumes

Commercially frozen peas (and beans) are the most popular green vegetables, yet their flavour cannot compare with that of home-grown peas, especially when they are picked as 'petit pois'—tiny, sweet peas. For ease at home, why not plant a hanging basket of snow peas or sugar snaps? For something a little different, try the asparagus pea, which is not a true pea and has winged seeds that are eaten whole and taste like asparagus. For great colour, look for purple peas.

Beans are one of the first of summer vegetables and will grow in just about

anything! Colours will range from the traditional green, through to blue, white, yellow and purple cultivars. If you are growing haricot beans (which have edible seeds), leave the pods till they turn yellow on the bush before harvesting them. If you're growing runner beans, choose a smaller variety so that it doesn't run out of ground area.

The ultimate health food, peas and beans are tremendously good sources of protein, amino acids, fibre, vitamins and minerals, and are low in fat and sugar to boot. They also contain phyto-oestrogens, which are beneficial to women suffering from premenstrual tension or going through menopause, and help protect men against prostate cancer. Soak dried beans for at least an hour and rinse and cook thoroughly (an hour or so) to avoid flatulence.

Asparagus

Asparagus are actually the tender young shoots that emerge each spring from a fern-like plant. Twenty plants should feed a family and blanched spears keep well in the freezer.

Asparagus is best suited to mild and cold climates, as each winter it rests during the cold weather and dies back to crowns. It can be sown from seed, but cull any female (berry-producing) plants as they have inferior spears. Alternatively, plant out two-year-old crowns in winter. Some people like to mound their plants to produce extra-long white spears, but whatever your practice, ensure that your soil is open and friable so that the shoots can spring up easily.

FAR LEFT AND LEFT: *Asparagus spears fresh from the garden; plump artichoke flower buds ready for picking.*

Cardoon

Sometimes called wild thistle, or referred to as the poor cousin of the globe artichoke, the cardoon has incredibly handsome silver foliage that looks spectacular in the garden, especially in the early morning when edged in dew. Unlike artichokes, it's the stems rather than flowers that are normally not eaten. Blanching, as often done with celery, will greatly improve the stems' texture and flavour. This is done by wrapping the lower part of the plant in cardboard and excluding sunlight for three to five weeks, but be sure to wear sturdy gloves when you do this as the leaves have sharp edges.

VITAL STATISTICS

Scientific name: *Cynara cardunculus*.
Family: Asteraceae.
Climate: Mediterranean climates are ideal, but most temperate and warm climates are suitable.
Culture: A beautiful and edible feature plant in the vegie patch.
Colours: Grey leaves with purple thistle-like flowers.
Height: About 1.2 m.
Planting time: From spring to early summer, from offsets.
Soil: Grow in well-drained soil with added organic matter and mulch.
Position: Plants need a full sun position and is best with wind protection.
Planting spacing: 1 m apart.
Fertiliser: Use liquid manure monthly.
Harvest: After about six months the cardoon will be ready to blanch, then harvest.
Propagation: Grow from seed or offsets.
Use: Prepare stems carefully so as not to hurt yourself on any sharp bits. A potato peeler can be useful to run down the back of the stems to remove strings. Cut into lengths and place into acidified water. Boil till just soft and then freeze or transfer to a frypan with oil, garlic and lemon zest, or bake with cheese sauce into a gratin.

Feature vegetable

legumes

1 Borlotti bean 2 Shelling pea 'Earlicrop Massey' 3 Stringless bean 'Blue Lake' 4 Broad bean seeds 'Aquadulce'
5 Snow pea 6 Stringless bean seeds 'Pioneer' 7 Pea seeds 'Greenfeast' 8 Butter bean 9 Dwarf snow pea seeds

10 Snake bean seeds 11 Broad bean seeds 'Crimson Flowered' 12 Pod pea 'Sugar Snap' 13 Lima bean seeds
14 Red kidney bean seeds 15 Beanettes 16 Bean seeds 'Scarlet Runner'

Summer

Sunburn. Glare. Sand, salt and sea breezes. Scorched leaves and faded flowers. Picnics, evening walks and heady scents. The drone of cicadas. Nature at full speed.

Overview of the season

Summer is the season for using and enjoying your garden—cricket with the kids on the back lawn, barbecues with friends (and the mossies) or simply breakfast on the deck.

With holidays, relaxing with the family and hot weather dominating the agenda in summer, it's hard to fit in any gardening other than lawn mowing and watering. It's easy to see why gardeners often refer to summer as the forgotten season, but if you choose reliable plants that flower generously and fit your lifestyle this can still be a great time to get things done in the garden and to enjoy all the benefits.

Take time to wander around your garden, taking note which plants are unable to cope with the effects of summer weather, such as reflected heat or drying winds. The impatiens that were pretty in spring now might be suffering from dehydration and to maintain their year-round good looks might need relocating.

Summer is not a traditional time for planting as the hot weather increases the stress on young root systems when they are planted out. Even so, this doesn't mean you can't put anything in, it just means you have to be more careful with watering and to ensure your purchases have a healthy (not pot-bound) root system (see 'Choosing a good plant at the nursery' on page 18).

A regular stroll through the garden will show you gaps that need summer colour. Fill these with annuals or potted plants so you'll have lots of flowers for Christmas. But remember, summer flowers have to be hardy to withstand the summer heat. Many tropical plants begin to perform well as the weather warms, so do try quintessential summer plants such as lilies, bougainvillea and frangipani.

Looking ahead

If you want a head start to your winter/spring flower garden, start sowing seeds now for flowers in about six weeks' time. Flower seeds that are started off now with temporary protection from the heat under shadecloth will be ready early in winter when not much else is flowering. Try pansies and violas, and pinch-prune any flowers when they are small.

This time of the year isn't right for major changes to be made to your garden, but maintenance and diligence are still necessary. Even the saddest, most neglected garden seems to look okay in spring, but if you're lazy now, your summer garden will really start to struggle.

LEFT: *Bees, like this one on a Bull Bay magnolia flower, get busy in summer.*

Weatherwatch

Prepare your garden for those summer 'scorchers' by watering and mulching, and erecting shading over heat-sensitive plants.

Summer protection

Summer is such a harsh season in Australia that we tend to do things in the reverse order to gardeners in the northern hemisphere.

They plan over their cold winters and work in a mild summer, but here we should plan when it's hot and work when it's cool.

Over summer the risk of sunburn and the possibility of skin cancer increases. It's widely known that Australians have the highest rate of skin cancer in the world.

After years of 'slip, slop, slap' advertising, many Australians are still not heeding the warnings. If you're out and about, put on a hat and sunscreen. Roll down your shirt sleeves, and try and keep out of the sun between 10 am and 2 pm.

In the garden the best protection from the sun is a tree, so why not plant one or more? Ask your nursery for a local tree species, or select something exotic and attractive—the choice is yours. Shade is so cool, you'll love it and so will the wildlife.

However, in the meantime, is there anything else you can do to protect your garden? Putting up a shadecloth or sun-shade structure is an obvious built response, and we look at that more closely on page 218. Alternatively, you could use a spray-on 'blockout' for plants. Yates DroughtShield® (formerly Stessguard) works by greatly reducing evaporation from the leaves. It protects against wind exposure, drought and sunburn, as well as transplant shock and frost, and should be used before the period of stress begins. It lasts for three months and is biodegradeable.

TOP: *This wisteria-clad arbour is a lovely cool haven on hot summer days.*

LEFT: *Pear trees have been trained into an arch to create shade and draw attention to the house beyond.*

Fires and storms

In the Australian summer, fire is a very real danger. All too often, blazes sweep through bushland, threatening people's lives, homes, animals and flora.

If your home is close to bushland and you have not already taken precautions, do so now.

• Make sure you clear away all flammable goods around the house and create a wide firebreak between the bush and your property. Many exotic plants have far more moisture in their leaves than native plants: ask your local fire authority and nursery which plants could help slow the speed of fire in your street.

• Ensure that you have plenty of hoses close to the house or easy access to swimming pools, dams and water reservoirs. Check that your auxiliary pumps are in good working order.

• Clear out the gutters around your house and be prepared to fill them with water in times of emergency.

• Work out a fire procedure with household members so everyone knows what to do in the event of fire. And, of course, always keep a portable radio with fresh batteries handy.

And don't forget your personal things. Gather all photo albums and other sentimental items together in a place that is readily accessible.

In the tropics, bushfires may not be such a threat, but cyclones are. Protecting your property against such forces is just as important. Pruning trees with brittle branches such as tulip trees, gums and robinias may reduce potential damage during the cyclone season.

In storms, remove any shade sails or tarpaulins, which can act as sails, and pull up and secure blinds. Lighter objects can be flung into buildings, causing great damage, so pack away garden furniture and kids' play things into sheds, if possible, or sink them in your pool as a temporary measure.

ABOVE: *Prune trees with brittle branches, such as robinia, to reduce damage in cyclones and storms.*

LEFT: *If you live in a bushfire-prone area, always keep your gutters clear.*

REMEMBER TO WATER Deep soakings are best, and if you haven't yet spread a thick layer of mulch around, you really should now. It will save you litres of water and countless hours later in the season.

HAVE YOU THOUGHT ABOUT A RAIN GARDEN?
This new trend in garden design aims to keep rain water (and its pollutants) from coursing into stormwater systems. Rain gardens are slightly depressed gardens, like a billabong. They're designed to capture run-off and are planted with species that are tolerant of 'wet feet'.

Summer watering

Watering plants can be a difficult task for some
gardeners to master—too much and the plant drowns,
too little and it wilts.

We should all take extra care not to
waste water. If your water bill is very
high, you might be wasting water on
your garden and lawn, which can often
be watered with recycled water or from
tanks. When you're watering, check
water doesn't run off down paths and
driveways into the gutter: sprinklers
should be set to water the lawn and
garden only. Watering systems do save
water. Sprayers and drippers apply
water where it's needed, at the roots of
your plants, but do check their nozzles
for any blockages.

In hot dry weather you only need to
water your lawn for half an hour, twice a
week. Anything more wastes water and
money. Some soils actually repel water
so consider using one of the new
generation soil wetters. These liquids
reduce the waxy coating on soil particles,
allowing water to penetrate further into
the soil to the roots of plants. This helps
to moisten pot and garden soils and to
stop water wastage from run-off.

Quality potting mixes contain water
crystals. These act as a reservoir so that
when the soil dries out, water can be
absorbed from the crystals. Once you
apply water the crystals are hydrated
again. They continue the swelling and

PIPE SAVVY If
you're laying irrigation
pipe, take a photo of
the area before you
cover it with grass
or mulch as a visual
reference in case you
need to dig in the
area later on.

shrinking process, providing plants with
water for up to six years. Use them at
planting time.

Watering wisely

- Water first thing in the morning or in the
cool of the evening. At other times the
water will mostly evaporate before it soaks
down to the plants' roots.

- Add a water penetrant to your water or
potting mixes/soils. This breaks down the
skin of many Australian soils and reduces
the water run-off that many potting mixes
and sandy soils suffer from. Seasol Super
Soil Wetter is a great liquid additive, while
Saturaid is a granular application perfect
for adding to pots.

- Plants need to be trained to go longer
between drinks in summer, and this means
deep soaks once a week to encourage
deep-growing roots, not surface roots.

Hoses

Most quality garden hoses have ultra-
violet stabilisers or protectors added to
the plastic, a sort of '30 Plus' for your
hose. Unless you take extra care of your
garden hose, however, it will still only
last a year or two in the hot summer sun.

To keep your hose working well for
many years:

- Put the hose away in the shade when it's
not in use.

- Get it off the driveway. The weight of the
car fractures the inner tubing, weakening
the hose.

- Regularly check all your fittings: if they're
loose or worn out, the nozzles and joiners
will leak, wasting water.

- Roll it up. To roll up a hose, first run the
hose out to its full length in a straight line.
Then, starting at the tap end, pull the hose
up into a circle or wind it onto a portable
hose reel. Keeping it rolled up also makes
it easy to roll out the hose, tangle free,
next time.

*When it's not in use,
your hose should be
rolled up and stored
in the shade.*

Plant a summer-hardy garden

The key to success at this time of year is preparation, plant selection and maintenance. Prepare the bed with added organic matter, such as compost, to help the soil retain what little moisture it receives. When selecting plants, keep these points in mind:

🍃 Plant groundcovers to help shade the soil, suppress weeds, contain moisture and reduce evaporation.

🍃 Examples of hardy plants for summer include bearded iris, euphorbia, geraniums, gazania and pigface.

🍃 Look for plants that are adapted for drought. Features include succulent leaves, hairy leaves or grey foliage and strappy or needle-like leaves. Avoid plants with large, shiny leaves—they have probably originated in rainforest or tropical areas.

🍃 Examine labels closely; many growers provide indications on the back of each tag for how drought-tolerant the plants are.

🍃 Start small. Plant tubestock and smaller-sized plants—these will grow and adapt into position and be inexpensive if you have small losses.

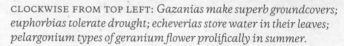

CLOCKWISE FROM TOP LEFT: *Gazanias make superb groundcovers; euphorbias tolerate drought; echeverias store water in their leaves; pelargonium types of geranium flower prolifically in summer.*

MAKE YOUR GARDEN A WATERWISE SUCCESS

Be wise with water by taking into account three design features:
Use permeable surfaces. Make sure a large proportion of the ground area consists of permeable surfaces to ensure that rain makes its way into the soil and water table where your plants can access it. Decomposed granite, decking (with water falling between the gaps in the boards to the ground below) or pebbles are alternatives to water-hungry grass. Mulched garden beds also allow water down into the plants' roots and help trap it there.

Create shade. Reduce evaporation by reducing your plants' exposure to direct sunlight. Plant a tree or erect a pergola, which can be covered in vines, for almost instant shade.

Build a water feature. A well-designed water feature might take the form of a mock billabong that fills with water when it rains, stockpiling run-off. In drier times, don't bother topping up the water constantly; instead, allow the stones or pebbles of its base to show through as an ornamental feature.

Water features

The alluring charm of a water feature is one of summer's underrated garden essentials. Water reflects light and cools the air, and moving water creates a peaceful ambience.

Many people would love to have a water feature, but the thought of pumps, digging huge holes, liners and the like is off-putting. Installing a pond in the garden is also a fairly expensive business. The easiest and cheapest way is simply to use a large pot.

Half wine barrels, stone and glazed pots, old coppers and plastic terracotta lookalikes are all suitable candidates. You can use any large container, but waterproof the inside with a sealant and ensure any drainage holes are plugged up (a cork, sealant, epoxy putty or silica gel will do the job).

To add life to your water, consider installing a pump. These are powered by a low-voltage, solar or regular 240-volt

motor, but make sure you have a safety switch. Usually the pump is submersible, and the spouts can vary from single jet options to multiple droplets or small gurgling devices.

Most flowering aquatic plants have distinct preference for the sun, with lilies, water poppies, reeds, Louisiana iris and lotus all suited to a sunny spot. If you have a shady area, try dwarf papyruses, arum lilies (either the green, white or dwarf types), syngonium, sedges and water lettuces.

You can also use floating pond weeds, but these grow quickly, so either stock fish to keep them in check, or scoop out the excess regularly to allow the other plants the room they need. Fish will also keep mosquito larvae under control.

Ponds take time to install but, once established, require less work than garden beds. Position is everything. Avoid placing ponds under trees, as overhanging trees also drop leaves and flowers that upset the biological balance of the water. When selecting water plants, take the position of your water feature into consideration. Arum lilies cope with shade, are long flowering and evergreen. Waterlilies have their own requirements: they don't like splashing water, need lots of sun and die down over winter, making them suitable for bigger ponds and still pools. Small pots may be capable of taking just a handful of floating weed.

Growing waterlilies

Not surprisingly, the waterlily is the world's most popular aquatic plant. Nothing could be more exotic on a balcony or in the garden than a pond filled with waterlilies.

You can grow waterlilies in either a large, shallow pond in the garden or in a pot on a verandah or sheltered rooftop

A water feature can be as simple as a shallow bowl with duckweed and sedge, like this, or as elaborate as a naturalistic pool with cascades.

WATERLILIES

Waterlilies have been featured in Arabic and Moorish gardens for centuries. In China, waterlilies are traditionally grown in large glazed pots raised on plinths in the middle of a courtyard, allowing them to be admired without any distractions. They really took off in Europe and then in the rest of the world in the late 19th century when heated glasshouses made it possible for the tropical species to be grown indoors in northern climates.

The French Impressionist painter Claude Monet featured them in a series of paintings set in his garden in Giverny, France. They are now the best known of all aquatic plants. There is a waterlily available to suit any climate, from tropical to cold zones. The miniature species *Nymphaea tetragona* (syn. *N. pygmaea*) is especially suited to pots. Very beautiful in flower, it is herbaceous, with the leaves dying back to a permanent rootstock as the weather cools. Rhizomes can be lifted during this dormancy, normally in late winter or early spring, and divided every two or three years.

garden, as long as it is a sunny position. There are shorter stemmed waterlilies available that are perfect for pot culture. Select a tub or decorative pot, about 30–40 cm deep and at least 50 cm wide, without a hole. Lined half wine barrels are ideal.

Grow waterlilies in a wire mesh basket lined with peat or coconut fibre or in a pot. Add a pinch of slow-release fertiliser to the compost and insert the waterlily root system. (Too much fertiliser will result in algal blooms in the water.) Then gently settle the basket into the water on the bottom of the pot,

or to a depth of about half a metre if you are planting in a pond.

Keep the water clean; fish will help keep the mossies at bay. After several weeks large leaves will appear, then huge, plump flower buds. Once water-lilies start flowering they keep blooming for months, and a number of species are perfumed.

If you're planning a water garden, it's a good idea to visit a nursery that specialises in aquatic plants. They'll have the biggest range of waterlilies and other water plants, and can give advice on growing them.

CONTAINERS
To grow waterlilies, use a container with a capacity of about 100 L. It will be very heavy once full of water, so make sure it's in situ and level before filling and planting.

Planting waterlilies

1

A waterlily root with some new shoots.

2

Insert the waterlily root into compost.

3

Mulch with pebbles.

CLOCKWISE FROM TOP LEFT: *Calla lilies are lovely, and have speckled leaves; blue pickerelweed (Pontederia cordata) has violet-blue (or white) flower spikes 50 cm tall in summer; canna lilies die down in winter and sprout fresh leaves in spring; hostas are loved for their colourful leaves; astilbes have feathery blooms of red, pink, purple or white.*

Bog gardens

In poorly drained areas of the garden, where the soil is constantly saturated, most deep-rooted shrubs and trees cannot get enough air. Some herbaceous plants—such as *Gunnera*, *Alocasia*, cannas, arums and Louisiana iris— will flourish here, and look great teamed with ferns, sedges and some bamboos that also thrive in these conditions. Other plants that prefer damp conditions include bottlebrushes, paperbarks, tea-trees, alders, swamp cypress, watergums, astilbes and hydrangeas.

It always makes good sense to work with the conditions, so rather than trying to improve the drainage, why not create a bog garden? They can look fantastic and display a wide range of flowering perennials that can be difficult to grow in hot dry climates. Beth Chatto made her Essex garden famous the world round by transforming her boggy hollows into just such a plant paradise.

AQUATICS

To keep the water clear and clean in your ponds, make sure you keep the sunlight off with a layer of floating aquatics that cover 70 per cent of the surface area. This will stop the algae from growing and keep your fish fed with their greens when you're away. Here, fairy moss (*Azolla*) and other plants do the job.

Planting Louisiana iris

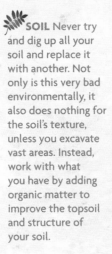

SOIL Never try and dig up all your soil and replace it with another. Not only is this very bad environmentally, it also does nothing for the soil's texture, unless you excavate vast areas. Instead, work with what you have by adding organic matter to improve the topsoil and structure of your soil.

1. Line a wire basket with coconut fibre. Add soil.

2. Trim the leaves on your iris before potting.

3. Carefully divide the plant.

4. Top up with garden soil.

5. Finish with pebble mulch.

6. Lower into the pond water slowly.

Louisiana iris

For fantastic flowers and foliage consider Louisiana iris, a group of five *Iris* species native to the swamps of Louisiana and Florida. They are great planted as marginals around a pond, or even as garden perennials, as long as they are given plenty of water. In cold climates, Louisiana iris become dormant after flowering. When their leaves become brown, trim them to about 15 cm tall and mulch them well.

LOTUS FLOWER

For centuries these stunning flowers have been held high as the bloom that rises up from mud, and in many Eastern cultures the lotus flower is a spiritual representation of our ability to rise above whatever dire circumstances we are in, and still be pure. In fact, this flower prefers still, putrid water and it won't grow where the water moves, so pots and ponds, and even dams are perfect. Known botanically as *Nelumbo*, the lotus comes in white, pink and dark pink, with doubles and almost peony forms. All are followed by a beautiful seed pod. The lotus root is also used as a root crop and can be pickled or eaten fresh. Young flower stalks and the seeds are also edible.

Free plants

Propagating plants from your garden is a very rewarding experience. So many plants are easy to propagate.

You can take cuttings and grow your own plants, and you don't even need a green thumb. Among the plants to choose from are lavender, box, camellia, fuchsia, rhododendron, pittosporum, azalea, gardenia, rosemary, osmanthus, daphne, eriostemon and photinia.

Propagating rosemary

Take semi-hardwood cuttings in late summer or early autumn. Plant them out when they have put on new growth, indicating they have put down roots.

1 Trim short lengths and remove the soft tip. **2** Remove all the lower leaves. **3** Take a thin layer off the stem to reveal the cambium layer, then dip the stem in some hormone powder. **4** Make a hole with a stick in a pot filled with a free-draining potting mix, and plant the cutting. Water the pot.

Softwood cuttings

At this time of year, most plants grow rapidly. Use this new growth to take softwood cuttings. The best time to collect cuttings is in the early morning before the sun heats up. Take a tip piece of stem (the 'soft' wood), about 8 cm long, from a healthy new shoot. Remove the lower leaves. If the remaining leaves are large, cut them in half to reduce the amount of water lost by transpiration. Dip the stem in hormone powder to encourage strong root growth. Fill a small pot with a free-draining potting mix, insert several cuttings around the edge and then water them in gently.

Cover the pot with a plastic bag and keep it shaded until the cuttings have struck. Alternatively, make a mini glasshouse by inverting a used coffee jar over the cuttings. This will provide a moist environment for the cuttings and help prevent them drying out.

In a few weeks, roots should have formed on each cutting. Then you can re-pot each cutting into its own pot.

Semi-hardwood cuttings

Semi-hardwood cuttings can normally be taken in summer too. Select pencil-thick new growth that has firmed up enough not to wilt once picked. Pieces should be about 5–8 cm in length, and have a sliver of tissue removed at the base of each to reveal the green cambium layer before dipping into hormone powder and placing in a pot with potting mix. Try taking these cuttings from shrubs such as camellias, azaleas, rhododendrons, escallonias, *Raphiolepis* and *Euonymus*.

For some shrubs, such as rosemary and lavender, a 'heeled' cutting gets the best results. This simply means pulling your piece off the main shrub (rather than cutting it) with a sliver of the parent branch still attached. This sliver will have the green cambium layer exposed. Dip into hormone powder and plant into containers of potting mix. Keep watered until the cutting is well rooted.

Hollow tubes, such as these bamboo canes, can be clustered together to make a habitat for native bees and other beneficial insects.

Organic gardening

Summer can be a particularly devastating time for our environment, but with organic gardening techniques you can help put back into the soil what has been taken out.

Organic gardeners use naturally occurring fertilisers and pest control methods, as well as lots of bulky, well-rotted material. This will improve not only soil fertility, but also microbial activity, soil structure, and the soil's water- and nutrient-holding capacity.

A thriving compost heap is essential in the organic garden, but you can also dig farmyard manure, leaf mould, seaweed and old mushroom compost into your beds. Any organic matter will feed your plants gently and encourage good soil organisms.

Keep the garden free of plant debris as many pests and diseases lurk among dying foliage. Encourage insects and birds—many of them are the natural predators of garden pests. For example, ladybirds and lacewings eat aphids. And bees will pollinate your fruit and vegetables, which will set much better crops as a result. To attract bees, plant buddleia (butterfly bush) and sedum.

Finally, mulching your garden well conserves moisture and protects it from the summer heat.

Each floret of the butterfly bush has an 'eye' like a target to help direct the butterfly's proboscis for feeding.

MULCH

The secret to a happy summer garden is mulch, the best strategy for getting the most from your garden and having it look fabulous over the holidays. It also maximises your efforts in the garden.

The value of blanketing your garden in a 10 cm layer of organic matter to keep the soil moist and the weeds away cannot be overestimated. Smother the soil around your plants with a thick layer of mulch to prevent the roots baking in the hot summer sun and to conserve moisture.

Mulch can be made up of any organic material. Leaves make good mulch but work best once they have decomposed—run over them with the lawnmower to speed up this process. Pine bark is popular for mulching. Use it with pelletised chicken manure as the bark can absorb nitrogen from the soil and rob your plants of this nutrient, turning them yellow.

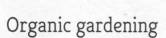

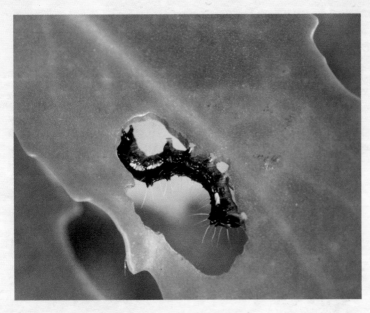

Caterpillars can destroy even tough tissue with their strong chewing mouth parts.

Plant problems and pests

Summer can be a difficult time for plants in the garden. The butterflies and moths of spring have laid their eggs, which have now hatched into grubs that are eating their way through your garden.

Do you reach for a spray at the first sign of a creepy crawly? Well, they may all give you the shivers, but there is a difference between friend and foe. All creatures, great and small, have a part in the food chain, and a little under-standing can go a long way towards coexisting with the insect world and still having a garden.

First, let's look at the way most people garden. We group plants together in ways that we find attractive and useful:

vegies in their own patch, roses in a rose bed and the annuals down the driveway. To insects, though, these are rather like neon signs pinpointing eating spots.

It would be much more sensible for us to mix everything up together. Hide your delicious vegetables in the garden and distribute the roses among other flowering shrubs. Such techniques also encourage beneficial insects in the garden. These insects parasitise aphids, mites and the like, controlling the 'bad guy' numbers naturally. To coax more 'good guys' into your garden, try planting some insect- and bird-attracting plants, including parsley, dill, elderberry, fennel, Queen Anne's lace (*Anthriscus sylvestris*) and nectar-rich flowering plants.

By practising all the principles of good plant cultivation (such as feeding, pruning, watering and mulching), in most cases you should minimise the opportunity for pests and diseases to take hold. Plants are often attacked because they are under other stresses, so always deal with the problem first, and the solution second.

If you still experience outbreaks after taking these preventive measures, follow these simple steps to outwit the craftiest crawly and slimiest disease!

1 Correctly identify the pest or disease. This may involve a trip to your local garden centre so you can ask a horticulturist to look at it.

2 At what stage is the pest or disease? In other words, will spraying catch the problem, or will it have flown away?

3 Not every problem will have a chemical solution: sometimes you'll have to rectify the way you care for your garden.

4 Don't overkill. Every time you use a spray to control a pest you may also be killing its natural predators.

ATTRACT THE GOOD GUYS

Flowers such as Queen Anne's lace (shown here) and elderberry attract beneficial insects to your garden. Ladybirds, for example, eat huge numbers of aphids, mites, mealy bugs and scales. Lacewings and parasitic wasps will also work for you, but chemical sprays will kill them as well as the pests.

Common summer problems

Silvering foliage

A wide range of insects attack different
plants but they all produce the same sort
of damage—silvery leaves. These insects
can be red spider, thrips and lace bugs.
Most people jump to the conclusion that
it is red spider (which is not a spider at
all but a mite), especially when this
damage appears on azaleas.

In fact, this sort of damage occurs
because of insects known as 'rasping
feeders'. They scratch away at the
undersurface of the leaf, causing it
to bleed sap, which they then suck up.
This rasping action permanently
discolours leaves on azaleas, fuchsias,
viburnum, roses and a host of other
commonly grown ornamentals.

To effectively control these pests, you
must identify them correctly. Make sure
you examine the underside of the foliage,
and take a few leaves down to your local
nursery, or a museum entomologist, for
identification.

The chemical control will vary
(see, for example, 'Azaleas' on page 206),
but one treatment is common to all—
keep the underside of your plant well
watered and hosed down once in a
while, especially if they are growing
in rain shadows, such as under your
house's eaves, where the problem can be
compounded. This will keep all these
plants clean and healthy, and far less
prone to significant attack. If large trees
are affected, treatment can be very
difficult, but adequate watering and
hosing down the foliage will reduce
stress in trees, and help them to rectify
any problems naturally.

DID YOU KNOW? Praying mantises are
great at eating all sorts of bugs in the garden.
So named because when waiting for prey, it
holds its front legs as if they are folded in
prayer. Despite this serene pose, the mantis
is a deadly predator.

ABOVE: *A lace bug
infestation caused
this severe damage
to azalea leaves.*

LEFT: *An adult lace
bug is only a few
millimetres long.*

Fruit fly

Fruit fly has been a problem for orchardists and home gardeners for years. The insect is about the size of a small housefly and you often see the pest sitting on fruit with its transparent wings waving back and forth. It lays eggs in the fruit and these hatch into little maggots or grubs, ruining the fruit. During the warmer months of the year the fly attacks ripening citrus and stone fruits such as peaches and nectarines and, in the vegie patch, tomatoes, eggplants and capsicums.

Monitoring for evidence of this pest is the first step towards its control. Hang baits from trees to attract the males—this will let you know if the flies are present. Then you can use a spray that contains an attractant and an inseciticide to kill them (see below).

Apart from spraying, two methods to reduce fruit-fly damage are:

- Grow early-maturing varieties of fruit trees. This means you'll harvest the crop before the fruit fly arrives. Your nursery will know the special fruit varieties to ask for.

- For those who are really keen, place muslin or a paper bag over the ripening fruit.

FLY HAVENS Be particularly careful growing winter-fruiting plants, such as loquats and kumquats, as these can harbour fruit fly over winter.

Thrips on fig

Now that standardised figs have become commonplace, certain problems keep recurring. If you notice that the new growth on your standard fig has curled, and you can see small ant-like creatures in this affected growth, Cuban laurel thrips (*Gynaikothrips ficorum*) are the likely cause.

The size of tiny aphids, thrips look like black dashes with pointed tails. There are normally lots of small dark droppings around as well. Thrips are a rasping feeder, sucking the sap from leaves, after scraping their surface. This causes leaves to become finely mottled or streaked on their upper surface.

Thrips attack large established trees as well as your standardised pot plants. Try cutting off the affected parts and placing them in a secure plastic bag, rather than in the compost bin. When the new growth starts to come back, spraying with PestOil® may help, especially if you combine it with a few drops of the insecticide Lebaycid®.

Keep the new growth moist with an atomiser, and make sure that the roots are not allowed to dry out as this will cause leaf drop and subject your fig to further stress.

Fruit fly killer

A bacteria-derived insecticide, spinosad, is registered for use with fruit fly and has the green tick of approval from eco-organisations. Applied as a spray, it comes with a protein bait, which attracts the fruit fly to feed on it. When the fly feeds on the spray, the spinosad kills it.

1 Measure out the correct dose, following the manufacturer's instructions.

2 Fill a spray bottle with the spinosad and add water to the correct level.

3 Spray onto the fruit tree's foliage. The whole plant need not be covered.

Millipedes

After summer rains you might notice that lots of insects seek the dryness of houses and verandahs. One such crawly is the millipede. At this time of the year they may come inside, especially one species, the black Portuguese millipede.

Millipedes are actually pretty harmless creatures. When their numbers build up in wet weather, they might eat soft fruit such as strawberries that grow close to the ground, but generally they feed on decomposing organic matter. If they become really hungry, they might eat some young roots, seedlings or seeds. They can be a problem with soft fruit, and squirmy gardeners!

Millipedes have a long segmented body that has a hard external covering, and are famous for their multitude of legs. Many pairs of legs line the sides of their bodies.

When disturbed, millipedes curl up in a flat spiral, and can be easily squashed or swept up. If they really are worrying you, Baysol® will kill them.

Disease alert

In tropical and subtropical areas, late summer is particularly humid, leaving many plants susceptible to fungal diseases such as leaf spot, mildew and rot. Diligent garden hygiene is a much better preventative measure than resorting to chemical controls.

- Remove leaves affected by fungal spots or mildew and throw them away—do not put them into the compost heap.

- Clear away fallen leaves.

- Allow good air circulation around your plants. This is very important, especially with roses—and feed them now to encourage new growth that will flower in autumn.

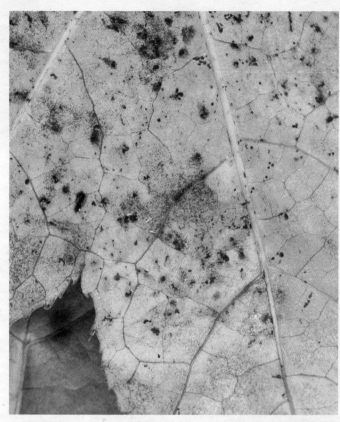

The tissue of this leaf has been destroyed by a fungus.

- Remove any weed growth at ground level to discourage fungus diseases like black spot.

- Crepe myrtle is in full flower now, and these magnificent small flowering trees are susceptible to powdery mildew. It's pointless to spray larger trees, the chemical just drifts in the air. If your tree is healthy, the mildew will not affect its growth or its flowering. Make sure your tree gets enough sunshine—this will also discourage fungus.

HOMEMADE REMEDIES

Many insecticides now are synthesised forms of pyrethrum. To make your own spray, finely chop the flowers and leaves of the pyrethrum daisy and immerse in water overnight. Strain the water through a muslin cloth and store it in a container. Use the mixture as needed as a contact spray for aphids and other sap-suckers. Other foul-tasting concoctions can be made from chilli, garlic, wormwood and quassia chips. See pages 233 and 234 for DIY insecticides using chilli.

Gardening at the seaside

Anyone who lives along the coast or who is lucky enough to have a holiday house there knows the problems associated with low soil nutrients, salt-laden winds and salty, and often sandy soils that hold little water.

BELOW: *Sea holly (Eryngium sp.) thrives on neglect and makes a striking sight in the summer garden.*

A well-planned seaside garden can enhance ocean views, provide shelter from strong sea winds, capture sunlight, and add colour and interest in the garden all year. The first task is to build up the soil with organic matter, compost, lawn clippings and decomposed leaves. Doing so will make the garden more productive and water retentive.

The trick to seaside gardening is to provide a windbreak shelter for weaker plants. Planting a screen of extremely hardy plants, such as banksias, she-oaks or paperbarks, is good for this purpose. All the varieties of the New Zealand Christmas bush (*Metrosideros* sp.) and coastal rosemary (*Westringia* sp.) are good for windbreaks and hedges.

Salt-tolerant bougainvillea, snake vine and agapanthus add colour through summer. Hebes come in a great range of colours, from the softest lilac to deep cherry pinks, and will cope with just about anything, from frosts to salt-laden wind and baking sun. Oleanders thrive on neglect, and an exposed seaside location is perfect for them.

Salt-tolerant grasses (such as *Festuca glauca* and *Carex buccananii*) and native groundcovers, like the cushion plant (*Leucophyta brownii*), are also useful. Indeed, the majority of grey plants grow naturally in harsh conditions, such as on the shoreline and in desert and alpine regions. Many silver and grey foliage plants originated in Australia and these soft silvery-grey colours make a great foil for sombre greens in the garden.

The grey and silver appearance is caused by white hairs on the leaf surface. The hairs reflect the harsh rays of the sun, reducing water loss and retaining moisture close to the surface. Silver and grey plants are perfect for inland and shoreline areas as they will thrive where other plants could not survive, but remember that they do need sun to create the shimmering effect: otherwise they are simply grey.

ABOVE: *Many ornamental grasses cope with salt-laden winds and 'dance' with each breath.*

Gardening in small areas

Small gardens can be very special additional rooms of the house—places for relaxing on sunny days and for eating on balmy evenings.

The direct warmth of the sun, small movements of the air, the sound of water, deep shadows and the dazzle of light on leaves, the fresh green of thriving plants—these are pleasures that no interior can achieve. But that is only half the charm of small gardens, for they also form vivid backdrops to daily life, fascinating display cases to be enjoyed from the comfort of the house.

The contained garden

Apartment and townhouse dwellings are becoming more and more common for more and more people, especially in our inner-city areas.

Do you have a tiny garden? Perhaps it's only a balcony or courtyard. Well, a great deal can be achieved in a limited space with a bit of imagination, and lots of ideas and books are available that focus on small gardens. Small spaces can be transformed into pretty, usable green extensions of your home's living space to make an outdoor room. These can be intimate—with lattice smothered in perfumed creepers—or cheery and portable, ideal for renters. Make small gardens appear bigger by planting cool colours at the back of the garden and warmer shades—such as reds, yellows and oranges—in the foreground.

Climate control

One of the difficulties facing courtyard and balcony gardeners is exposure to prevailing winds. Even in cool shaded areas, wind will quickly dry out pots and hanging baskets so some form of protection is required. For a balcony this could be a reinforced glass screen that neither obscures views nor blocks out the sun. In a courtyard a panel or two of lattice supporting a hardy climber will stop the draughts.

TOP: *This black glazed pot features shade-loving black cordyline, variegated* Euonymus *'Silver Pillar' and variegated liriope.*

ABOVE: *The cottagey effect of a stone sink filled with slow-growing thyme and dianthus requires full sun.*

The choice of plant material in a small garden will be determined by the amount of sunlight available. This will vary according to the aspect as well as the height and proximity of neighbouring buildings. The ideal aspect is an easterly one which receives gentle morning sun and is protected from the fierce afternoon heat of summer.

Plants suitable for containers

Virtually any plant can be potted, as long as it is treated properly. This may require root pruning every few years (in effect 'bonsaiing'), or taking cores of the rootball out each year. This can often be an arduous task, especially considering the weight of heavy cement pots or moist potting mix. The best way to get around this problem is to choose dwarf or smaller growing specimens where you can.

Terrific examples of these include:

- **Fruit trees:** 'Nectazee', 'Pictazee', flying dragon rootstock on citrus or smaller growers such as 'Meyer' and 'Lisbon' lemon, kumquat, 'Honey Murcott' mandarin, Ballerina apples, and Trixzie pears and cherries.

- **Screening trees:** dwarf lilly-pillies, small pittosporums ('Silver Song' and 'Tom Thumb'), and smaller sasanqua camellias such as 'Yuletide' and 'Mine-no-yuki'.

- **Flowering shrubs:** dwarf duranta ('Blue Boy' or 'Towards 2000'), dwarf apricot oleander, Elfin series daisies, dwarf *Murraya* 'Min-a-Min', and 'Petite' and 'Little Lianne' sasanqua camellias.

- **Natives:** dwarf lilly-pillies ('Blaze', 'Bush Christmas', 'Tiny Trevor'), *Banksia* 'Birthday Candles', small wattles (such as *Acacia fimbriata* dwarf) and the new dwarf brush box called 'Billy Bunter'.

CLOCKWISE FROM TOP LEFT: Pittosporum *'Tom Thumb'* has dark purple leaves that contrast well with its bright green new growth; nemesia flowers for many months in a pot; the frothy pink flowers of this gaura work well with the dramatic form of variegated cordyline.

ABOVE: *Colanders, a watering-can and other items can make off-beat containers.*

LEFT: *Cloud topiary is a style characterised by cloud-like balls of foliage that are clipped into balls on top of the stems.*

Pruning techniques

There are three main pruning techniques that can be used on a wide range of plants to keep them smaller, which makes them ideal for small gardens.

1 Topiary, or clipping plants into shapes, can be a way of introducing formality or even whimsy. You could prune your favourite hedging plant into a bird, watering can or simply an obelisk. Easy, fast-growing plants suitable for topiary include lilly-pillies, box, box honeysuckle (*Lonicera nitida*) and creeping wire vine.

2 For the traditional standard, or 'ball on a stick' look, choose from golden broom, daisies, fuchsias, roses, potato vine, azaleas and ficus. (See the project on page 209.)

3 Espalier is a French word meaning 'trellis', and this pruning technique involves training plants to grow flat against a wall or frame. Try using fire thorn, sasanqua camellias, bougainvillea or nasturtium bush (*Bauhinia galpinii*); most fruit trees can also be espaliered. Remember that while elaborate candelabra patterns are fantastic, espalier can be simply achieved by just cutting away outward growth and tying back the remainder.

Potting with unusual containers

You don't have to use standard plastic or terracotta pots for your potted garden: collect some unusual containers and pot them up with quick-growing plants such as verbena and lobelia. Check your kitchen cupboards or local garage sales for some suitable potting containers. Colanders, old baths, bird cages, ancient walking boots, buckets, kettles, you name it—all can be pressed into service. Just make sure you use good-quality fresh potting mix.

BLOOMING BAG

To brighten up a patio, balcony or balustrade, buy a 'blooming bag' from you local nursery. These are strong green plastic bags, with slits cut down one side. Fill the bag up in levels, planting seedlings in the pockets as you go. Impatiens look great planted in this way, as do lobelia, nasturtium and strawberries or mixed cottage selections. Choose the right seedlings for each spot, and you'll have colour in the sun or shade.

Hanging baskets

Every home has a transition zone, the space that connects the inside to the outside. Whether it's a porch, verandah or a large pergola-covered entertaining area, this area can be the most enjoyable of all to be in.

One of the most satisfying gardening activities is to grow plants in a hanging basket in this space linking the house with the garden. Choose annuals filled with seasonal colour or a mass planting of mixed seedlings, pendulous plants and a small shrub or two.

In recent years many improvements have been made to moisture-retaining products, potting mixes and fertilisers, making growing plants in baskets much easier. Water crystals act like a reservoir in the soil by holding water in the basket. Potting mixes have improved enormously. Controlled, slow-release fertiliser means plants need only be fed once every nine months, and generally that's sufficient for the life of the display.

Top-quality potting mixes contain all three products: slow-release fertiliser, water crystals and wetting agents.

There is also a new product for lining the inside of the basket. In the old days paperbark was removed from tea trees under licence and used for lining the insides of hanging baskets. New liners made from sheep wool waste are environmentally friendly and recycle an excellent product.

Which plant where?

The arrangement and placement of plants is important in achieving an overall, pleasant effect. Pots should be uniform, all terracotta or all plastic, not a mixture. Place them in some logical order, perhaps grouped around a large central pot with a feature plant.

Choose your plants to suit the conditions in your garden. A sunny exposed site may be perfect for a Tuscan theme with bright red geraniums in terracotta troughs. Window boxes or troughs are ideal for long narrow spaces. To add height, grow potted standard bougainvillea, which flower for months and love the basking sun, as do potted gerberas. For a damp and shady spot, try dwarf arum lilies, begonias, ferns and impatiens.

Perfect potted plants

The biggest problem facing plants in pots is drying out. A good-quality potting mix is essential, and some added peat moss means it will hold more water. If the potting mix does dry out, break up the surface with a small fork or the water will run off the soil without being absorbed. If you need further help with water absorption and retention, use wetting agents and water-storing crystals. All potted plants are best fertilised with slow-release fertilisers. If you add some nutrient solution to the water your plants will thrive.

Maintenance tips

- Group your pots together to reduce the impacts of exposure when you're away.

- Pinch back shoots to help plants bush out.

- Dead-heading is essential for most flowering plants to maintain flowering over a long period.

🌿 **ON THE MOVE**
Often balconies are several storeys up, so remember that smaller items make everything easier to take with you if you're renting.

These hanging baskets complement the colour scheme of the house and brighten it up at the same time.

project

1

2

3

Make a ball basket

Baskets filled with colourful flowering plants simply look fabulous. You can hang them from the walls of your home and use them to decorate your patio, pergola, verandah or courtyard, or hang them from established trees in your garden.

4

5

1 Choose the biggest basket that you can lift. The bigger the basket, the easier it will be to keep the root system happy. You'll find it easier to work if you balance the basket on top of a stand, such as an old can. Use plastic baskets or attractive wire baskets that can be teamed with a liner, such as wool, coco fibre, sphagnum moss or bark. It should fit snuggly inside the wire frame. Cut slits in the sides of fitted liners to allow plants to grow into a ball of colour.

2 Line the basket with sphagnum moss.

3 Use a premium quality potting mix that contains water-holding crystals and slow-release fertiliser.

4 As you fill the basket, position the seedlings and then plant the top section.

5 Planted with wishbone flower (*Torenia* sp.), viola and alyssum, this basket will be a mass of flowers in a few weeks.

BASKET SIZE As a rule, the bigger the basket, the less often you'll have to water and the more scope there will be in plant selection, so choose something at least 300 mm wide.

FROM TOP: *A potted poinsettia for Christmas; a 'Just Joey' rose for a Joseph or Josephine; a pink begonia for the festive season.*

Wish list

Summer, being Christmas time, is a great time to think about giving plants as gifts. There are so many plants that make wonderful living gifts at Christmas, and a lovely change from red poinsettias is the pretty, small-flowered azalea called 'Christmas Cheer'. Wax or bedding begonias in white, pink or red with the leaves purple, red or green also make an excellent choice for Christmas presents.

Down under, many Australian natives evoke the feeling of Christmas just as effectively as holly and mistletoe. Combine Christmas bells with their dainty yellow-and-red trumpet flowers, stunning New South Wales Christmas bush, red kangaroo paws and red-flowering gum to make a wonderful Yuletide bouquet.

Kangaroo paws come in all shades of red, green and yellow, and many hybrids grow well in a wide range of climates. Their festive colours make lovely floral arrangements that last in even the hottest weather.

Christmas bells are not so easy to grow but worth a try, which makes it a great thrill when they actually flower. Specific winter temperatures are one of the factors that induce flowering.

The New South Wales Christmas bush starts flowering in late spring, but it is the seed calyces behind the flowers that grow larger and turn red, giving this tree its beautiful colour in summer. Now there's a variety of improved flower colours available: 'Albery's Red' for early red flowers; 'Wildfire' for deep red; 'White Christmas' for its less vigorous

white form; and 'True Blue' for its silver variegated leaf.

Make sure you prune after flowering as this keeps the bush looking good, compact and healthy.

Birthdays, births and christenings

Many plants are named after people, and matching a plant's name with the person you're giving it to is an especially lovely touch. Examples include camellias such as 'Jennifer Susan', 'Vanessa' and 'Susan'; and roses such as 'Cecilia', 'Carla' and 'Sexy Rexy'. There are less common ones too, such as a magnolia called 'Elizabeth' and a tibouchina named 'Kathleen'. Ask at your local nursery for more ideas.

A special gift for a newborn or a christened child is a tree that can grow with them. If it is going to be planted in the garden, choose something that doesn't grow too big, such as gordonia.

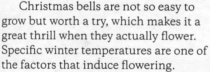

LOOKING AFTER LIVE CHRISTMAS PRESENTS
- Acclimatise plants slowly from being indoors to full sun by placing them in a shaded position for a few weeks.
- Don't let plants sit in saucers of water. Lift them up out of the tray with a brick or pebbles so that their roots don't rot.
- Feed Christmas trees in autumn to ensure they look great for the next year.

Christmas is not the only time to think of giving plants as a gift. Not only do they give us pleasure long after the occasion has passed, they continue to remind us of the giver and their kind thoughts.

The pale lemon luminous flowers of Magnolia *'Elizabeth' would surely make any 'Liz' pleased to receive one as a gift.*

Alternatively, suggest that the local park may need greening up with a native gum.

If none of these suggestions suits, perhaps you could choose the child's birth flower. There is a floral emblem, both native and exotic, for each month of the year.

Weddings and anniversaries

For weddings and anniversaries many plants have names that suit perfectly, like the azaleas named 'Ruby Glow' and 'Silver Anniversary' or the roses called 'Gold Medal' and 'Wedding Day'. Another nice idea is to plant up a basket with a matching colour scheme, such as a silver foliage combo for a silver wedding anniversary.

Remembrance

A living gift is a thoughtful way of remembering the loss of a loved one. It can be planted at the memorial site or at the home of a close relative. Pick something hardy and understated. A white camellia or gardenia is always nice, and old-fashioned roses and bulbs are great survivors at cemeteries. For indoors, a peace lily makes a thoughtful gift, or give rosemary, which is associated with remembrance.

House warmings

The happy plant (*Dracaena deremensis*), like the jade plant, is supposed to be good feng shui and bring good fortune to the household.

St Valentine's Day or Easter

If you're looking for a low-kilojoule gift on this day of traditional chocolate indulgence, buy pots of chocolate cosmos and chocolate mint, both of which are chocolate scented, to accompany a red rose.

Father's Day and Mother's Day

Tomatoes are perfect Father's Day presents. Dads seem to love the competitive aspect of tomato growing, and early spring is just the right time to be planting young seedlings.

Chrysanthemums, affectionately known as 'Mums' in the cut flower industry, are given by the bucketful each Mother's Day in Australia, but do remember that in other countries and even Japan, chrysanthemums are traditional funeral flowers.

CLOCKWISE FROM TOP LEFT: *Chocolate cosmos is perfect for the diet version of a Valentine or Easter gift; lavender, which is a symbol of remembrance, is hardy enough to cope with gravesite conditions; the purity of a white camellia suits many occasions perfectly.*

BIRTH FLOWERS

This northern hemisphere list of birth flowers is not definitive, but it's a start.

January	Carnation
February	Violet
March	Daffodil
April	Sweet pea
May	Lily-of-the-valley
June	Rose
July	Larkspur
August	Gladiolus
September	Aster
October	Marigold
November	Chrysanthemum
December	Holly

TIPS FOR CUT FLOWERS

- Re-cut the stems just before you place your flowers in the vase.
- Change the water daily or add a drop of bleach to the water to stop algae growing.

We're all going on a summer holiday

Before you go away on holiday, whether it's for a week or well over a month, make sure you've done enough maintenance in the garden so it still looks great when you return.

A quick 'short back and sides' on your garden is worth the effort.

Get things in order

🌢 Stake and tie back taller perennials. Rake, edge and tidy up. Most weeds set seed in summer so it is vital that you weed before this happens.

🌢 A light trim all over will help give hedges a still lived-in look. Removing old flowers, and even flower buds, can promote bushy growth and help conserve energy.

🌢 Water your garden with a wetting agent to help any light showers penetrate into the soil. Dig water-storing crystals into dry areas: they will act as water reservoirs.

Hydrate water crystals before digging them in.

🌢 Mulch the whole garden, pots included, with a thick (10–15 cm) layer of organic matter. Water everything thoroughly, as both the mulch and the soil below need to be wet. This will help keep the roots cool and moist, and reduce evaporation.

🌢 Cut the grass just before you leave, but not too short.

🌢 Spray your lawn with a hormone treatment to slow down growth while you're away.

🌢 Cut a big bunch of flowers and buds for any relatives you're visiting—after all, they'll go to waste in the garden.

PROTECT POT PLANTS

🌢 Pots dry out quickly at the best of times, so move them into a shady corner, and group them together, with the toughest on the perimeter. This will make it easier for your neighbour to water, and also reduce the impact of wind and sun on those plants in the centre.

🌢 Saucers can also help, but remove them when you return so that roots don't rot. Any really precious pot plants should be plunged in a moist area of the garden, and dug back up when you get home.

🌢 Put indoor plants in the bath on an old towel, water them thoroughly, and if possible leave the tap dripping slightly. Make sure the plug is not in place. Water will get sucked up through the towel to the rootballs, and the room will stay cool and moist, further protecting your plants.

LEFT: *Gardenia flowers are quintessentially summer and perfume your whole house with a few in bud vases.*

ABOVE: *Wax flower (Hoya sp.) can be grown inside or out in the shade and will reward with scented flowers year after year.*

Sensuous summer

Fragrant shrubs like gardenias and buddleia are heavenly during daytime, while *Cestrum nocturnum*, or night jessamine, casts its magic spell once the sun has set. Many fragrant plants are also useful for encouraging pollinators to the garden.

The breath of flowers is far sweeter in the air...than in the hand.

FRANCIS BACON

An often overlooked flowering shrub with a delightful perfume is *Bouvardia longiflora*. This small shrub tends to be a bit floppy, and may require some support and protection, but its wonderful, pure white tubular flowers are worth the extra effort.

Climbers can be trained over pergolas, on trellises near windows or on tripods in pots. Hoya, stephanotis, poet's jasmine and honeysuckle will all do the job for delicious daytime scent, while the moonflower (*Ipomoea alba*) will charm you in the evenings.

Although most bulbs have finished in spring, the November lily (*Lilium longiflorum*) and the oriental lilies are both highly perfumed and worth keeping in pots to put on tables both inside and out when they are in flower.

Trees can be easily forgotten, especially when it comes to planting for perfume. If you have room, frangipani is a wonderful old favourite which is famous the world over. A slightly smaller and lesser known tree, dais or South African daphne (*Dais cotinifolia*) has attractive mottled bark and clusters of scented pink flowers in summer.

The cool hues of summer blues

In the world of flowers, blue is the ultimate cool colour. That slice of the colour wheel that includes the blue hues of mauve, purple, grey-green and cobalt helps you feel cooler. It takes only a glimpse of sparkling blue water to offer relief from the heat of summer, and blue flowers in the garden create the same feeling.

Louisiana iris (see also page 141) flower superbly when planted in ponds and damp areas, where the water reflects their blooms.

Blue is a distant ethereal colour, and planted en masse can seem sombre. Coming from the cool side of the colour wheel and traditionally associated with spiritual things, blue conjures a mood of innermost peace, is restful and even slightly contemplative. Along with green, blue is the most agreeable of colours in the garden, combining readily with hot or cool colours.

This cooling colour comes in many flowering forms in late spring: the frothy mass of plumbago, fragrant yesterday-today-and-tomorrow (*Brunfelsia* sp.), blue agapanthus and the unforgettable jacaranda tree to name only a few.

A good approach is to use blue as a base for highlights such as white, contrasting yellow or with harmonies of pinks and violets. It's a delight with pink, cream, lemon yellow and silver, or contrasted with orange to add vibrancy. Watch out that blue doesn't become dull and flat in red and purple partnerships. Use silver foliage plants—such as lamb's ears, wormwood, artichokes and cotton lavender—to enhance the effect of your flower colour. To exaggerate the blueness of foliage, combine it with plants that have yellow-green leaves or creamy flowers, such as catmint and hosta.

Blues, silvers and greys seem to recede into the distance, suggesting a larger space.

At dusk blue flowers have special value. Together with whites they remain

visible longer than any other colour. You can take advantage of this effect by concentrating blue and white flowers around the areas where you like to sit on summer evenings.

A planting of blue and white agapanthus makes a sensational evergreen border in parts of the garden exposed to hot full sun. Ornamental allium, liriope and cassimentas can also create similar effects.

True blue

Plenty of plants describe themselves as blue, but are actually shades of lilac and mauve. There are, however, a few plants that fall into that elusive category of 'true blue'.

- **Plumbago.** Originally from South Africa, *Plumbago auriculata* grows best in warm climates, to 2 m, and smothers itself in sky blue flowers through the warm months. Plumbago can be grown as an informal hedge or trimmed as a formal hedge. The variety 'Royal Cape' has more intense blue flowers and is more tolerant of frost and drier conditions.

- **Leschenaultia.** This groundcover is native to the Perth region of Western Australia and needs a dry, sunny spot. Its brilliant blue flowers are short-lived but it strikes easily from cuttings.

- **Tibetan blue poppy.** *Meconopsis betonicifolia* is from the Himalayan region and tends to be a tricky plant to grow successfully outside its natural habitat, as it needs partial shade from sun, constant moisture, fertile lime-free soil and a dose of good luck. It is, however, an exquisitely beautiful 2 m-tall flower and many gardeners try to grow it, though mostly it works out to be an annual rather than perennial treat.

DID YOU KNOW? Blue roses are being developed by mixing the genetic material from blue pansies and splicing it into roses. One day, there may be a true blue rose.

Blue bulbs and other groundcover plants help to make the floor of the garden a mirror of the sky.

CLOCKWISE FROM TOP LEFT: *The gentian-blue flowers of* Lithospermum *look great at the edge of paths and the front of borders; blue sage repeat flowers in warm climates;* Chinese plumbago (Ceratostigma sp.), *hardy in warm and colder climes, will flower all summer.*

Blues for all occasions

Many blue-flowering plants are easy to grow and disease free. They can all be grown in association with each other. For example, hydrangeas grow well in the shade of the pretty blue-flowering jacaranda and come into flower as the jacaranda finishes.

The perennial *Otacanthus* 'Little Blue Boy' is a much under-utilised plant that flowers for many months from late spring to the end of autumn in the warm temperate garden. It grows to about 1 m high and 1 m wide, strikes easily and is a perfect choice for filling up holes in the border.

Another species to consider is blue sage (*Eranthemum pulchellum*), which grows to 1–2 m as a rounded shrub, and also flourishes in both subtropical and warm temperate gardens. Flowering in late winter and early spring, there is also a white form that's very pretty. Both forms need protection from frosts.

Blue thou art, intensely blue;
Flower, whence came thy dazzling hue?

JAMES MONTGOMERY

Get the look

Annuals

Forget-me-not, love-in-a-mist (*Nigella*), salvia, pansy, lobelia, viola, verbena, cornflower, petunia, baby-blue eyes, browallia

Perennials

Aster × *frikartii*, Easter daisy, delphinium, perennial salvia, Stokes' aster, campanula, balloon flower, iris, *Geranium* 'Johnson's Blue', Russian sage (*Perovskia atriplicifolia*), borage, agapanthus, globe thistle, gentian

Bulbs

Grape hyacinth, bluebell, alliums, hyacinth, triteleia, ranunculus, anemone

Grasses

Blue-eyed grass, *Festuca glauca*, *Elymus arenarius*, *Themeda* 'Mingo', *Poa* 'Eskdale', *Dianella* 'Cassa Blue'

Groundcovers

Periwinkle, fan flower (*Scaevola*), catmint (*Nepeta*), bugle flower (*Ajuga*), convolvulus, evolvulus, dampiera, leschenaultia, prostrate rosemary, perennial verbena, brachyscome, lithospermum, *Veronica* 'Oxford Blue'

Climbers

Clematis, blue trumpet vine (*Thunbergia grandiflora*), blue potato vine (*Solanum seaforthianum*, *S. wendlandii*), bluebell creeper (*Sollya*), blue passion flower, wreath vine

Shrubs

Lavender, felicia (blue daisy), hydrangea, ceanothus (California lilac), rosemary, echium, Rose-of-Sharon (*Hibiscus syriacus*), blue potato bush (*Solanum rantonnetii*), blue butterfly bush (*Clerodendrum ugandense*), buddleia, blue sage, plumbago, duranta

CLOCKWISE FROM TOP LEFT: *Browallia is a charming annual; Easter daisies give reliable autumn colour; blue passion flower needs a frost-free climate; blue butterfly bush grows to 2 m;* Eupatorium *has many beautiful species;* Otacanthus *'Little Blue Boy' grows to 1 m; hydrangeas flower for months;* Solanum wendlandii.

Checklist
Jobs to do now
Annuals, perennials and bulbs

🍂 Prune petunias, violas and pansies, and fertilise them for another show.

🍂 Lay snail traps around the new shoots of your dahlias and hostas.

🍂 As flowers finish, prune foxgloves, campanulas and lupins.

🍂 Prune lavender, stake dahlias and dead-head agapanthus.

🍂 Stake or tie chrysanthemums to prevent the weight of the buds breaking the stems; disbud plants for single blooms.

🍂 Top-dress dianthus and lavenders with lime and potash.

🍂 Divide and re-pot late-flowering cymbidiums.

🍂 Re-pot all begonias, including Rex, tuberous, angel-wings and foliage types.

🍂 Trim back paper daisies as they finish.

🍂 Trim faded flowers to keep plants tidy and prevent seed from setting.

🍂 Lift and divide bearded iris. Discard old, gnarled rhizomes.

🍂 Prune spring-blossoming perennials to encourage bushy growth and even more flowers.

🍂 When planting new season's annuals, especially impatiens, add water-storing crystals and a wetting agent to the soil.

🍂 Prepare your garden beds with lots of organic material before planting your spring bulbs. If you are growing tulips, hyacinths and Dutch iris, it's a good idea to put them in the crisper part of the fridge now and leave them there until late autumn when the temperature of the soil has dropped.

🍂 Lift any gladiolus while there are still some leaves and allow them to dry off. After the stems have completely withered, dust them in derris and store them in plastic bags.

Grasses, groundcovers and climbers

🍂 Keep the lawn mown, but not too low.

🍂 Check the lawn for early signs of grub damage.

🍂 A blast with hose-on fertiliser and weedicide will smarten up your lawn.

🍂 If you must water the lawn, do it deeply twice a week. Never water during the heat of the day.

🍂 Remove excess growth on wisteria vines to maintain control of these vigorous climbers.

🍂 Strike star jasmine in pots of sharp sand that has been mixed with one third peat moss.

🍂 If you live in a bushfire-prone area, keep an eye on ornamental grasses: some can become fire hazards if you don't keep them trimmed.

Set snail baits to protect susceptible plants such as hostas.

Trim spent blooms of lavender a few centimetres below the flower spike.

Remove coneflowers to encourage another flush.

Shrubs and trees

🍂 Mulch azaleas, camellias and daphne with decomposed cow manure.

🍂 Prune back spring-flowering shrubs (such as philadelphus, viburnums and lilacs) which have finished flowering for the season.

🍂 Prune back azaleas now for compact, disease-free growth. Keep a careful watch for lace bug in case it has started to attack fresh foliage. A few early sprays with Baythroid® or PestOil® under the leaves can reduce the infestation.

🍂 Keep roses well watered and remove spent blooms to promote further flowering. Your roses will flower especially well if you trim the hips off.

🍂 High humidity can be a problem for rose lovers. Pick off and destroy any leaves affected by black spot and mildew, and spray with a specific fungicide.

🍂 Fertilise roses to prepare them for the autumn flush.

🍂 Keep a check on tea-trees and bottlebrush for webworm. This pest forms thick webs among the smaller branches and can cause quite a mess if it is left unchecked. Prune off affected areas.

🍂 Snip off old flowers from New South Wales Christmas bush.

🍂 Trim rondeletia.

Herbs, fruit and vegetables

🍂 Cut back and tidy herbs, even if you're not using them, so that they don't go to seed.

🍂 Look for signs of powdery mildew on vegetables, caused by high humidity, and spray with fungicide.

🍂 Feed passionfruit with pelletised manure.

🍂 Mulch fruit with chicken manure.

🍂 Prune pawpaws.

🍂 Thin out and remove excess growth on fruit trees. Feed stone and pome fruit at the end of summer.

🍂 Stake tomato plants and remove side shoots.

🍂 Water tomatoes frequently.

🍂 Cut artichoke plants to the ground to promote fresh growth.

🍂 Celery is one of the easiest and most attractive vegies to grow in the home garden. It can be harvested over a long period and used in a range of hot and cold dishes.

🍂 Keep whitefly in check with a regular spray of Baythroid® or Permaguard®.

🍂 Feed vegetables with a liquid fertiliser to keep them growing rapidly and to prevent bitterness.

Click-on 'weed and feed' lawn treatments are easy to apply.

Mildew can attack vegies in summer. For treatment, see page 247.

Remove laterals from tomatoes for maximum cropping.

Plant now

Annuals, perennials and bulbs

◗ Summer is a tricky time for annuals as they are between seasons. Plant alyssum, lobelia, dwarf snapdragons dwarf marigolds and chrysanthemums (both *C. paludosum* and the bedding variety of *C. grandiflorum*) to fill up any gaps.

◗ Calendulas, renowned for providing winter colour, have flat daisy-like flowers which cheer up the garden and help control pests such as whitefly and aphids. Poor man's orchid, which looks a bit like a bright small orchid, is inexpensive and easy to sow from seed.

◗ Plant window boxes and hanging baskets with colourful trailing plants such as lobelia, torenia and pigface. They'll fit the bill beautifully.

◗ Plant out seedlings of zinnias, impatiens, salvia, verbena and petunias.

Petunias can still be planted for late-season blooms.

◗ You can still plant asters, celosia, coleus, dahlias, amaranthus, portulaca, nasturtium (the Alaska hybrids), sunflowers and marigolds.

◗ Begonias make a stunning massed display and are great for brightening up any holes in the garden. They also adapt to sun or shade.

◗ Plantings of artemisias and senecio create wonderful swathes of grey foliage colour.

◗ Cottage gardens can be given a lift with fresh displays of phlox, cosmos, gypsophila, cleome, rudbeckia, Swan River daisy (*Brachyscome iberidifolia*), zinnia, gerberas, verbena and *Oenothera* 'Ballerina'.

◗ Plant cyclamen seedlings out, or raise them from seed.

◗ Order spring-flowering bulbs and store them in the crisper (not freezer) until bulb-planting time. Most bulbs should be planted in early autumn, although hyacinths and tulips should be planted in late autumn.

◗ Sow bulbs of spider lily, crinum, colchicum, belladonna lily and zephyranthes.

Grasses, groundcovers and climbers

◗ Plant couch lawns from seed, runners or turf sods.

◗ Plant rooted gazania offsets to create a stunning groundcover in the sun.

◗ Plant tropical climbers such as thunbergia.

Shrubs and trees

◗ Geraniums can be planted from cuttings or seedlings.

◗ Plant a hedge—now that shrubs are in their growth stage, you'll be amazed at just how fast they form a screen. Try viburnum, photinia, murraya or lilly-pillies for a fast, attractive informal or formal hedge.

◗ Soft-tip cuttings of fuchsia will strike easily now. It's also time to strike camellias and gardenias.

◗ Plant rainforest trees now, provided you keep the water up to them.

Herbs, fruit and vegetables

◗ Annual herbs such as dill, parsley, coriander and basil can all be replanted.

◗ All tropical fruit can be planted now.

◗ Grafted passionfruit are available for planting throughout summer and will crop well the following year.

◗ Plant potatoes in garden beds free of lime. Use a fresh garden bed that has not been planted for a season—crop rotation, wherever it's possible, reduces the chances of disease. Potatoes can be planted when soils are still warm—up to early summer in cold regions and late summer in warmer areas.

◗ Plant lettuce, radish, silverbeet, beans, beetroot, cabbage, carrot, cucumber, spinach, squash, cauliflower, sweet corn, pumpkin, zucchini and melon. Others to plant include eggplant, tomato, capsicum and chillies.

CLOCKWISE FROM TOP LEFT: *Zinnias are great for garden colour and cutting; marigolds come in large- and small-flowered types; gazanias are hardy to sun, salt and wind; mussaenda loves the tropics; the shimmering blooms of the Cape chestnut tree; daylilies are prolific bloomers; the South African daphne has a lovely perfume; the red passion vine will cover quickly.*

Flowering now
Annuals, perennials and bulbs

🌺 Annuals such as ageratum, alyssum, amaranthus, asters, begonias, celosia, cosmos, foxglove, linaria, larkspur, lobelia, marigolds, nasturtiums, petunias, phlox, poor man's orchid, portulaca, rudbeckia, salvias, snapdragons, sweet William and zinnias.

🌺 Perennials such as acanthus, aquilegia, cannas, crinum, daylilies, delphiniums, gazania, gerbera, milfoil, perennial phlox, Shasta daisies and sunflowers.

🌺 Bulbs such as agapanthus (lily of the Nile), belladonna lily, gladiolus, Jacobean lily, Japanese iris and kniphofia (red hot poker).

Grasses, groundcovers and climbers

🌺 Flowering ornamental grasses such as blue fescue, feather reed grass, Gray's sedge, Japanese sedge, quaking grass, oatgrass, ribbon grass, sand love grass, squirrel tail grass.

🌺 Groundcovers such as ajuga, cerastium, convolvulus, erigeron, lamb's ears, native violet, verbena.

🌺 Climbers such as allamanda, bougainvillea, campsis (orange trumpet vine), mandevilla, pandorea (wonga-wonga vine), podranea, thunbergia, stephanotis, hoya.

Shrubs and trees

🌺 Shrubs such as abutilon, buddleia, geraniums, gardenias, hebe, hibiscus, hydrangeas, lavender, murraya, mussaenda, pomegranate, tecoma.

🌺 Trees such as forbidden fruit (*Acokanthera*), black bean, Cape chestnut, dais (South African daphne), flame tree, frangipani, fringe tree (*Chionanthus*), kurrajong, poinciana, silk tree (*Albizia julibrissin*), South African ironwood (*Millettia grandis*).

🌺 Crepe myrtle, *Tibouchina* 'Kathleen', golden shower tree (*Cassia fistula*).

Herbs, fruit and vegetables

🌺 Herbs such as basil (prune the flowers), coriander (keep the flowers for the seeds), lavender (spot flowers), rosemary, sage.

🌺 Fruit such as berry fruits, melons, olives, stone fruits, tropical fruits.

🌺 Vegetables such as eggplants, tomatoes, zucchini, capsicums and young corn.

Annuals, perennials and bulbs

No plants give your garden a splash of colour quite like annuals, perennials and bulbs. More than any other season, summer yields the festive feel of flowers—from sunny yellows to cool blues—and lots of them.

Summer is a stressful time for young plants, with the heat affecting their immature root systems, so protect your young charges under shadecloth or leave them under a tree to acclimatise slowly. The heat also means you have to be more careful with your watering.

If you want a head start to your winter/spring flower garden, start sowing seeds now. Flower seeds that are started off now under shade will be ready early in winter when not much else will be flowering in the garden.

Plants that love the summer sun have vibrant colours and, in combination, create a dazzling massed flower effect. The sunny yellows of helianthus, sunflower, marigolds and rudbeckia, the reds and burnt oranges of dahlia, salvia, pigface and perennial portulaca, and the lipstick pinks of verbena and begonias create a splash of colour as bright as the summer sun.

ABOVE: *The spider flower (Cleome sp.) will self-seed in your garden, providing delightful summer surprises.*

RIGHT: *Late-flowering pansies have the ability to bloom for months, and come in many shades. These yellow ones are like a ray of sunshine.*

Annuals

Summer annuals can be big, bold and blowzy perfumed affairs.

Gaudy reds, pinks and tangerines can be found in succulents such as sunjewels and portulaca, and in upright growers such as sunflowers and zinnias. Softer, cooler colours for subdued background plantings can be found in spider flower (*Cleome* sp.), foxgloves (*Digitalis* sp.) and cosmos, while asters, phlox, lobelia and floss flower provide long-lasting foreground selections.

Seedlings

Growing seedlings, whether they're flowers or vegetables, can be a bit tricky. So, when choosing your punnets of seedlings at the nursery, always select fresh young stock and avoid tired, root-bound plants that are past their prime.

Select the coolest part of the day for planting and place the seedlings in a handful of peat or compost in the soil and then surround them with straw or lucerne hay for immediate support.

Water them in with a seaweed solution. This helps to settle in the roots and initiates growth without encouraging new leaves. The seedlings will be established after a week or two. At that point, apply liquid blood and bone to strengthen the stems. Use a complete fertiliser when the flowers or fruits appear.

ABOVE LEFT: *The bright faces of sunflowers turn towards the sun throughout the day.*

ABOVE: *Foxgloves add height to the garden with their spires of bells.*

Summer set lip to earth's bosom bare, and left the flushed print in a poppy there.

FRANCIS THOMPSON

Planting seedlings

1 Dig a hole large enough to accommodate each plant.

2 Separate the seedlings, taking care not to damage the roots.

3 Plant each seedling and then backfill. Water well.

SEEDLING CARE
Keep your seedlings moist until they have grown into their new positions, and use seaweed solution to ease their transition.

Pansies and paludosum daisies make for a beautiful potted colour display.

complementary colour. Leaf colour can also be used with dramatic results.

Fill a pot or trough to the rim with plants then feed them with a liquid fertiliser. Within weeks you'll be rewarded with the same colourful and prolific growth. Select your main plant, perhaps a gardenia or conifer, then surround it with spillover seedlings such as convolvulus, sweet Alice, lobelia or small-leafed trailing ivy in complementary colours.

Feeding summer flowers

Don't pull out plants that have already been flowering for a few months. They can be revived to flower again before summer ends.

If petunias have been damaged or look tired and lifeless, prune them back by at least half, then feed them up with a liquid fertiliser. They'll bloom within ten days.

Four o'clock plant

Four o'clock plant (*Mirabilis jalapa*) is an unusual species with flowers of white, cerise or yellow, or even streaked and mottled. The blooms open only in the afternoon, hence its common name. It is also known as the marvel of Peru, as it is native to tropical America. It grows about 1 m tall and is sensitive to frost, but otherwise it's fairly trouble-free.

Perfect potted colour

Ever wondered how those glossy garden magazines get wonderful pictures of potted plants filled with colour and perfect growth? Of course they employ very skilled photographers, but the secret lies in the selection and quantity of the plants being used.

At home most of us tend to be a bit stingy and plant only one shrub or a couple of seedlings in each pot, and then expect them to look like the photographs in the magazine. But if you look closely at the photographs you'll see that there are always several plants in any one container, and sometimes one or two main shrubs with a dozen annuals of a

Impatiens

Impatiens are one of the most bountiful flowering plants of all time. Balsam or busy Lizzies are different names for the same plant, which loves shade to filtered sun. There is also a sun-tolerant type called Sun Lizzies. The stems are succulent and quick growing with large flat flowers about the size of a 50-cent piece. Flower colours include white,

DID YOU KNOW? Impatiens are known as 'busy Lizzies' in the United Kingdom and 'patient Lizzies' in the United States.

pinks and reds, with the newer varieties including orange and yellow. Some have coloured leaves, which results in a lovely display. You can prune impatiens reasonably hard, keeping them compact, then feed them with organic fertilisers, which will ensure they'll flower until the end of autumn. *Impatiens walleriana* come in doubles and singles. The Congo cockatoo (*I. niamniamensis*) is a fabulously gaudy flower that attracts butterflies, bees and birds. It, too, prefers a shady spot (or a sunroom) and moist soil, and flowers for many months.

Vincas

Vincas (*Catharanthus roseus*), also called periwinkles, are very similar to dwarf impatiens, but will happily grow in full sun and take the heat that their lookalikes don't. The flowers are five-petalled in shades of pink, maroon and white, often with a contrasting darker eye. Vincas are perennials that do well in a frost-free climate. They need pruning in early spring to stay bushy and tidy.

Phlox

In almost every North American landscape, from prairie to tundra, you can find phlox. So it's no surprise that phlox come in all shapes and sizes— some taller and ideal for cutting and others, great low groundcovers. The Astoria range is perfect for containers and comes in 11 colours, ranging from white to blue, pink, cream, red and apricot. Its season runs from late spring

through summer and into autumn, and the plants reach about 0.5 m in height. Keep dead-heading them throughout the growing season, or bring them into the house as a cut flower to prolong flowering. At the end of flowering, cut them back to the ground.

The Alpine phlox (*Phlox subulata*) is also worth having in your garden as a rockery plant. Like other phlox species, it is available in many colours and will be so smothered with blooms that you'll hardly be able to see the foliage. It grows to about 50 cm wide and 10 cm tall and looks very attractive planted in clumps or with other flowers in a border.

Verbenas

This genus *Verbena* contains a tremendous group of garden plants. Its annuals are eye-catching plants that flower all spring and summer, provided they are dead-headed, and they grow to a good, neat height of about 30 cm. But it's the perennials that are the stars, available in myriad colours, from lilac and apricot through to red, white and candy-stripe pinks. They sprawl and self-root, which makes them perfect for rockeries, gentle slopes and hanging baskets. They all prefer full sun and well-drained soil, and benefit from regular dead-heading and a monthly application of liquid fertiliser.

Verbena blooms include doubles, singles, miniatures and cascading types. They come in every colour except true blue and orange.

LEFT TO RIGHT: *The Congo cockatoo impatiens is an unusual show stopper; vinca flowers (here in white) bloom all summer; hardy and heat-proof verbena.*

Petunias

It would be hard to name an annual that has enjoyed more breeding and improvements than the petunia. The wild species were originally purple and white, but 150 years of cultivation has resulted in the sturdier, showier types we are familiar with today. These include doubles, singles, miniatures and cascading types in an extremely wide range of colours.

Unlike most annual hybrids that you would be familiar with dating from 50 years ago, like 'Bobby Dazzler' or even those from 20 years ago, such as 'Lilac

ABOVE: *The trumpet-style annual petunia.*

RIGHT: *Regular dead-heading of petunias, especially after rain when their petals spoil, will encourage new blooms.*

EVERLASTING PETUNIAS

Calibrachoa, which look like tiny petunias, have been crossed with *Petunia* sp. to produce hybrids called *Petchoa*. The dainty flowers of Million Bells, Super Bells, Chimes and Can Can collections are the breeding offspring of these hybrids. Daintier plants are the *Calibrachoa* 'Million Bells' from the Chimes collection and Nature's Decor Can Can collection. They have tiny, ten-cent-piece-size, petunia-like flowers held in multitudes on a shrub 30 cm high, 50 cm wide. Colours include red, white, violet, cherry, gold, coral, peach and terracotta. They flower virtually nonstop, and are more smothered than usual in spring, in warm climates when grown in full sun; they are very heat tolerant. They do need to be fed and watered consistently, however, to maintain this pace!

Cascade', these new hybrid plants are now mostly perennial (annual in cold areas) and include great groundcovering or basket types.

Sometimes called Supertunias, or Happytunias, these have thicker stems, more like a shrub, and a single plant will grow 60 cm wide and only 10 cm tall. The most commonly available type is 'Raspberry Blast'—its flowers are cerise pink, edged slightly darker violet—but there are others, such as 'Royal Velvet', 'White' and 'Citrus'. A particularly dazzling one is 'Pretty Much Picasso', with pink flowers edged in lime green.

Some are upright growers, others have tiny bell-shaped flowers (see box, opposite), some are prostrate, while still others have the traditional larger trumpet-like blooms. They all produce wave after wave of flowers throughout the warm weather, and if they enjoy their position they can flower for up to nine months of the year. These perennial petunias love a warm, sunny position. They are sensitive to cold conditions, and also react poorly to high humidity. Being vigorous growers, they like plenty of regular fertilising and a few good haircuts a year (in late winter and again in summer) to keep them from becoming straggly.

Petunias are prone to a few pests. Slugs and snails love them. Watch out for aphids too, which you might only notice by the damaged, puckered leaves that grow as a result of their sap-sucking ways. Insecticidal soap sprays will keep most things at bay, but you also might need Dipel bio-insecticide (*Bacillus thuringiensis*) to keep caterpillars from becoming a problem.

DID YOU KNOW? The word 'petunia' comes from the French word *petun*, which means tobacco, and is a reference to the tobacco family, to which petunias belong.

Nicotiana

This ornamental form of tobacco is a cottage garden favourite thanks to its delightful self-seeding habit, which means it effortlessly pops up in nooks and crannies of the garden. Its dainty bell flowers, which are perfumed, especially at night, range in colour from red and pink through to greens, yellows and whites.

VITAL STATISTICS

Scientific name: *Nicotiana.*
Family: Solanaceae.
Plant/bulb type: Annual.
Height: 60–120 cm.
Planting time: Spring, after last frosts.
Soil: Well drained, fertile.
Position: Full sun.
Planting depth and spacing: Press seeds lightly into the soil and plant in groups about 20 cm apart.
Watering: Water regularly over summer.
Fertiliser: Every fortnight with liquid fertiliser is ideal, or spread pelletised manure once established.
After-flowering care: Dead-head throughout the season until late autumn, when you may wish to let them go to seed and come up the following season.
Comments: Perfect for a cottage garden. Many types are highly perfumed.

Feature annual

CLOCKWISE FROM TOP LEFT: *Purple Easter daisies make wonderful cut flowers; white ageratum is both lovely and hardy; gaillardia looks beautiful even when its petals drop, as the discs remain attractive for many months.*

Perennials

To ensure that you get to enjoy idle summer afternoons, fill your garden with fuss-free plants that showcase stunning colour and attractive foliage.

Oops a daisy

Sunny as a daisy, the family Asteraceae boasts some of the world's great plants. From late winter through to autumn, various daisies flower continuously, which makes them unsurpassed as flowering plants. There are daisies for every position and use.

Annuals such as zinnias, sunflowers, cosmos and marigolds give superb colour for summer. Place them strategically in pots or plant them in pockets around the garden.

Chrysanthemum paludosum is a wonderful, long-flowering annual with white daisy-like flowers. It will bloom from spring through summer provided it is regularly dead-headed.

Ageratum can be an annual or a perennial, depending on the species. Both types are well worth growing.

For perennial display, aurora daisies, gazanias, rudbeckias and gaillardias look fabulous from late spring onwards.

The cottage garden would be incomplete without favourites like marguerites, milfoil (yarrow), Shasta daisies and asters.

Many daisies—such as gerberas, dahlias and sunflowers—make long-lasting cut flowers, while others—such as chamomile, wormwood and feverfew—have herbal uses.

DID YOU KNOW? The Asteraceae family will repeat flower if old blooms are cut off.

SEASIDE DAISY

Like the other members of the Asteraceae family, the seaside daisy (*Erigeron* sp.) is a great filler. Native to northern America, the common white type has happily settled into many new countries, and in Australia care should be taken not to plant it too near bushland, where seeds may spread and crowd out native species. In urban areas, however, this habit of spreading is all part of its charm, softening walls, paths and flagging by growing in crevices and flowering for so many months that it's hardly seen without a bud. There is also a form called 'Pink Jewel', which has larger pink rays on slightly longer stems than the usual white type.

Blooms aplenty

It's high summer and the garden is at its flowering peak. Your home should be filled with fresh flowers.

- Dahlias, flowering from early summer right through to Easter, are top of the list. Liquid feed them now to encourage more flowers. Stake them to support the heavy summer growth.

- Shasta daisies are tough and drought hardy. They love the sun. Pick them for posies and you'll encourage more flowers.

- Lavender is another favourite cut flower. The French and Italian lavenders grow best in warm areas as they love hot and dry conditions. English lavender prefers a cooler climate and dislikes humidity.

- Hydrangeas are lovely in vases. Pick them early in the morning and submerge them in water for an hour before you arrange them. Modern varieties are more compact and don't require much pruning. Buy them now while they're in flower and plant them in the shade.

- Lilies and bulbs, from agapanthus to Jacobean lilies, from liliums to tuberoses, are uniquely beautiful.

- Zinnias are both beautiful and long lasting.

CLOCKWISE FROM TOP LEFT: *French lavender; Italian lavender; tuberose; daylily; white hydrangea; pink hydrangea; red zinnias; Shasta daisy.*

LEFT AND ABOVE: *Flowering from spring to autumn, African daisies* (Osteospermum sp.) *are available in pinks, yellows, oranges, reds and whites.*

African daisy

African daisy is the common name given to members of two different genera, *Arctotis* and *Osteospermum*. *Arctotis* flowers profusely through spring to autumn, and is distinguished from its relatives by its grey and silver leaves. This plant flowers in pinks, oranges, reds, whites and yellows, and also comes in special varieties in lilac and plum shades. All have the characteristic black and gold centres. The flowers close in the late afternoon.

Osteospermum species, also called veldt daisies, make a great groundcover or a bank planting and are very popular in coastal gardens. They come in a wide range of bright colours and do best in full sun. The Serenity range includes the varieties 'Serenity' and 'Tradewinds'.

Alstroemeria

Alstroemerias (commonly called Peruvian lilies or princess lilies) make beautiful cut flowers and have charming azalea-like blooms about 60 cm long. Their sausage-shaped tubers can easily spread in any well-draining soil. They like sun, but will happily grow in semi-shade too, especially in warmer climates. Some cultivars are dwarf and others have attractive variegated leaves.

Water well in summer but do not overwater in winter. For best results, each spring dig in some manure, and mulch well.

1 *Alstroemeria* 'Elaine' 2 *A.* 'Sara' 3 *A.* 'Ariane' 4 *A.* 'Daniela' 5 *A.* 'Letizia' 6 *A.* 'Fabiana'

Alstroemeria

Salvia, summer's lavender

The mint family (Lamiaceae) is huge,
comprising mints, salvias, lavenders,
rosemary and many Australian natives,
such as prostanthera and westringia.

Salvias are proving invaluable for
use in cottage and flower gardens, herb
gardens and as an integral part of
drought-tolerant landscapes.

For diversity of habitat, colour,
texture and leaf fragrance, it's hard to

go past salvias. Loved by bees and easy
to grow in any temperate climate, they
add colourful splashes of blues, purples,
pinks and reds to the garden from spring
through to late summer and autumn.

The best known in this group is
common sage, although it is only one
among a genus of 900. Some of the
deepest blues and truest reds can be
found among the flowers of this genus
and many have stunning colour-
contrasting foliage, but the square
stems, opposite leaves and scented
foliage can identify them all.

To make your selection easier, here's
a guide to some of the best salvias.

🍃 **Common sage (*Salvia officinalis*).** The grey-
green leaves and blue-mauve flower spikes
in spring are familiar to any keen cook and
herb grower. Said to cure anything from
headaches to fever, from greying hair to
palsy, sage has long been a popular home
remedy. The aromatic leaves are also used
for flavouring pork, veal, poultry, stuffings,

GROWING TIPS FOR SALVIAS

🍃 Most salvias like a free-draining soil and will not tolerate heavy
   frosts. Although drought tolerant, they respond well to watering
   over summer, and will flower longer if fed and tip pruned.
🍃 Prune salvias back hard at the end of winter, then mulch with
   manure to promote new spring growth.
🍃 Salvias look terrific as low informal hedges (similar to lavender),
   among herb borders (where their aromatic foliage will make a
   contribution), in pots and other containers or in the flower garden.
🍃 Salvias also look terrific combined with other perennials such as
   daylilies, iris and catmint, or companion planted with any member
   of the cabbage family.

and cheese and egg dishes. Common sage also comes in a dwarf form as well as pink- and white-flowering cultivars. For a wonderful foliage contrast, try planting the golden-, grey- and purple-leafed forms together in clumps.

- **Annual or scarlet sage (*S. splendens*).** Many may recognise this popular bedding plant, which flowers scarlet throughout summer and autumn. There are various cultivars, growing from 15 cm to 1 m tall. This type makes a fabulous Christmas display and, with a cut back and feed each autumn, will add colour for about two or three seasons.

- **Mealy-cup or lavender sage (*S. farinacea*).** Although the red-flowering form has been a popular bedding plant for years, the blue and white forms of mealy sage are now the most popular, with their spikes of lavender-like flowers gracing many displays. A 1997 variety called 'Chorus Line' is also popular.

- **Pineapple-scented sage (*S. elegans*).** This 1.5 m shrub is a fine choice for your herb garden. The leaves are fruit-scented and can be used for flavouring drinks and salads. Throughout autumn this sage is crowned with stunning (and edible) scarlet flowers. The golden form is a winner in the garden with yellow leaves and non-stop flowers.

- **Gentian sage (*S. patens*).** So named after the incredible gentian blue flowers, this is one of the best flowering sages. Throughout summer it is smothered with flowers on stems to 1 m, and looks great when planted in masses with the paler blue form.

- **Bog sage (*S. uliginosa*).** This perennial is hardier in heavy soils, and tolerates shade and poorly drained soils. It is an excellent spreading plant for any garden border, although it can romp if left unchecked. The flowers, sky blue-lipped with white markings, smother the shrub over summer and autumn.

- **Mexican bush sage or autumn sage (*S. leucantha*).** A most durable species, Mexican bush sage grows to 1 m with white

woolly hairs all over the stems, underside of the foliage and flower buds. The plant flowers from summer to winter with spikes of velvety, purple-lipped flowers, which keep their colour well when dried. It flowers in semi-shade and, once established, grows well with little water.

- **'Mexican Bandit' (*S. greggii*).** Not to be confused with Mexican bush sage, these newish cultivars make a really colourful display from late spring to late autumn. With red, cerise pink or white flowers, 'Mexican Bandit' reflowers if trimmed and fed after each flush.

- **Giant yellow sage (*S. madrensis*)** has huge spires of yellow flowers nearly 1 m tall. It also goes by the name of forsythia sage.

- **Germander sage (*S. chamaedryiodes*).** The deep blue flowers and grey down-like leaves make this sage a great foliage contrast in the garden. Although hard to come by, it is well worth the effort taken to find it.

Mexican bush sage tolerates drought, copes with heavy frosts, and flowers prolifically for many months of the year.

False sage

While quite a few plants are called sages, not all are true sages (members of the *Salvia* genus). They are, however, equally worthy of a place in your garden.

Of particular beauty is Jerusalem sage (*Phlomis fruticosa*). Throughout summer it is covered with yellow hooded flowers that stand out superbly against the silvery grey foliage. Growing only to 1 m tall, this is a hardy and reliable plant as long as the drainage is good.

The giant blue sage (*Brillantaisia subulugurica*) is actually in a completely different family (Acanthaceae) to the true sages, but it has very sage-looking square stems and giant 1 m long stems of blue flowers through summer and autumn. Given that the shrub is only about 1 m tall itself, these flowers make quite a statement.

Also in the same family is a plant often called blue sage (*Eranthemum pulchellum*). It has 'true blue' flowers, handsome foliage and grows to about 1 m tall in a neat bush that will even cope well when planted in shade. It does not like frost, however, so in cold climates it will need to be grown in a shade house or glass house. The white form is also very beautiful. Both forms flower in spring.

Blue sage, a member of the Eranthemum *genus, is native to parts of India and China.*

THE LAMIACEAE FAMILY

This family of mainly annual or perennial herbs and the odd shrub is characterised by aromatic foliage, square stems and flowers with a tongue-like appearance; the 'tongue' acts as an insect landing pad. It comprises about 200 genera (including *Salvia*, *Thymus* and *Lavandula*) and 3200 species. It is an economically important family, as many plants contain essential oils for cooking, perfumery and medicines. The mint family in particular can be found around the world: mint in Europe and Africa; basil in Asia, the Pacific islands and the Middle East; and *Westringia* species in Australia.

Variegated ginger

Euphorbia 'Snow on the Mountain'

Lamium 'White Nancy'

Liriope variegata

Variegated Lamium

Hosta 'White Edge'

Hemizygia 'Candy Kisses'

Variegated white foliage

Plants with white-edged variegation act as highlights, especially in shaded areas. Variegated ginger has lovely blue flowers in summer; Euphorbia 'Snow on the Mountain' is a useful annual for drought-prone areas; Lamium 'White Nancy' has a metallic sheen to its leaves; Liriope variegata (lily turf) has a white edge to its strappy foliage and lilac flowers; variegated Lamium is a mat-forming groundcover; variegated hostas love the shade; and Hemizygia 'Candy Kisses' has white-splotched leaves and pink spikes of flowers.

Calla lilies

1 Calla lily 'Ivory Gem' **2** Calla lily 'Hot Chocolate' **3** *Zantedeschia aethiopica* 'Hercules'
4 *Z. aethiopica* 'Green Goddess' **5** Calla lily 'Elliottiana' **6** Calla lily 'Sunrise' **7** Calla lily 'Lilac Mist'
8 Calla lily 'Florex Gold' **9** Calla lily 'Pot of Gold'

Red valerian

Red valerian or, as it's sometimes called, keys to heaven, shares a name and family with the plant from which valerian the drug is made (*Valeriana officinalis*). Come summer, it is covered in clusters of fragrant red flowers. Very easily grown, it can become invasive provided the drainage is good. Before planting it, check whether it's likely to become a weed in your area.

VITAL STATISTICS

Scientific name: *Centranthus ruber*.
Family: Valerianaceae.
Plant/bulb type: Perennial.
Height: 60 cm.
Planting time: Plant seed in late winter, or division in spring.
Soil: Any, dry or moist.
Position: Sun or semi-shade and even by the seaside.
Planting depth and spacing: 40 cm apart.
Fertiliser: Not needed.
Flowering: Hermaphrodite flowers all summer in shades of pink, red or white that are delightfully fragrant.
Watering: Not needed.
After-flowering care: Trim off flowers as they fade to prevent self-seeding.
Comments: Attracts bees.

Feature perennial

Calla lilies

Calla lilies are among the easiest of all cut flowers to grow, and certainly present value, with each tuber producing about 20 flowers. When planting, leave the top of each tuber exposed slightly, with any 'eyes' pointing upwards. Ensure that they receive some direct sunlight, otherwise they will not bloom well.

Begonias

Begonia is a genus of many varying species. They are mostly native to tropical and semi-tropical regions, and can be grown outside in the shade in frost-free areas. In cooler areas, it's best to grow them in shade- or green-houses. They come in annual/biannual (semperflorens begonias) and perennial forms, and many are useful foliage plants as well as reliable flowerers.

The main perennial types are: rhizomatous begonias, which can make great pot plants; rex begonias, which have spectacular metallic leaves; cane-like begonias, which make hardy free-flowering screens in the shade; shrub-like begonias such as *Begonia fuchsioides*; thick-stemmed begonias; and trailing/scandent begonias, perfect for hanging baskets. Tuberous and semi-tuberous begonias and elatior begonias make beautiful indoor flowering plants.

Cane begonias flower from late spring to winter.

Cannas love a warm, frost-free climate, but if you live in a cool area, mulch generously: this will protect the rhizomes from the cold. Propagate cannas in spring by dividing the rhizomes. Water diligently for the first six weeks while it establishes itself.

ABOVE: *Looking stunning in the garden, canna flowers don't keep well in a vase, though their foliage does.*

ABOVE RIGHT: Canna glauca *has steel-blue foliage and dusty pink blooms.*

Cannas

Cannas are the great all-rounder. Known also as Indian shot, they cope with anything, look great for nine months of the year, and have stunning foliage and flowers, which range in colour from the common yellows, reds and oranges to pink, cream and apricot. They also work in with a variety of gardening styles, from Victorian to tropical Thai or the modern perennial border. 'Striata', 'Tropicana' and 'Bronze' are all worth planting. Harder to come by is the soft apricot-flowered and grey-leafed 'Glauca'.

Shady ladies

A shady refuge on a hot summer's day is one of life's simplest pleasures. Some people associate a shady garden with a dark, dingy, flowerless grotto. Happily, this need not be the case, because many perennials relish some protection from scorching sun.

For flowers that will remain in the shade throughout summer, consider columbines (aquilegia), native violet (*Viola hederacea*) and storm lilies (*Zephyranthes candida*). For spectacular foliage as well, try oyster plants (*Acanthus mollis*) with their bold, deeply dissected

IRESINE
Also known for its spectacular foliage, bloodleaf (*Iresine* sp.) is beautiful in the garden for lifting shaded areas with its bright pink, green and gold or purple-red leaves. It won't cope with frost, but looks good all year round in warmer temperate areas. 'Aureo-reticulata' is a form with red veins and green and yellow leaves, 'Wallisii' is a dwarf purple/black and 'Brilliantissima' is the crimson beauty.

FAR RIGHT: *The white variegated leaves of* Brunnera *give a lift to shady areas.*

RIGHT: *Granny's bonnets, as aquilegias are also known, have dainty blooms and charming foliage reminiscent of a maidenhair fern's.*

leaves and flowers on tall spires; these make wonderful background plants. Harmonise them with hostas, some of the most elegant of plants with their shiny leaves of various colourings—some sea-green, others lime-gold and some cream-striped. The palest of lavender or white flowers, some with a pleasant perfume, appear in early summer.

Hostas

Of all the foliage perennials, hostas, or plantain lilies, are perhaps the most striking. Popular herbaceous plants for shady glens, they prefer a moist spot and are perfect for growing near water or in bog gardens. Wait until they are in flower before you choose one because many of them are scented.

These plants have been bred and hybridised to produce marbled, white, gold, bluish green and various other foliage variegations. Most, such as *H. fortunei*, have lavender bell flowers on spires 1 m tall. Some, such as the blue-green round-leafed *H. sieboldiana*, have white flowers. Hybrids of *H. ventricosa* have pointed leaves, and one of the nicest is 'Gold Edger', which has pale green leaves with a yellow edge and prolific lavender flowers.

Unfortunately, hostas succumb easily to snails, which can destroy their tender young leaves. Make an environmentally friendly snail trap by half-burying a partly filled beer bottle in the soil.

Heuchera and Brunnera

Heuchera species, or coral bells, are well suited to a semi-shaded area. The newer coloured-foliage cultivars, such as 'Berry Smoothie', 'Chocolate Ruffles', 'Amethyst Myst' and 'Marmalade', are well suited to a wider range of climates, coping with heat and humidity.

Also charming are *Brunnera* species. These are closely related to forget-me-nots and borage (the small blue flowers are a giveaway) and, like them, prefer positions under trees with adequate moisture. There are also many pretty leaf forms, such as 'Jack Frost', that lift a shady garden enormously with their white/silvery markings.

 SNAIL ALERT
The cool, moist places that hostas favour are also snail havens, so you need to be vigilant to guard against tatty leaves.

ASTILBE
Flowering late spring and summer with their plume-like blooms of red, white, pink and lilac, astilbes look almost like a gardener's feather duster with such fluffy flowers on stiff stalks. Best suited to shady areas (note that their fern-like leaves will burn if not well mulched), they are absolutely perfect near ponds and water features.

Bulbs

Spring is the season usually associated with bulbs, because most bulbs grown are from cool climates and have adapted to shoot as soon as the weather warms.

ABOVE: *Daylily cultivars come in a wide range of colours and forms. The blooms, which are edible, are widely used in Asian cuisine.*

ABOVE RIGHT: *The Jacobean lily forms a thick clump of strappy green foliage, which makes a nice backdrop for the stunning red blooms.*

There are, however, also many bulbs that flower later and have adapted to drought and heat. Those gardeners with mild climates are blessed with a range of summer-flowering bulbs that includes sea squill (*Urginea maritima*), fairy's fishing rod (*Dierama pulcherrimum*) and South African bugle lily (*Watsonia* sp.).

Summer bulbs

Many summer bulbs come from Africa and will thrive in hot summers. As delightful as white daffodils and every bit as fragrant is the rare subtropical bulb, the eucharist lily. The white trumpet-shaped flowers have a sweet scent. Belladonna lily also has a lovely fragrance with large showy bells of pink, streaked subtly in white and yellow. Also known for its enchanting scent is the summer-flowering tuberose, a favourite in bridal bouquets. Another South

African bulb, crinum, or veldt lily, has fragrant white or pink flowers.

For warm tones and fabulous cut flowers, try Peruvian lily (*Alstroemeria* sp.) (see pages 175–6). For a dash of red, try the stunning Jacobean lily, jockey's cap lily, vallota or climbing gloriosa lily.

Pineapple lily (*Eucomis* sp.) is a worthy addition to the cutting garden. Its large cylindrical flower spikes, made up of masses of greenish white petals, last for weeks in water.

A day in the sun

Some flowers are simply not made to last. They have a flash of brilliance and then quickly fade away. Luckily for us, though, many of them flower anew each day, thus staying fresh and fabulous for weeks. Daylilies and the walking stick iris are two fine examples.

Daylilies are pretty much foolproof. They're easily grown in a wide range of conditions, with new flowers over a long period. Their colour range includes shades of tangerine, butterscotch, lemon, magenta and purple in both singles and doubles—ideal for a hot summer border. Some varieties may be deciduous in winter, although most are evergreen in warm temperate climates.

The walking stick iris is actually the common name given to two different plants. The first is *Neomarica gracilis*, which has light blue and white flowers, and the second is *Trimezia martinicensis*, which has golden yellow blooms. Both have great strappy foliage to 60 cm and belong to the iris family (Iridaceae), spreading outwards by rhizomes. They attract bees and butterflies, though are poisonous to humans if eaten. They are best used in mass plantings, either as large clumps or in long borders.

Swamp and spider lilies

Crinums love the subtropics, where they flower throughout late spring and summer. They especially enjoy moist areas, which gives rise to their common name, swamp lily. Often scented, crinums come in pink, yellow or white, depending on the species, with some native to Australia. All stay evergreen if the climate is warm enough, though they will become deciduous if they need to cope with cold.

Very similar is the spider lily (*Hymenocallis* sp.)—a native of the Caribbean—which has daffodil-like white cup flowers with tassel-like stamens. Its stout stems bear their perfumed flowers in summer, rising out of clumps of strappy evergreen leaves about 60–70 cm tall. Both crinums and spider lilies belong to the same family of bulbs, the Amaryllidaceae.

Agapanthus

Agapanthus lilies tell of summer like no other in warm temperate gardens, where they thrive. Native to Africa, they are sometimes known as the Nile lily, and modern breeding over the last decade or so has resulted in many new cultivars, some dwarfs and others with more intense shades of azure or bearing hundreds of flowers at a time. Hardy beyond belief, they are a favourite choice for council roadside plantings, and will tolerate both wet and dry conditions, and even act as fire retardants in bushfire-prone areas. Do not, however, plant them near bushland unless they're a sterile cultivar as some types seed too readily. So be vigilant removing flowers as they fade—not only will your clump look tidier, but it will also stay put.

Perfect for driveways and edging paths, they will help bind soil and prevent erosion on steep sites or in poor soils.

To create a storm, look out for a cultivar named just that. More compact than traditional types, 'Storm' also flowers longer, with many more blooms. Another sterile form is 'Queen Mum', which has stunning extra-large white flowers with blue touches upon 1.5 m stems. A near-black-stemmed, deep-purple form called 'Back in Black'—bred in Holland—is another show stopper, with 65 cm tall flowers. 'Strawberry Ice' is a pretty soft pink that grows to 80 cm; 'Finn', a white sterile dwarf, only grows 30 cm tall; an ultra-dwarf type called 'Agapetite' reaches half that height.

Eucharist lily

Also known as the Amazon lily, the Eucharist lily (*Eucharis amazonica*) is in fact native to the Andes Mountains of Colombia and Peru. The flower is a most exquisite daffodil-like bloom, pure white and divinely perfumed. It's perfect for containers and massed planting under trees, and can even be brought inside when flowering for the most beautiful, scented display.

DID YOU KNOW? Today's daylilies have come a long way from the yellow single daylily brought to England from East Asia in the 16th century.

A sea of white and blue agapanthus makes an impressive sight in the early days of summer.

Lovely liliums

Easy to grow, liliums provide a feast of colour, perfume and floral display from early summer into autumn. Liliums flower for three or four weeks, but the bulbs last for decades in the ground and multiply in the soil, producing even more flowers the following year. For a small, initial investment for your first bulb, within five years you'll have a dozen or more for free.

The November or Christmas lilies are the first to display their elegant,

Picture-perfect pink oriental lilies make beautiful, fragrant pot plants.

Leopard lily

So named because of the attractive spotted apricot flowers, the leopard lily is also sometimes called blackberry lily after the berry-like seeds that follow the blooms.

VITAL STATISTICS

Scientific name: *Belamcanda chinensis.*
Family: Iridaceae.
Climate: Grows best in frost-free semi-tropical areas with hot summers.
Culture: Lift and over-winter if you're in a marginal climate.
Colours: Flowers are apricot spotted with orange.
Height: 1 m flower spike and clump 25 cm wide.
Planting time: Re-plant rhizomes in early spring.
Soil: Slightly acid sandy loam with added organic matter.
Position: Full sun or part shade.
Planting spacing: Plant rhizomes 20 cm apart.
Fertiliser: Apply a complete plant food after the new growth appears.
Pests/diseases: None.
Cutting: Remove spent flowers and continue watering until the foliage dies off.
Propagation: Strip bulblets off the main bulb and plant them out.
Storage: Lift clumps in late winter or early spring.

Feature bulb

pure white trumpet flowers. As they finish, up pop the very tall regal lilies with trumpet-shaped fragrant flowers in many delicate shades. A few weeks after that, in late summer, the shorter but richly coloured Asiatic lilies spear through the ground and bloom. Then it's the turn of the oriental liliums to flower into autumn.

Liliums need prepared, well-drained soil enriched with manure, although some varieties can be grown in pots. Ask your nursery when to plant them, as some need to be planted in autumn, others in spring.

Gloriosa lily

Also known as glory lily, this must be the star of all lilies. With its crimson wings and golden hearts, the upturned flowers resemble exotic butterflies in mid-flight, touching down upon glossy green, tendril-tipped leaves. Provided it is in a well-drained spot sheltered from frosts (the fleshy roots remain dormant till late spring, so early frosts present little risk), it's surprisingly easy to grow.

The main problem with the gloriosa lily is its habit of working downwards into the soil. If it buries itself too deep it might forget to come up, so every few years lift the tubers and replant them to about 5 cm below the surface.

Flowering in summer and into autumn before dying down, gloriosas are dormant for about six months of the year, so store the tubers in a cool dry place indoors if the outdoor conditions are not perfect.

Alliums

Many of us are familiar with allium family members onions, garlic and leeks, but too few gardeners have dabbled with ornamental alliums, grown for their pompom-like blooms. There are several hundred different species, many of which have fabulous beauty and are hardy and disease resistant, making them perfect bulbs for the garden, if you can find them. Start looking in autumn when your traditional bulbs get to stores,

or order them and have them mailed to you ready for planting. Flowering is in spring and summer, depending on the type, and colours vary widely, though pink and purple tones predominate.

The gloriosa lily makes a stunning addition to the garden or conservatory.

But who will watch my lilies,
When their blossoms open white?
By day the sun will be sentry,
And the moon and stars by night!

BAYARD TAYLOR

Grasses, groundcovers and climbers

A sweeping expanse of lawn, a wall with spill-over plants cascading gently, a lovely groundcover or an arbour draped in fragrant climbers—these elements are charming in their own right, but also help to link buildings to their surrounds and soften hard landscaped features such as paths and retaining walls.

ABOVE: *The passion flower* (Passiflora *sp.)* *is a spectacular summer-flowering climber.*

LEFT: *This walkway, planted with wisteria and Boston ivy, provides shade in summer.*

Grasses

Summer is grass-growing season. Every weekend somewhere in the suburbs the buzz of a lawnmower can be heard as it carves its way through another backyard.

Most gardeners lower the mower's blades for a 'close shave' to extend the time between cuts, but this is the worst thing you can do. Lift the mower blades in early summer because short grass is stressed grass, and far more likely to turn into a browned-off dust bowl than a bowling green. Let your lawn grow a little taller as this helps stressed grass cope with wear and tear. Cut just a little, more frequently, and you'll be rewarded with lush growth.

Make sure you keep your mower blades sharp, as torn grass edges brown quickly in the summer heat.

Lawn fix

Nothing sets off your garden better than a backdrop of green, healthy lawn. Build up strong roots and emerald green leaves with a dose of balanced lawn food and your lawn will be able to cope with weekend cricket matches.

Together with summer's high temperatures and, in some areas, high humidity, come a set of troublesome lawn problems, pests and diseases. Army worm can devastate a lawn. These grubs (they're not actually worms) can breed up into massive numbers and move through the soil like a wave or encroaching troop line eating the roots of grass. Soon the lawn is stone dead. Another lawn pest is the sod webworm, a 25 mm long green caterpillar that chews through the crowns of grass, causing dieback. They feed at night and move en masse through the soil.

Check for both of these pests by placing a hessian bag on the lawn overnight. The grubs will crawl between the layers of hessian. The next morning you can squash them and feed them to the birds. Also, beware of applying too much nitrogen during summer, as it can encourage soft leafy growth. It can also burn turf if applied on a hot or dry day.

Drought-tolerant grasses

As summer comes on, we need to look for drought-tolerant lawns that are less dependent on watering. Hybrid couches and fescues are the hardiest, while bluegrass and buffalo grasses are reasonably tolerant. Good old kikuyu is also tough (but does require regular mowing), and Empire™ Zoysia is one of the most drought-resistant new lawns on the market today. The grasses to avoid contain rye grass and bent, so check seed mixes carefully when sowing.

Fairy rings

After rain you might find fairy rings popping up in your lawn. These are small to large circular rings of dead grass. The soil under the dead areas is frequently packed with white thread-like fungal growths that cause the grass to die by depriving it of nutrients and water. The fungi start growing at one point, but gradually spread out into a circle so that the rings expand each year. Often the grass in the centre of the ring is green, as it is only where the fungi

The fine texture of couch and its fast recovery time from wear and tear make it popular in warm-climate regions.

actively grow that it does any damage. These fairy rings are common in turfed areas and pastures, and can grow for many years unless treated. They are spread via the mushroom-like fruiting bodies, especially in warm and moist conditions.

The main treatment is to ensure adequate water penetration into the areas where the fungus is actively growing. Hollow tyne forking or coring the affected areas as deeply as possible will assist water penetration, as will wetting agents.

Breathless, we flung us on the windy hill.
Laughed in the sun, and kissed the lovely grass.

RUPERT BROOKE

GRASS VERSUS PAVING

As backyards shrink and artificial landscapes become a popular choice for urban dwellings, consider the cooling effects of grass versus paving. Turf reduces the surrounding ambient temperature by about 3°C and a natural lawn produces the same cooling effects as 9 tonnes of air conditioning—enough for two average-sized homes, so it makes green sense to stick with grass where you can. Also, replacing a natural turf surface with concrete will limit natural rain absorption, likely causing problems with water run-off. This is a particular concern during the hot months where long dry spells are often followed by heavy rainfall. Another fact that has come out of recent research is that lawns act as excellent water filters, removing particles from run-off that might otherwise cause turgidity in water courses.

Problem patch

Do you have a troublesome patch of lawn where any water applied simply runs off and it's hard to get a good grass surface going? Even well-prepared soil can compact over the years, stopping water or fertiliser from penetrating the surface. This makes the maintenance of even a small patch an endless chore.

To beat the problem, first water in a product called Clay Breaker®, which comes in a container that clicks on to your hose. This contains gypsum, which helps break down the heavy compacted soil below the grass roots. It chemically reacts with the soil and flocculates it, which means helps form peds or balls of soil rather than a flat pan of clay. It's better than lime and it doesn't change the acidity or pH levels of the soil. (There are several soil wetters on the market that do a similar job.)

After a few weeks, apply a fine pelletised lawn food, which helps to feed the grass and break up the subsoil. The organic matter contained in the lawn food will encourage earthworms, the best free workers in the garden. Finally, water in a wetting agent, also known as a penetrant, to help break down any water-repelling wax coatings on sand and soil particles.

Variegated *Dietes* 'White Tiger'

This clump-forming, low-maintenance, grass-like plant has the rare ability to grow in dry shade, as well as full sun. Drought-tolerant, it works well in gravel gardens or difficult spots such as beside driveways. The white-streaked leaves are attractive year-round and the iris-like white flowers bloom for most of the year.

VITAL STATISTICS

Scientific name: *Dietes* 'White Tiger'.
Family: Iridaceae.
Climate: Frost hardy and salt-tolerant.
Culture: Flowers for many months from late winter to late autumn.
Height: Plants grow 60 cm high, 50 cm wide.
Planting time: Any time from pots.
Soil: Easily grown in any garden soil. Suitable for soil stabilisation, seaside plantings and waterside conditions.
Position: Full shade or partial sun.
Watering: Not needed once established.
Fertiliser: Not needed.
Pruning: Remove unwanted foliage if it has become straggly.
Propagation: Divide clumps in winter.

Feature grass

Groundcovers

Next time you have to mow your lawn, take the time to consider some alternatives to grass. If your garden has a turfed area that could be transformed by a groundcover, now is the time to be making plans.

Uplifting groundcovers

A groundcover can be a clumpy, spreading perennial, a creeping one or even a climber that sprawls over the ground rather than growing upwards. These plants cover the ground to give it a soft appearance, smothering weeds and integrating built features with planted-up areas.

Ideal candidates are pennyroyal, dichondra, mazus, pratia, isotoma and even Corsican mint. These have tight, rounded leaves that can cope with occasional foot traffic. Many groundcovers flower over summer, creating a colourful carpet. Gazanias, dead nettle (*Lamium* sp.), bindweed (*Convolvulus* sp.), lamb's ears and plectranthus are just a few that create a sea of splendour. Silver-leafed groundcovers are another lovely way of lifting an area.

A delightful flowering mass could be achieved through summer by planting a garden pink called *Dianthus deltoides*, candytuft (*Iberis*) or thrift (*Armeria*), which forms a low, cushion-like carpet with flowers that vary from white to crimson, making it an excellent choice for the edge of a herbaceous border.

ABOVE:
Plectranthus nicoletta *is fabulous planted beneath trees, where it creates a thick, silvery mat.*

ABOVE LEFT:
Canberra grass (Scleranthus sp.) makes a lovely moss-like groundcover.

CLOCKWISE FROM TOP LEFT: Gazania tomentosa *creates a thick and hardy cover; candytuft is a springtime pleasure; lamb's ears is covered in soft hairs that give it its common name; snow-in-summer is pretty year-round with its grey foliage; cats love the smell of Nepeta, or catmint.*

Gazanias

Treasure flowers, or gazania, are so named because 18th-century gardeners thought the flowers' centres were like pearls on velvet. But they could well be called treasure flowers because of the shining golden flowers or silver-plated foliage. Certainly, gazanias are invaluable as summer flowers. They are sturdy and easily grown from seed or root division and they're perfect for any inhospitable area such as by the seaside, as a groundcover for the nature strip or for any tub that dries out quickly. Their only enemy is severe frost and lack of sun, as their flowers close when the sun fades away.

Lamb's ears

Lamb's ears (*Stachys byzantina*) has thick silvery leaves that are covered in grey felt. During summer it will produce purple flowers on tall spikes. This plant provides flashes of silvery contrast in a mixed border, and its soft woolly leaves growing in a rosette formation make it an attractive groundcover for a shady position. There is also an unusual golden-leafed form.

Gold and silver chrysanthemum

This pretty chrysanthemum (*Ajania pacifica*) forms a low mound 30 cm tall and 1 m across. It's named for its very attractive silver-edged leaves and gold daisy-like flowers that bloom through late summer and autumn.

Silver bush

This plant (*Helichrysum petiolare*) is half groundcover and half sprawling shrub. It's particularly suitable for slopes and embankments because it grows easily and roots where it touches the ground, helping to bind the soil. Although the commonly grown form is silver, there is also a stunning-looking gold form. Both clip well too.

Catmint

If you have a cat, it will love you for planting catmint (*Nepeta* × *faasenii*). It is a low-growing herbaceous plant with attractive mauve flower spikes. The serrated leaves are mainly grey-green. It likes a well-drained soil with full sun to part shade and in the right conditions will layer itself, quickly spreading into a matting groundcover. Ideal for rockeries or grown against walls, it can also be grown as a clumpy dwarf hedge in a border.

Snow-in-summer

A carpet-like plant, snow-in-summer (*Cerastium tomentosum*) has silvery grey foliage and masses of white cup-shaped flowers in late spring. This is a fast-growing groundcover, making it great for rockeries and hanging baskets. Plant it in a well-drained position with full sun and water it well during dry weather. It will grow to around 15 cm tall and spread to about 1 m wide.

Dead nettles

Dead nettles (*Lamium* sp.) are ideal groundcover plants for shady areas under trees. The leaves are very attractive: some have striking silvery white markings, such as *L. maculatum* 'White Nancy'; others have golden variegation or a central white stripe. *Lamium* sp. tend to be a little invasive for small gardens or herbaceous borders, but have foliage that looks striking when massed as a groundcover.

Quicksilver

Also called spiderwort, this groundcover is a variegated and much less vigorous form of the weedy wandering Jew.

VITAL STATISTICS

Scientific name: *Tradescantia fluminensis* 'Variegata'.
Family: Commelinaceae.
Climate: Suitable for growing in warm climates or indoors and patios or in heated glasshouses.
Culture: Flowers from early spring through to late autumn.
Height: 10 cm high, 50 cm wide.
Planting time: Propagate by soft-tip cutting any time indoors or summer outside.
Soil: Will grow in any soil and any pH, though it loves moisture.
Position: Will tolerate a sunny position, but it prefers shade.
Planting spacing: 1–3 m apart.
Fertiliser: Feed with a slow-release fertiliser in spring.
Watering: When dry.
Pruning: Pinch prune to keep it from getting straggly.

Feature groundcover

RIGHT: *A variety of house leeks makes for a beautiful and hardy potted collection.*

BELOW: *This variety of century plant has gold-edged leaves.*

Succulents for pots

More and more frequently, gardeners are having to look again at plants that need less water. With water becoming more expensive, lawns, the biggest guzzlers of water, will become too costly to maintain. Xerophytic, or drought-tolerant, plants that store water in their stems, leaves or roots are a major solution to this dilemma.

Succulents are unquestionably tough, surviving hot summers without water and in 50°C heat, but they can also be breathtakingly beautiful. Their symmetrical, statuesque and organic shapes often resemble an underwater landscape, yet they can survive on a dribble of water.

Their colour range is fabulous too: black, purple, grey, pink, red, gold, green and combinations of the lot can be found in their foliage. They look like glamorous plants and yet they are as

LEFT: Echeveria albicans *forms tightly packed rosettes of silvery grey.*

BELOW: Echeveria graptoveria *'Debbie' has a rosy coloration.*

tough as old boots, provided you give them adequate drainage. They are perfect for pots, coastal landscapes, gravel gardens, as accent plants, and yes, for Grandma's front porch!

For information on propagating succulents, see page 295.

Agave

One of the most popular plants in modern landscapes at the moment is the century plant (*Agave attenuata*). There is also a beautiful golden variegated form (*A. attenuata* 'Variegata'), which looks extra special when used in pots.

Echeveria

For impossible locations the versatility of succulents is hard to beat. They cope with dry conditions superbly, both in extreme heat and shade, surviving the harshest of conditions. Despite this hardiness, some are surprisingly

beautiful. For rosettes as attractive as any rose, try growing echeveria, a succulent with a stunning array of colours, from grey to pink, blue, deep purple and green. Without a doubt they are the plant of the future. As water becomes scarcer for garden usage, these toughies will excel. After all, not many things survive summer in 50°C temperatures without water.

DID YOU KNOW? In Mexico, two alcoholic drinks are made from agave. The heart (or *piña*) of *Agave tequilana* is made into tequila, and the sap of *Agave filifera* is fermented to make *pulque*.

Climbers

In small gardens where space is restricted, climbing plants can be grown on walls, fences and trellises. A wall of colour will be a feature and can even camouflage an eyesore, such as a carport or a water tank.

There are lots of choices for supports for your climbing plants; some of them can be decorative features in their own right, but make sure your support is anchored firmly. A climber in full leaf acts as a sail; any strong wind blowing on it can exert tremendous pressure.

Freestanding trellis panels, pergolas, arches and arbours can all be clothed with climbing plants. To decorate a fence you can attach wires or plastic netting to allow the climber to be fixed into place. Climbing roses can be grown over walls, arbours and archways but they also look good decorating an ornamental pillar.

A few climbers, such as ivy, cling on with their roots. Ivy will climb walls, fences and tree trunks too if you let it escape. Some plants have tendrils with which they grasp the support. Sweet pea is a good example. Just make sure they have something to climb on and that they climb in the right direction. Climbers naturally grow upwards to seek the light, so twine them sideways rather than upright for a bushy thick cover.

One species, *Parthenocissus sikkimensis*, is a climber-cum-ground-cover. It has evergreen leaves that form a flat mound on the ground and will cope with dry shade, or it will climb using its sucker pads if there is a support.

Two fragrant climbers

Two related climbers that require very little effort and give so much in return are hoya and stephanotis. Mostly from tropical South-East Asia and northern Australia, hoya are slow-growing climbers which can last for 30 years in the same pot, flowering every year. Commonly called wax vine or porcelain flower because of their unique porcelain-china-like flowers, hoya prefer semi-shade but can tolerate full sun.

ABOVE LEFT: *Hoyas have a delicious fragrance that will enhance outdoor living in summer.*

LEFT: *The flowers of stephanotis are commonly used in bridal displays.*

Paradise vine

Sometimes called giant potato vine or Costa Rica nightshade, this sensational climber has masses of lavender flowers borne in large trusses from early summer to late autumn. Watch out for the hook-like spines it uses for climbing.

VITAL STATISTICS

Scientific name: *Solanum wendlandii*.
Family: Solanaceae.
Climate: Frost-free, temperate climates are preferred; it will become deciduous if cold.
Culture: Support on fence, trellis or railing.
Colour: Lavender.
Height: 5 m.
Planting time: Plant in spring from pots.
Soil: Free draining.
Position: Full sun with protection from cold winds.
Fertiliser: Complete fertiliser in spring.
Pests/diseases: None.
Pruning: Cut back by half after flowering.
Propagation: Cutting.

Feature climber

Hoya love to be root-bound in the pot, so neglect is perfect. Don't prune them or pick the flowers, as new flowers grow from the same spurs as the old ones. Water them and you'll get flowers every summer!

There are the Hindu rope hoyas with twisted and contorted leaves, and there is also a variegated leaf form. 'Shooting Star' has a white and purple flower head like exploding fireworks. One variety has burgundy-coloured flowers, each 5 cm across; the head of ten or twenty blooms is simply breathtaking.

One very popular but often ignored climber is stephanotis. In the 1920s and '30s they were popular in bridal bouquets and are now starting to enjoy a resurgence. Their pendulous creamy white and sweetly perfumed flowers are irresistible. You don't need a botanical garden to grow them—just some manured soil and a position in the warm morning sun.

Stephanotis comes from Madagascar which has a similar climate to much of Australia. The plant performs best in a frost-free aspect where it can grow along a fence or trellis. Don't prune it, just twine the stems in and through the lattice or over a garden arch. If you want more blooms and richer, greener leaves, simply feed them some fertiliser and manure, and water them well in summer. Stephanotis never becomes rampant and invasive, as some climbers can; in fact, it grows slowly, giving you enough time to train the stems to the preferred position.

So if your garden has a small, warm, neglected spot where you can improve the soil, why not put up a trellis and plant a stephanotis.

INDOOR CHARM
Both stephanotis and hoya grow indoors quite well, provided there is enough light. In cold areas they prefer to be indoors.

Bougainvilleas have masses of flowers but the stems are armed with thorns.

PRUNING A GRAPEVINE

Unless the grape is a fruiting one, its growth can be kept in check by summer pruning. Remove wayward long tendrils back to the secondary growth or older wood. In this way you'll keep only the water shoots required.

Fabulous tropical climbers

Many climbers are native to the warm-temperate climates in the rainforests of the southern hemisphere. The best season for these frost-tender climbers is summer, when their spectacular blooms are at their peak.

Bougainvilleas

Perhaps the most popular and easily recognised climber for warmer climates is the bougainvillea. The papery bracts of bougainvillea are long lasting and showy, making a dazzling display in spring and summer. They need strong supports and hard pruning to keep them in check, and are perfect for great cascades, hiding a shed and climbing over old trees; they can even be standardised or planted in hanging baskets. They love a warm-temperate or tropical climate. Most climb using hard, hooked thorns, but new plant breeding has developed many dwarf double-flowered near-thornless varieties, so choose carefully. There are over 100 varieties of bougainvillea, some of which have variegated leaves as well which make a year-round feature. All tolerate drought once established and will grow happily in tubs.

CRUEL TO BE KIND Bougainvilleas love neglect, so be careful not to overwater or use nitrogen-based fertilisers that promote leaf growth at the expense of flowers.

Passion flowers

The edible passionfruit is the best known feature of the passionfruit vine, but there is more to this vine than just the fruit. The South American climber requires a warm, frost-free position in order for its fruits to reach maturity, but the flowers themselves are also special.

Catholic missionaries in Central and South America used the flowers to describe Christ's Crucifixion. They are highly intricate, consisting of ten greenish-white, pink-tinged petals surrounding rows of thin purple, blue and white filaments, which in turn surround five stamens and three styles. The petals look like the crown of thorns, the three styles represent the three nails in the cross and the fruit is the blessing of Christianity.

The common eating type of passionfruit (*Passiflora edulis*) is not the most spectacular species. The red passion flower (*P. coccinea*) and blue passion flower (*P. caerulea*) are more ornamental, with the latter developing orange-yellow egg-shaped fruit throughout summer before ripening in autumn. A soft pink, miniature-flowered cultivar called 'Kiss and Run' is also a pretty addition to a subtropical garden trellis. For perfume, try the vigorous giant granadilla (*P. quadrangularis*), which has red and purple flowers and edible fruits up to 25 cm long.

Passionfruit respond well to generous feeding. Lightly dress with high-nitrogen fertilisers every month.

Brazilian firecracker

Many vines can outstay their welcome, getting out of control in the garden and requiring constant cut backs to keep them in check. Not so the Brazilian firecracker vine (*Manettia luteorubra*), which is a genteel grower with bright red, yellow-edged, cigar-shaped flowers. It meanders gently through your garden shrubs, or up a small fence or even works in a hanging basket, where it will trail and grow up the hooks that support it.

Thunbergia

The best known of all species of thunbergia is commonly called black-eyed Susan (*Thunbergia alata*) because of its black centres, nestled in orange petals. This restrained annual climber is ideal for a hanging basket or post.

The other thunbergias are not as well behaved, and can in fact be weeds if allowed to get out of hand. Bengal clock vine or skyflower (*T. grandiflora*) is highly vigorous, and will quickly cover a support if not restrained or killed off by a hard frost. It has jacaranda-blue flowers in summer.

There are, however, three other species that are worth growing—the golden glory vine (*T. gibsonii*), which has masses of orange flowers; *T. fragrans*, which has white, very fragrant flowers; and *T. mysorensis*, which has yellow and brown flowers that grow in long pendulant clusters.

Allamanda

Magnificent in semi-tropical and temperate areas, *Allamanda cathartica* bears clusters of golden yellow flowers from spring to autumn, giving rise to its common name, golden trumpet vine. There is also a purple allamanda (*A. violacea*) often sold as 'Cherry Ripe'. Some new blood-red and brick-orange cultivars have also been developed. Cut allamanda back in winter, taking care to wear long sleeves as the milky white sap is poisonous. It can become overly vigorous so make sure it doesn't become weedy.

CLOCKWISE FROM TOP LEFT: *Black-eyed Susan is a good choice for hanging baskets; coral vine reaches 3 m in height; the Bengal clock vine flowers for many months; red passion flower blooms spectacularly; the dainty Brazilian firecracker is ideal for small gardens.*

Antigonon

Coral vine (*Antigonon leptopus*) is another tropical delight that is native to Mexico. The coral-pink flowers are borne en masse from early summer to mid-autumn. Its leaves are heart-shaped and the tubers are edible. Once established, it tolerates drought and will survive the occasional frost. Trim after flowering and cut back to ground level in winter, mulching to protect from the cold if the climate requires.

DIG DEEP

Climbing plants are usually left in the same position for many years, so prepare the soil well before planting.

Flowers beyond reach are sacred to God.

INDIAN PROVERB

Shrubs and trees

Three words describe shrubs and trees in summer: green, cool and lush. But that needn't mean an upper storey devoid of flowers. Many shrubs and trees, the structural plants of the garden, feature colourful and fragrant flowers at this time of year—some are dainty and pretty while others are striking and vibrant.

Of course you want your garden to look good at this time of the year, but keeping up with the family next door can be a hard slog if your garden isn't planned well with hardy summer plants.

At no other time does the value of trees and shrubs become more important than over summer. Gone are the flowers from spring, and instead the shade of trees and the privacy of shrubs become crucial for enjoying outdoor leisure time.

ABOVE: *This deciduous white rose of Sharon is a frothy mass of cascading blooms.*

LEFT: *Rain tree's beautiful sprays of summer flowers simmer at the tips of all the branches.*

I never before knew the full value of trees. My house is entirely embosomed in high plane trees, with good grass below. and under them I breakfast. dine, write, read and receive my company.

THOMAS JEFFERSON

CLOCKWISE FROM TOP LEFT: *Abutilon flowers come in myriad colours; white oleander adds a splash of coolnesss to a hot day; two bauhinias,* B. galpinii *(terracotta blooms) and* B. tomentosa *(yellow blooms); Hawaiian hibiscus basks in the heat.*

Shrubs

Shrubs are the mainstays of a garden. They require little maintenance, form a background to flowering 'fillers' like annuals and cottage plants, and will always look green and healthy if they have been chosen and maintained well.

There is a beautiful array of colourful plants available for growing at this time of the year. The fluffy flowers of *Calliandra* (powder puff tree) and the exotic flowers of *Ixora* are great choices for the tropical sun. Heat-loving shrubs include grevilleas, wattles, bauhinias, hibiscus and bottlebrush. They are all good-value plants that last for years, while improving in size, performance and impact every year.

Gardeners in temperate climates can enjoy the large heads of hydrangea. Fuchsias are beautiful in the shade with their tutu-like flowers of sky blue, indigo, cerise and white. Plant them in baskets, pots or in clumps of three for the best effect.

Oleander is easy to grow and long flowering. It has had a bad reputation because all parts of the plant are poisonous, but providing you don't have children who are too young to heed a warning, oleander is the perfect summer plant. Provided it receives sun it will grow almost anywhere, flower profusely and can even be trimmed into tall standards. During summer the flowers put on a magnificent display in a limited range of white, pink and red shades. There is also a variegated leaf form and a dwarf apricot form.

Almost as hardy as the oleander is hibiscus. If you live in a cooler area, stick to rose of Sharon (*Hibiscus syriacus*), which is quite frost-hardy; in warmer areas, plant Hawaiian hibiscus (*H. rosa-sinensis*), the best known of tropical flowers. If you like hibiscus, but don't have a sunny spot, try your hand at their close relative, Chinese lantern (*Abutilon × hybridum*), which has pendulous flowers and likes more protection.

BELOW: *A selection of abutilons, including variegated leaf forms.*

Gardenias are 'handle-with-care' plants because they easily bruise or are burnt by the sun.

Summer shrubs for shade

Three summer-flowering old favourites thrive in shady places.

Gardenia

Native to the subtropical south of China, this highly fragrant shrub wins many hearts. Its white flowers appear from late spring through to mid-autumn, and they always have a lavish perfume that refreshes, even on the hottest days.

Popular varieties include 'Florida', a bush to 1.5 m with mid-sized flowers (8 cm across), and 'Magnifica' (up to 15 cm across), which is bigger and better but less prolific and looks rather like a big white rose. 'Radicans' is the smallest cultivar and can be used in pots or as a groundcover. It has smaller flowers. Some single varieties of gardenia are also starting to make a comeback.

Close relatives of the gardenia include coffee and bouvardia, although the plant known as tree gardenia is actually not a gardenia but a member of the *Rothmannia* genus (see page 224).

Hydrangeas

When it comes to summer flowers, the appeal of hydrangeas remains timeless. Their clusters of flowers in red, pink, purple, blue and white are perfect for classic bunches of flowers in vases, for brightening the shady south side of the house, or in pots. They also have a traditional feel about them, which makes them appropriate for plantings around older-style homes.

These bushy, generally deciduous shrubs originated in China, Japan and North America. Growing up to 4 m tall, they are long lasting and extremely versatile. Although they are drought-tolerant once established, they will wilt in the heat and love a hose down!

The common or mop-head hydrangea (*Hydrangea macrophylla* var. Hortensia), with its large showy heads, is the most widely grown, but there are many other types that are popular with both collectors and keen gardeners.

- **Lacecaps.** These delicate blooms resemble lace doilies, with the centre buds made up of tiny fertile flowers, and the surrounding blooms the larger infertile flowers that form the basis of the common hydrangea. Lacecaps, which comprise a group of *H. macrophylla*, come in white, blue and pink, and also a variegated leaf form that is useful for lightening up dull corners of the garden.

- **Japanese forms.** These are a variation on the common type, but have tightly curled florets that look more like rose buds.

- *H. paniculata* **'Grandiflora'.** This has upright, 25 cm long conical heads of creamy white bracts that turn pink with age. Grows to 2 m.

- *H. villosa.* This North American species flowers later in summer than the traditional type. Pink-white infertile flowers surround

HYDRANGEAS: PRUNING

Some people make a fuss about how tricky it is to prune hydrangeas, but the truth is it's a simple task, providing you understand them a little.

If you like large, showy blooms, cut the plants back by about one third each winter, until you find a pair of fat double buds. Trim them neatly here. To have masses of smaller blooms, just trim off the old flower heads at the end of autumn, lightly shaping the plant.

Don't hard prune the entire bush, or the following season you'll have lots of healthy green growth, but not many flowers.

the scattered deep blue bracts of fertile flowers. Grows to 3 m.

🍂 *H. quercifolia.* Known as the oak-leaf hydrangea, it has clusters of white fertile and infertile flowers in summer. The deeply lobed leaves colour red and burnt orange in autumn before falling.

🍂 *H. petiolaris.* This climbing hydrangea is quite rare in Australia, but can be successfully grown in cooler temperate areas. The flat heads of white flowers smother the plant throughout summer, making it ideal for decorating shady fences and walls. It climbs by using adventitious roots (like ivy), which means it self-clings.

Caring for hydrangeas

Hydrangea literally means 'water loving', which makes them ideal for the dark, moist parts of the garden where most shrubs won't flower. They do cope with sun, provided they receive an adequate amount of water. Try combining water-storing crystals with your soil, and add some rich compost and leaf mould to help keep the roots cool.

The magic surrounding the colour-changing ability of hydrangea flowers all comes down to pH. The lower the pH, or the more acid the soil, the bluer the flower, while the higher the pH, or the more alkaline the soil, the redder the bloom becomes.

To change the colour of hydrangeas, start feeding in autumn with either lime, for pink flowers, or aluminium sulphate, also called bluing tonic, for purple and blue flowers. Keep this up until the buds have formed in early summer.

If you're wondering how to change the colour of your white hydrangea, you can't. White hydrangeas are unaffected by pH levels.

CLOCKWISE FROM TOP LEFT: *Hydrangea paniculata 'Grandiflora' flowers late in the season but is worth waiting for; lacecaps have showy blossoms surrounding small bud-like blooms—blue (top) and pink (bottom) forms are shown here.*

NEW WAYS FOR OLD FAVOURITES

🍂 **Standards.** Hydrangeas can be trained to make fabulous summer specimen plants. Simply trim off all side shoots till the desired height is reached, staking the plant firmly as you go. Nip the top from the leader when it's the right height and trim to a round ball.

🍂 **Pots.** Hydrangeas make classic container plants. Used extensively in Italy for decorating outdoor living areas, they can also be brought inside for a lasting flower display. Place a saucer under each pot to keep up the water during hot, dry weather.

🍂 **Drying.** Hydrangea flowers can be either dried on the bush and picked in autumn once they've greened, or cut fresh and placed in glycerin solution so that they keep their colour.

1 *Hydrangea serrata* 'Libelle' **2** *H. macrophylla* 'Variegata' **3** *H. macrophylla* 'Pia' **4** *H. formosa* (fertile flowers only) **5** *H. macrophylla* 'Variegata' leaf; *H. macrophylla* 'Pia' leaf (dwarf type) **6** *H. serrata thunbergii* 'Plena' (faded flowers) **7** *H. serrata thunbergii* 'Plena' (fresh flowers)

Hydrangeas

8 *H. macrophylla* 'Endless Summer' **9** *H. macrophylla* pink mop-head **10** *Hydrangea Japanese* form 'Ayesha'
11 *H. paniculata* 'Grandiflora' **12** *H. macrophylla* blue mop-head **13** *H. macrophylla* 'Benelux'

To keep your azaleas looking their best, a small amount of summertime maintenance is a sound investment.

Azaleas

To keep azaleas bushy and producing the maximum quantity of flowering branches, lightly trim your azalea bushes now. Remove any tall, irregular sucker-like growths as these will make your plants look misshapen and encourage them to become leggy.

Mulching with cow manure will slowly feed and protect the shallow roots during the heat of summer. Don't use powdered fertilisers as they can cause burn.

By autumn you may notice silvery grey leaves on your azaleas and rhododendrons, but by the time the damage is visible it's too late—the insect has gone, leaving the problem behind. Now is the time to control lace bug, the pest that causes the silvering. Have a look on the reverse of your azalea leaves: if you can see black blotches and small winged insects, they're lace bugs. It won't be long before they start sucking the sap from the foliage, and if left unchecked, will seriously reduce the health and vigour of your plants.

The controls are very specific and effective. Hose down the underside of the foliage before spraying with an insecticide. Baythroid®, Confidor®, Natrasoap® or the new-generation and safer Mavrik® will kill the insects. One follow-up spray several weeks later will protect your azaleas for the season.

Treating lace bug

To treat azalea lace bug, either use a timely application of a contact insecticide, or instead, place some tablets of Confidor® in the soil at the base after flowering in spring. This will stop them feeding in summer and autumn when their numbers reach a peak.

1 Dissolve insecticide in bucket of water and fill according to instructions.

2 Pour over affected plants, but not when in flower, to avoid harming bees.

Tropical foliage

For years, gardeners have obsessed about plants from the tropics. In essence, it's all about plant palette, celebrating dramatic form and exotic foliage, as found with canna lilies, castor oil plants and tree ferns. Lusty plants with architectural lines, gargantuan leaves, coloured foliage and vibrant flowers are found with bananas, angel's trumpet, dracaenas and Gymea lilies.

British garden author Christopher Lloyd experimented and popularised 'exotic' gardening at his home, Great Dixter, and this, coupled with a desire for many of us to recreate our favourite holiday resort at home, have thrust 'tropicals' back into the limelight no matter what climate you actually live in.

To create a colourful kaleidoscope with year-round interest, mix the vivid red cordyline, yellow gold-dust plant, pink acalypha, blue-grey bismarckia palms, orange crotons and green ginger lilies. The strappy leaves of flax or zebra grass combine well with broad, interesting-looking leaves like those of *Philodendron* 'Xanadu' or cycads.

An amazing addition to the tropical garden is the tall amaranthus or Joseph's coat, which has multicoloured leaves. While some varieties have red, cat's tail-like flowers, there is another form that has striking hot-pink-coloured leaves. This plant grows to about 1 m or more tall and puts on a fantastic display in autumn at the back of the flower border in full sun.

Strobilanthes

This often overlooked group of plants belongs to the Acanthaceae family and are mostly shrubs. They thrive in warm temperate areas, where they will flower for many months. The most common is *S. anisophyllus*, also called goldfussia. Its lilac bell flowers bloom prolifically, and they show up extra well against the purplish green foliage. Growing to about 1.5 m tall, it will happily flower in the shade too. For amazing foliage, it's hard to go past purple Persian shield

(*S. dyeranus*), which has stunning purple leaves with a metallic shimmer to them. A great shrub for the shade too, it will reach about 2 m and looks wonderful in its glittery outfit throughout the year. Silver Persian shield (*S. gossypinus*) is dense, requires no pruning and grows to about 1.2 m. Native to the mountains of South India and Sri Lanka, its coat is hairier than its namesake and looks silver and gold in the sun. The Chinese rain bell (*S. flaccidifolius*) will also grow in shady places, where it flowers from late summer into winter and copes in very ordinary soil. Growing to 1.5–2 m in height, it is particularly popular in regional gardens as it strikes so easily, so it can be shared among friends.

CLOCKWISE FROM TOP: *Cordylines with pink and purple leaves lift the garden to a whole new level; bismarckia palm brings elegance to a tropical setting; the shimmering foliage of purple Persian shield* (S. dyeranus) *will add some 'bling' to your garden.*

Summer shrubs for sun

Duranta

Duranta is a great plant, with sky blue or white flowers in summer, followed by golden chains of fruit in autumn. There are also golden-leafed forms that add a bright spark to the garden. It is tough, coping with heat, drought, frost and hard pruning. You can manipulate this ability to bounce back by growing it into hedges and even training it as a standard. There is also a particularly vivid flowering bicolour form called 'Geisha Girl'.

Silver sensations

Butterfly bush (*Buddleia* sp.) is another wonderful shrub that will grow anywhere except the most tropical and the very coldest zones. Its silver foliage shows off its flowers beautifully.

Two other fabulous shrubs for the summer garden are blue mist bush (*Caryopteris* sp.) and Russian sage (*Perovskia* sp.). Blue mist is a late summer bloomer that will attract both attention, butterflies and bees to the garden with its feathery puff of smoky blue flowers that look great against its silvery grey foliage. Russian sage is a very useful plant for a sunny spot. It has pungent, insect-resistant silver leaves and stems and lavender-like panicles of lilac throughout summer. Cut it back after flowering to keep it bushy. Both plants are tough, coping with drought and virtually indestructible by anything but prolonged damp.

Hibiscus

One of the most rewarding plants to grow is hibiscus. Needing full sun, each bush can produce hundreds of flowers over six or eight months of every year.

Although sometimes known as Hawaiian hibiscus, it's actually native to China. The Latin name is a giveaway—*Hibiscus rosa-sinensis*, the rose of China. Australia could lay claim to this popular plant because our breeders have created more hybrids than any other country.

Able to cope with sun or shade is *Hibiscus cooperi*, which has a marvellous variegated cultivar with white splotched leaves and bright red flowers. There is also a stunning pink foliage form.

The underused rose of Sharon (*H. syriacus*) is a deciduous hibiscus that comes in blue, pink and lilac shades, and there is also a very pretty white form that has a slightly pendulous nature and looks like seafoam in flower.

To get the most out of hibiscus, ensure they get plenty of sunshine. Give them blood and bone, cow manure and a sprinkle of pelletised fertiliser, all with extra water throughout the growing seasons of spring, summer and autumn.

Another tip is to prune hibiscus heavily every year after all frosts in late spring because they only flower on new season's branches. If you don't, you eventually get fewer and fewer flowers. Be brave: cut them back hard in late spring, feed and water them, then stand back and admire the display.

The honey scent of buddleia makes it attractive to bees, butterflies and gardeners alike.

Plant training

Standards are simply plants grown into a 'ball on a stick' shape. You can either buy them ready-made, which costs more but could be worth the time saved, or train your own young plant into a standard by cutting off lower branches and lifting the crown till you reach the desired height, then trimming the top into a ball. This is quite a simple process provided you choose a seedling with a single trunk.

Continue to keep your standard in shape by trimming off side branches and tip pruning the main ball to keep it thick and lush.

1 *Duranta erecta* 'Geisha Girl' is a terrific shrub for training as a standard. Other candidates include fuchsias, abutilons, gardenias, oleander, hibiscus and, of course, roses.

2 Prune the lower branches, and pinch off any growth from the stem, leaving only the growth at the top.

3 Cut the leader, or main shoot, from the crown.

4 Lightly trim the growth at the top.

5 Keep the top trimmed into a ball shape and within a few years your shrub will grow into a lush 'ball on a stick'.

ABOVE: *Silvery pink, single blooms appear continuously on 'Dainty Bess'.*

ABOVE RIGHT: *'Falstaff' is a crimson David Austin rose with a heady fragrance.*

Summer roses

Heritage roses

Heritage roses are always in fashion. They are easy-care and disease-resistant, and their stunning perfume makes them a charming addition to any garden. 'Lady Hillingdon' is a lovely coppery pink with purple and bronze foliage; 'Crepuscule' has masses of semi-double, apricot-gold flowers virtually all year; 'Mutabilis' has flowers that start out pink and fade to a coppery yellow; and 'New Dawn' has delicate, sweetly smelling shell pink flowers perfect for making jellies, jams and sorbets.

Not every rose is a flouncy mass of petals. Some of the most charming are single roses. Look for 'Dainty Bess', 'Wedding Day', 'Frühlingsmorgen', 'Canary Bird' and 'Altissimo'.

Standard roses

Standard roses are becoming increasingly popular. Standards are grafted on top of a long stem and can range in height from 60 cm to 2 m. They are wonderful as features, and have the added bonus that the flowers are raised up to eye height. Check the ties each winter to make sure that they are secure, and that borers aren't attacking underneath the ties. Ties that have some stretch in them, such as budding tape, Velcro or even strips of old stockings, work best.

Nowadays, growers are making standards even more interesting by grafting more than one variety of rose onto each stem, sometimes at staggered heights to create poodle-like features in an array of colours.

Thornless roses

The thornless rose first appeared in a Californian garden during trials designed to create disease-resistant roses. It became apparent that some stronger new seedlings had no thorns and fewer diseases. These characteristics were then enhanced and passed on to more new rose varieties, which are now available in Australia. They are sold as 'Smooth Prince', a deep pink flower colour; 'Smooth Romance', a soft shell pink; 'Smooth Angel', a delicate shade of apricot; and 'Smooth Velvet', a red. The best new releases include 'Smooth Sambilli', 'Smooth Shining Spirit', 'Smooth Little Treasure' and 'Smooth Jamie's Boy'. Not all have a strong fragrance, but they don't have any thorns (although the odd thorn might appear over time).

SUMMER ROSE CARE Prune and fertilise repeat-flowering roses, removing all twiggy growth. For proper hardening of canes for winter in frost-prone areas, do not fertilise after late summer.

ABOVE: *Standard red roses make a strong colour impact in the garden.*

FAR LEFT: *'Angel Face' has mauve double petals and a lovely fragrance.*

LEFT: *Rose pink, a bloom that perfectly matches the colour after which it is named.*

TOP: Grevillea sericea, *or pink spider flower, prefers some sun, but it will flower happily in semi-shade, such as the dappled light under gum trees.*

ABOVE: *The tooth-brush flowers of* Grevillea *'Gaudi-Chaudi' appear from spring to summer.*

Grevilleas

For a quick-growing screen it's hard to go past the Australian native grevilleas, or spider flowers, which can quickly grow to 3–4 m. Most fantastic of all is that they flower for so long one is hardly ever without a bloom, and these are a valuable food source for birds, possums and insects. Many have large flowers, and the colours range from 'Misty Pink', with its pale pink blooms, to 'Moonlight', which has soft lemon spikes, and the golden yellow 'Honey Gem'. Smaller flowered reds such as 'Ivanhoe' and 'Hookeriana' look great clipped almost into a formal hedge, as their tight foliage lends itself well to this. They grow about 5 m tall and recover well from regular

pruning. For great lower-growing shrubs to about 2 m you can't go past 'Superb', with its apricot flowers and the red 'Robyn Gordon'. All grevilleas need good sunlight and regular pruning to keep them looking bushy, and excellent drainage will get the best out of them for the longest time. Take care not to feed them with a phosphorus-based fertiliser, however, as being members of the Proteaceae family they can suffer from fertiliser burn.

Summer blockouts

Privacy is something that all of us crave, particularly when it comes to our own home. In our own backyards most of us would like to step outside to the clothesline without feeling as if we're being observed by every stray eye, and to have lunch with friends al fresco without feeling you need to invite the neighbours too.

There are many options to backyard privacy, varying from fencing, to planting trees, hedges and screens, to attachable cladding and even training climbers up and along wires to create a barrier. Each has its advantages and disadvantages, its own style and cost.

Fencing

The traditional paling fence is the most common option for backyard fencing. It's cheap, can be easily painted or stained or left to weather to a silvery grey, and can be adapted: the 'neighbour-friendly' fence has palings on both sides of the rails so that neither side gets the 'back'. Wire fencing is a lovely option for heritage homes, as are picket fences; they're also a great way to add old-age appeal to house frontages.

You can also buy steel panels that are painted in a range of colours to match your roof and gutters. These make a termite-free fence that won't chip or rot. It's also hard to climb (good for security), non-combustible (good for fire-prone areas) and gap-free (good for privacy). On the downside, in hot climates plants can struggle growing directly against them due to the heat retained in summer.

Walls of brick or stone look attractive and can be very long lasting if built correctly. You can imitate this expensive look much more cheaply, however, with a rendered board wall or stacked stone veneer. On the downside, these products will not have the same durability.

Cladding is another option for tarting up an old wall. Products such as bamboo, brush panels, reed and even artificial stone panels can all be attached to an existing, sound fence, a great way to disguise eyesores or create a look. Corteen steel, which has a rust-like appearance but is treated so that it does not deteriorate, can be laser cut into decorative panels with real style.

Semi-transparent options, such as woven willow, lattices and stainless steel cables, will create garden 'rooms' (and can be used as 'roofs' too) that still give glimpses into the next area. The Alhambra gardens in Spain are famous for this, as are the Japanese with their bamboo trellising and redwood screens.

The traditional look of a clipped hedge not only screens but also creates 'rooms' in the garden.

Forest bell bush

If you are looking for a reliable flowerer for the shade, then this is a winner. The lilac bells flower in sprays throughout summer. It's perfect for screening a fence, and can be trimmed into shape or left to cascade softly in an informal froth of blooms.

VITAL STATISTICS

Scientific name: *Mackaya bella*.
Family: Acanthaceae.
Climate: Temperate.
Colours: Trumpet-shaped, purple-veined lilac flowers in trusses.
Height: 3 m high, 2 m wide.
Planting time: Spring to autumn.
Soil: Soil enriched with organic matter.
Position: Able to cope with dry shade or full sun, though is slightly frost tender.
Fertiliser: Feed in autumn with fertiliser and manure to encourage fresh new growth, which will flower profusely in summer.
Pests/diseases: None.
Cutting: Lightly prune after flowering in autumn.
Propagation: Take semi-hardwood cuttings in autumn.

Feature shrub

Grevilleas

1 *Grevillea* 'Honey Gem' **2** G. 'Misty Pink' **3** G. 'Sylvia' **4** G. 'Honey Gem'
5 G. 'Moonlight' **6** G. 'Flamingo' **7** G. 'Blood Orange'

8 *G. sericea*   9 G. 'Elegance'   10 G. 'Pink Lady'   11 *G. buxifolia*   12 G. 'Sandra Gordon'
13 Seeds of G. 'Honey Gem'

LIVING BOUNDARIES
Living boundaries increase the value of your property and extend your outdoor living area. Plants as boundaries can also diffuse where boundaries start and finish, merge into borrowed views and can also be used to create garden 'rooms'. Compartmentalising your garden can actually make 'rooms' with specific purposes in the garden and also add the element of surprise, anticipation, allure and reveal.

Walls have tongues, and hedges ears.

JONATHAN SWIFT

RIGHT: *This elaeagnus hedge has variegated foliage to provide year-round interest. It needs pruning twice a year to keep it in check, and tolerates drought and resists frost.*

Hedging

A garden hedge is far more than just a property boundary, keeping out unwanted animals and people, and providing privacy. Hedges are a positive feature in any garden design, providing a framework and background to the life within. They can be used as the 'skeleton' of your landscape, helping to create garden 'rooms' for you to decorate, conceal utility areas and unsightly views, and act as a windbreak.

Small hedges form borders along driveways and paths. Tall hedges provide windbreaks and shelter from salt spray and hot, drying, dust-laden winds. Hedges offer more protection than a solid wall because plants slow down the wind, filtering the air in the process. Solid walls, on the other hand, provide a barrier, increasing the turbulence in your garden.

Formal or informal, flowers or foliage, there are hedges suitable for all garden areas. The traditional garden hedge is close clipped and neat, usually screening the front garden from the street and masking traffic noise, but there is a huge number of attractive shrubs that will form low-maintenance, informal hedges. Just match the final height of a mature plant to the hedged height of about half to two-thirds of the size you are hoping to have—that way, you're not constantly pruning to maintain it.

ALL SHAPES AND SIZES
Before planting your hedge, consider the eventual height, purpose and time you've allowed for growth. Fast growers may screen quickly but their vigour will mean more maintenance later on to keep them in bounds.

- Conifers (for example, Leyland cypress) form a fast-growing hedge which, being evergreen, is a perfect windbreak or screen. Many reach enormous heights, so be prepared. Height: 3–6 m.
- Australian natives—such as grevilleas, lilly-pillies, hakeas and tea trees—make fast-growing flowering screens that attract birds. These may need replacing every ten years or so. Height: 2–3 m.
- For a formal low hedge, try yew, box, lonicera, euonymus, dwarf lilly-pilly or dwarf murraya. Height: 0.5–1 m.
- Taller flowering hedges of escallonia, pittosporum, elaeagnus, perfumed murraya, photinia, viburnum and sasanqua camellias can all look spectacular. Height: 2–3 m.
- Deciduous hedges are popular in cold climates and many species can also be pleached. Try beech, limes (*Tilia*) and hornbeam. Height: 2–6 m.

Keeping trim

Hedges require regular trimming to keep them looking good. Start trimming from the bottom so that the clippings fall clear. A hedge should be wider at the base than the top. This allows vital light to reach all parts. Hedge trimmers and shears give more control, especially if you want a particular shape. Don't use a mechanical pruner on large-leafed plants as it damages the leaves.

If your hedge has grown out of control, check that the shrub will reshoot after pruning. Most conifers will not. Start by cutting the top of the hedge first, then one side. Wait until that side has greened up before you prune the other side.

Feed your hedge and mulch it to keep it looking good for years to come.

How to plant a hedge

1 For a really straight hedge, mark out the run with a string line. Dig a trench at least 60 cm wide and 45 cm deep.

2 Incorporate lots of well-rotted manure or compost. Fill the trench back in, which will create a small mound. (Omit this step with phosphorus-sensitive natives.)

3 Using a measuring stick, space out all the plants. Dig a hole for each plant, add some slow-release fertiliser and water crystals, and plant, ensuring that the soil has not built up around the trunks.

4 Tip-prune all new shoots to encourage branching. Do this for the first few seasons so that a well-branched, thick-to-the-base hedge is developed.

5 Trim to shape. Secateurs allow precise cutting and are suitable for pruning conifers and all informal hedges. They are ideal for the initial shaping of young plants. For larger plants in an informal hedge, use shears: they produce the best shape and leave the foliage unmarked. They can also be used on formal hedges for a perfect, but time-consuming cut, or you can use electric hedge trimmers in slow, even cuts.

Pruning a hedge

1 Measure the height you want your hedge to be. **2** Tie the string to the hedge at one end. **3** Run the string along the hedge and then tie it at the other end at the same height from the ground. **4** Cut the top of the hedge first with a hedge trimmer or shears.

POLLUTION

As house blocks and gardens get smaller and our suburbs become choked with noisy traffic, lack of privacy and pollution are becoming greater problems.

While solid fences and walls block out the view of traffic, they can also create an air vacuum behind the wall and suck in the sound. On the other hand, a combination of trees and shrubs of varying heights and leaf textures improves the view, increases privacy and filters pollution and traffic noise.

Add some more pleasant noises, such as the sound of splashing water in a small fountain, and you'll be amazed by how much the traffic noise is reduced.

Trees

The value of trees becomes very clear in summer. Their cooling green canopy is a great relief on a hot summer's day, but many people don't realise that trees have more than leaves to offer in summer.

Many trees, especially those that are native to tropical and temperate regions, have dramatic, vibrant flowers. The fabulous silk tree (*Albizia julibrissin*) has long silky stamens in ruby red, and then there is the silk floss tree (*Ceiba speciosa*). The rosy pink, five-petalled flowers look spectacular blossoming on bare wood. Beware, however, of the thorns that grow on the trunk and branches that would scare off any climbing animal or unsuspecting victim. Silk floss trees follow their flowering with a pear-shaped capsule that is filled with 'silk floss'. This is often used for stuffing cushions and mattresses in its native South America.

Two other trees to consider are Cape chestnut (*Calodendrum capense*), which blooms profusely in mauve-pink, and poinciana (*Delonix regia*), which has brilliant scarlet-orange flowers.

If you want to give your garden a Midas touch, try the golden shower tree (*Cassia fistula*), with its pendulous clusters of perfumed yellow flowers, or golden rain tree (*Koelreuteria paniculata*), which has large clusters of yellow flowers.

Flowering in late spring and summer, the jacaranda is a beautiful tree. Its graceful, fine fern-like leaves turn golden bronze in winter before they fall. Many towns have capitalised on its beauty with streets lined with that blue haze of blossom. There is also a white-flowering variety called 'White Christmas'.

Ideas for a tranquil garden

If your block is bare, your home and garden exposed to the full glare of the sun, you need shade! A living canopy creates a serene atmosphere, so cast a peaceful and cool spell with shade trees. Alternatively, structures both permanent and temporary are available.

Pop-up shade

Sometimes waiting for a tree to grow is just not fast enough and you might want to erect shade in the form of a structure. There are many options. The most plant friendly among them would be to erect a pergola. This is also a quick option, as many climbers will have covered the roof of such a structure within two years.

However, if you require man-made shade there are many alternatives. Market umbrellas are the simplest and can be inserted, in many cases, through the middle of your outdoor dining table to provide shade directly overhead. They require a sandbag weight at their base, and steel sleeve in most instances to hold them securely so that they don't become airborne on a windy day. Portable gazebos are another alternative, being cheap and easy to put up, though are best not left up.

For more permanent options, shade sails and shade wings are probably worth considering. They can either be cantilevered from a post or attached to the house itself with stainless-steel cables. Some are adjustable, too, so that they can be angled to suit where the sun is coming from. The material itself

The golden shower tree is a South American native that grows to about 5–8 m high. Its spectacular blooms set it apart.

can vary from shadecloth, which is permeable and comes in different percentages (indicating density), to silicone-coated fabrics that also repel the rain and create a waterproof cover.

The most sophisticated of all is probably the remote opening roof systems such as Vergola. At the touch of a button you can adjust the louvre blades' angle to give you control over sunlight and ventilation.

For temporary shade over sensitive plants, consider erecting a cloche. These are usually bell-shaped covers that protect a plant during its early life. They could be made from glass, bamboo and even clear plastic. Or, you could make your own tunnel from filter fabric or shadecloth, irrigation tubing and tent pegs.

It's recommended to use 30 per cent shadecloth for leafy vegies and seedlings, and 12 per cent for sun lovers like tomatoes and capsicums.

Choosing a shade tree

Trees create a cool microclimate that can drop the temperature by up to 10°C, and they add value to your home. So, how should you go about choosing the dominant plants in your garden?

The critical consideration is the root zone. Direction and division are the key things: make sure that the roots are oriented outwards, with no circling, and that they branch uniformly right out to the fine hairs.

Other indicators of a good tree include its ability to support its own weight, and having an even taper from the trunk collar to the tip. Disease-free foliage is a clue to the tree's vigour.

Regular watering is essential for the first six weeks while the tree establishes itself. Water-storing crystals will help because they act as a reservoir in the soil.

Feed again next autumn with another application of slow-release fertiliser. Keep the grass, or other ground covers, away from the trunk right out to the drip line, as these can compete for food and moisture and slow the growth of your tree.

White-flowering crepe myrtles produce a snowy mass of blooms in summer.

Great backyard trees include trident and Japanese maples, crepe myrtles, dwarf gums and the silk tree.

Crepe myrtles

The crepe myrtle is a tree for all seasons. The smooth mottled bark makes it a feature in winter, it flowers spectacularly in late summer and early autumn, and its leaves, butter yellow turning to scarlet, make it a feature in late autumn. Choose 'Indian Summer' hybrids, because they are resistant to powdery mildew.

Also consider multi-stemmed shrubby varieties around 3–4.5 m tall such as 'Acoma' (a weeping white), and 'Hopi' (bright pink). There are also miniatures growing to 1 m or less, such as lavender-blue 'Cordon Bleu' and mauve-pink 'Delta Blush', which are perfect for very small spaces or tubs.

Gum trees

Most gum trees are too big for the average house block, often growing 60 m tall, though many mallee types have similar habits to the crepe myrtle. The red-flowering Western Australian gum (*Corymbia ficifolia*) is one of the country's most spectacular flowering trees. It's a reasonable-sized tree for the garden, growing to about 6 m tall and spreading to 5–6 m. The 'Summer Beauty' variety is pink and 'Summer Red' has vibrant scarlet staminous flowers followed by large woody seed pods in the classic gumnut shape.

There are also some other small growers, including the dwarf Sydney red gum (*Angophora costata* 'Little Gumball'), which grows to only about 5 m and has wonderful mottled bark, and the stunning clear yellow blooms of the bell-fruited mallee (*Eucalyptus preissiana*), which also has beautiful blue-grey foliage.

Ivory curl tree

In the garden the ivory curl tree (*Buckinghamia celsissima*) will probably grow to about 8 m tall by 5–6 m wide, which means it is good for small gardens. It tolerates a wide range of conditions, from sandy coastal soils to heavy clays, as long as it receives heat and the sun.

It's also ideal for a hedge, but it's the creamy white flowers that are the real attraction. They're spidery in appearance and the birds just love them. The tree is smothered in flowers in summer and autumn, while the large new leaves open pinky red in colour then age to glossy dark green.

Trees with stamina

Staminate blossoms are particularly common in the family Myrtaceae. Think lilly-pilly, gum blossom and even the New Zealand Christmas bush

ABOVE: Azara celastrina, *known in Chile as lilén, has perfumed yellow flowers followed by white berries that look like speckled eggs.*

RIGHT: *The golden penda has stunning yellow blooms 15 cm across.*

(*Metrosideros* sp.), which is also called rata or pohutukawa. Golden penda (*Xanthostemon chrysanthus*), native to Queensland, is an extremely beautiful yet underused Australian native with gorgeous golden flowers. Both tree and dwarf forms are available. They have glossy foliage, and are prolific flowerers, starting in spring and blooming through till autumn. Now that's stamina!

Patagonian native *Azara celastrina* is another underused plant. It, too, flowers in summer, when a mass of golden blooms smother foliage and their vanilla-like scent lies heavy in the air. Growing into a large shrub or small tree, this is a perfect species for small gardens.

A FEW DO'S AND DON'TS
- Do find out how big your tree will grow; make sure it will fit your garden without the need for constant pruning.
- Do feed your tree to encourage new growth and stake it for the first year only.
- Don't plant your tree closer than 5 m to your house. It could damage foundations and block drains.
- Don't pave close to your tree. Allow space for the trunk to develop and for air and water to penetrate down to the roots.
- Don't prune your tree at the wrong time of year. Autumn is the best season for pruning as the sap flow slows down at this time of year.
- Don't expect grass to grow beneath your tree once it's mature.

Creating a rainforest garden

For a different style of garden try planting your own rainforest. Not only are they inspiring places, but they also contain a wonderful diversity of plants, some with delicious perfumes, others with stunning flowers, colourful foliage or edible fruit.

The rainforest garden has become popular because it's both attractive and easy to maintain. Once established, it becomes self-sufficient, needing little water, and producing its own mulch, which keeps the weeds down. It also is a great habitat for animals and birds due to its diversity and safe hiding places, and can be recreated in a normal suburban-sized block providing small trees are selected, such as the ivory curl tree.

Create some shade

A rainforest is defined as 'a tree-dominated community with a closed canopy', so trees are obviously important. It was once thought that eucalypts and wattles should be the pioneer plants for establishing a cover for lower-growing plants. Nowadays it's believed that these cast too much shade and have competitive roots that smother new seedlings. It's probably better to plant lilly-pilly (*Syzygium* sp.), lemon-scented myrtle (*Backhousia citriodora*) and blueberry ash (*Eleocarpus reticulatus*) instead.

Popular rainforest trees for the garden include the firewheel tree (*Stenocarpus sinuatus*), tree waratah (*Alloxylon flammeum*), ivory curl tree (*Buckinghamia celsissima*) and the Illawarra flame tree (*Brachychiton acerifolius*). These are not only flamboyant feature trees, they also bring birds and insects into your rainforest garden.

The built landscape

A water feature, such as a small rockpool, will add ambience and interest as well as increase the humidity and allow a greater diversity of plants, such as ferns and mosses, to be grown.

Rocks are very much part of the rainforest landscape, and should be exposed if found on the site. You can build a 'dry' creek bed by placing river pebbles and boulders along a depression, then softening it with terrestrial orchids and ferns. Perhaps add a small bridge made from weathered tree stumps or recycled railway sleepers.

The final touches

A rainforest is made up of layers of vegetation, so plan for 'storeys' of plants: trees as the top floor, palms and ferns as the first floor, and groundcovers like the native violet (*Viola hederacea*) or false sarsaparilla (*Hardenbergia violacea*) to carpet the ground.

To create the feel of a real rainforest, tie epiphytes such as rock orchids and staghorns onto tree trunks. Only use rainforest trees as hosts, as gums will develop rot and insect damage from the constant moisture.

ABOVE: *The wonga-wonga vine has clusters of white flowers.*

RIGHT: *A Western Australian native, bluebell creeper is now available widely. It may become a weed in some regions.*

For added effect, grow flowering climbers such as wonga-wonga vine (*Pandorea* sp.) or bluebell creeper (*Sollya* sp.) over trunks and old tree stumps, and on fences.

Sweet surrender
Fill your rainforest garden with perfumed understorey plants. Native tree gardenia (*Randia* sp.), parvetta, Macleay laurel (*Anopterus macleayanus*) and native daphne (*Pittosporum undulatum*) all have flowers with heady scents.

Relax
Simply string up a hammock and enjoy your own rainforest.

Classic combinations
Some plants look good by themselves, but look even better in combination with a contrasting plant that flowers concurrently. A classic mix, such as roses and clematis scrambling over an arbour together, is one such example. It's easy to overlook the tree canopy when creating these perfect pairings, but that's often where the most impact is made.

In the temperate regions of Australia, one strikingly successful combination is the jacaranda and the Illawarra flame tree; the brilliant scarlet-red flowers of the flame tree complement the purple bells of the jacaranda (*Jacaranda mimosifolia*). This colour combination is frequently punctuated by the golden spires of the silky oak (*Grevillea robusta*), and the result is a fireworks display in the early summer skyline.

Planted nearby, the Illawarra flame tree (left) and the jacaranda (right) are a match made in gardening heaven.

PLANTING ROUND A POOL
If you are siting a swimming pool in your backyard, it is impractical to have overhanging trees casting shade or dropping leaves. Instead, plant lower-storey palms around the perimeter, or ferns, which don't drop any foliage, by the pool.

Tree gardenia

Gardenias are some of the most sought-after plants in warm, frost-free areas because of their to-die-for perfume and lush glossy foliage. But there are other plants with similar appeal.

The single *Gardenia thunbergia* is one such plant. It is a small tree or large shrub, grows in any rich, well-drained soil in a similar climate to the doubles, and is exceptionally beautiful. The long white tubular flowers are fragrant and prolific in summer.

The other tree gardenia, *Rothmannia globosa*, is closely related. It is an upright tree with a narrow crown, suitable for

Another tree-sized 'gardenia', the paper gardenia (Tabernaemontana cerifera) flowers all through summer.

Cape chestnut

This stunning tree is from the Cape in South Africa. Its orchid-like, sweetly scented blooms adorn the tree throughout summer in such abundance that there is hardly any foliage left visible beneath the pink flowers. Try to purchase a grafted specimen, as not only will the flowers be a mid-pink (some seedling types can range from near white to pale pink) but it will also be many years earlier to bloom than with seed-grown trees.

VITAL STATISTICS

Scientific name: *Calodendrum capense*.
Family: Rutaceae.
Plant type: Semi-deciduous tree, losing its leaves just before blooming.
Planting time: Spring.
Climate: Warm temperate.
Height: 6–20 m.
Aspect: Full sun.
Soil: Well drained, fertile.
Spacing: Plant 15 m apart.
Watering: Regularly over summer.
Fertilising: Use a slow-release fertiliser annually.
Flowering: Late spring through summer.

Feature tree

tight spaces in regions that experience a tropical or temperate climate. The bell-shaped creamy white flowers are fragrant and appear in the thousands.

Lilly-pillies

Lilly-pillies are terrifically flexible and can be allowed to grow into spreading trees or trimmed to shapes such as hedges, cones and standards. A few genera are called lilly-pillies, but all are characterised by glossy foliage, gum blossom-like flowers and shiny edible berries, known as riberries. Often lilly-pillies have attractive new foliage with pink, apricot or lime tinges.

There are many dwarf cultivars available, such as 'Lillyput', 'Tiny Trev' and 'Bush Christmas', and all are suitable for growing in containers.

This is the time of year to watch out for infestations of psyllid, a sap-sucking insect which if left untreated can destroy your plants. Prune any infected growth before spraying the plant with white oil. Put the prunings in a plastic bag and place them in the garbage bin; do not put them in the compost bin.

This lilly-pilly, Syzygium wilsonii, is famous for its fabulous new growth. Be sure to be on the lookout for psyllid attack.

Treating a psyllid infestation

Lilly-pillies are susceptible to attack by psyllids, which cause unsightly damage to the foliage. Here's how to treat an infestation of these sap-suckers.

1

2

3

Lilly-pilly leaves that have been badly mutated by an infestation of psyllid.

Trim any psyllid-infested growth. Place the prunings in a plastic bag before throwing them out.

Spray with white oil to prevent reinfestation.

Fresh herbs are always welcome in the kitchen.

Herbs, fruit and vegetables

If there is a season for the edible garden, then surely this is it. Your spring plantings have come to fruition, and now there's a glut you can share with friends. Extend harvest time to late autumn with repeat planting.

Fragrant basil with ripe tomatoes, or sweet melons and passionfruit, epitomise summer. But as summer vegies finish, think about planting vegetables for the new season. Prepare the soil with a good soil conditioner. Home-made compost is the best. A light dusting of lime is a good idea too.

At the end of the season you can sow seeds of traditional winter vegetables, but also think about including popular Asian herbs and vegetables, which are also available as seeds. Choose from tender Chinese cabbages such as pak choy and wombok, the Japanese greens tatsoi and senposai, and lemongrass, a perennial lemon-scented grass.

FAR LEFT: *The young stems of lemongrass are perfect for teas and Thai curries.*

LEFT: *Passion flowers unfurling. These need plenty of action from bees to create fruit.*

Herbs

Summer produces a glut of all the best herbs. They are so fast growing that many annual types, like parsley, basil and rocket, can still be planted out as seedlings and eaten in four weeks' time. As they grow, keep them well trimmed by consuming them regularly or by picking bunches and drying them. They will bolt into flower and lose their flavour if you neglect them.

Basil

There are several types of basil, all of which have a different flavour. Genoa or sweet basil is the best known and most common. It has a spicy smell and is used extensively in Italian cooking. Opal basil has purple leaves, Greek basil has smaller leaves and a pungent flavour, and Thai or holy basil complements Thai and South-East Asian dishes.

Basil should be torn, not chopped, and added to hot food at the last moment to preserve the flavour. It doesn't dry well. It can keep frozen if first made into a pesto or herb butter.

ABOVE: *Basil flowers should be removed to encourage leaf growth and plant longevity.*

RIGHT: *The near-black foliage of opal basil makes a lovely colour contrast in the garden.*

Sowe Carrets in your gardens, and humbly praise God for them, as for a singular and great blessing.

RICHARD GARDINER

Underplanting tomatoes with basil

Clear a small space for the seedling, being careful not to disturb the roots.

Remove seedlings from the pot. Divide into bunches of two or three plants.

Plant around your tomato plants and replace mulch.

SUMMER HERBS
Don't forget to include a wide range of summer herbs such as lemongrass, verbena, various mints, and French, Chinese, Italian and curly parsley for fabulously tasty and fresh meals.

ABOVE: *Tansy, sometimes called bitter buttons, can be used in the pantry.*

ABOVE RIGHT: *As the name suggests, wormwood was traditionally used to treat intestinal worms. It is useful for repelling many other bugs too.*

Protection

If you choose the right plants for your garden you can help keep mosquitoes and other insects at bay—naturally.

One downside to the onset of summer is the explosion of the creepy-crawly population, but your garden can help solve pest-control problems, with certain plants working in tandem with, say, a citronella candle to keep you comfortable outdoors.

The oil contained in many plants will help deter many pesky insects, from flies and fleas to ants and mozzies. Simply planting pyrethrum (*Chrysanthemum cinerariifolium*), however, won't help at all as it's the dried flowers that are used in sprays, not the leaves. These have the intensity and concentration to work effectively. Instead, it is essential to choose plants that release their oil when the foliage is bruised, and to plant them next to footpaths, doorways, between pavers or potted up and placed on tables.

If you don't have anywhere suitable near your entertaining areas to grow these herbs, try rubbing your table, legs and arms and even pets with fresh leaves or bruising leaves and then strewing them underneath a tablecloth where the oil can take effect as you dine.

Nature's insecticides

1 Lad's love (*Artemisia abrotanum*) works wonders with mozzies, fleas, fruit fly and various moths (including the dreaded cabbage moth).

2 Tansy (*Tanacetum vulgare*). This pretty and hardy perennial, with its tiny button-like flowers, was once grown in monastery herb gardens to repel mosquitoes and fleas. When planted near fruit and nut trees, vegetables and berry fruits, it discourages fruit fly, ants, beetles and aphids. Tansy will also repel cabbage moth and cabbage white butterfly. Sprinkled on pantry shelves, its dried flowers discourage flies and ants.

3 Pennyroyal (*Mentha pulegium*) gets rid of silverfish and ants in the cupboard if sprinkled when dried and crushed. Rub it onto your dog's coat after washing as well as scattering it among your pet's bedding to keep fleas at bay.

4 Wormwood (*Artemisia absinthium*), one of the most bitter herbs known, tastes so hideous it repels a variety of insects. For centuries it has been used to repel insects, including fleas, flies and moths, and was once used as an ingredient in ink to stop mice eating old letters. Strangely, it is also a major ingredient in apéritifs and herb wines, such as absinthe and vermouth. Legend has it that as the serpent slithered out of Eden, wormwood sprang up in the impressions left by its tail on the ground, and it has been used ever since to keep away evil spirits. Pick wormwood leaves for drying in summer, and mix them with dried mint and lavender in sachets to keep your clothes fresh and free of moth holes. (See 'Tarragon and wormwood' on page 432.)

5 Rue (*Ruta graveolens*), a sturdy evergreen herb with blue metallic, feathery leaves, is useful as a disinfectant and as an insecticide. Plant it by doors and windows to repel mosquitoes, flies and other insect pests, in the garden to discourage beetles and slugs, and rub it over pets to help reduce fleas.

Planting a mint garden

1 Place the mint in a pot and add potting mix.

2 Dig a hole and insert the pot of mint. The lip of the pot should protrude so that the runners won't easily spread into the surrounding soil.

3 You can do the same thing with other varieties of mint, such as the spearmint shown here. Remember to mulch the pot and water well.

COMPANION PLANTING Grow chives under fruit trees to guard against the diseases leaf curl and black spot.

6 Mozzie geranium (*Pelargonium citrosum* 'Vaneenii') has attractive flowers and foliage that, when crushed, smell like citronella. It is a perennial, and its year-round foliage will help keep mosquitoes away through the year.

7 Coriander (*Coriandrum sativum*). This pretty aromatic herb has a strong pungent scent that discourages aphids. Bees and other beneficial insects are attracted to the umbels of its tiny white flowers.

Mint

There are many species of mint, including apple mint, spearmint, eau de cologne mint, pineapple mint and pennyroyal. Apart from its culinary uses, mint repels many pests, especially fleas and beetles, which dislike the smell. Dried mint sachets in the wardrobe will freshen clothes and keep moths at bay. Fresh mint in the pantry will deter ants.

Rub fresh mint leaves on your hands, neck and face to protect your skin from mosquitoes. Plant mint around a dog kennel or strew near animal cages to repel flies. Rub fresh mint around the eyes and mouths of horses or cows to discourage pesky flies. Mint is the perfect companion plant for cabbages and tomatoes because it repels cabbage white butterfly, aphids and whiteflies— all insects that can ruin your crop.

Plant a mint garden

Mint's oil-rich leaves have long been used to flavour teas, condiments and salads. The menthol improves digestion and has antiseptic and decongestant properties. Mint can, however, grow like topsy, so to inhibit its spread, plant it in a container, leaving a small ridge above soil level. Split established clumps in spring, and store roots in peat, compost or potting mix over winter in cold zones. For fresh leaves out of season, these can be forced in a conservatory or on a warm windowsill. All mints have their own unique character and flavour.

Apple mint (a variegated form is shown) is lovely mixed with cream cheese and spread on crackers.

Gardens are not made by sitting in the shade.

RUDYARD KIPLING

1 Peppermint (*Mentha × piperita*) **2** Lemon mint (*M. × piperita citrata* 'Lemon') **3** Eau de cologne mint
(*M. × piperata citrata*) **4** Apple mint (*M. suaveolens*) **5** Moroccan mint (*M. spicata* 'Moroccan')

Mint

6 Variegated apple mint (*M. suaveolens* 'Variegata') **7** Spearmint (*M. spicata*) **8** Water mint (*M. aquatica*)
9 Hot mint (*Persicaria odorata*) **10** Common mint (*M. spicata*) **11** Chocolate mint (*M. spicata* 'Chocolate Mint')

CLOCKWISE FROM TOP LEFT: *Galangal tastes similar to its cousin ginger, only with citrus notes; though turmeric is native to tropical India, it will grow in any mild climate that is free of frost; cardamom's seed pods are highly sought after.*

Tropical herbs

For most Australians today, Asian stir-fries and curries are a staple part of our diet. Lemongrass (*Cymbopogon citratus*), cardamom (*Elettaria cardamomum*), ginger (*Zingiber officinale*), galangal (*Alpinia galanga*) and turmeric (*Curcuma longa*) can all be grown in your garden, providing you live in a frost-free, mild climate or in a tropical area.

Cardamom is the world's second most expensive spice (after saffron). The whole seed pod or individual seeds are ground with a mortar and pestle and are used for flavouring curries, pickles and custards. With galangal, ginger and turmeric the rhizome is either finely chopped or ground into powder for use in many Eastern dishes.

A pretty addition to the herb garden is lemongrass. The white, bulbous base of lemongrass is used to flavour curries, while the leaves can be dried and made into tea.

Chillies are also indispensable. Their heat is known and loved in Thai dishes, Indian curries and Malaysian laksas. The curious thing is that they are not native to any Asian country.

The red hot chilli peppers

The origin of the chilli is thought to be South and Central America, where it was a staple of the Incas and Aztecs. Chillies are now grown throughout the world, and are used extensively in Thai, Mexican, Cajun, Asian, Hungarian and Portuguese cuisines.

The rest of the world was introduced to them by Christopher Columbus when he sailed to the West Indies in 1492. He believed the various fiery varieties of capsicums used by the locals were pepper, and brought plants back to Spain. As a result, the name pepper has stuck (even though true peppercorns grow on a vine) and 500 years later we still often call them chilli peppers.

There are many chillies to choose from. Some varieties add pep to savoury food, some can be used in desserts and some are simply ornamental.

TUSSIE MUSSIE

A tussie mussie or nosegay is a posy of flowers and herbs that has some meaning or purpose. Traditionally tussie mussies were intended to ward off disease, but throughout the 18th century they eventually came to spell out a message using the language of flowers. Most often this message was an expression of love for one's sweetheart, but it could also be other emotions, such as hate, grief or thankfulness.

Here are some examples:

angelica	inspiration
balm	sympathy
basil	good wishes
forget-me-not	true love
lavender	distrust
mint	virtue
parsley	festivity
rose bud	pre-love
tansy	war
violet	modesty
zinnia	thoughts of absent friends

Spring is the season for sowing peppers. There are at least ten different species of *Capsicum*, although only three main types are commonly grown in home gardens in Australia.

1 **Ornamental chilli.** This is a non-edible variety with much smaller fruits that change with maturity from green or purple to yellow, orange and scarlet. The fruits, or berries as they are often called, are extremely hot, so take care to keep young children away from them.

2 **Edible chillies.** Either cherry-like, conical or the typical long-pointed shape, hot chillies are eaten either green or red, and can be used fresh, pickled or dried. Dried, ground chillies can be made into cayenne pepper and paprika, while fresh chillies can be kept in oil and, after a few months, added to sauces like tabasco.

3 **Capsicum.** The large fruited, non-hot varieties are also known as bell peppers, sweet peppers and pimentos. These can be eaten unripe (green) or ripe (yellow or red), raw in salads, cooked in sauces or char-grilled for antipasto.

Hot stuff

All hot peppers should be handled with care, as they are known to cause inflammation on contact with broken skin, eyes and mucous membranes. If you have sensitive skin, wear rubber gloves, wash your hands thoroughly after handling them and be careful not to rub your eyes because doing so can cause severe burning. To reduce the intensity of the heat, consume milk, yoghurt or other dairy products. The hot compound in chillies, capsaicin, is in its most concentrated form in the seeds, so remove these if you are worried about the intensity of your chillies.

Apart from their value as cooking ingredients, chillies are effective when incorporated into a spray for deterring possums, rabbits and sap-sucking insects such as aphids. (See the recipe for 'Chilli water', right.)

Use a pair of secateurs to cut the ripe chillies from the bush.

Here are five 'hot shots' from which to choose:

1 **Habañero'.** This is a bell chilli with an intense heat. As they ripen, the fruits change from dark green to orange or red, and is similar to 'Scotch Bonnets'.

2 **'Jalapeño'.** The best known chilli available, the 'Jalapeño' is a green, ripening to red, long thin tapering fruit with medium heat that can be used in any dish that needs spicing up.

3 **'Thai Hot'.** This variety has a small, conical red fruit with lots of seeds and a lingering heat, which makes it perfect for Asian cooking. It is also known as 'Birds Eye'.

4 **'Pimiento'.** This is a traditional hardy variety of chilli with beautiful heart-shaped, deepest red fruits that are of unrivalled sweetness.

5 **'Long Cayenne'.** The scarlet red, 9 cm long thin fruit has a medium heat with some smoky overtones.

CHILLI WATER
For a spicy, environmentally friendly insecticide, use a food blender to purée 20 or so chillies to form a paste. Mix the paste with water, then leave it to stand so the pulp can settle. Use the strained 'tea' on a still day so that it won't blow into your eyes.

How to grow chillies

Chillies are warm-season plants and susceptible to frost, which means the best sowing time is from spring to early summer. They need a warm, sunny position with shelter from strong winds. Chillies prefer fertile soil with added organic matter and a mixed fertiliser. Water regularly and spread a mulch in dry weather.

Once the small white flowers have appeared, start feeding with a liquid fertiliser every two to three weeks. This will encourage prolific fruiting.

Regular harvesting encourages chilli plants to set more flowers and produce more fruit, which means it's a good idea to keep picking.

How to use chillies

The benefit of using members of the chilli family in cooking is the sweet, fruity flavour notes that are conveyed, as well as the stimulating effects given by the 'bite' of heat. When chillies are dried, the sugars are caramelised, which is why dried chillies taste so different from the fresh kind.

Normally, fresh chillies are used in quick-cooking Asian dishes, while slow-cooked soups, stews and curries use dried chilli.

CHILLI AND SOAP SPRAY

For an organic pesticide, add soap flakes to a spray bottle that is nearly full of water. Then add about eight chopped chillies. Shake the contents vigorously and spray your DIY insecticide onto any plant.

Shiso

The leaves of the shiso plant are used in Korean and Japanese cuisine. They have an anise or liquorice flavour and can be used stir-fried or pickled and as wrappers like vine leaves around rice and fish or meat.

VITAL STATISTICS

Scientific name: *Perilla magilla* and *P. frutescens*.
Family: Lamiaceae.
Climate: Enjoys damp or humid areas. Plant after frosts have finished.
Culture: Can be grown in the ground or in containers. Mostly annual so needs re-seeding annually or take cuttings and leave them in a sheltered position over winter till bringing out again in spring.
Colours: Blue flowers.
Height: 70 cm.
Planting time: Early spring in frosty areas, up until late autumn in frost-free areas.
Soil: Light, well drained with added organic matter.
Position: Plant in a sunny position or in light shade. They need to be frost free.
Planting spacing: 50 cm apart.
Fertiliser: Liquid feed every few weeks.
Pests/diseases: None.
Propagation: Soft-tip cuttings or seed.

Feature herb

The Apiaceae family

The Apiaceae family contains about 200 genera, distinguished by aromatic foliage and umbels of many small flowers. Planting members in the garden will help attract hover flies and other beneficial insects.

The family is important economically for products used for food, condiments and as ornamentals. Carrot, parsnip, celery, parsley, chervil, fennel, lovage, angelica, caraway, dill, sea holly (*Eryngium* sp.) and Queen Anne's lace are all popular members of this family. Not all members are, however, edible: hemlock and fool's parsley are both notoriously poisonous. Introduced to Australia from Europe, hemlock has become an environmental weed.

Cooking with coriander

The most popular herb for Asian cooking is likely to be coriander, also known as cilantro or Chinese parsley. You can use the leaves, stem and root, and each has its own purpose. Use the roots in curry pastes, the stems when a strong coriander flavour is needed, and add the leaves to a dish at the end of cooking, both as a flavouring and an attractive garnish. It may surprise you to learn that it's native to Britain, and was a popular herb in England until Tudor times; it has, in fact, been cultivated for more than 3000 years (seeds were found in Tutankhamun's tomb). It is a tender annual used fresh or as dry seeds. There is also a perennial form (see page 114).

Coriander's pungent scent discourages aphids, while bees and other beneficial insects are attracted to the tiny white flowers. Always plant from seed direct into position as this helps stop it from bolting.

DID YOU KNOW? The Greek philosopher Socrates was sentenced to death by drinking a cup of hemlock.

CLOCKWISE FROM TOP LEFT: *Angelica attracts bees to the garden, and its stems can be turned into candy; chervil is a popular herb in French cuisine; coriander flowers are edible and also make a charming garnish.*

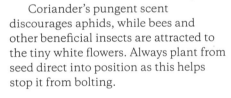

DILL

Dill (*Anethum graveolens*) is often synonymous with pickles, where it is frequently the flavouring ingredient present in either (or both) seed or foliage, flavouring vinegars, mayonnaise and dishes that involve seafood. Native to Asia and Europe, it has been known to be used as long ago as 3000 BC in Eygpt. Its leaves look very much like those of fennel—thin and feathery—but it is a smaller grower, and so perfect for pots as well as in the garden.

Fruit

One of the best things about summer is its fruit. Delicious tropical fruit, mouth-watering stone fruit and succulent berries are all part of this season's rich, sweet palette.

CLOCKWISE FROM TOP LEFT: *Avocado trees take about three years to bear fruit; lychee trees have pretty red-skinned fruit; star fruit (or carambola) are related to oxalis; pawpaw can be eaten when green, shredded as a salad.*

Tropical delights

Nothing evokes the feeling of summer quite like succulent juicy fruit. A ripe fragrant mango dripping down your chin and hands, passionfruit over ice cream and strawberries on pavlova go hand in hand with a traditional Australian summer.

What may come as a surprise is that most of the country enjoys such a mild climate that we can also grow delicious tropical fruits. Even in cold areas, a north-facing sheltered aspect can usually harbour a passionfruit vine or a hand of bananas.

The range of tropical fruit continues to increase, with rare and interesting plants being 'discovered' in remote rainforest communities and introduced into our country by devoted collectors.

Top ten

The best choices for the home garden have a delicious flavour and are easy to grow to fruiting stage. In alphabetical order, here are my top ten.

1 Avocado. One of the most nutritious fruits in the world, avocado is high in many vitamins. It's best to pick grafted trees in order to guarantee fruit quality. Regular water is important, as avocados have a poor root system for their size (10 m).

2 Banana. In many countries where rice, wheat and potatoes are not known, the banana is the major source of carbohydrate. Although referred to as a tree, the banana really is an evergreen perennial, and should be grown in rich fertile soil where it has plenty of space to spread.

3 Custard apple. The white flesh of the custard apple has a melting, juicy texture which is delicate, sweet and rich. Trees range in size from 3 to 10 m, are normally grafted, and are suitable in climates as far south as Sydney.

4 Lychee. Capable of withstanding cold to −2°C once established, lychees are related to rambutans and longans, and are extremely popular in Asia. The tree reaches 7 m, although it can be a little slow at first. The fruit is pinkish red on the outside and grape-like inside.

5 Macadamia. This is the first native food crop commercially grown in Australia. It is closely related to grevilleas and able to withstand light frosts. The spidery cream flowers are produced first, followed by the sweet-tasting nuts. The macadamia tree may reach 10 m high, so make sure you have the space before planting.

6 Mango. Believe it or not, the mango is a close relative of the cashew nut, and is native to India where it has been cultivated for 4000 years. For high-quality fruit, choose a grafted tree, as common mangoes can have a high fibre content and lack juice.

7 **Passionfruit**. Even if you can't fit in a tree, consider planting a passionfruit vine. Grafted passionfruit like 'Nellie Kelly' are hardy, disease-resistant and fast-growing.

8 **Pawpaw**. Paw paw can be bisexual, male or female. Females produce the best fruit but you need at least one male tree to every ten females. They are best grown in tropical or subtropical regions, and need shelter from strong hot or cold winds.

9 **Pineapple**. A member of the bromeliad family, the pineapple likes tropical conditions and won't stand frosts. It will grow in cooler areas, however, and responds by fruiting every two years.

10 **Star fruit**. This small tree (about 6 m high) bears fruit with ridged sides and a crisp, apple-like flavour.

For those of you bewitched by these tropical tastes, don't stop there. There are other flavours, from chocolate to custard to citrus and beyond to be enjoyed. Pomegranates, mangosteens, guavas, persimmons, rambutans, longans, jackfruit, lilly-pillies and sapotas are all worth investigating if you live in a warmer climate.

If you think your area is too warm to grow stone fruit successfully, consider subtropical stone fruit varieties such as 'Nectared', 'Flordaprince', 'Sundowner' and 'Flordagold'. One of the most ancient of fruits, the fig, grows in any warm climate.

Protect your harvest

It's very demoralising to nurture your fruit trees and vines only to watch birds and insects feast off the pick of the crop before harvest time. Keep birds from attacking your ripening harvest with such devices as painted plastic pots, cat cut-out silhouettes, fake hawks, bits of foil strung in trees and netting.

Try scaring away birds and insects with painted pots and foil strips in trees.

ABOVE: *Pick sapote when it's green, then allow it to soften indoors.*

LEFT: *Jackfruit is so sticky that oiling your knife beforehand will help cut it.*

TROPICAL FRUIT TIPS

- Grow tropical fruit in a frost-free area, or cover during winter. If you live in a marginal zone, try using DroughtShield® over winter—it's like dressing your plants in a spencer!
- Add lots of moisture-holding organic matter to your soil, so that your plants think that they're at home in a forest.
- Make sure the drainage is adequate, even if that means raising the beds or planting into mounds. Collar rot and root rot affect most tropical fruits.
- Check with your local horticulturist on whether you need to buy a grafted specimen (to cut down fruiting time) and whether you need male and female plants for pollination.
- Many permaculture textbooks will explain how you can plant different varieties underneath each other to double up on cropping and help feed your family.

ABOVE: *Cherry tomato vines are prolific bearers.*

BELOW: *A solution for excess crops: tomato relish.*

Tomatoes

We love our tomatoes in Australia, something that may have been encouraged by our large numbers of Italian and Greek migrants. Tomatoes abound in summer, and provide a higher yield for space occupied than any other vegetable—2-5 kg per plant on average.

Tomatoes are frost susceptible and need a season of about three months to fruit, so all areas of Australia are perfect for tomato cropping, from early summer to mid-autumn. Buy healthy young seedlings and avoid any that look yellow or starved or are flowering prematurely. Don't rush into buying too early in spring—wait until the weather begins to warm up, especially in cool districts.

There are more varieties of tomato than any other vegetable crop, but for real tomato flavour, pick when red-ripe on the vine and choose a flavoursome cultivar such as 'Ox Heart', 'Sweetie' or 'Beefsteak'.

Tomatoes can be grown from seed sown direct or in punnets or as grafted plants. You can even use prunings from your existing bushes—simply poke the pieces into the soil for a succession of ripening fruits.

With so much fruit there are bound to be pests eager to munch away at the crop. Watch out for whitefly, a real pest for tomatoes. You shouldn't spray just as you are about to harvest them, so paint a piece of board bright yellow, coat it with grease and place it among your tomatoes. The whiteflies are attracted to the yellow board where they get stuck in the grease. Holes in the fruit may indicate the presence of snails or hornworms, caterpillars that feed on fruit and foliage. Both pests can be hand-picked. For fruit fly either spray or lay baits; alternatively, try ripening green tomatoes indoors next to bananas.

Excess tomatoes

At the end of tomato time, you may wish to dispose of your remaining crop. You can enjoy the delicious flavour of home-grown tomatoes throughout winter by trying some of these preserving ideas.

Apart from pickling, making chutneys and relishes, you could try sun-drying or semi-drying your tomatoes. Core and slice them lengthways and place them on a rack cut side up. Sprinkle with sea salt and bake for up to eight hours in a slow oven (75°C) until the excess moisture has evaporated. The tomatoes should be completely dry and almost leathery, but not crisp. Cool and

DID YOU KNOW? When tomatoes first arrived in Europe they were gold, not red.

store them in sterilised jars in the fridge for up to six months. To sterilise jars, rinse them in hot soapy water and dry them in the oven for ten minutes along with the tomatoes.

Or store whole, unblemished tomatoes in a jar. Just cover the ripe fruit with olive oil and keep them in the fridge.

These young tomato seedlings are ready to be pricked out and potted on or planted in the ground.

Tamarillo

Also known as the tree tomato, this is a small, soft-wooded evergreen shrub from the subtropical areas of South America. Pale yellow to purple in colour and the size of an orange, the fruit ripen in early autumn and have a leathery rind. Inside there are many seeds surrounded by edible flesh. These are fast-growing and fast-fruiting plants with attractive heart-shaped hairy leaves, spring perfumed flowers and summer and autumn fruits for use in salads, eaten raw like passionfruit or made into jams. The dwarf species is very pretty, but be warned: its fruit is inedible.

VITAL STATISTICS

Scientific name: *Cyphomandra betacea.*
Family: Solanaceae.
Climate: Warm, frost-free climate.
Culture: They require little pruning and are generally free of disease, but watch for fruit fly.
Colours: Skin is either yellow, orange or red, and the flesh is orange and red.
Height: 3 m.
Planting time: Spring when soil is warming.
Soil: Plenty of soil moisture, especially in summer, though good drainage is critical; pH slightly acid.
Position: Full sun and coastal as they love humidity.
Fertiliser: Dress with complete fertiliser in late winter.
Pests/diseases: Fruit fly.
Pruning: Tip-prune the first shoot to encourage multi-branching when young.
Storage: Jams, chutneys and syrups.

Feature fruit

Tomatoes

1 'Jaune Flammee'   2 'Red Fig'   3 'Gold Nugget'   4 'Siberian'
5 'Wapsipinicon'   6 'Black Russian'

241

7 'Green Zebra' 8 'Martino Roma Red' 9 'Black Koim' 10 'Green Sausage' 11 'Sugar Lump'
12 'Cream Sausage' 13 'Tigrella'

Keep your vegetable garden well watered and mulched so that the soil stays moist and the roots cool.

FEED LETTUCES
Lettuces will 'bolt' into flower if they are not fed enough or if the weather is too hot. Giving the plants light side dressings of nitrogen fertiliser or liquid feeds every 10–14 days helps.

Vegetables

In summer almost anything you plant will grow. Greens, melons, cucumbers and zucchini are prolific.

Salad greens

Leafy salad crops such as mignonettes and perpetual lettuces are terrific at this time of the year. The young leaves grow quickly and will be sweet and tender for summer salads. It's not until you have tasted home-grown salads that you realise just how tasteless and uninspiring shop-bought produce can be.

By growing your own, you can guarantee that your salad will be fresh.

Take advantage of the huge range of varieties that are available in seed packets such as Romaine (cos), kale, radicchio and sorrel. Salad vegetables need fertile soil with plenty of well-rotted organic material incorporated into it. Most salad vegetables need a sunny, open spot with plenty of water. They can be planted and plucked from about two weeks, but on average four to six weeks of fast growing will see them out of the soil and into your salad bowl. The faster you grow them too, the sweeter the flavour. Healthy plants make it difficult for pests and diseases to gain hold, so keep your garden free of weeds as they attract diseases.

Many types of lettuce are available, but keep in mind that the darker the leaf, the better the nutritional value.

'Mesclun' is baby lettuces plucked at this early stage. They are often the oak leaf type or coloured, fancy-leaf types that don't heart and can be continuously sown and harvested making them excellent for pots. By nature lettuce is a cool season crop, but breeders have ensured that you can now sow it all year-round in each climate zone of Australia. And do grow rocket, which, with its lovely nutty flavour, continues to grow in popularity. It's also an annual that can be sown at any time of the year.

Sprouts

Over the past decade or so there's been an incredible growth of interest, from nutritionists and gardeners alike, in microvegies or various sprouts. Incredibly easy to grow, especially for children, who are impatient gardeners, sprouts contain lots of antioxidants.

Cress and mustard seeds have always been harvested for their young leaves, but the value of sprouts wasn't appreciated until the advent of alfalfa. Principally grown as a garnish, back in the 1970s alfalfa used to be the only sprout available, but today we have bean, broccoli, mung, daikon, radish, snow peas and onion sprouts, just to name a few. They all begin life as seeds, and may be in the form of grain or dried legumes. Once they are soaked in water then drained, germination starts and their nutritional value rockets. Harvest them between two days and two weeks, depending on the variety.

How to grow sprouts

1 Buy certified edible seeds from a supermarket, health food shop or nursery. You can get them organically certified too.

2 Soak the seeds for 4–6 hours or overnight, then drain.

3 Place the seeds in a jar and cover with a fine gauze material such as a clean stocking or cheesecloth.

4 Leave in a cool spot.

5 Rinse with fresh water daily and drain.

Germinated seeds, or sprouts, are both easy to grow and great for you.

Crazy about cucurbits

The warm season vine crops, often referred to as cucurbits, are a fabulous addition to the summer vegetable garden. All of them require frost-free conditions, with seeds sown immediately after the last frost, or kept indoors until the weather is more dependable. To help flowers and fruits form, prepare the richest soil you can manage, keep the water up to plants and add a side dressing of blood and bone.

Melons

The sweet, delectable flavour of today's melons is a testament to plant breeding. Melons are, in fact, a relative of zucchinis, cucumbers, pumpkins and marrows, and have been turned into such delicious fruit through hundreds of years of selection and hybridisation. Like their relatives, they are vine crops, needing a fair bit of space to sprawl over the ground, or a strong trelliswork if you are training smaller melons vertically.

Two main parents, the rockmelon or cantaloupe (*Cucumis melo*) and the watermelon (*Citrullus lanatus*), are responsible for the wonderful colours and tastes of melons such as the honeydew melon and the champagne melon. A rockmelon is ready to pick when the stem pulls easily from the fruit, while a watermelon is ready when the side lying on the ground turns yellow and the fruit sounds hollow when you tap it.

Cucumbers

Cucumbers too have come a long way since they were first cultivated in south Asia over 3000 years ago. Now they are green, yellow, white, spotted or even 'horned'. The shapes vary even more—from round to globe-shaped, long and short, large and small—and the flavour has also changed from sweet to tangy to low acid; a quarter are even burpless.

The method of growing cucumbers has also changed: some new varieties are small bushes and don't require any support or trellising, unlike the old types. These more compact plants

ABOVE: *A mixture of marrows, zucchini and zucchini flowers, button squash and cucumbers.*

RIGHT: *The 'netted' skin of rockmelon makes it distinctive.*

Peanuts

Native to Peru and Brazil, this high-protein South American crop has become a staple in Africa and Asia where it is eaten as a nut and grown for its oil.

VITAL STATISTICS

Botanical name: *Arachis hypogaea*.

Family: Fabaceae.

Climate: Night temperature should be consistently more than 15°C, so grow from mid-spring to the end of summer in temperate climates, or throughout the year in warmer subtropical areas.

Culture: The flowers form pods in the ground, making an underground kernel.

Colours: Flowers are white.

Height: Grows to 30 cm and normally planted as a groundcover between taller crops such as corn.

Planting time: Sow seeds in spring after all cold snaps have finished.

Soil: Free draining. Being a legumous crop they will produce their own nitrogen and are often used as a living mulch.

Position: Full sun for half of the day is plenty and will help guard against heat stress. Shelter from prevailing winds and excess heat.

Planting depth and spacing: Plant the nuts directly into the soil 3 cm deep and 5 cm apart.

Fertiliser: None, though dig in the spent crop to enrich the soil.

Pests/diseases: None.

Harvest: When leaves begin to yellow, fork them out, washing them thoroughly to remove any soil.

Propagation: Fresh, unprocessed peanuts from a health food shop are fine to use.

Storage: Fresh, or roasted in a pan, or puréed and made into peanut butter.

Feature vegetable

have come about because plant breeders acknowledge that most of us have smaller gardens today.

Cucumbers are very easy to grow and there is still time in warm areas to grow one more crop before autumn comes around. Give them a try; you can harvest them early for pickling or let them grow fresh from the patch for summer salads. Remember, cucumbers are 96 per cent water so don't let your plants dry out.

Keep cucumbers well mulched and watered so that they bear well.

DID YOU KNOW? Alfalfa, or lucerne, is a perennial of the pea family. The word 'alfalfa' comes from the Arabic word al-fasfasah, meaning 'the best sort of fodder'; it used to be used as cattle feed. It contains amino acids, vitamins B1, B2, B3, B6, B12, D, E, F and K, plus calcium, iron, potassium, zinc, carotene, folic acid and phyotoestrogen.

Zucchini

Zucchini, or courgettes, are picked when immature, about 15 cm long, to encourage continuous cropping. They are quick and easy to grow, and their flowers, lightly battered then cooked in olive oil, are especially delicious, just make sure you pick out the stamen and stigma before cooking. Summer squash too are related, though these tend to be button-shaped and come in yellow or green.

Crop rotation

Crop rotation has been around for hundreds of years. Back then phases of the moon were taken into account and the whole process took on almost mystical qualities. Today there are two main reasons to undertake crop rotation for greater success with your vegetables. One is rotating for nutrients and the other is minimising pests.

In the garden vegetable patch it is very wise to plant with these relationship and cycles in mind.

To maximise your nutrient cycles, always plant legumes first. These will add nitrogen to the soil via their specialised roots that can extract atmospheric nitrogen. Once you harvest, ensure you dig their leaves through the soil as a green manure crop. Next, plant a leaf crop such as lettuce, which can make use of these nutrients. Follow these with a crop of fruiting plants such as tomatoes, zucchini or eggplants, and then plant a root crop such as turnips, beetroot or carrots, as these will benefit from the stripped soil. Next, go back to a legumous crop—either peas or beans would be a good choice.

To help minimise disease, also try to change up plant families successively in the same bed. Avoid planting vegies that are in the same family season after season in the same bed—do not, for example, plant tomatoes after potatoes or cabbage after broccoli.

It was Charles 'Turnip' Townsend who introduced the turnip to England from Europe in the early 1700s and advocated its use in crop rotation. The turnip is from a different family to the potato, the most popular root vegetable, so farmers could alternate their root vegetable crops and still practise crop rotation successfully. This basic rotation of crops stops any soil-borne insects and diseases, from remaining in the same garden bed year after year, and avoids the depletion of certain soil nutrients that results from planting similar vegetables in the same plot.

Zucchini flowers are delicious, but be sure to pick out the stamens from the centre before cooking.

LIVING STAKES Climbing beans are sometimes planted next to corn plants, which act as living stakes. The beans, with their nitrogen-fixing roots, feed the corn as they grow.

Treating mildew

In summer, many plants (especially cucurbits) get mildew. This organic treatment is easy.

1 Harvest a generous bunch of garlic chives from your vegetable garden, or buy some.

2 Roughly chop the garlic chives. Add the garlic chives to a watering-can.

3 Cover with boiling water and steep for at least an hour before using.

4 Pour over leaves. Mildew can also be treated using milk or preparations made with baking soda and oil.

Root crops such as carrots are the last plants in your nutrient cycle. Next season, the beans beside it will be planted here to enrich the soil with more nitrogen.

Autumn

Brisk walks. Long shadows across the lawn. Warm days, cool crisp nights. Crunchy leaves, clippings and compost. Golden hues. Harvest and finale.

Overview of the season

There is a sense of fulfilment and maturity in autumn that no other season evokes. Gone are the floral tributes of summer, and in their place we have plenty—ripening fruit, delicate seeds, the last of the season's flowers, bright berries and, loveliest of all, colouring leaves. To really make the most of this season, plant a selection of foliage, fruit and flowering plants. Deciduous trees, chrysanthemums, dahlias and the hot and spicy colours of tropical plants all combine to promote a feeling of warmth and harmony.

Harvest

Gathering berries, collecting seeds, storing nuts and squirrelling away treasures are all part of autumn. As the weather becomes colder, remove crops such as tomatoes, eggplants, squash and melons. Gorge on the last of their fruits, or bottle, dry or marinate them in oil for later use. Store hard-skinned pumpkins in a dry place, and dig up old potatoes. When at last your larder is full and the cupboards are bursting, autumn is drawing to a close.

Hard work

As far as the climate is concerned, autumn is one of the most pleasant times for gardening. This is fortunate, as there is much to do. Your secateurs get a real workout tidying many perennials, pruning shrubs and taking cuttings.

In early autumn, it's also a good idea to feed your plants with some general fertilisers, especially those containing a high level of phosphorus. This essential element encourages root growth and cell repair, which are both important at this time in the garden's cycle.

If you live in a frosty area, you need to prepare your plants for the cold by covering and protecting them.

Planting

Don't underestimate the benefits of autumn planting. Although most of us are tempted to buy plants when they're in flower over spring and summer, the cool night temperatures and warm autumn soils make this a better time for root growth, which means quicker establishment and fewer losses than at other times. By planting now, you will also have another nine months before the heat of summer arrives in which to establish your new plants.

Select deciduous shrubs and trees for coloured foliage during their autumn display to ensure that your plants will perform exactly as you'd hoped. You can also transplant existing specimens now to lessen the shock of the move (see page 327).

LEFT: *Autumn's bounty is rich: berries, late flowers like fuchsias, bulbs such as nerines, even pine cones—all form part of the garden's texture.*

Weatherwatch

Never work when the earth is sodden. Wait until it is damp and crumbly before planting out.

Bring your soil to life

With the frenzy of summertime growth in the garden it is easy to overlook your soil—after all, brown earth is not as appealing. Many gardeners put all their efforts into the above-ground parts of their garden, forgetting what is going on below soil level. Half of every plant lies hidden in the soil, feeding and supporting the leaf and flower growth above.

All really grim gardeners possess a keen sense of humus.

W. C. SELLAR AND R. J. YEATMAN

To cater for your whole plant, it is important to understand soil, compost, mulching, fertilising and the organisms that make it all happen. There are three main factors in improving the soil in your garden—humus or compost, fertilisers and mulch.

Composting

The breakdown and decay of animal and vegetable materials produces humus or compost. This organic content, which is essential for sustaining living plants, brings your soil to life. Without organic matter your soil is 'dead'.

The composting process is a complex one, employing myriad micro-organisms

Making a compost pile

1 Spread a 10 cm layer of leaves, kitchen waste or other vegetative matter over a square metre or so of bare earth—this is great for encouraging beneficial animals, such as earthworms, slaters and millipedes, into your pile.

2 Cover this with a layer of soil, then with a layer of animal manure. Repeat the layers as vegetative matter becomes available. You can use shredded prunings, leaves and grass clippings, and keep the pile topped with straw to shed rainwater.

3 Add a bucket of soil and a handful of blood and bone to encourage the rapid multiplication of soil bacteria and fungal decomposers. Lime helps to balance pH, as the other materials are very acid.

4 Once the pile is about 1 m high, spread 2 cm of soil on top and press it down to help keep the heat in and the rain out. Cover your heap with black plastic. To speed the composting process, turn the pile over with a spade every few weeks.

Build up your compost heap with alternate layers of wet and dry material. Wet material (such as grass clippings), which is high in nitrogen and low in carbon, helps to break down dry material, which is low in nitrogen and high in carbon. A compost heap works faster if some things are already broken down—that is, if the material already includes organisms. Lime helps to balance pH, as the other materials are very acid. As both blood and bone and chicken manure are high in nitrogen and contain living organisms, they help to break down other materials.

to bring about chemical changes in organic waste matter. These microscopic workers like plenty of air, heat and a little moisture in order to perform their composting duties; they also rely on a good carbon/nitrogen ratio. You can achieve this ratio in your compost heap by incorporating a balanced mix of dry (for example, leaf litter) and wet (kitchen scraps and grass) ingredients, as well as by regularly turning the mix.

Adding compost to the garden is a natural way of aiding water retention and maintaining a rich, quality soil. Compost is in effect nature's miracle tonic. Composting can convert bulky 'rubbish' into a fertiliser that is of great benefit to the soil. If you add organic matter to your soil in the form of compost on a regular basis, you can transform even a poor soil into a rich, friable organic loam that will be teeming with worms in no time. You can create a compost pile, or use a bin or tumbler.

The compost tumbler

Tumblers are possibly the quickest way to make compost. Manufacturers of compost tumblers claim the tumbling process takes just a fortnight to convert a load of fresh organic matter into rich, crumbly compost. You do not add

COMPOSTING TIPS

Don't add persistent bulbous weeds, such as onion weed or oxalis, to your compost.

Hasten the composting process by growing comfrey, nature's compost herb, near your pile. Add it between layers.

Composting worms, bought for compost heaps, are very effective in reducing organic waste such as lawn clippings and kitchen scraps into valuable garden nutrients. Compost worms will eat their way through kitchen scraps and garden waste, producing castings that can be used on the garden.

material day by day. Tumblers are designed to make the whole aeration process easier. There are different models and brands available, but the best ones spin on their long axis, like a raffle barrel, rather than end to end, which can be hard going when the tumbler is getting full and falls heavily from one side to another.

1 Completely fill the tumbler with four parts of fresh organic material to one part of dry.

2 Make sure the mixture is not too wet. If it is, add more dry material such as grass clippings.

3 Turn the tumbler 5–6 times each day to aerate the mixture so the heat builds through the centre.

SOIL TONIC
A tap at the bottom of the bokashi bucket can be used to drain off the liquid. When watered down, this makes fabulous fertiliser. The solid waste from the bokashi bucket also supplies your soil with nutrients.

The bokashi compost system

Bokashi is a composting system that breaks down organic matter by a fermentation that uses special micro-organisms (the bokashi 'mix'). Many people with small gardens, or no garden at all, use this method, which uses just one bucket or, better still, two.

First place a few handfuls of the bokashi mix—a combination of sawdust and bran that's infused with composting micro-organisms—in the bucket.

Place your daily kitchen waste on top, followed by another handful of the mix, and so on, until the bucket is full.

Put the bucket aside for 12–14 days and start working on your next one. When this one is full, bury the contents of the first bucket in a hole in the garden. Fill this bucket again in the same way while the other one ferments.

The benefits of worms

Worms are natural recyclers, converting vegetative matter into nutrient-rich worm castings. Once introduced, worms will multiply rapidly, greatly increasing the aeration of the soil as well as its nitrogen content. The 'earthworking' worm species has been shown to improve soil structure and fertility; these worms increase water penetration into the soil and reduce both water run-off and the subsequent loss of topsoil through erosion. Soils with increased earthworm activity display increased crop yields.

Worms are often accused of killing grass and of eating the roots of pot plants and vegetables. The truth is worms in the garden help to aerate the soil, improving drainage and soil structure. They consume organic waste materials and convert them into humus. That's what those small mounds of worm castings are on your lawn.

So worms don't damage grass or plant roots. Overusing fertilisers and insecticides discourages worms but, by adding organic matter, such as compost, you encourage these beneficial friends of the garden.

A worm farm

A typical worm farm comprises three different layers—the top layer of paper scraps and organic matter, a centre layer where worms nest, and a bottom layer of castings (worm poo). Add food scraps to the top layer and, as the worms consume them, keep adding more food. Note, however, that worms do not like banana, citrus, onion or garlic. You can keep adding layers and the worms will migrate to the new layer and begin the process again. As chambers fill with waste, empty them into the garden or into pots. Start your worm farm with about 500 worms; after a year it should have about 30,000.

If you occasionally pour water into the farm, it will filter through the worm castings into the bottom layer. Just collect the liquid waste via a tap and use it diluted 1:10 with water as a fertiliser.

The actual worm farm can be anything from a proprietary system of bins to a stack of polystyrene boxes, even a wheelie bin that has had drainage holes drilled into it. Place the worms in a bedding layer of cocopeat or humus, top it with scraps and cover it with a layer of wet newspaper or plastic. Keep it in the shade and, hey presto, you have a farm.

LEFT: *This rectangular box system can keep quite a few worms in business making your waste into valuable fertiliser.*

PHOSPHATE-FREE DETERGENT Choose phosphate-free laundry, kitchen and cleaning products and, if they are 'eco-friendly', consider using grey water on your citrus trees for top-up waterings.

Adding worms

1 Place a base layer of moistened cocopeat or peat moss into the bin.

2 Add the worms, together wiith finely chopped vegetable scraps.

3 Cover with wet newspaper or moistened cardboard to keep the worms moist. Place a bucket beneath the farm's tap to collect nutrient-rich 'worm wee'.

1 Blood and bone
2 Milled cow manure
3 Slow-release fertiliser
4 Complete plant food
5 Soluble fertiliser
6 Pelletised chicken manure

Fertilisers

The 'organic' approach—compost—is always best, as nature intended it that way. But if, for some reason, you either can't use compost or prefer not to, you need to consider the implications of using fertilising products. For example, phosphorus, one of the essential elements required by many crops, is in short supply worldwide, and many people think we will reach 'peak phosphorus', causing agricultural meltdown, before we reach 'peak oil'.

Occurring naturally in bird and bat manure and mined from caves and atolls, phosphorus is a very finite resource. As it is highly soluble, it can be easily washed away into streams and other waterways, contributing to their pollution, so applying it as a more stable, slow-release pelletised product may well be a better 'environmental' strategy.

Fertiliser types

Fertilisers can be separated into natural or organic fertilisers, such as seaweed extract and various animal manures, and artificial combinations or chemical fertilisers. Each type offers benefits, but they are of different kinds. Organic fertilisers encourage soil organisms and lead to soils with a better structure. Chemical fertilisers can be fast-acting and balanced, and many are designed to cater for the specific needs of certain plants, such as ferns, natives, flowers, roses, citrus and fruit trees. They have no effect on soil structure.

Fertilisers are classified according to their component ratio of nitrogen, potassium and phosphorus, known as the NPK ratio. These are particularly important elements, as they are not only needed for basic plant growth and function but are also used in relatively large quantities. Like phosphorus, nitrogen and potassium are highly soluble, so if you apply excess fertiliser, it washes straight into waterways and eventually causes algal growth. It is particularly important to remember this when you are feeding your lawn.

LIQUID FERTILISER Make your own liquid fertiliser from blood and bone, chicken manure pellets or seaweed. Steep any of the above in hot water, allowing it to sit for a few weeks, then use a cup of the liquid in about 10 L (a watering can) of water.

HANDY FEEDING HINTS

Always fertilise when the soil is moist, and water thoroughly after you have completed the application.

If in doubt, apply fertiliser at half-strength twice as often.

Plants don't need much food in winter, so don't bother feeding them then. Spring, summer and autumn feeds are better value.

Nitrogen is responsible for leaf growth, but too much nitrogen can cause floppy growth and poor flowers.

Phosphorus, vital for strong roots and stems, is generally in low supply in Australian soils. Light doses bring some benefits, but apply it to Australian native plants in the Proteaceae family with caution, as you can poison these plants if the level of phosphorus is too concentrated.

Potassium maintains the rigidity of plants and is important for promoting flowering.

1 Coarse woodchip

2 Fine woodchip

3 Woodchip
 (stained redwood)

4 Leaf litter

5 Pine bark

6 Finely chipped
 cypress pine

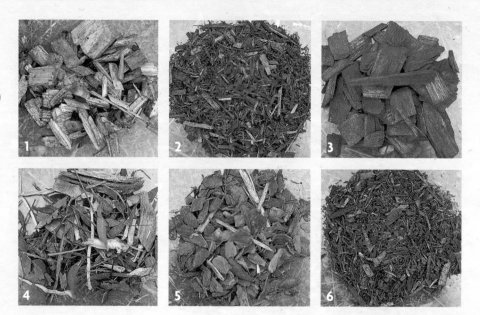

Mulch

Mulch provides a blanket layer over your soil. Normally about 10 cm thick, mulch has three main benefits. It:

- regulates soil temperature, by keeping roots cool in summer and warm in winter;

- conserves moisture and cuts down on watering requirements by reducing evaporation from the soil surface and increasing water penetration; and

- controls weeds by preventing weed seeds from germinating.

Mulches are available in many forms, both organic and inorganic. Organic mulches include leaf mulch, pine bark, red gum chips, newspaper, compost, lucerne, straw, rice husks and sugar cane. An effective mulch should not be dislodged by wind and rain, and should have a loose enough structure to allow water to soak through easily.

Some mulches—for example, lucerne, compost and sugar cane—have a high nitrogen content. These mulches improve the soil fertility, but they rot down quickly and need to be replaced every few months. Finely chipped cypress pine, which repels termites, makes a particularly good mulch in termite-prone areas.

Inorganic mulches—such as black plastic, weed control mat, scoria and decorative gravels—are not really 'garden-friendly': they add nothing to the soil structure and, once these mulches are in place, it's difficult to

PEBBLE MULCH

If you want to use pebbles for decorative effect, it's best to use them as toppings on pots or along garden bed edges, where they can be seen and admired without getting in the way of maintenance.

USING A WEED MAT TO SUPPRESS WEEDS

Weed mat is a woven fabric made up of plastic strands. Unlike plain sheets of black plastic, it still allows water to penetrate to the soil below. As an alternative, you could use layers of old carpet or newspaper to help suppress weeds. Newspaper and carpets (made from natural fibres) will break down over a period of time, but by then you will have the weeds under control. There are also manufactured versions of paper-filled weed control mats, which are perfect to use in the vegetable garden where an 'organic' approach is preferable.

incorporate soil additives. They tend to raise the soil temperature, and some can even stop your soil from breathing, which can lead to serious problems.

Depending on the time of year at which you mulch, you can influence soil temperatures. For example, if you add mulch towards the end of autumn, you will keep the soil warmer for longer; conversely, adding mulch in early spring will keep the soil cooler and prevent heat being trapped in summer.

Soil pH

Gardening books often speak of the pH range. The pH is a measure of acidity and alkalinity, based on a scale of 1 to 14, with 1 being extremely acid and 14 being extremely alkaline. Test your soil to see if your plants are compatible with its pH level. Most native plants, as well as proteas, citrus, gardenias, azaleas, rhododendrons, blue-flowering hydrangeas, camellias and many herbs require a range of 4.5 to 5.5 (acid). Most garden plants—including roses, bedding plants, annuals, mints, grasses and ferns—prefer slightly acid to neutral soils.

Nearly all members of the pea family (wisteria, peas, beans, sweet peas and clovers), iris, lilac, pink-flowering hydrangeas and many rockery plants and herbs prefer alkaline soils with a pH range of 6.5 to 7.5.

Foliar feeding works regardless of soil pH, and is handy in some cases. Use diluted liquid fertiliser over the leaves so they can absorb nutrients directly.

Make your own pH test kit using red cabbage

Red cabbage contains a pigment called anthocyanin that changes colour depending on the pH. You can take advantage of this property to make your own pH test kit (see instructions below). Your home-made kit comprises a number of paper strips. To test the soil, first take a soil sample and add water to it, then soak one of the strips in the watery sample. The strip will turn a colour: very acidic soils will turn the strip red, neutral will be purple, while alkaline soils will turn the paper greenish yellow.

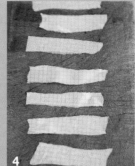

1 Chop about two cups of red cabbage and add to a kitchen blender.

2 Add enough boiling water to the blender to cover the cabbage. Pulse the blender for a few minutes to release the cabbage's colour into the liquid.

3 Strain the coloured liquid into a bowl. This liquid is at about pH 7. Soak strips of filtered paper in the liquid. (Coffee filter paper works well for this.)

4 Allow the paper strips to dry, then store them in an airtight container until you are ready to test your soil. When using them, compare the colour to the table below. For example, if a strip turns red, your soil has a pH of 2. If it turns blue, your soil has a pH of 8.

Red cabbage pH indicator colours

pH	Colour		pH	Colour	
2		Red	8		Blue
4		Purple	10		Blue-green
6		Violet	12		Greenish yellow

Checklist
Jobs to do now
Annuals, perennials and bulbs

🍂 Prune any diseased or twiggy growth from perennials, such as pelargoniums, cannas and salvias.

🍂 Prepare your garden beds for sowing sweet peas in early autumn. Acid soils need a dressing of lime or dolomite, and plenty of well-rotted manure. Dig this in now so it can settle before planting.

🍂 Remove old annuals and think about some of the new releases for autumn.

🍂 Allow your dahlias to die down naturally—don't cut them back, just trim off old flowers.

🍂 Feed chrysanthemums regularly with liquid fertiliser, and disbud them for extra large blooms.

🍂 Don't prune spent perennials if they are self-seeders you want to encourage; others can be removed.

🍂 Feed zygocactus (winter cactus) with phosphorus-based, low-nitrogen fertiliser. This will encourage more flowers and better quality blooms.

🍂 Take off any older, tattered leaves from your gerberas and divide them if required. Watch for tiny green scale on the underside of the foliage; treat this with an oil spray.

🍂 Move cymbidium orchids out into more sun now that it isn't as strong.

🍂 Enjoy the last days of perennials— such as Shasta daisies, stokesia, Easter daisies and perennial phlox—but be ready to pick the last bunches for the house before dividing and replanting the others. Artemisia, delphiniums, perennial phlox, anemone, canna, agapanthus, campanula and rudbeckia are just some of the many perennials that can be lifted now.

🍂 Prepare your garden beds by digging in lots of organic material in readiness for planting spring bulbs.

🍂 Tidy bearded iris and make way for new growth by cutting it back. The more sun the rhizomes get, the more flowers you'll have.

🍂 Lift any gladiolus while they still have some leaves and allow them to dry off. After the stems have completely withered, dust them in derris and store them in plastic bags.

🍂 Water windflowers to prolong their season.

🍂 Separate liliums.

🍂 If you are growing tulips, hyacinths and Dutch iris, don't forget to put them in the crisper bin in the fridge in early autumn and leave them there till late autumn when the temperature of the soil has dropped.

Grasses, groundcovers and climbers

🍂 Autumn feeding will rejuvenate the lawn and green it up in time for winter. Rake up fallen leaves. Edge your lawn and define garden beds.

🍂 Check for the presence of lawn grub or army worm. Dead patches

Cut flower stems that have 'done their dash' back to the ground.

Rake up fallen leaves from your lawn to allow the grass to 'breathe'.

Tidy dahlia beds by trimming off the old flowers.

or a line of damage on the lawn could be signs of pest attack.

◆ Cut flower heads from ornamental grasses if self-seeding is a problem.

◆ Dead-head summer-flowering groundcovers—such as gazania, brachyscome and pigface—to encourage flowering before winter.

◆ Divide and replant groundcovers.

◆ Trim vigorous climbers, such as jasmine and potato vine, which tend to get out of control.

Shrubs and trees

◆ Give mature hedges a trim. This will save doing them again in spring, a great timesaver for the lazy gardener.

◆ Cut back anything that has just finished a flush of flowers. The only exceptions would be cold-sensitive or tropical plants, especially if you live in a marginal area.

◆ Mulch azaleas, camellias and daphne with decomposed cow manure.

◆ Feed camellias and azaleas, applying granular fertiliser at the recommended rate onto moist soil, then water in well. This should be completed by early autumn. Subsequent liquid feeds will encourage strong plants.

◆ Start thinking about transplanting and remodelling your established shrubs. Autumn is a great time for moving plants about, as the air temperatures have cooled sufficiently to ease 'sunburn', but soil temperatures still encourage root growth.

◆ Trim long canes on philadelphus, abelia and weigela.

◆ Prune any diseased or twiggy growth from abelia, hydrangea, buddleia, hypericum and any other summer-flowering shrubs.

◆ Buddleia looks beautiful at this time of year. The flowers attract butterflies and come in lots of colours—pink, white, purple, near black, yellow and white. Water buddleias when they are in bloom to help make the flowers last.

Herbs, fruit and vegetables

◆ Lift and divide horseradish and comfrey.

◆ To control thrips, dust derris or diatomaceous earth on your vegies.

◆ Watch out for caterpillars, citrus leaf miner, slugs and snails as well as pear and cherry slug.

◆ Fungal diseases are all prolific at the moment, so be vigilant.

◆ Check ripening grapes. Cover fruit with netting if birds are a problem.

◆ Prepare strawberry beds by adding blood and bone.

◆ Remove mummified stone fruit clinging onto fruit trees, as they carry brown rot.

◆ Cut back asparagus and mulch the bed with pulverised poultry manure.

◆ Harvest remaining herbs and cold-hardy greens.

Remove twiggy or diseased side shoots and understock from grafted trees.

Use the clippers to trim back any overgrown hedges.

Cold-hardy greens such as sorrel can be harvested, outside leaves first.

Plant now
Annuals, perennials and bulbs

🌰 Plant out linaria, pansies, violas, stock, poppies, nemesia, schizanthus, polyanthus and sweet pea seedlings.

🌰 Plant out cyclamen seedlings, or raise them from seed.

🌰 It's time to sow cinerarias, which are the most glorious winter annuals for semi-shaded positions, and godetias, which resemble jewel-coloured poppies.

🌰 Don't forget to consider some of the taller annuals. Foxgloves, yarrows, Canterbury bells, delphiniums, penstemons and larkspurs are all great for cutting, although they take longer to come into flower because of their height.

🌰 Look out for summer-flowering bulbs. Liliums and similar bulbs are now just starting to come into nurseries. It's not too late to plant bulbs, and many nurseries will have them at reduced prices at this time of the year, so you could get some bargains. Hunt around.

🌰 Try planting some autumn crocus between the gaps in crazy paving.

Grasses, groundcovers and climbers

🌰 Oversow cool-season grasses in lawns.

🌰 Plant groundcovers such as ajuga, nepeta, stachys and santolina.

🌰 Choose deciduous vines when in leaf colour.

Shrubs and trees

🌰 Plant camellias, deciduous plants and transplanted specimens.

🌰 You will start to see roses appear in nurseries, so order some from your local garden centre. At this time of year you can order roses that are bare-rooted, or wrapped in bags. It is not essential to buy roses like this (potted roses can be bought at any time of the year), but it does give them an excellent start, and it's also much cheaper.

🌰 Autumn is the best time of year to plant any native trees, conifers and shrubs.

Herbs, fruit and vegetables

🌰 Plant chives, cress and mustard from seed.

🌰 It's a great time for new citrus trees—imagine all those fresh oranges and tangelos ripening in your garden.

🌰 Plant rhubarb crowns into deep, well-drained soil. Incorporate large quantities of cow manure, and choose sturdy crowns with thick stalks.

🌰 May is the ideal month for sowing anything in the onion family. Seedlings transplant easily when they are 10 cm high, and should be spaced every 7 cm.

🌰 Sow root vegies such as beets, carrots, turnips, swedes and Jerusalem artichokes; leafy greens such as spinach, silverbeet and rocket; the Brassica family, which includes cabbage, broccoli and cauliflower; and peas and broad beans.

🌰 Cut up sprouted potato 'chits' and plant them in garden beds free of lime. Use a fresh garden bed—crop rotation will reduce the chances of disease.

🌰 Plant celery and wrap it with black plastic or cardboard to create that 'blanched' stem look.

🌰 Grow Chinese cabbages so they'll mature while temperatures are moderate, otherwise they'll bolt to seed.

Blanch celery using cardboard or plastic to exclude sunlight.

Cut sprouted potato 'chits' into pieces; each should have an eye.

CLOCKWISE FROM TOP LEFT: *Variegated liriope looks good year-round and sends up lilac flowers in autumn; fuchsias flower for many months; buddleias attract butterflies; Camellia sasanqua 'Setsugekka'; Thai basil; cosmos; purple-leafed fountain grass; white plume flower (Justicia sp.).*

Flowering now

Annuals, perennials and bulbs

🌷 Annuals such as salvia, amaranthus, China asters, snapdragons, Californian poppies, celosia, globe amaranth, candytuft, French marigold, verbena, nasturtium, mallow, sweet Alice, zinnia, floss flower and joe pye weed.

🌷 Perennials such as bedding and tree dahlias, gerberas, daisies (including Michaelmas daisies), gaillardias, salvias, coneflowers, Stokes' aster, coreopsis, obedient plant, statice, chrysanthemums, windflower, phlox, convolvulus, carnation, monkshood, *Aster* sp., larkspur, helichrysum, helianthus, geraniums and penstemon.

🌷 For bulbs try nerines, clivias, belladonna lily, autumn crocus (*Zephyranthes candida*) and saffron crocus (*Crocus sativus*).

Grasses, groundcovers and climbers

🌷 Grasses such as zebra grass, liriope, silver spike grass, pampas grass and fountain grass.

🌷 Groundcovers such as ivy geraniums, Swedish ivy, campanula, pinks and alpine phlox.

🌷 Climbing plants such as allamanda, Rangoon creeper, Azores jasmine, coral vine (antigonon), dipladenias and Chilean jasmine (mandevilla), bleeding heart vine and Carolina jasmine.

Shrubs and trees

🌷 Shrubs such as geraniums, fuchsias, camellias, oleanders, buddleias, hibiscus, bouvardia, luculia, Chinese bellflower, osmanthus, justicia, calliandra, ceratostigma, ixora, plumbago, abelia and roses.

🌷 Trees such as tibouchina, firewheel tree, red-flowering gum and African tulip tree.

Herbs, fruit and vegetables

🌷 Basil, bergamot, *Plectranthus caninus*, ginger, pineapple sage, oregano, rosemary and coriander.

🌷 The remaining flowers on pumpkins and zucchinis can be eaten as there is not enough time for them to develop into fruits.

Annuals, perennials and bulbs

No need to lie low just because the weather is cooling. Imaginative planting will brighten any grey day with its own sunshine.

Annuals

Autumn can be a difficult time for annuals, as many of them die, or at least start shutting down in preparation for cold weather. Make use of long-lasting summer annuals such as dwarf and tall snapdragons, amaranthus, salvia and begonias, which have more than one flush of flowers. Don't be too quick to pull out alyssum and lobelia either, as you can grow these all year round.

The marigold that goes to bed with the sun. And with him rises weeping.

WILLIAM SHAKESPEARE

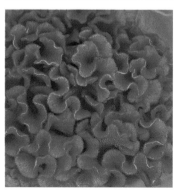

The hot bed

Although it's a quiet time for most flowers, there are still some that can warm up your garden in shades of red, tangerine and gold. Sparks seem to fly when reds, oranges and yellows are concentrated together. Their vitality and strength can cheer you up and brighten the greyest of autumn days!

Each flower has its own charm. Children love snapdragons because the flowers will snap open and shut when squeezed at the sides. Asters are still blooming, and make wonderful cut flowers, while zinnias self-seed, coming up the following spring and flowering in profusion from summer onwards.

Not so pleasant smelling but just as showy are marigolds. They come in cheerful colours, both singles and doubles, and establish easily, often flowering right into winter. Tansy, like

ABOVE LEFT: *Mountain marigold* (Tagetes lemmonii) *foliage smells like passionfruit.*

CLOCKWISE FROM TOP LEFT: *The feathery plumes of celosia; colourful Joseph's coat; the crested head of cockscomb; and the bright purple buttons of purple globe amaranth.*

marigolds, another useful organic insecticide, has charming golden button flowers into autumn and soft, fragrant fern-like foliage in fresh leaf green or golden yellow.

Technicolour dream

If zany colour and wild foliage appeal to you, try one or more of the members of the amaranth family, including purple globe amaranth (*Gomphrena globosa*), Joseph's coat (*Amaranthus tricolor*), celosias, cockscomb (*Celosia cristata* var. *childsii*), love-lies-bleeding (*Amaranthus caudatus*) and the Australian wildflower, mulla mulla (*Ptilotus* sp.).

Some amaranths have the most stunning variegations, such as those on Joseph's coat, with its large decorative leaves in shades of red, bronze, yellow and green. Others have quite remarkable flowers, such as the long, tassel-like purplish red blooms of love-lies-bleeding, known as grain amaranth in the Andes, where it is used as a leaf green and source of protein.

The purple globe amaranth, also called 'Little Buddy', and the native silver and pink mulla mulla (also called pussy tails) are not dissimilar, with the latter being distributed over all arid areas of mainland Australia.

The celosias are also chameleons. Some have soft, feathery plume-like flowers in pink, amber, lemon and carmine, while the crested variety has glowing crimson, red, orange and yellow clusters of tiny flowers.

All members of the amaranth family thrive in a sunny spot in just about any type of soil. They are also extremely tolerant of dry conditions, and dislike being overwatered. See also pages 264–5.

Zany highlights

To add to the kaleidoscope of colour created by these flowers, why not add a splash of foliage magic too? *Coleus* 'Kiwi Fern' and *Solenostemon scutellarioides* 'Frogs Foot' have beautiful yellow and green or red and green leaves, depending on the form; the deeply toothed margins of these plants add the wow factor. Suitable for sun or shade, they can be easily grown from cuttings, creating a border or repetition with plenty of impact at a reasonable cost. They tend to be treated as annuals but can in fact overwinter in frost-free areas.

Other foliage plants include *Iresine herbstii*, great for fast hedges to 1 m, borders and, of course, foliage contrast. The most commonly available cultivar is 'Wallisii', a dwarf, purple/black-leafed form, but another interesting type is 'Aureo-reticulata', with green and red leaves and yellow veins. Frost kills them, but they can overwinter in warmer areas.

CLOCKWISE FROM LEFT: *Its cerise and beetroot markings make iresine a sought-after foliage plant; coleus, such as this purple-centred type, are great for colouring up shady areas; mulla mulla flowers en masse in early spring and makes a stunning meadow or wildflower display in a sunny, well-drained spot.*

264

Celosia and amaranthus

1 *Amaranthus hypochondriacus* 'Green Thumb' **2** *Celosia cristata* 'Orange' **3** *Gomphrena globosa*
4 *C. spicata* 'Orange' **5** *C. cristata* 'Carmine' **6** *C. cristata* 'Nana Jessica Yellow' **7** *C. cristata* 'Orange'

8 *C. cristata*   9 *A. caudatus*   10 *A. hybridus* 'Opopeo'   11 *C. cristata* 'Pink'

ABOVE: *Violas tend to pop up where and when they like.*

RIGHT: *Honesty, which is grown for its attractive seed heads as well as its flowers, also pops up by itself.*

Flowers for spring

Now the weather has cooled, it's time to plant flowers that bloom in spring. In sunny spots you can plant virtually anything. Probably best are pansies and violas, which grow into carpets of colour. They are good value, as they last from autumn to early summer.

In shade or semi-shade, plant cinerarias, primulas and honesty. Primulas are good for those difficult spots under trees and come in shades of pink and white. They will grow in full sun but need plenty of moisture.

Many annuals can be grown as cutting flowers. It's nice to have a special bed in full sunshine for this purpose. Plant perfumed stocks, which come in such lovely colours as deep rose, clotted cream, a soft terracotta and a deep

Zinnia

Zinnias are the happiest, most joyful flowers to add to the garden. They give many months of blooms, which have the added bonus of making great cut flowers.

VITAL STATISTICS

Scientific name: *Zinnia* x *hybrid*.
Family: Asteraceae.
Climate: Temperate and warm. It doesn't like cold conditions or sudden drops in temperature.
Uses: Great for cut flowers, cottage gardens, borders, especially dwarf types.
Colours: Double or single types in many warm shades such as red, pink, orange, yellow and buttery white.
Height: Grows up to 1.5 m.
Planting time: Plant in spring after all chance of frosts has passed, for summer and autumn blooms.
Soil: Moist, well-drained soil with added organic matter and mulch.
Position: Full sun.
Planting spacing: Plant about 30 cm apart.
Fertiliser: Use a liquid fertiliser.
Harvest: They take eight weeks to bloom.
Propagation: Raise in punnets of seed-raising mix or sow direct into the bed.

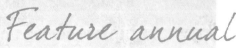

Feature annual

mulberry. Stocks last well in a vase if you change the water regularly.

Poppy flowers add brilliant splashes of colour to the garden in spring, and look stunning grown as a mass planting or among perennials. They are also excellent as cut flowers. With their delicate, silken, crepe-like blooms held high on slender, downy stalks that sway in the breeze, Iceland poppies (*Papaver nudicaule*) are the most popular. The Gallipoli or Flanders poppy (*P. rhoeas*) has a single tissue-paper-thin scarlet flower with a black blotch. It grows wild in the fields of Flanders and has become a symbol of the lives lost in the First World War. Such apparent fragility masks the true nature of these brilliant survivors, some species of which grow wild in the fields of Europe, Asia and North Africa. The Shirley poppy is another cultivar of *P. rhoeas*, but it has pink or white flowers. The dried latex of the opium poppy (*P. somniferum*) is made into the narcotic opium; its seed is used to flavour curries or decorate cakes and bread.

At the back of the bed try the giant larkspur, with its stately flower spikes that reach up to more than a metre, and of course, the ever-popular sweet pea grown on trelliswork.

RIGHT: *Shirley poppies, cultivars of the Flanders poppy, self-seed in the garden, coming up of their own accord where they are happiest. They make excellent cut flowers, and do best in cooler climates.*

SPOT FLOWERING

Although autumn can be a quiet time in terms of flower colour, there are plenty of plants that 'spot' flower. That simply means that they have a smaller show, in addition to their main flowering flush, as an autumn bonus. Great value plants such as these include azaleas, campanula, rhododendrons, Carolina jasmine, Brazilian plume flower (*Justicia carnea*) and bottlebrush (shown, and see also page 318), which has a major second showing in autumn after its spring splendour.

PERENNIAL PEA

The sweet pea family contains many other species, but the annual one is the most popular. The perennial pea (*Lathyrus grandiflorus*) is a semi-climbing perennial suited to temperate climates, perfect for covering an old stump. It has rosy red flowers in seemingly endless supply in spring and summer. Cut it right down in autumn. Another species, also known as the perennial or everlasting pea, is *L. latifolius*. This herbaceous perennial climber bears attractive mauve and pink flowers and is evergreen when grown in temperate climates.

Fragrant and ideal for cut flowers, sweet peas bloom for months, and the more you pick, the more you get.

Sweet peas

In Australia, St Patrick's Day is traditionally the time for sowing sweet pea seeds. Sweet peas (*Lathyrus odoratus*) need plenty of sunshine and a tall, sturdy trellis in order to grow well (although you can grow dwarf varieties in pots). A wall of these sweet-smelling blooms will provide you with cut flowers for up to six weeks in spring.

A fence in full sun is perfect. Just attach some chicken wire to support the climbing tendrils. To prepare the soil, add some well-rotted animal manure or compost and cultivate deeply. Apply a liberal dressing of complete fertiliser (about half a cup per square metre) and a handful of lime per square metre (unless your soil is alkaline). Lightly cultivate this fertiliser into the top 15 cm of soil and water well.

Allow a week for the soil to settle before sowing your sweet pea seeds. Failure to germinate is usually due to overwatering or rainy conditions. Once the seeds are sown, just damp down the soil. Do not water them again until the seedlings appear. Always plant two seeds in each hole, just to be sure, or as the Irish say, 'to be sure, to be sure'.

THE PAPILIONACEAE FAMILY

Many genera belong to this interesting family—wattles (subfamily Mimosoideae), sweet peas (subfamily Faboideae) and bauhinias (subfamily Caesalpinioideae).

What makes this family so interesting are the roots. All members have roots with nitrogen-fixing nodules, which take nitrogen from the soil and convert it into an available form for the plants to use as food.

As a result of this adaptation, many members of this family are used as green manures or nutritious mulches. Lupins, peanuts, lucerne pea manure and clover all fall into this category.

The peanut (*Arachis hypogaea*) is a frost-tender annual that grows as a groundcovering legume, improving the soil by fixing nitrogen from the air.

Bamboo trellis

If you don't have a sunny wall, you can create your own support for sweet peas, making light bamboo trelliswork. Choose a sunny spot in the garden. The more sun sweet peas get, the more they flower, so all day is best. Pinch sweet peas as they reach about 15 cm high to create three or four laterals that can be trained upwards. Frequent picking of blooms encourages flowering.

1 First, assemble the materials you'll need: 10 × 1.5 m bamboo stakes, lime, twine, potting mix, two terracotta pots, secateurs and sweet pea seedlings.

2 Insert the first bamboo stake at an angle of about 60 degrees, making sure that the stake is firmly embedded in the ground. Insert four more stakes parallel to the first, about 20 cm apart.

3 Push in the other five stakes, this time working at the same angle but in the opposite direction. This should form a diamond-shaped lattice.

4 Secure each junction neatly with twine, cutting off any loose ends.

5 Place two pots, each filled with potting mix and a handful of lime, in front of the trellis, then plant the sweet pea seedlings. As the seedlings grow, feed them weekly with diluted liquid fertiliser.

Perennials

Although it is a quiet season for flowers, there are some perennials you can weave through your garden beds for autumn colour. Most popular of all are the chrysanthemums, with their array of scarlet, gold, bronze, dusky pink and white flowers, but there are also other, more unusual gems.

ABOVE: *This lovely border flowers through spring, summer and late into autumn, thanks to the chrysanthemums, euphorbias, salvias and ornamental grasses.*

RIGHT: *Gaillardia will give many months of blooms and provide fuss-free colour for years.*

Everything's coming up daisies

Create a daisy theme with Easter daisies, gaillardia and coreopsis. For shady areas, plant swathes of Japanese windflowers and enjoy their long stems dancing in the breeze.

Coneflowers

The 'Marmalade' or 'Gloriosa' daisy (*Rudbeckia hirta*) makes a vivid summer and autumn display. Great for cutting, this showy annual has gold discs with a mahogany centre. Closely related is black-eyed Susan (*R. fulgida*), which is also known as orange coneflower. This species is wonderful for mass planting

ABOVE: 'Sunny-side-up': a windflower in close-up.

LEFT: En masse, windflowers gently sway in the breeze, as their name suggests.

in wide drifts, as if your garden were an enormous flowering meadow.

The other 'coneflower' is *Echinacea purpurea*, or purple coneflower. Native to the great prairies of North America, the medicinal echinacea is said to increase the body's resistance to infection. It displays handsome plum-coloured blooms that feature a black eye, very similar to those on rudbeckias, but also comes in pink, white, yellow, orange and double forms. Echinaceas start blooming in summer and continue to early autumn, and when the flowers finish you don't need to dead-head them as they have decorative seed heads that look stunning right into winter.

Windflowers

One of the prettiest perennials in the autumn garden is the Japanese windflower (*Anemone × hybrida*). It bears dainty white or pink flowers—in double, semi-double and single forms—over many weeks. Their long stems make them ideal as cut flowers, and give rise to their common name 'windflower', because they gently wave in the breeze.

The foliage is present for most of the year, and the plant forms a clump that spreads widely from fleshy rhizomes that you can easily divide and propagate on. The leaves are broad and handsome, so the foliage is a feature in its own right.

The great thing about windflowers is their adaptability. Related to buttercups, and just as easily grown, they grow in full sun to semi-shade, and need little or no attention. Just dig in a little leaf mould and they're ready to go.

If you haven't tried windflowers, you are missing out on one of the easiest and most rewarding of shade growers. They are an invaluable addition to gardens, blooming into early winter when little else does.

WINDFLOWER CARE Keep your windflowers looking great with extra watering during flowering, and by regularly dead-heading spent blooms. Watch out for leaf nematode. This microscopic worm-like pest damages leaves, leaving a spilt-ink-like effect. Affected plants are best destroyed. Mulch well to stop water splashing from plant to plant and spreading the problem.

RIGHT: *Goldenrod can fill up boggy spots in the garden with great vigour.*

FAR RIGHT: *This pink form of Stokes' aster will give many years' joy in the garden and many days in a vase.*

The early days of autumn bring with them the best bloom of the Michaelmas Daisies, the many beautiful garden kinds of the perennial Asters... and in glad spring-like profusion, when all else is on the verge of death and decay, gives an impression of satisfying refreshment that is hardly to be equalled throughout the year.

GERTRUDE JEKYLL

Asters and their relatives

The blooms of many perennial daisies look their best in autumn. Easter daisies, also known as Michaelmas daisies (*Aster* sp.), are rewarding and easy to grow in a sunny position. Just water them in dry weather, stake tall flower stems, cut back the clump to the base after flowering and divide in spring. The colours range from purple and red to pink and white; there is even a black foliage species called 'Lady in Black', which has star-like white flowers with purple–black leaves.

If you love cornflowers you'll adore Stokes' aster (*Stokesia laevis*), the summer version, which also flowers into autumn. If you dead-head the flowers regularly, this plant will flower for months. The lavender–blue, white, rose pink and lilac flowers last well in a vase.

Goldenrod (*Solidago* sp.), a yellow aster cross, produces tiny daisy-like yellow flowers and grows easily in full sun or part shade. Some species can be too vigorous, so select specially bred garden types.

The kingfisher daisy or blue marguerite (*Felicia amelloides*) and Swan River daisy (*Brachyscome multifida*) are both superb in spring, but their autumn display is also a worthy addition to the garden border. With its sky-blue flowers with yellow centres and long-flowering period, from late spring to autumn, the kingfisher daisy is a great standby in the garden. The Swan River daisy is a long-flowering Australian native groundcover, its spreading habit making it great for rockeries or hanging baskets. The delicate daisy-like flowers are mauve-pink among pale green, deeply cut, lacy foliage. Renew it every few years, as it is not long-lived. Both plants benefit from regular trims after each flush of flowers.

ABOVE AND LEFT:
*These Easter daisies
are among the
greatest of all
autumn flowers.
They come in small,
dainty blooms, as
well as larger
doubles. All are
prolific and make
great cut flowers.*

A spidery-petalled chrysanthemum. The range of flower shapes, colours and styles is vast.

Chrysanthemums

Chrysanthemums are traditional Mother's Day flowers in the southern hemisphere. The Japanese improved them over thousands of years, and the chrysanthemum is their national flower as well as the flower of the Imperial Royal Family. These popular and showy perennials are still being hybridised and crossed, which makes it almost impossible to track down their origins.

Short day lengths trigger flowering and can be manipulated with blackout curtains in glasshouses to produce year-round blooms.

CHRYSANTHEMUMS: GROWING TIPS

- Provide chrysanthemums with rich, well-drained soil.
- Grow them from seed sown in spring or from soft-tip cuttings.
- Stake the taller varieties.
- Prune your plants after flowering to produce a second flush.
- For indoor display, try potted chrysanthemums, which are more compact than the old garden varieties.
- Feed them with liquid fertiliser in autumn and remove excess buds for larger blooms.
- Watch for black aphids that cluster around the buds, as these will spoil the flower display if you don't control them.
- If you spot dying leaves, you may have leaf nematode. Spray with a systemic poison as soon as you notice the damage and identify the pest.

Dahlias

The longest-flowering perennials for the warm-season garden are bright and blowsy dahlias, flowering from mid-summer to the end of autumn. There are many different flower shapes and sizes—some are like cactus, some have simple single petals and others are spidery. Some strike as cut blooms, others as bedding plants for foliage contrast.

Magnificent purple–black foliage types include 'Redskin'; 'Bishop of Llandaff', with its electric red single and semi-double flowers; 'Le Coco', a yellow single with a red central disc; and 'Yellow Hammer', with soft buttercup yellow flowers that turn peachy orange in the hot summer sun.

LEFT: *Dahlias are not only many and varied in form and colour but also excellent as cut flowers, lasting a week in a vase and free-flowering in the garden for many months. The yellow and red bicolour form is called 'Le Coco'.*

DID YOU KNOW? Dahlias were originally imported into Europe as a food source because the tubers, like potatoes, are edible.

Mammoths of the perennial world

The magnificent tree dahlia (*Dahlia imperialis*) towers over most perennials, easily reaching about 2 m. The large trusses of bell-like blooms hang on throughout mid- and late autumn. The flowers are usually a soft lilac, but occasionally the white and pink forms are available, and there are even doubles. Support your plants with sturdy stakes or grow them near a fence, as the hollow stems are quite brittle and don't stand up to windy weather very well. Pieces strike easily from 30 cm sections.

Look out for the tree daisy (*Montanoa bipinnatifida*), which grows up to 5 m tall, producing trusses of white daisy-like flowers with a yellow eye from late autumn to early winter. Then there is the tree marigold, or Mexican sunflower (*Tithonia diversifolia*), which has yellow disc flowers held upon a 3–5 m shrub throughout autumn, winter and spring. In tropical climates both plants tend to get out of control, so if you don't live in a climate where winter knocks it back a notch or two, keep an eye on it.

Another 'tree daisy', which grows up to 3 m high and is sometimes called giant sowthistle, *Sonchus arboreus* looks like a tree succulent with deeply divided, almost fern-like grey–green leaves. The daisy flowers are yellow and start

blooming in spring, but the foliage itself is a year-round pleasure.

Seek out the Californian tree poppy (*Romneya coulteri*), which makes a lovely addition to a perennial border, for its white flowers in summer as well as its lovely grey, felted foliage, which looks great throughout the year. The shrub tends to sucker, so it can spread to 2.5 m high and also wide if you let it go. It is also drought-tolerant and likes any well-drained soil. Plant it in situ, because it dislikes being moved.

The wackiest and wildest of all these supersized perennials is the giant tree daisy (*Podachaenium eminens*), which has spicy-scented leaves 40 cm in diameter. It grows to about 5 m tall, then bears white dinner-plate-sized sprays of daisy-like blooms atop all this splendour. It's nothing short of magnificent.

> **DAHLIAS: GROWING TIPS**
> - Plant tubers in spring, about 7 cm deep into enriched soil.
> - If the position is windy or the variety you're planting is tall, insert stakes about 7 cm away from the tuber.
> - When the leader reaches about 50 cm, pinch out the central shoot to encourage side shoots.
> - Fertilise your plants as buds appear, and disbud if you want to encourage fewer but larger blooms.
> - In late autumn, after the plants die down, cut off the stems 15 cm above ground level. Dig up the clumps, remove surplus soil and store in a cool, dry place in sawdust or bark chips.

BELOW LEFT: *Montanoa or tree daisy will flower from autumn to winter and make a spectacle of itself.*

BELOW: *Tree dahlias shoot skywards like garden firecrackers.*

Perfect pastels

A palette of mauve, soft blues, pale pinks and white is easy to use, and can be carried into autumn with popular flowers such as asters, phlox and delphinium. Some lesser known additions, however, will add great charm.

If you find gardening tricky, try obedient plant (*Physostegia* sp.). It is easy to grow and tolerates dry conditions, but flowers better with moisture. The willow-like stems bear spikes of bell-like flowers.

A similar-looking perennial is penstemon, a close relative of both foxgloves and snapdragons, which bears spires of bells that bloom from summer through autumn. Native to North America, it is great in dry gardens; the species *Penstemon barbatus*—native to the arid states of Arizona, Mexico, Texas and Utah—does particularly well in dry conditions, and its gorgeous scarlet-red blooms are very showy. More common are the blue, purple and white cultivars, which form part of the flower borders in the rose gardens at 'Sissinghurst' in Kent, in the United Kingdom. If you cut your penstemons back at the very end of winter, they will re-shoot with a fresh batch of foliage and flowers.

The vanilla-scented heliotrope (*Heliotropium* sp.) is a useful plant for a warm, sheltered position. The colourful flowers are used to scent herbal bouquets and potpourri. The dark-leafed form, 'Lord Roberts', and the golden-leafed form, 'Aureum', make good foliage contrast plants with bonus flowers.

Foliage, form and texture carry this garden through the year. Even when many flowers have finished, the spent seeds of sea holly (Eryngium sp.) look great against the upright stems of giant feather grass (Stipa gigantea). See also pages 148 and 290 respectively.

CLOCKWISE FROM TOP LEFT: *Heliotrope smells like vanilla ice-cream; sometimes called spurflower,* Plectranthus *bloom for many months; butterfly bush is named for the dainty flowers that look like hovering butterflies; the pincushion flower comes in white, pink, purple or lavender;* Plectranthus *species will happily bloom in the shade.*

The pincushion flower (*Scabiosa* sp.), which is used as a herbal remedy, blooms from spring to autumn. The papery shells left by the flower heads are decorative in dried arrangements. Perhaps the longest flowering of all, however, is the dainty *Gaura lindheimeri*, which features multitudes of butterfly-like flowers on thin, wiry stems, giving the impression they are hovering above the garden. There are many cultivars of this species, some with beetroot-coloured foliage and others with golden leaves, such as 'Corrie's Gold', but their foliage doesn't quite hit the mark so, if you are in doubt, go for the plain green

form, and choose from white-, pink- or cherry-coloured blooms.

Plectranthus

Plectranthus is an often overlooked genus of plants. Its members come from various subtropical areas, and can be grown for their quantities of mauve–blue flowers in autumn, or for their foliage. Some species have soft grey felted leaves, some have maroon undersides, and others look similar to fresh fern fronds. Ageratum, joe pye weed and tweedia are also useful for touches of purple in warmer zones. A selection of them is shown on pages 378-9.

God Almighty first planted a garden; and, indeed, it is the purest of human pleasures.

FRANCIS BACON

The cigar plant is constantly in bloom. Available flower colours range from white to scarlet.

Cupheas

Cupheas are true year-round performers, flowering constantly in warmer climates. There are several species, and they all share this propensity to flower. The most common is probably *Cuphea hyssopifolia*, which bears white, pink or purple flowers. Its glossy green foliage can be grown as a small, clipped hedge, and it self-seeds readily, so you can make up a row quickly and cheaply. The cigar plant (*C. ignea*) works really well as a container plant, border or edging plant, and the Matchmaker® series includes a pink, white, orange and scarlet form.

With its long, tubular flowers, the giant cigar plant (*C. micropetala*) looks similar to the cigar plant but grows taller. *C. llavea* is sometimes called tiny mice or Mickey Mouse plant and even bat plant, as its blooms have red 'ears' flying out of a black heart. Like the other species in this genus, it grows to only about 30 cm in height and can be treated as an annual if there is a cold snap capable of killing them off in an unsheltered position.

All of these *Cuphea* species are very tolerant of dry conditions and will cope with drought. Low-maintenance, easy-care plants that don't attract disease, cupheas have the added bonus of attracting insects and nectar-feeding small birds.

Delphinium

Delphiniums' tall stems rocketing up through the flower bed are a must for cut flower enthusiasts and show-offs, as well as cottage garden lovers.

VITAL STATISTICS

Scientific name: *Delphinium* 'Pacific Giants'.
Family: Ranunculaceae.
Climate: Temperate and warm.
Uses: Great for cut flowers, cottage gardens, cutting gardens and the rear of borders.
Colours: Lavender, blue, pink and white in both double and semi-double blooms, sometimes with contrasting centres.
Height: Grows to 1.5 m.
Planting time: Autumn.
Soil: Grow in well-drained soil with added organic matter and mulch.
Position: Plants need full sun, preferably with wind protection and staking.
Planting spacing: About 1 m apart.
Fertiliser: Fertilise with manure and ensure plants are well mulched.
Harvest: They take 20 weeks to bloom.
Propagation: Raise seeds in punnets of seed-raising mix and transplant when seedlings are 3–4 cm high.

Feature perennial

Larch (Larix sp) cones

Bog arum (Calla palustris) seeds

Honesty (Lunaria) pods

Old man's beard (Clematis aristata)

Zebra grass (Miscanthus sp)

Coneflower (Echinacea sp) seed heads

Pods and seeds

The range of seed heads, cones and fruits is huge. In autumn, leaving some of the more spectacular types on the bush will ensure winter curiosities. The cones of conifers, bright winter berries, and dried seed heads of many perennials add whimsy and a new dimension to the garden as flowers fade.

Bentham's cornel (Cornus capitata) berries

Bulbs

Now that autumn is here, it's time to think about planting spring-flowering bulbs. Lying within each inert-looking package is a little bit of sunshine, just waiting to burst into bloom. Every bulb contains what is necessary for its journey to flowering, with food, protection and blossom wrapped up inside a rather dull-looking exterior.

ABOVE: *Jonquils, some of the earliest bulbs to break into bloom, are a welcome splash of sunshine in winter when trees are still bare. 'Soleil d'or', which translates to 'golden sun', could not be a more accurate cultivar name.*

LEFT: *Harlequin flowers (Sparaxis sp.) add a cheery note to any garden. Here they are teamed with bluebells and tulips.*

There is an endearing self-sufficiency about bulbs. Each is a masterpiece of packaging, complete with food storage and protection for the next year's precious plant in miniature.

JANE EDMANSON

Nature's hidden treasures

Most bulbs need a sunny well-drained spot in order to flower well. Some initial soil preparation will help the bulbs settle in and flower year after year—before planting, add some compost or soil conditioner to improve the soil texture and drainage.

For extra colour in the ground, plant groundcovers over planted bulbs so that, once the leaves have yellowed and died down, you won't be looking at bare summer soil. Plant hardy perennials such as catmint (*Nepeta* sp.), which flowers during summer when most spring-flowering bulbs are over. Other spreading groundcovers include sweet alice (*Alyssum* sp.), which grows into a lovely white carpet, and snow-in-summer (*Cerastium tomentosum*), which is good in hot, dry areas. Blue bugle (*Ajuga* sp.), planted over bluebells and grape hyacinths, is better in cool, moist, shaded areas.

ABOVE: *Plant* Ajuga *in conjunction with shade-loving bulbs (bluebells, grape hyacinths and so on) to help cover the ground when they die down.*

LEFT: *Beautiful white tulips add a dramatic touch to the garden.*

TINY TOTS

New miniature varieties of spring bulbs are now available. These will grow well in pots in a courtyard or on a balcony. Varieties include *Narcissus* 'Tête-à-Tête', 'Hoop Petticoat' and 'Jetfire'; *Narcissus* 'Minnow'; *Ipheion* 'Spring Stars'; and rockery-type tulips (*Tulipa* sp.).

1 Grape hyacinth   2 Ranunculus   3 Cape cowslip (*Lachenalia aloides*)   4 *Gladiolus* × *colvillei* 'The Bride'   5 Anemone
6 Ixia   7 Blubell   8 Freesia   9 Dutch iris   10 Watsonia   11 Hyacinth   12 Tulip   13 Snowflake   14 Daffodil

BULBS: GROWING TIPS

- Daffodils are probably the most popular bulbs, available now in pink, white and cream as well as yellow. As with all bulbs, they look best when planted in informal clumps or drifts.
- Ranunculus grow from tiny tubers. Just one can produce up to thirty blooms, ideal for cutting. Make sure you don't overwater them, as they are susceptible to rotting in wet soils. Ranunculus tubers should be planted with the claw-like end pointing downwards.
- As bulbs can remain in the ground for many years, add some bulb food to the soil each year as the new shoots come through the soil.
- Daffodils no longer flowering? Divide them every three years by removing the offsets and replanting them separately into freshly dug over, improved soil.
- Because bulbs have evolved to withstand cold winter temperatures, it's important to wait until the heat of summer has completely gone before planting. Early autumn is probably best, although tulips are an exception: wait until late autumn, once the temperature of the soil has dropped.

- If lifting your bulbs and replanting them sounds like a drag, select old-fashioned favourites that pretty much look after themselves. Plant them in bold drifts with cool-season grasses that don't need regular mowing. This technique is called naturalising. Don't restrict yourself to daffodils; try freesias, ixias, babianas, sparaxis, autumn crocus, baby gladioli, bluebells, watsonias and triteleia.
- While most bulbs like a full-sun position, some will tolerate more shade. If you have a shadier garden, plant bluebells, grape hyacinths, snowdrops, freesias and triteleia.
- Some bulbs have perfume. Jonquils, freesias and hyacinths are particularly renowned for their heady scents.
- If you're growing them as cut flowers, place potted bulbs in the shade for a while to lengthen the flower stems. Gradually bring them out into full sun, then plant seedling annuals between the new shoots.
- Use a premium potting medium when growing bulbs in containers. Free-draining, enriched composts with added peat moss, which helps retain nutrients and moisture, are vital.
- Top off bulbs in pots with annuals such as alyssum, lobelia, primula and Virginia stock, which help support the stems of finer bulbs, such as freesias and ixias, so you won't be left with pots of unattractive bare earth later.
- After flowering, maintain watering and feeding until the leaves yellow and collapse. This will give you the best display the following year. Never trim or plait the leaves while they are green.

BULB DIEBACK
Always allow bulbs in the lawn to die down naturally before mowing. Use winter or cool-season grasses when oversowing bulbs as these grasses will not need mowing as frequently as warm-season grasses.

Stakes, flags or, in this case, a pitchfork, indicate where bulbs are emerging, so that the new shoots are not mown over by accident.

COOL STORAGE
If you want tulips and hyacinths to re-flower, dig them up in autumn and store them in string bags until the following year. When it comes to planting time again, gardeners in warmer climates will need to trick their bulbs into believing they're in a colder climate by placing them in the fridge's crisper; store them neatly in an egg carton.

Plant a hyacinth bowl

Many bulbs look charming when they are used as a one-off indoor flowering display. The sturdy stems and delightful fragrances make hyacinths, paper whites and colchicums ideal candidates.

You can plant bulbs either in gravel and water (see the instructions at right) or, if you prefer, into free-draining potting mix, then oversow with grass seed once you have brought them out into the light. The grass makes an attractive carpet by the time the bulbs come into flower.

1 Fill a ceramic bowl with gravel, then place the bulbs on the gravel.

2 Fill the bowl with water just to the base of the bulbs. Keep the water level topped up to this point until the roots start to appear. This will take about two weeks.

3 Freshen the water every week until the flowers finish, then throw the exhausted bulbs away.

ABOVE: *A bowl planted with hyacinths makes an attractive and fragrant indoors display.*

Planting bulbs in the garden

Bring your bulbs out of cool storage, ready for planting.

Dig a hole for each bulb to a depth 2–3 times the width of the bulb. For daffodils, it's about 8 cm.

Place each bulb in its hole so that the growth point (that is, the narrow end) faces upwards.

Once the bulb is in the hole, backfill with soil.

Flowering gingers

There are many plants known as ginger lilies. Although they're commonly associated with the tropics because of their fragrant, showy flowers and lush foliage, ginger lilies are also tolerant of temperate climates. The most popular species is *Hedychium gardneranum*, a Himalayan species that has perfumed pale yellow and red flowers from late summer into autumn. The blue ginger (*Dichorisandra thyrsiflora*) is the next best for a temperate climate. Flowering in autumn, it grows to a height of 2.4 m.

But surely the most sensational of all is the torch ginger (*Nicolaia elatior*), which has a stunning red bloom on top of a 1.5 m stem.

Other plants, suited for tropical gardens only, include the beehive ginger (*Zingiber spectabile*). The *Curcuma* species have stunning perfumed flowers that grow from between large bracts, and the best known of these is turmeric (*Curcuma domestica*). All make super indoor floral arrangements. The edible ginger is a *Zingiber* species (see 'Tropical herbs' on page 232 in 'Summer').

Long-flowering blue ginger loves shade.

Snake lily

Also called voodoo lily or devil's tongue, the snake lily has incredible markings on its stem (shown at far right) that resemble snakeskin. At about three years old, this herbaceous, tuberous perennial sends up a flower, which looks like a pale pink arum lily, directly from the ground. Odourless by day, the flower smells like decaying flesh by night.

VITAL STATISTICS

Scientific name: *Amorphophallus bulbifer*.
Family: Araceae subfamily Aroideae.
Climate: These beauties need a subtropical or tropical environment when planted outside, but can also be grown in pots as a conservatory plant.
Plant/bulb type: Tuber.
Colours: Pale pink.
Height: About 1 m.
Planting time: Spring.
Soil: The soil should be freely draining, especially in the winter months.
Position: Semi-shade to full shade.
Planting spacing: Plant tubers 1.5 m apart.
Watering: Water regularly over spring, summer and autumn.
Fertiliser: Use liquid seaweed in summer every fortnight.
Flowering: Summer.
Propagation: Propagate by division.

Feature bulb

CLOCKWISE FROM TOP LEFT: *Pink crocus, meadow saffron, yellow crocus and storm lily. All four are known by the name crocus, despite being unrelated.*

Known as the autumn daffodil, *Sternbergia lutea* has golden crocus-like flowers in autumn. Plant them in natural drifts, and leave them undisturbed to grow into large clumps.

Meadow saffron (*Colchicum autumnale*) has pale lilac flowers that emerge before the leaves. A white form called 'Album' and a double called 'Waterlily' are also delightful. All parts of the plant are poisonous, so don't use it as saffron!

Hippeastrum

The brassy flowers of the hippeastrum make a sensational potted houseplant. Plant the bulb while it is dormant in early to mid-winter, feed it with blood and bone occasionally and let the foliage die down.

Bulbs that flower in autumn

If you enjoy your spring bulbs, why not think about mixing in some summer- and autumn-flowering bulbs such as liliums, naked lady (*Amaryllis*), mini hippeastrum, spider lily (*Nerine* sp.) and crocus.

Autumn crocuses

For a touch of spring on the opposite side of the calendar, look no further than autumn crocuses. Botanically speaking, these plants are not true crocuses, but they certainly have the charm of their namesakes.

First to flower are the zephyr or storm lilies (*Zephyranthes* sp.); the botanical name is Greek for the West Wind. They bloom after the first of the autumn rains, and will not be tricked by your sprinkler into flowering! White is the most common (*Z. candida*), although there are pink (*Z. rosea*) and yellow (*Z. citrina*) species. Most are evergreen in temperate climates.

Potted hippeastrums make a striking feature.

PLANT A HIPPY
To plant a hippeastrum, keep the neck of the bulb (about a quarter) above the soil level. Plant it into good quality, free-draining mix and water once, then not again until buds appear, then weekly. It should flower annually if you cut the flower stalks close to the point of origin after fading.

Nerines and spider lilies

Two other beautiful autumn-flowering gems, *Nerine* sp. and surprise or spider lily (*Lycoris* sp.), which both flower in white, cream, red, pink and yellow, are often confused with each other. *Lycoris*, a genus native to East Asia, is dormant throughout summer, when the weather is at its hottest, then it sends up flowers before any foliage—something that summer rains usually trigger. It blooms throughout autumn, and when the flowers fade, it starts to produce foliage, which continues to grow throughout winter into spring. *Lycoris* is almost always grown from bulbs, as the seeds take about five years to reach maturity.

The nerines, on the other hand, come from Africa, where they are used to any extremes in the weather. *Nerine bowdenii*, the pink nerine, flowers in autumn and then doesn't send up any foliage until springtime, so it is quite tolerant of cold conditions. *N. flexuosa* 'Alba' is the white form, and is most floriferous, with 15 flowers appearing on each stem. It's happy in sun or shade, whereas the tangerine (*N. fothergillii major*) and red nerine (*N. sarniensis*) both prefer more sun.

The strange-looking Scadoxus *prefers a well-drained, shady position with protection from snails and slugs.*

Bizarre but beautiful

Another member of the bulb family Amaryllidaceae is the paintbrush or blood lily, which bears extraordinary flowers in autumn. The African blood lily (*Haemanthus coccineus*) is a very useful plant for shade and grows happily under large trees, flowering in autumn in any frost-free area, or in pots, protected over winter, in cooler climates. The red paintbrush-like flowers tipped with yellow appear before the leaves, and are followed by a pair of dark green leaves, which die down again at the end of summer. There is also a white (*H. deformis*) and pink (*H. humilis*) species.

Closely related to the blood lily is the snake lily (*Scadoxus* sp.). In the wild it produces berries that are eaten by monkeys in its native habitat—tropical Africa—but elsewhere are enjoyed by birds. The spikes of blooms vary from species to species, but are often clusters of small orange to red stars held on a spotted stem. They also come in white and gold, but these forms are quite rare.

BELOW: *The golden spider lily.*

BELOW RIGHT: *The beautiful white nerine flowers in autumn and early winter.*

Grasses, groundcovers and climbers

Autumn is a good time to repair elements in the lawn that have become neglected or worn. The weather is generally fine, although cold nights mean that plant growth has slowed to a 'catch-up' pace. The seasonal slow-down affects the whole garden.

Dandelion, with globe of down,
The schoolboy's clock in every town…

WILLIAM HOWITT

Grasses

Autumn can also mean a lack of colour, with the lawn's lush green fading and demanding extra care.

Now is a great time to feed your lawns and encourage a strong, healthy grass cover for the next six months. A vigorous grass will also be weed- and drought-resistant, with a deeper root system and more coverage. Autumn is the best time to fix problems so weeds don't take hold over winter.

Lawn fixes

Try these sure-fire fixes to rejuvenate a tired-looking lawn.

Oversow

Autumn is a good time to restore worn patches in couch, buffalo and kikuyu lawns. Nurseries sell a range of lawn seed mixtures, and they all contain cool-season grasses, such as perennial rye grass and fescue, which will withstand the cold winter temperatures. The seeds should germinate rapidly and fill in the bare patches, keeping your lawn looking green and lush throughout winter.

Feed

Before and after applying a complete lawn food, thoroughly water the lawn. Avoid using sulphate of ammonia, as it only softens the grass and turns it green temporarily. Balanced lawn fertilisers will encourage a strong root system, more stems and lots more leaves.

Dethatch

To deal with a thatch build-up and help activate a new flush of growth, scarify your lawn by raking it with a steel-tined rake. Scarifying or dethatching removes the mat of old leaves and decaying plant

A lawn serves both decorative and practical functions, including as a soft-surface hard-wearing kids' play area. Autumn is the time to do a little repair work.

Oversowing lawn seed

1 Prepare bare patches for seeding by raking the ground to a fine tilth. Add topsoil to level out any depressions in the ground.

2 Mix together the lawn seed and starter fertiliser and apply them at the same time. Using a spreader will ensure even distribution of the seed.

3 Tamp down with a rake. Don't be tempted to bury the seed under more soil as doing so will reduce seed germination.

4 Water in, then keep moist for the next 7–10 days in particular, while the seeds germinate and seedlings take root.

matter. If you neglect to do this, the thatch can form a waterproof barrier and stop added nutrients and rain penetrating to the roots where they are needed.

Aerating the lawn

Improving the drainage will always help your lawn remain healthy. Use spiked shoes or a garden fork to puncture any compacted layers; this will leave tiny holes that allow air to travel down into the soil. For larger areas it is more efficient to use specialised equipment, such as hollow-tined forks and tined rollers, which you can purchase or hire from most equipment centres, hardware stores and nurseries. You can either leave the holes open or top-dress them with a free-draining mixture, such as coarse river sand.

Aerating your lawn is of particular benefit to heavy soils with a high clay content, as these tend to compact easily with traffic. In worst-case scenarios, or where important trees and shrubs are affected by compaction, you can hire a machine that injects air into the soil, filling the resulting air pockets with a proprietary foam so they stay open.

CLOCKWISE FROM TOP LEFT: *Lawns need regular care to keep them at their best: a good soaking during hot weather; feeding to encourage vigour and discourage weeds; using spiked shoes to aerate compacted soil; and dethatching with a rake to remove old grass leaves.*

Giant feather grass

Texture in the garden is an important design consideration, as is adding vertical elements to the design. This beautiful ornamental grass ticks all the boxes. It's dynamic, swaying in the gentlest of breezes, yet hardy and architectural too. Cradles can be used to keep the grass upright. Mixing it with flowering perennials adds grace and charm to your planting combos.

VITAL STATISTICS

Scientific name: *Stipa gigantea*.
Family: Poaceae.
Climate: Hardy to extreme cold.
Culture: This species looks particularly beautiful mixed with flowering perennials.
Colours: Golden oat-like flowers glisten and shimmer.
Height: Grows up to 2.5 m.
Planting time: Plant seed in spring; clumps can be divided in winter.
Soil: Moderately fertile, well-drained soil.
Position: Full sun.
Planting spacing: Plant about 1.2 m apart.
Fertiliser: Apply fertiliser in spring after pruning to the ground.
Propagation: By seed or division of clumps.

Feature grass

Mowing

It's tempting to mow your lawn as close as possible to the ground, to try and prolong the period before needing to mow again. But when the grass is left just that little bit longer, the roots go deeper and the grass develops a stronger, thicker cover.

DID YOU KNOW? Real estate experts estimate that a feature lawn adds 15 per cent to the value of a property.

Your children and pets will love its softer, friendlier surface. Longer grass is more resilient to traffic and resistant to periods of drought, and weeds will find it difficult to get a foothold in the thick, luxuriant lawn. The best advice is not to cut more than one third of the blade of grass at one time; otherwise, your grass will start to suffer stress.

Also, avoid mowing in extreme heat or cold (or if such conditions are forecast) or if the ground is sodden, as this will place more stress on the turf.

Feeding and liming the lawn

All plants need feeding and watering, but grass seems to need more regular attention. Mowing removes nutrients in the growing tips, so you have to return these, either by feeding or by letting lawn clippings lie and rot, thus returning to the roots as humus.

Many commercial lawn fertilisers are available. You should vary the amount of nitrogen in feeds, according to the time of year. Late summer and autumn feeds should contain less nitrogen than spring feeds. A slower-acting fertiliser that contains a lower proportion of nitrogen and higher ones of both phosphate and potassium will help promote strong root growth and repair through autumn.

Application of lawn fertilisers gradually increases soil acidity, which actually prevents many nutrients being available to the grass. An annual application of lime will rectify this and sweeten the soil.

Turf grows best with a neutral pH (that is, around 5.5), so a simple soil test will show you whether liming is necessary. (See 'Soil pH' on page 257.) If the reading is below 5.5, the soil needs sweetening. Do not use lime on neutral or alkaline soil.

When liming, always wear gloves, as lime (calcium carbonate) can burn the skin. Only apply lime in calm weather conditions, and always water in well afterwards. Hot, windy days can result in burnt grass, health hazards and chemicals leaching into the environment.

Reducing lawn acidity with lime

Over a period of time, lawn soils tend to become more acid, which impairs growth. Use a pH test kit to check the acidity of the soil. If the lawn soil is acid, apply lime at the rate specified on the bag—about 100 g per square metre. It's vital to water in the lime after applying it. Always apply lime in calm weather.

1 Wear gloves when applying lime to protect your hands from being burnt.

2 There's no need for a spreader—just use your gloved hand.

3 Keep a steady pace to ensure even distribution.

4 The limed lawn is ready for watering.

Groundcovers

Good groundcover plants should provide value and interest as ornamentals throughout the year, rather than be just a means of smothering weeds and covering bare soil.

What is a groundcover?

A groundcover is defined as a plant that quickly smothers weeds and covers bare earth. It usually requires only a small amount of maintenance, especially when planted on a sloping site.

Ideal groundcovers are plants that divide and propagate themselves by clumping, carpeting (using runners or spreading with underground stolons or rhizomes), or simply by sprawling or creeping low to the ground over a good distance. These characteristics help them bind the soil, combat erosion and reduce the amount of space available to those opportunistic weeds.

Flowers underfoot

There are some autumn-flowering groundcovers, including cottage pinks, ajuga, ivy geraniums, true geraniums, the spot-flowering Alpine phlox, campanula, fanflower and Swedish ivy (see 'Feature groundcover', opposite).

Gardeners in frost-free areas can enjoy flowering nasturtiums right through autumn and winter. When the flowers fade, coloured leaves—such as those in the silver ground-hugging forms of artemisia, snow-in-summer and *Lamium* 'White Nancy'—provide the perfect foil for larger background plantings and flowers.

Another stunning foliage perennial is the *Heuchera* genus. Native to North America, these beautiful low-growing plants are ideally suited to growing as groundcovers in rockeries, pots and at the fronts of borders. The various cultivars have pink, grey, bronze, gold and silver markings that cast a unique, almost stained-glass like pattern. 'Plum Pudding', 'Purple Palace', 'Chocolate Ruffles', 'Caramel' and 'Citronelle' are just some of the cultivars, with flowers

CLOCKWISE FROM TOP: *Alpine phlox,* Lamium *'White Nancy' and* Heuchera *'Beauty Colour'. The ground can be just as pretty as the rest of the garden with a mixture of foliage and flowering plants.*

Swedish ivy

Often sold as an indoor plant or basket plant, Swedish ivy, which is actually native to South Africa, also makes a fabulous groundcover under trees, as it copes with heavy shade and root competition.

VITAL STATISTICS

Scientific name: *Plectranthus verticillatus*.

Family: Lamiaceae.

Climate: Warm temperate or tropical.

Colours: The flowers are spikes of pale lavender, white or pink.

Height: About 30 cm.

Planting time: Plant in spring, summer or autumn.

Soil: Plant in free-draining soil, although it loves water. It's reasonably drought tolerant when established.

Position: Shade; also glasshouse or shade house.

Planting spacing: Plant 1 m apart.

Fertiliser: Use an annual top dressing of leaf mould and slow-release fertiliser.

Propagation: It strikes very easily from soft-tip cuttings.

Feature groundcover

of white, coral or pink appearing in spring to autumn. They are hardy in full sun and part shade, and cope with some dryness, although they will thrive in humus-rich soil.

Autumn division

Autumn is a good time of the year for propagating many groundcovers by division. This can be done in one of the following three ways.

1 Simply pull off a rooted portion of a plant and replant it where required.

2 Use a spade or knife to cut big chunks from a large established plant.

3 For herbaceous perennial clumps that often die in the centre and need breaking up to refresh them, insert two forks back to back in the centre of the clump and use them to lever it into smaller pieces, which can then be broken up and planted.

Break up clumps of groundcovers using the backs of forks.

Some people are like wheelbarrows, useful only when pushed and very easily upset.

HENRY S. HASKINS

Succulents

Many succulents grow effectively as groundcovers. The variety of foliage colour combined with their adaptability make them ideal for a wide range of positions, while their dramatic forms make them great potted plants.

Sensational sedum

Known as 'stonecrop' (*Sedum* sp.), this diverse group of plants varies in appearance and form, from jellybeans to rosettes and upright growers that fit perfectly into a perennial flower garden.

As with most succulents, you can grow sedum virtually anywhere that drains freely—ideal spots are pots, edging, rockeries or tucked into notches between rocks. Use your imagination to find a position that heightens the beauty of these treasures.

ABOVE: *These rosette-shaped echeverias are hardy, flower-like plants with year-long 'blooms'.*

RIGHT: *This sedum matures from pinkish red flowers in summer to rust red blooms in autumn.*

FAR RIGHT: Sedum rubrotinctum *gets its common name of jellybean plant from its colourful leaves.*

Kalanchoe

Kalanchoe seem to be the masters of disguise. These plants range from dainty pot and basket specimens to tree-like monsters with elephant ears! The most common species is flaming katy (*Kalanchoe blossfeldiana*), which makes a spectacular potted plant in sun or part shade. Also adaptable to various conditions is the delightful cascading lavender scallops (*K. pumila*), with its lolly pink flowers and silver-white powdery foliage. The most tactile is the panda plant (*K. tomentosa*), also known as pussy ears. The furry leaves are silver with chocolate-coloured tips, and it is best suited to a garden bed in full sun. Another kalanchoe worth mentioning is the Madagascan feltbush or velvet elephant ear (*K. beharensis*). It has enormous grey velvety leaves and grows tree-like to 6 m.

DID YOU KNOW? Compounds found in *Kalanchoe pinnata* have been found to have medicinal properties that fight tumours.

Propagating succulents

When potting succulents, you'll find that no matter how careful you are, leaves will break off from the mother plant. Don't throw them out. Succulents readily propagate themselves from these leaf cuttings. If you let them dry out for a week or so, the wound will callus over, preventing the cuttings from rotting off. Plant these cuttings to a shallow depth in 10 cm tubes. The new plants will grow from the calluses, supporting themselves on the stored energy inside the discarded fleshy leaves. Once they're well-rooted and of adequate size, replant them in the garden as an instant hedge, give them away to friends or add them to your own potted collection.

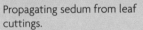

Propagating sedum from leaf cuttings.

A new rosette forming from a leaf cutting of *Sedum* sp.

LEFT: Kalanchoe beharensis *is a highly unusual succulent from Madagascar with spectacular felted foliage.*

FAR LEFT: *The silver-grey leaves of* Kalanchoe *'Quicksilver' contrast beautifully with the musk-pink flowers that emerge in spring.*

Climbers

Although summer shade is essential in hot climates, winter sun is just as desirable. A pergola on the northern or western side of your home will shade your windows from the afternoon sun and create an outdoor room for leisure and summer entertaining.

TOP: *The blue butterfly bush flowers for many months of the year.*

ABOVE: *The bridal veil clerodendrum is a dainty-looking charmer.*

Bleeding hearts

Native mainly to the tropics and subtropics, this genus includes more than 450 species of trees, shrubs and climbers, known by various names, such as glory bower, pagoda flower, butterfly bush and bleeding heart.

Bleeding heart vine (*Clerodendrum thomsoniae*) is so named because of the unusual appearance of the flower. The large, showy white calyx has a crimson corolla shooting out from its centre, almost like a drop of blood. There is a hybrid (*C. thomsoniae × splendens*) with a dull red calyx, and another species with intense scarlet flowers (*C. splendens*).

Other clerodendrums include the blue butterfly bush (*C. ugandense*); pagoda flower (*C. paniculatum*), which is a loose, trailing shrub to 1.5 m with similar flowers to its namesake; and

Virginia creeper (Parthenocissus quinquefolia) *is a fast-growing deciduous vine perfect for instant shade and autumn colour.*

Brazilian firecracker vine

This charming climber can be grown in hanging baskets, through perennial beds or up along fences and trelliswork where it will flower virtually non-stop with its cigar-shaped red blooms, tipped in yellow.

VITAL STATISTICS

Scientific name: *Manettia luteorubra.*
Family: Rubiaceae.
Climate: Needs frost protection or can be grown in sunrooms and glasshouses easily.
Colours: Red tipped with yellow.
Height: 1–2 m.
Planting time: Any time of year when conditions are mild.
Soil: Tolerates moderately fertile soils with good drainage.
Position: To ensure best flowering, plant in full sun; will grow in part sun with fewer flowers. Protect from the wind.
Watering: Keep moist at all times.
Fertiliser: Apply a complete fertiliser in spring.
Pests/diseases: Risk of spider mite in glasshouses.
Propagation: Soft-tip cuttings in spring.

Feature climber

C. wallichii (syn. *C nutans*), which is a dainty white-flowering shrub with the same butterfly-like flowers.

They all flower over summer and autumn, and seem to do as well in a sheltered warm-temperate climate as in the tropics. If you live in a cooler zone, you can grow them indoors or in glasshouses, where the twining species can look delightful trailing in a large basket or growing up trelliswork. Failing this, grow *Dicentra* sp., also known as bleeding heart.

Chilean beauties

A stunning plant, native to Chile, is the sacred flower of the Incas (*Cantua buxifolia*). This semi-climbing shrub flowers profusely in spring with trumpet-shaped bells in rose–purple, pink and white. There is also a variety with pink- and white-striped flowers. It likes a mild climate and a sunny position in moist, well-drained soil.

Also known as dipladenia or Chilean jasmine, mandevilla (*Mandevilla* sp.) is an excellent choice for a warm, sheltered position with some protection from the summer afternoon sun.

Mandevilla laxa has clusters of deliciously scented white trumpet flowers, and is deciduous in cool areas. *M. splendens* has lipstick pink flowers, although there are many new cultivars that include shell pink and musk tones. It grows best in temperate areas. Both species flower for much of the year—from summer through to late autumn. They require ample watering during hot weather.

The Chilean bell flower (Lapageria rosea) is the national flower of Chile. This cultivar is 'Arco Iris'.

Shrubs and trees

Autumn can be a particularly colourful time if you plan it
well. Many plants are still flowering, while others produce
displays of a different nature. Berrying plants are extremely
ornamental features throughout autumn with a range of
colours that is a seasonal delight.

*Still water magically
reflects the sky
canopy above,
creating 'twice' the
garden picture with
its mirror image.*

*Season of mists and mellow fruitfulness,
Close bosom-friend of the maturing sun;
Conspiring with him how to load and bless
With fruit the vines that round the thatch-eaves run;...*

JOHN KEATS

Shrubs

Your garden can include shrubs that reach their peak of flowering now, providing privacy, perfume, colour and texture when other plants are shutting down for winter.

Flushes of colour

The warm-toned hibiscus, ixora, Cape honeysuckle and Chinese bellflower can add colour to a shrub border. Large flowering shrubs such as the tibouchinas and *Camellia sasanqua* are a wonderful sight in autumn, especially if they are given enough room in which to grow to their natural shape.

Garden staples such as geraniums, fuchsias, lavender and roses continue to produce flushes of flowers if you lavish extra care, such as tip pruning and feeding, on them.

Plumbago also has a second flush in autumn. It is one of the easiest shrubs to grow, coping with virtually any soil, withstanding drought and tolerating light frosts. The only thing that puts people off growing plumbago is that it can become unruly, suckering where it's not wanted, so prune it back fairly heavily after flowering in spring and again after its autumn flush. There are white, blue and dark blue cultivars. Use it as a hedge or to screen ugly walls and fences.

However, much of the autumn garden's beauty lies beyond flowers. Foliage, both deciduous and evergreen, can be a highlight in its own right or act in a 'supporting role' to the flowers in season.

Many shrubs—such as the purple tones of cannas, flax and coleus—have fabulous coloured leaves all year, and these can work particularly well in a shrub border that contains autumn-turning leaves of berberis, smoke bush and viburnum. Even evergreens can colour at certain times of the year. Mahonias display autumn tints in late autumn and early winter, and bergenia and heuchera can colour brilliantly as the weather cools.

CLOCKWISE FROM TOP LEFT: *The fragrant blooms of* Viburnum × burkwoodii; Mahonia aquifolium *has beautiful sprays of blue berries;* Iochroma fuchsioides *has red, fuchsia-like blooms in autumn; frog's foot coleus has interesting bicoloured foliage year-round in mild areas; a pretty salmon canna with steel-grey foliage; true 'Blue' geranium will send up sporadic flowers for many months.*

DID YOU KNOW? The fruits of both berberis and mahonias can be made into jams and jellies that go very well with roasted meat.

300

The Rubiaceae family

1 *Coffea arabica*   **2** *Gardenia augusta* 'Florida'   **3** *Pentas* 'Light Pink'   **4** *Ixora* 'Apricot Delight'   **5** *Pentas* 'Dark Pink'

Tropical delights from the Rubiaceae family

Some plant families enrich our lives in both practical and sentimental ways. Rubiaceae is one such family. Imagine starting your day without a morning coffee—enter *Coffea arabica*, the most widely grown commercial member of this group. Think too of a world without the scent of gardenias (see page 202), although there are many other worthwhile contenders for the most heavenly scented prize, including *Bouvardia* (see page 314) and the stunning and equally fragrant *Posoqueria*, a shrub that grows to 3 m, with shooting star-like blooms darting out from its glossy green leaves.

Other members of this family make up for their lack of perfume with the sheer brilliance of their display. The *Ixora* genus, for example, includes the 'Prince of Orange', a shrub that grows to 2 m with showy orange heads. Dwarf cultivars—with yellow, pink and gold flowers—tend to grow to about 1 m. Ixoras flower from summer to late autumn, but longer in the tropics.

From Madagascar comes a plant called flaming beauty (*Carphalea kirondron*), which looks a bit like an ixora crossed with a Christmas bush. It bears lovely red star-like 'blooms', called calyxes, for many months of the year, provided it is growing in a warm tropical area and receives lots of regular water and at least half a day of sunshine. You can grow these plants in pots or in the ground, where they can reach 3 m.

Perhaps the more unusual member of this family is the Bangkok rose (*Mussaenda* sp.), native to Thailand, which attracts attention with showy bracts rather than flowers. The most commonly grown is *M. frondosa*, which grows to about 2 m tall, with creamy bracts and yellow flowers. There are also pink and red cultivars, but it is the *M.* 'Queen Sirikit' and 'Tropic Snow' forms that take your breath away. Both have felted leaves, which form the showy bracts, and grow to about 2 m in semi-shade or sun, flowering from the middle

of summer through autumn and into early winter. In cooler climates they tend to become deciduous in winter and require protection from frosts.

Pentas lanceolata should be included more often in borders in frost-free areas. They grow to 1 m tall, flower profusely and really only pause for a spell when you take time out to prune them back, saving them from becoming straggly. They come in a wide range of colours, including red, pink, candy stripes, violet and white, and there is also a variegated leaf form called 'Touch of Ice'. The dwarf varieties grow to about 40 cm tall.

The mirror bush (*Coprosma* sp.) is native to New Zealand and other Pacific islands. Unlike so many other members of this family, it may not feature showy flowers but it has other superb qualities, such as salt and drought tolerance and soil adaptability, which has helped it to become a garden escapee in some areas of Australia. However, some cultivars have wonderful foliage variations that make them great features for hedging and foliage contrast. Look for 'Karo Red', for beetroot-coloured leaves; 'Evening Glow', for a sunset splash of colours, including gold; and 'Fireburst', for some beautiful shades of pink.

ABOVE LEFT: *Pentas is a genus of perennials that flower reliably in warm temperate and subtropical gardens.*

ABOVE: *The white flag bush* (Mussaenda frondosa) *is known for its creamy bracts (modified leaves).*

CLOCKWISE FROM TOP LEFT: *Perfect for filling in big spots in a shaded shrubbery,* Strobilanthes flaccidifolius *looks like a dainty fuchsia; polka dot plant* (Hypoestes phyllostachya) *makes a useful edging plant in the shade; purple Persian shield* (Strobilanthes dyeranus) *is an eye-catching year-round beauty to 2 m.*

The Acanthaceae family

For many years the useful foliage plant goldfussia (*Strobilanthes anisophyllus*), with its lovely purple-tinged leaves and dainty bell-like lavender flowers, which appear in spring but bloom for months, has been popular in gardens. The flowers look great against the dark foil of the leaves. Goldfussia is hardy, copes with salt and neglect and grows to a tidy 1 m or so.

For a foliage contrast, look for silver Persian shield (*S. gossypinus*), which has lovely felted leaves with a silver sheen on one side and an almost copper-like look on the other. It too happily grows in sun or shade, and looks great against any other coloured-leaf plant. Obligingly, it also grows in pots.

Another commonly grown species is purple Persian shield (*S. dyeranus*), which has marvellous lavender-coloured leaves with a silvery sheen that dance and shimmer. Flowering in autumn with spikes of light blue flowers, it is also useful for pots, foliage contrast and semi-shaded positions, as long as the position is moist and frost-free.

Ruellia brevifolia grows to 60 cm. The leaves are a bright green with prominent leaf veins. The bright red tubular flowers appear in late summer and autumn and occasionally at other times of the year. A shaded position is ideal. *R. brevifolia* self sows readily without becoming weedy. Plant in a warm position in the garden as it is frost tender.

For a winner of a plant, look out for firecracker flower (*Crossandra infundibuliformis*), which usually has beautiful apricot flowers that appear almost year-round. Reaching only 60 cm or so, it can be grown outside in frost-free places, filling the gaps in many a garden, from temperate to tropical areas. There are other species of *Crossandra* from which to choose, including a greenish blue flowering plant sometimes called shamrock flower. The yellow 'Lutea' and blood red 'Nile Queen' are more popular cultivars, however.

Justicia, another genus in the Acanthaceae family, is a fabulous group of autumn-flowering gems. Most common is the Brazilian plume flower (*Justicia carnea*), which grows to about 1.5 m in height and features lovely pleated leaves of glossy mid-green. It will do well in partial shade, flowering after the summer rains then throughout autumn, spot flowering whenever it's inclined. The white form, 'Alba', is particularly lovely.

Once found in everyone's garden and known as shrimp plant or beloperone is *Justicia brandegeeana*. The apricot- to red-felted flowers appear at the end of a spike or showy bract for many months, and the plant itself grows to about 40 cm tall and likes a well-drained soil in full sun, with lots of mulch. There is also a lovely yellow shrimp plant called *Pachystachys lutea* (syn. *Beloperone guttata*), which grows bushier and taller, to about 70 cm, with glossier foliage. Native to Mexico, it likes full sun or shade, and is useful for conservatories and potted gardens due to its long flowering period.

Purple shrimp plant (*Justicia scheidweileri*) is known by a number of other common names, including blue shrimp plant, Brazilian fireworks and maracas. It has attractive white-veined leaves, and spiky deep pink to red bracts that enclose light purple flowers. Growing only 20 cm high, it makes a good groundcover plant, and flowers through the warmer months of the year.

Brazilian fuchsia (*J. rizzinii*) is another great garden plant. An evergreen shrub to about 60 cm that prefers semi-shade, its tubular yellow and red flowers (similar to the cigar plant on page 278) bloom from autumn until spring, making it a really valuable addition to both the garden and the conservatory in frosty areas.

And lastly, don't forget another shade-loving member of the family—*Acanthus mollis*, the oyster plant (see page 39), which has vertical spires of blooms and striking deep green leaves.

CLOCKWISE FROM TOP LEFT: *Yellow shrimp plant* (Pachystachys lutea) *grows well in the shade, where it flowers from autumn to spring, as does Brazilian fuchsia* (Justicia rizzinii), *with its lovely yellow and red blooms. The pink Brazilian plume flower* (J. carnea) *is showier than its relatives but just as hardy.*

The Acanthaceae family

9 Giant blue 'sage' (*Brillantaisia subulugurica*) **10** *Ruellia makoyana* **11** *Justicia rizzinii* **12** *Ruellia brevifolia*
13 *Strobilanthes anisophyllus* **14** Purple Persian shield (*Strobilanthes dyeranus*) **15** Firecracker flower (*Crossandra infundibuliformis*) **16** *Odontonema tubaeforme* **17** Goldfussia (*Strobilanthes anisophyllus*)

Fabulous fuchsias

In the botanical world, fuchsias lend a touch of whimsy—they dance from bending boughs like ballerinas in tutus, making them a charming plant for any shaded spot.

Named for the German botanist Dr Leonhart Fuchs, fuchsias were 'discovered' by Europeans in South America during the late 15th century, then found their way to the northern hemisphere during the great plant-trading era of the late 18th century. Their popularity has waxed and waned over the years, but fuchsias are now a mainstay of the hanging basket and conservatory growing cultures throughout the world.

There are more than 8000 varieties of fuchsia, so it pays to narrow your choices down to the less troublesome—those that reward you with blooms throughout the milder months from autumn to the end of spring.

CLOCKWISE FROM LEFT: Fuchsia 'Winston Churchill' is a showy double, pendulous small shrub type; F. magellanica is a species fuchsia, as is F. × bacillaris 'Cottinghamii'; F. 'Campo Thilco' is one of the simplest and most reliable of all fuchsias.

Fuchsia types

From groundcovers to taller shrubs, there is a fuchsia to suit almost every position. Many of these plants are used for hanging baskets, which highlight their cascading habit and gorgeous pendulous flowers.

Basket fuchsias To fully appreciate the cascading growth habit and exquisite blooms of the basket varieties, hang them at eye level. Basket fuchsias, which tend to be easy varieties to grow, include *Fuchsia × hybrida* 'Derby Imp', 'La Campanella', 'Streamliner', 'Pink Marshmallow', 'Lyric' and 'Blue Satin'. Plants in baskets are liable to dry out rapidly and be damaged by strong winds, so place them in a position where you can water them easily.

Small shrubs Smaller upright growers are excellent as border or bedding plants. Grow them in a row to create a dramatic display, or dot them about the garden in groups of three. Try some of these recommended varieties—*Fuchsia × hybrida* 'Cotton Candy', 'Cecile', 'Pinwheel', 'Winston Churchill', 'Lord Byron' and 'Countess of Aberdeen'.

Tall shrubs The taller rambling varieties are the tough stalwarts of old gardens. They will trail over garden walls, grow against a wall and thread their way through latticework. Choose from *F. magellanica* var. *gracilis* and *Fuchsia × hybrida* 'Eva Boerg', 'Display', 'Pixie' and 'Enfant Prodigue'.

Standards Growing fuchsias as standards is a lovely way to set off their 'teardrop' blooms. *Fuchsia × hybrida* 'Peppermint Stick', 'Harbour Bridge', 'Voodoo' and 'Swingtime' all make successful standards.

project

Propagating fuchsias

Fuchsias strike easily from semi-hardwood cuttings—that is, cuttings that don't wilt after about five minutes from cutting (they should still be firm). Cut a 10-20 cm long piece of the parent plant, dip it into rooting powder and place in potting mix. Keep moist.

1 Once the cutting is well established, it is ready for transplanting.

2 Plant the struck fuchsia in a suitable pot.

3 Add potting mix.

4 If you're growing your fuchsia as a standard, tie it to a stake with budding tape. If you're growing it as a bush, tip prune the leader and encourage side shoots.

Species fuchsias

While there are thousands of modern varieties, with their uncomplicated blooms and often striking grace, the straight species types have their own charm. They tend to be more shrub-like and less taciturn, showing off an abundance of simple flowers.

The lilac fuchsia (*F. arborescens*) is a perfect example. Growing up to 3 m tall, it is smothered almost year-round with a profusion of lilac flowers—in their native habitat, a favourite with hummingbirds. Following the flowers are attractive and edible sweet purple fruits. Another undervalued species fuchsia is the Bolivian fuchsia (*F. boliviana*), which also has edible reddish purple fruits, but it's the exquisite flowers, which literally drip like the crystals on a chandelier, that make it so desirable. The straight species has clusters of long pure red flowers, whereas the flowers on the cultivar 'Luxurians' have red-tipped white tubes. Growing to 5 m, this somewhat straggly shrub needs a frost-free position but, such is the beauty of its year-round blooms, you'll feel blessed to behold them.

Then there is *F. denticulata*, which usually grows to 1.5 m. Juicy red berries

Fuchsia boliviana is hard to find, but it's a delightful shrub once sourced.

Fuchsia is a dancer
Dancing on her toes
Clad in red and purple
By a cottage wall;
Sometimes in a greenhouse
In frilly white and rose,
Dressed in her best for
the fairies' evening ball!

CICELY MAY BARKER

FUCHSIAS: GROWING TIPS

- Fuchsias need a protected spot in a reasonably shaded area that receives sufficient light for you to take a photograph without using a flash.
- Most varieties are also frost tender, so place them in a protected spot in winter, or cover them lightly with shade cloth at night.
- Severe pruning can kill fuchsias. Tip prune them throughout their growing season and dead-head them after flowering.
- Feed fuchsias with liquid fertiliser once every fortnight after watering.
- The best way to water a potted fuchsia is to immerse it in a bucket of water. Air bubbles will rise when the soil is thoroughly watered and the plant is ready to be removed for draining.

follow its green-tipped pink flowers, and the green leaves with a pinkish tinge to their venation make it an unusual and handsome foliage plant. Even more spectacular for foliage is the *F. triphylla* 'Gartenmeister Bonstedt' series, which has beautiful bronze foliage and stunning orange, pink or red blooms, depending on the form. More sun-tolerant than most, it is a lovely addition to the garden, where it will flower sporadically for most of the year.

There are thousands of modern hybrid cultivars, mainly the offspring of *F. fulgens* and *F. magellanica*. All cultivars are suitable for growing in pots, hanging baskets and in the garden.

This fuchsia has the simple elegance of a clean white 'top' over a pink 'skirt'.

Brazilian red cloak

The glossy green, deeply veined foliage of Brazilian red cloak (also called red justicia) is the perfect foil for its bright red plumes, which flower through summer and autumn. A light trim after flowering will keep this shrub looking compact and encourage new growth and further flower flushes.

VITAL STATISTICS

Scientific name: *Megaskepasma erythrochlamys*.
Family: Acanthaceae.
Climate: A frost-free position, or tropical or subtropical climate.
Colours: Red-scarlet flowers in plumes.
Height: Grows 1.5–3 m tall.
Planting time: Any time of the year from pots.
Soil: Plant in humus-enriched soil for best results.
Position: Sun to part shade.
Planting spacing: Plant 1.5 m apart.
Fertiliser: Fertilise each spring with slow-release fertiliser.
Propagation: Soft-tip cuttings in spring or semi-hardwood in summer.

Feature shrub

The bush garden

Many 'wild' flowers from the southern hemisphere have great integrity as garden plants. For some, autumn is their main flowering period.

Correas and croweas

Two delightful plants with similar-sounding names—correas and croweas—are wonderful additions to the autumn bush garden.

Correas are small Australian natives to about 1 m with distinctive flowers—they look a bit like a chef's hat. Three varieties of correa that are worth adding to your garden are the white correa (*Correa alba*), which has very pretty grey foliage and white flowers, and can be pruned into a hedge; the common correa (*C. reflexa*), which looks like a miniature red fuchsia with white tips; and mountain correa (*C. lawrenceana*), which has soft green flowers.

Correas like a sandy, well-drained soil, and they grow in sun or shade. The coastal correa and common correa will even tolerate salt winds, while the mountain correa will cope with frost. Croweas are related to boronias and look very similar when in flower, but they don't have the heavenly perfume that boronias produce. The very hardy correas have bell-shaped flowers similar

ABOVE: Correa baeuerlenii *is commonly known as chef's hat due to its greenish, strangely shaped flowers.*

RIGHT: *White correa (*C. alba*) has beautiful grey foliage that can be clipped into a hedge.*

FAR RIGHT: *Rock correa (*C. glabra*) makes a lovely small shrub.*

to fuchsia blooms, which has resulted in their common name of native fuchsia.

Croweas are evergreen shrubs reaching about 1 m high and spreading to 1.5 m wide. They have a very long flowering season, producing masses of bright pink flowers from autumn through to the end of spring. In cooler, sheltered positions, flowers will continue through summer.

Hardy in hot or cold climates—as long as they are protected from severe frost in winter—croweas can be grown in full sun or partial shade. The soil is the crucial factor, and needs to be free-draining. In heavier soils, mound and raise the beds. Fertilise croweas with slow-release granules in late winter to early spring, and occasionally liquid feed. This plant flowers profusely in both autumn and winter, and is highlighted by pretty bronze-red new growth.

Croweas are also ideal rockery or tub plants. They will grow in full sun or part shade and prefer their soils to be well mulched, as this keeps their root zone cool. Light tip pruning at the end of spring to remove spent flowers will encourage dense, bushy growth.

Banksias

Banksias are in full flower in autumn, with blooms that last for many months before turning into large cobs.

The range of banksias is huge. The best species for the east coast of Australia are probably the heath banksia (*Banksia ericifolia*), which forms lovely golden yellow candles; coastal banksia (*B. integrifolia*), which has softer lemon flowers and grows into a small tree; and the hairpin banksia (*B. spinulosa*), which looks like honey-coloured candles. The west coast of Australia can grow the more tantalising colours of *B. coccinea*.

All banksias grow in full sun, although they will take some shade. Good drainage is essential, except for the swamp banksia (*B. robur*), which forms greenish blue flowers.

Some banksias are quite large, but the range of dwarf varieties and even groundcovers now available makes it possible to grow a banksia in a pot or rockery in a small garden. Among the dwarf banksias are 'Birthday Candles', 'Stumpy Gold', 'Cherry Candles', 'Little Eric' and 'Black Magic'; two ground-cover varieties are 'Roller Coaster' and 'Pygmy Possum'.

ABOVE LEFT: *The heath banksia (B. ericifolia), a native of the eastern sea-board, will attract honey-eating birds to the garden.*

ABOVE RIGHT: *The stunning flowers of the scarlet banksia (B. coccinea) are sought after in the cut flower industry.*

DID YOU KNOW?

The genus *Banksia* is named after Sir Joseph Banks, the naturalist who accompanied James Cook to Botany Bay, where he became the first European to collect specimens of these plants.

ABOVE: Tibouchina
'Jules' makes a lovely
low shrub or pot
plant to about 1 m.

RIGHT: The flowers'
anthers look almost
like spiders' legs
on these two
tibouchinas.

Tibouchinas

Also commonly called lasiandras or glory bushes, tibouchinas are spectacular plants that flower at a time when most of the garden is shutting down for winter. Their rich purple flowers adorn the autumn garden, and carry into winter.

Tibouchinas originate from Brazil, where they grow in semi-rainforest conditions with warm weather and regular rainfall. When growing one in your garden, try to mimic this habitat. A thick mulch of leaf litter, regular summer watering and night-time temperatures above 7°C will all bring out the best in your tibouchina.

Tibouchinas make wonderful street trees or small evergreen shade trees. Their bright green leaves are attractive all year and look great in most garden styles, ranging from the tropical to the traditional, although do guard against placing them in front of red brick houses, as the colours can clash. Prune them lightly after flowering and you'll keep them looking thick and bushy.

Australian cultivars

The Australian plant breeder Ken Dunstan made great progress with the development of these plants. A visit to the northern rivers region of New South Wales will reveal the impact of his work. In the town of Alstonville, streets lined with tibouchinas have given rise to the Tibouchina Festival. The cultivar 'Alstonville' was named after the town. Other famous hybrids—'Jules', 'Noelene' and 'Kathleen'—Dunstan named after members of his family.

The fabulous sprays of purple on *Tibouchina lepidota* 'Alstonville' are a sight to behold. If you don't have room for this 3 m shrub, plant one of the dwarf 'Jules' varieties, which grow to only about 1 m tall. For something a little different, keep an eye out for 'Kathleen', which becomes smothered in lipstick-pink flowers. Or try 'Noelene', which has flowers that begin as white, then turn a lilac-pink shade as they age.

A recent cultivar, called 'Peace Baby', bears white flowers on a compact bush that grows to about 1 m tall, making it perfect for containers and small spaces. The smallest yet developed is 'Groovy Baby', which grows to only 60 cm in height and 80 cm in width. It produces a profusion of large purple flowers and is more cold-tolerant than most types. Simply pop it in a pot and enjoy months of blooms. Remember to trim off flowers as they fade.

DID YOU KNOW? The Australian native *Melastoma affine* has very similar flowers to a tibouchina. Its fruit are sweet and edible, and will stain your tongue blue!

Tibouchina granulosa *in all its autumnal glory.*

CLOCKWISE FROM TOP LEFT: *Double bouvardia (pink); double bouvardia (lilac);* Luculia gratissima; Osmanthus fragrans; *and* Luculia gratissima *'Fragrant Cloud'.*

A fragrant few

For those who appreciate perfume, four of the best flower in autumn. Bouvardia, luculia, osmanthus and Angel's trumpet are essential shrubs for the scented garden.

Bouvardias

Bouvardias have a reputation for being perfumed, but only one species—*Bouvardia longiflora*—actually is. This has beautiful star-shaped white flowers, and comes in a green foliage form as well as a variegated foliage one called 'Silver Star'. Some people regard them as cool-climate plants, too temperamental to grow in a humid subtropical zone such as Sydney. The truth is they are closely related to gardenias, and require a frost-free position; they are, in fact, only cold-resistant down to 7°C.

What bouvardias do need is continuous shaping, as they will look untidy unless you regularly trim them and pinch out the growing tips. Bouvardias like a rich, well-drained soil with heavy watering in summer, and diluted liquid fertiliser during the flowering season.

Luculias

Another heavily perfumed shrub with a bad name for itself is *Luculia gratissima*. It is sometimes disappointing, dying suddenly for no apparent reason, but it is well worth the effort, as it bears stunning clusters of fragrant pink flowers, not unlike a hydrangea, over autumn and winter. It likes a sunny spot with a cool root run that is protected from hot, drying winds. Beside the house is ideal, as the roots can hide under the foundations. There is also a divine white form (*L. grandifolia*) and a beautiful, larger-flowered pink cultivar called 'Pink Spice'.

Luculias are notoriously difficult to grow, and need excellent drainage. Root rot is usually the cause of their demise, so a dose of an anti-rot fungicide will often save sick plants.

Osmanthus

If you want something tougher, you cannot go past osmanthus or sweet olive. To be frank, the tiny off-white flowers, held close to the leaves where they are difficult to see, are uninspiring, but nature has given it a rich, intoxicating apricot nectar fragrance to attract pollinators. Osmanthus is as tough as old boots and will grow anywhere, in any soil. For foliage contrast, try planting the holly-like leaf of *O. heterophyllus*, which also has a gold-edged form called 'Auromarginata' and a purple form called 'Purpurea'. 'Variegatus' has leaves with white margins. These cultivars all flower in autumn.

Angel's trumpet

Angel's trumpet (*Brugmansia* sp.), a relative of tobacco, is the perfect night-time plant for temperate and tropical regions, as the flowers have a dreamy perfume that is most noticeable in the evening. The large flared trumpets hang down in their hundreds—white (in both double and single forms), yellow, burnt gold, orange and apricot. Train them to a single stem by removing any suckers, or keep them shrubby, to about 3 m, by repeated hard pruning. There is also a green- and red-flowered form called *B. sanguinea* as well as an unusual frilly black-edged flower, *B. metel* 'Fastuosa'.

Another plant, commonly called blue angel's trumpet (*Dunalia australis*), is actually from a different genus. It flowers profusely for many months—including spring, summer and autumn—and will tolerate a wide range of soils.

The lingering fragrance of Brugmansia *has a heavenly lemon-scented edge.*

TUBULAR BELLS

Similar in flower to both species fuchsias and angel's trumpet are the members of the *Iochroma* genus, part of the Solanaceae family and native to South America. They too flower in summer and autumn, with flush after flush of long, tubular-bell-like blooms in cherry red, bluish purple or orange and scarlet, depending on the species. Plant them in semi-shade to full sun in a frost-free position, and cut them back hard after flowering.

Shrubs with autumn colour

While most of us think of trees when we imagine autumn's display, there are many shrubs—such as berberis, viburnums, euonymous and even hydrangea—with a brilliant show at leaf fall. The oak-leafed hydrangea (*Hydrangea quercifolia*), famed for its splendid white summer blooms, is one such shrub, with leaves that turn scarlet during autumn.

There is also the *Fothergilla* genus, which includes *F. gardenii*, better known as the witch alder, and *F. major*. Both are bushy shrubs to about 1 m with toothbrush-like, creamy white flowers in spring, but it is in autumn when their true brilliance—of orange, red and yellow foliage colour—is so rewarding. Both species prefer semi-shade in hotter areas. Water them well and apply an annual top dressing of lime to sweeten the soil.

Easy to care for is Chinese plumbago (*Ceratostigma plumbaginoides*), a small shrub that only grows to about 75 cm tall, with red-tinged leaves that become richer and more intense in colour as the weather cools, when they can fall in colder regions. Although the flowers are similar to those of plumbago, the deeper, truer blue flowers of this plant bloom in spring, summer and autumn. They are marvellous when mass planted in almost any well-drained soil, rewarding you well for very little effort.

Members of the *Cotinus* genus are commonly called smoke bush due to their unusual, smoke-like flowers. They are a classic for autumn, but also beautiful year-round, with shades of purple (*Cotinus coggygria* 'Royal Purple'), green ('Daydream') or gold ('Golden Spirit') in summer, depending on the variety. Some also display the classic rich tints of autumn at other times of the year. Cut them back hard each spring to encourage new foliage.

A rarer edition worth hunting out is *Franklinia alatamaha*, a member of the tea family, which boasts large, camellia-like white flowers with a beautiful scent in summer and autumn. As the name suggests, it was named in honour of Benjamin Franklin. It is grown either as a small tree or a larger, multi-stemmed shrub. In autumn, however, the normally glossy, dark green foliage colours crimson before falling to the ground, revealing a textural, vertically striped bark, a lovely thing in itself.

Another beautiful small tree or large shrub, depending on how you treat it, is *Cercis canadensis* 'Forest Pansy', which is perfect for courtyards. Its heart-shaped purple leaves change to a rich russet in autumn before dropping in winter. Late winter reveals lilac flowers on the bare stems and trunks, which give the tree a purple haze, just before it reshoots its leaves in spring. If you want a slightly smaller, and very similar-looking plant, hunt out *Disanthus cercidifolius*, which has heart-shaped leaves that turn scarlet in autumn. It will thrive in acid soils.

One of the very best golden-leafed shrubs for autumn colour is the Japanese spicebush (*Lindera obtusiloba*). The leaves turn buttery yellow in autumn before dropping, then yellow flowers appear in winter on the bare branches. Its glossy, tri-lobed or mitten-like leaves are pretty throughout summer, and the plant will survive and even thrive in shade, growing to 2 m tall and colouring well.

BELOW: *The oak-leaf hydrangea's leaves will turn a deep claret colour before falling in late autumn.*

BELOW RIGHT: *Smoke bush has year-round purple (or gold) leaves, but they colour up to fiery orange before dropping in early winter.*

Roses

Autumn is really the best season for rose blooms—the autumn flush is so much lovelier than the spring one. If you pruned your roses at the end of summer, you should have lovely blooms in mid-autumn. It is well worth visiting the many gardens that are open for inspection at this time to see roses and perennials in full flower, or you could visit rose nurseries to select and smell rose varieties while they are in full flower. Choosing a rose is a task that should not be undertaken lightly, so perhaps visit a rose show at a nursery. It's not like buying a punnet of poppies...a rose can live for 60 years or more!

Autumn rose care

Roses should be making good growth, ready for their autumn flush of flowers. Keep them thriving with deep watering about every fourth day but don't wet the foliage, as this encourages black spot fungus, which is prevalent in areas with high humidity. If your roses are infected (yellow leaves with black spots), you can use a Triforine® spray every ten days.

And watch out for aphids—tiny insects that breed quickly and smother the new growth, sucking the sap and spoiling the blooms. Remove them by hand with a damp tissue or use a pyrethrum or diatomaceous earth spray.

In their growing season, roses need a handful of pelletised manure each month, until late summer. Mulch them well with lucerne straw to enrich the soil, keep the roots cool and keep weeds in check.

The more you pick roses (and bring them inside), the more blooms you will encourage.

Gather therefore the rose, whilst yet is prime,
For soon comes age, that will her pride deflower:
Gather the rose of love, whilst yet is time,
Whilst loving thou mayst loved be with equal crime.

EDMUND SPENSER

ROSE HIPS

The seed pods that develop from the finished rose flower, hips have traditionally been made into rose hip jelly and also tea. Some roses set hips well, while others do not. *Rosa rugosa* (shown here) sets lovely hips that are bright red and orange in autumn. A few other roses that produce hips include *R. brunonii* (long, pale orange–apricot hips), *R. giraldii* (clusters of small hips), *R. longicuspis* (small, dark red hips), 'Wedding Day' (clusters of small orange hips) and 'Geranium' (bright red hips).

Seeds, dried seed head, flowers and leaves of
the beautiful firewheel tree.

Trees

Trees, the 'roof' of a garden, not only add a sense of human scale to buildings but can also provide privacy, add colour and attract wildlife. Not all climates enjoy colour changes and leaf 'fall' in autumn, but that does not mean they are without colour. In warmer areas there are some stunning flowers—including those of the African tulip tree, firewheel tree and berried rainforest plants—providing seasonal interest and colour.

The firewheel tree

One of Australia's showiest native trees, the firewheel tree (*Stenocarpus sinuatus*) forms masses of red spoke-like flowers, which attract lorikeets and rosellas in summer and autumn. The glossy green, wavy leathery leaves make this tree handsome regardless of the season.

The crown is narrow-domed, making it a perfect choice for small gardens. It grows very slowly, normally only reaching about 8 m, and loves a warm,

frost-free spot. It flowers well in a warm climate and tolerates moderate frosts once it is established. Plant the firewheel tree in a moist spot and add organic matter and water-retaining crystals. Buy a grafted tree, otherwise you might have to wait 15 years for the flowers!

Bottlebrushes

Every Australian garden should have a bottlebrush (*Callistemon* sp.). They are tougher than old boots, growing in clay, sand, flood and drought conditions, even coping with salt spray and frost. However, they don't just survive, they thrive, and will flower in spring and then again, just as heavily, in autumn, attracting native birds with their beautiful nectar-rich stamens, which is what the Greek translation of their botanical name means.

While most species are red, some are green (*C. pachyphyllus* 'Green form'), white (*C. viminalis* 'Wilderness White'), pink ('Matilda's Dream' a dwarf variety about 1.5 m in circumference, 'Reeve's Pink' and 'Taree Pink') and even purple ('Mauve Mist' and 'Purple Cloud') and yellow (*C. formosus* and *C. pallidus*); the latter species grows to 3 m.

Depending on the species or variety, bottlebrush can grow from 0.5 m to 12 m tall, although most are around the 3 m mark and will also cope with a wide range of pruning tactics, from the preferred trim after flowering to the 'man prune', or basal prune as it's known botanically, where all the branches are taken back to just above ground level, and anything in between! This means you can hedge and shape them, or simply let them grow into small trees—whatever you desire.

Bottlebrush also respond well to a native fertiliser (low-phosphorus) application in spring and again in autumn. The willow bottlebrush (*Callistemon salignus*) is also known as one of the tallest, reaching 12 m, with lovely papery bark, red or pink new growth and white, pink, greenish, red and mauve forms, making it a tough and beautiful street tree. For me the best of all the reds, however, are *C. viminalis* 'Wildfire', which has slightly weeping branches, grows about 2 m tall and round and has very plump, showy vivid red flowers; 'Harkness', which grows about 3 m tall and has lovely pink new growth; 'Kings Park Special', another taller grower to 5 m, with masses of crimson flowers and pendulous tips; 'Little John', dwarf to 1 m, with blue-green foliage and many red flowers; and 'Rocky Rambler', which is small and wide (0.5 m × 1 m) with pink new growth and red flowers tipped with yellow.

The flowering gums

For many years gardeners have shied away from planting gums because of their size and unpredictability. But with modern breeding and horticultural techniques, you can now safely plant a range of spectacular flowering gums, including the red-flowering gum from Western Australia (*Corymbia ficifolia* syn. *Eucalyptus ficifolia*).

This autumn-flowering tree is probably the most spectacular of all gums, with huge fluffy flowers, varying from near white through to salmon, vermilion and pink. Unfortunately, this colour variation has always been a problem, in that the colour of seed-raised plants cannot be guaranteed.

With grafting techniques not only can you buy a bright, brilliant red-flowering gum that is tolerant of Australian soil types, you can also now get a lovely grafted pink called *Corymbia ficifolia* 'Summertime'. This Western Australian gum is a smallish tree, growing to about 10 m with a broad-domed crown shape. The foliage is thick and leathery, with a nice sheen to it when it's healthy. For best results, plant in a well-drained position in full sun.

LEFT: Eucalyptus leucoxylon *'Rosea' is also known as flowering yellow gum, though the blooms can range from white through to pink and yellow.*

BELOW: *Bottlebrushes are hardy and under-utilised. Keep them trimmed after flowering and they will stay bushy and bloom twice a year.*

Gums

1 *Eucalyptus plenissima* 2 *E. caesia* 'Silver Princess' 3 Mottlecah or rose-of-the-west (*E. macrocarpa*)
4 *E. haemastoma* 5 *E. ropantha* 6 Coral gum (*E. torquata*) 7 Alpine cider gum (*E. gunnii*) 8 *E. hypochlamydea*

9 Small-leaved mottlecah (*E. macrocarpa*)   10 Tallerack (*E. tetragona*)   11 Argyle apple (*E. cinerea*)
12 *E. youngiana*   13 *E. gillii*   14 Scarlet pear gum (*E. stoatei*)   15 Red-flowering gum (*Corymbia ficifolia*
syn. *E. ficifolia*)   16 Redwood (*E. transcontinentalis*)

Abutilons, also called Chinese lanterns, come in compact forms such as the cultivars of the 'Bella' series. Pale pink, pale yellow and orange forms are shown here.

The hibiscus family

The Malvaceae family includes many useful flowering plants such as abutilons, hibiscus, rosella, mallow, hollyhocks, lavatera and alyogyne.

The abutilons, or Chinese lanterns as they are often known, have the daintiest of flowers, with their bell-shaped blooms in pink, yellow, red, apricot and white flowering from early autumn to spring. There is also a blue species, known as flowering maple (*Abutilon vitifolium*), and a variegated groundcover type, *A. megapotamicum* 'Variegatum', which bears dainty fuchsia-like red bells with a prominent yellow stamen. It looks great grafted onto longer stems and trained as weeping standards. Abutilons prefer a semi-shaded but still bright position, much like fuchsias.

The rosella (*Hibiscus sabdariffa*) is an annual sown in spring, and harvested as an edible flower throughout summer and autumn (see page 120). A very pretty addition to the kitchen garden, it grows to 2 × 1.2 m and likes a sunny place in which to thrive. You can preserve the flowers for later consumption in a sugar syrup—they look divine when placed in a glass of sparkling wine.

TROPICAL GARDENS

As the nights are getting cooler, you might not think a tropical garden is appropriate, but if you have a look around at what's in flower now, you might be surprised. Frangipani (pink form shown), hibiscus, golden shower tree (see 'Summer', page 218), tibouchinas, bougainvillea and strelitzia are all in full bloom, creating a tropical paradise. Gardenias (see 'Summer', page 202) and summer jasmines are also still flowering, adding to the heady fragrance of the frangipani blooms.

The fabulous African tulip tree (*Spathodea campanulata*) is still holding its summer display of large, frilled yellow and scarlet bell-shaped flowers, which contrast superbly with its glossy, deep green foliage.

In fact, autumn, not summer, is the time when many of these 'tropical' plants flower the most. Hibiscus, for example, spot flower in summer, but their main flush is now. So if you want to extend the feel of summer, and enjoy those sunny autumn days to the fullest, plant out your own paradise with a touch of the tropics.

The Hawaiian hibiscus (*H. rosa-sinensis*) is the most popular of its genus (see page 208). However, other species are well worth hunting out, such as the Australian natives *H. tileaceus* and *H. heterophyllus*, and the Norfolk Island hibiscus (*Lagunaria patersonia*). The first of these is known commonly as cottonwood, which grows into a small tree, to 6-8 m tall, with a dense canopy that makes it ideal for screening. Tolerant of a wide range of conditions, including coastal and wet, boggy areas, its yellow flowers appear throughout summer and autumn. There is also a copper foliage form called 'Rubra', which shows off these blooms to great advantage. The Norfolk Island hibiscus, which grows to about 8 m tall and features lilac flowers with a yellow stamen and blue-green foliage, is probably best known for its fibreglass-like seeds, which can stick to your skin and cause itching.

Another Australian species is *H. heterophyllus*, the native rosella, a large shrub with flowers of yellow, apricot, white or red, depending on the cultivar. It will grow in a wide range of positions and soils. It also has edible flowers, new leaves and shoots, which can be cooked up like spinach.

DID YOU KNOW? Another interesting member of the Malvaceae family that can be found in the kitchen garden is okra (*Abelmoschus esculentus*), an essential ingredient in gumbo. Plant it in spring and harvest it in summer and autumn.

CLOCKWISE FROM TOP: *This delightful double apricot Hawaiian type grows to 3 m tall; Hibiscus 'Apple Blossom' is a taller shrub to 5 m, making it an excellent screen; an unusual Australian native hibiscus; the single pink H. 'Flower Girl' bears prolifically; foulsapate marron (H. boryanus), from Mauritius, is a rare, beautiful shrub to 2 m.*

Leopard tree

A waterwise and fast-growing tree, with stunning spotted bark and yellow blooms in summer, the leopard tree is semi-deciduous, dropping its leaves just before putting on new growth. Its common name derives from its distinctive mottled bark. It's the perfect small feature tree for paved areas or as a specimen in a garden bed.

VITAL STATISTICS

Scientific name: *Caesalpinea ferrea.*
Family: Fabaceae sub. family Caesalpinia.
Climate: Tropical and subtropical.
Colours: It bears yellow pea flowers in summer and autumn.
Height: Up to 6 m.
Planting time: Plant any time from pots.
Soil: Plant in well-drained, fertile soil.
Position: Full sun.
Planting spacing: About 5 m apart.
Fertiliser: Use an organic fertiliser each spring.

Feature tree

Flowering cherries are prized for their spring blooms and autumn hues.

Create a rich tapestry

Deciduous trees come into their own each autumn or 'fall', their canopies of coloured leaves creating a marvellous rooftop for the garden below. Autumn's sunset brilliance, ranging from buttery yellows to fiery oranges and russet reds, is governed by many factors. When temperatures drop at this time of the year, the leaves of deciduous plants change colour and fall. This change is due to the green pigment chlorophyll disappearing from leaves, allowing the natural colours of carotene and other pigments to shine through.

In general, the cooler the climate, the more pronounced the process and the better the autumn colour, although persimmon and crepe myrtle colour well in the subtropics.

LEFT: *The golden ash lights up like a beacon as it starts its autumn display.*

BELOW: *Autumnal maple leaves (top) have an iridescent delicacy and brilliance to them; the maidenhair tree (bottom) is actually a deciduous conifer (see page 417).*

Autumn in felted slipper shuffles on.
Muted yet fiery—Autumn's character.

VITA SACKVILLE-WEST

ABOVE: *The first signs of leaf change on a Chinese tallow tree, which will later glow red.*

RIGHT: *The magnificence of Chinese pistachio in full swing.*

TOP 10 TREES FOR AUTUMN COLOUR

1 Golden ash (*Fraxinus excelsior* 'Aurea'), which looks like a ball of gold, is a very tough and drought-tolerant species and grows to about 6 m, or larger in ideal conditions.

2 The full-moon maple (*Acer japonicum* 'Aureum') is one of the most dazzling trees, with leaves that colour beautifully in autumn. It rarely reaches more than 10 m, and is even more stunning than the more commonly planted Japanese maple.

3 The maidenhair tree (*Ginkgo biloba*) has buttercup yellow leaves. Fastigiate or columnar in shape, growing to 20–30 m, this lovely tree has leaves shaped like maidenhair fern fronds, which change from green to clear yellow in autumn before they fall, making a lovely carpet beneath the tree. Watch the tree closely as it grows for signs of borer attack, as ginkgo is susceptible, particularly in warm temperate areas.

4 In autumn the leaves of Chinese pistachio (*Pistacia chinensis*), which grows to 8–10 m, develop a rainbow of shades from yellow to scarlet.

5 The American tupelo (*Nyssa sylvatica*), which grows to about 20 m, is a spreading tree with 'layers' of foliage that turn to stunning reds, clear yellow and orange at the same time. Its scientific name means 'water nymph', and the whole genus is great for damp and poorly drained soil.

6 The Japanese maples (*Acer* sp.) make superb courtyard specimen trees. There are hundreds to choose from. Some of the finely dissected varieties will need to grow in semi-shade so the sun does not burn the tender leaves. Most of these maples prefer moist, rich soils. Some have pretty red leaves in spring and others colour gold, bronze and russet in autumn. Depending on the species and variety, the height of these maples varies from about 1 m on short grafts up to 20 m for spreading trees.

7 The trident maple (*Acer buergerianum*) is upright to about 8 m and colours really well, even in warm temperate areas.

8 If you have a smaller garden, consider one of the dogwoods (*Cornus* sp.), loved for their attractive spring flowers and very deep, shining red leaves in autumn. Depending on the species, these trees grow to 3–8 m.

9 Suitable for average-sized gardens, claret ash (*Fraxinus angustifolia* 'Raywood') has deep green leaves that change to rich burgundy. It grows to 8 m.

10 The Chinese tallow tree (*Triadica sebifera* syn. *Sapium sebiferum*) has pretty, heart-shaped leaves that turn bright red, then a lovely deep claret colour. It grows to approximately 10 m and develops a rounded crown, making it a good choice as a courtyard or street tree.

Transplanting

Enthusiastic gardeners often tend to overplant, underestimating the mature size of a plant or simply mixing up a combination. Trees and shrubs that might be in the way of home extensions or pool constructions may also need relocating. So take stock now and make a few moves in the garden.

When to transplant

In mild climates, autumn is a good time for transplanting evergreens, as many shrubs are dormant and will successfully transplant to a new location over the next few months. Only dig up plants you can physically manage. Two or three people should be able to easily handle a plant that is 1–2 m tall.

Don't transplant tropical plants, such as palms, until summer, as they like the warm weather to help them settle in. Winter is best for deciduous plants and *Camellia japonica*. You should choose a cool, calm day for digging up your plant.

The main reason transplants die is water stress. Following these simple steps will increase the likelihood of a smooth, trauma-free transition. Watering with DroughtShield® by Yates will help reduce transplant shock.

Preparation

Before you lift your tree or shrub, dig a large hole in the new spot and improve the removed soil by adding well-rotted manure and compost. Then add just a sprinkle of water crystals and use this improved soil for backfilling.

1 Using a sharp spade (see the tools listed in 'The garden shed' section, page 356), cut through the roots in a circle at least 40 cm away from the trunk (or ten times the width of the trunk). You'll need to widen this trench in order to get under the roots.

2 Slide the spade under the roots and lift the tree onto some hessian or an old sheet, trying to keep as much soil on the roots as you can.

3 Wrap the rootball in the hessian or sheet. This method is called 'ball and burlap'.

4 Use the wrap to slide or lift the plant into its new position.

5 Place the plant in the prepared hole, backfill with the improved soil, then water in well using a watering can with a little soluble seaweed solution added to the water. Spray your plant with an anti-transpirant to reduce stress. Prune off any damaged growth, and cover it with an old sheet or shadecloth to protect it from the sun. Keep the soil evenly moist, especially if the weather turns warm or windy. It will take up to six weeks for the plant to re-establish itself in its new home.

6 Insert a stake if your transplant seems top-heavy and unstable, or if it is in an exposed position, but take care not to damage the rootball. Use three stakes if necessary and attach them with flexible ties—such as budding tape, old stockings or hessian webbing—in a figure eight. This allows the trunk to bend with the breeze but still remain stable.

ORIENTATION

As plants grow, they have a definite front and back side. Try to position them in their new home with their best side facing forward. Failing this, orient them in their original aspect so they don't become sunburnt as easily.

After digging through the roots, carefully wrap (or 'ball and burlap') the rootball in hessian (left). The final step is to insert a stake alongside the rootball for stability (right). Take care not to put the stake through the roots.

Herbs, fruit and vegetables

Autumn is a time of ripening fruits and nuts, and storing away for winter. As the weather becomes colder, store hard-skinned pumpkins in a dry place, and dig up old potatoes. Remove crops such as tomatoes, eggplants, squash and melons, pickling and bottling any remaining fruits. When your pantry is full and the cupboards are bursting, autumn is drawing to a close.

Pumpkins of all shapes and sizes are part of every harvest festival in autumn.

Herbs

Harvest and preserve herbs for use in winter, prune hedges of evergreen herbs, such as rosemary and lavender, collect seeds and dress beds with manure.

Preserving

Preserving herbs for later use can be achieved in various ways. The most common method is drying. For this to work, you need to either hang stems upside down in a cool, dry place until they dry out, or place them on baking paper on trays and dry them in a very low oven (80°C). Once the leaves are dry, they can be stored in airtight containers.

You can also preserve herbs in oils and butters. First, warm the oil, add the leaves of your choice and cover. After a few days, remove the leaves from the oil, especially if they are soft like basil leaves, then store the infused oil in sterilised containers and use the herb oil as required. You can also make pestos, combining macerated herbs with oils and nuts to form pastes, then freeze them for later use.

To make your own herb butter, chop up fresh herbs and add them to softened butter, then form the butter into a roll, cut it into slabs and freeze them so you can use the individual slabs for instant bursts of flavour whenever you need them.

Some fresh herbs, such as mint and chives, can be chopped up then frozen with water in ice cube trays, to be used later in soups and stews (see box, opposite). Or you could pickle herbs in vinegar solutions, or even extract them in alcohol to make tipples. The most common example of this technique is vanilla extract (see box, opposite).

DID YOU KNOW? A spice is any part of a plant, other than its leaves, that is used to flavour food.

Freezing mint

1 Remove the leaves from the stems.
2 Chop the leaves.
3 Pour water into the tray. Add the chopped mint and freeze.
4 Use your mint ice cubes in summer drinks or add them to curries.

ROSEMARY

Highly ornamental, with long-lasting fragrant flowers that attract bees, rosemary has strongly aromatic, leathery leaves that are dark green above, and white and felted beneath. Some plants have an upright bushy habit, making them perfect for hedging and topiary, while other types have a sprawling habit, making them useful for rock walls and sunny banks.

Traditionally, rosemary was thought to bring good fortune and fertility; Henry VIII's fourth wife, Anne of Cleves, wore a rosemary wreath at her wedding. She didn't bear the king children but at least she survived the marriage!

Rosemary literally means 'seaside dew'. It grows well in nutrient-rich, semi-shaded areas. Harvest the leaves before the flowers open. Sow seeds or take cuttings or divisions in spring, then plant them 45 cm apart in the garden. Divide plants every three years. Cut rosemary back to the ground in autumn and feed it with manure or compost.

There's rosemary, that's for remembrance.

WILLIAM SHAKESPEARE

VANILLA EXTRACT

Vanilla is a spice produced from the seed pods of a climbing tropical orchid (*Vanilla planifolia*) from South America. Pure vanilla extract is easy to make at home. Simply split two vanilla beans and put them in a sterilised glass jar or bottle with 1 cup of unflavoured vodka. Cap and store in a cool, dark place, shaking gently every few weeks. It will be ready to use in two months but lasts for ages.

Dried chrsyanthemum flowers

Rosemary

Mint

Tea please

Herb teas have been consumed since ancient times. A small handful of fresh or dried herbs can be made into tea by either pouring boiling water over sprigs (herb tea) or simmering herbs and water in a pan for a few minutes before straining (herb brew). Try the flowers of German chamomile, jasmine, lavender and bergamot, and the leaves of mints, lemon balm, lemongrass or verbena, hyssop, oregano, parsley and rosemary, various thymes and sages. Pick tender young leaves before the flowers open and before the heat of the day.

Thyme

Orange blossom

Sage

Rose hip

BERGAMOT
Native to North America, bergamot (*Monarda* sp.) replaced Indian tea in many American households following the Boston Tea Party of 1773. The common name, bergamot, comes from an Italian word because the scent of the crushed leaf resembles the aroma of the bitter Italian orange used in aromatherapy, perfumes and cosmetics. Native Americans used it for colds.

Edible flowers

There was a time when a plant had to be useful to justify its space in a garden. This could mean growing herbs for medicinal purposes, or for dying cloth or weaving, perhaps for stock fodder or simply for the flowers, which could be eaten in their own right. Many flowers fall into the medicinal category (think lavender and calendula). Some help repel insects or attract pollinators and other beneficial insects to the garden, but what many people are only just discovering is that they can be delicious.

Flowers are our forgotten harvest. Some edible flowers commonly found in the garden are calendula, roses and carnations (the white heel or base of pinks must be removed, as this is very bitter), orange and lemon flowers, cornflowers, fuchsias, salvia, violets and geraniums.

A dish or drink graced by flowers should be a celebration of a distinctive and lovely scent. Try them. Some are sweet, and make an elegant dessert decoration when dipped in egg white,

rolled in caster sugar and dried. Others, such as chive and nasturtium flowers, have nutty or peppery flavours and also add colour when tossed fresh into salads.

Citrus flowers can be added to water for a delicious summer drink or, for the ultimate in relaxation, try a Pimms, dry ginger ale and borage blossoms—it reinvigorates the spirits! Mexicans are partial to a drink infused with Jamaica (or rosella) flowers (*Hibiscus sabdariffa*), while Europeans flavour wine, fruit compotes and jams by stirring sprays of elderflowers into them. Try freezing flowers into ice cubes or a flower bowl for festive occasions.

Cloves (*Syzygium aromaticum*) and capers (*Capparis spinosa*) are flower buds. Clinging to walls, the caper bush seems to scorn soil and water but love heat.

Mediterranean and Middle Eastern cuisines have long traditions of using flowers, creating jasmine tea and rose-flavoured Turkish delight. Draw some inspiration from them and experiment with flowers from your garden.

CLOCKWISE FROM TOP LEFT: Rosa rugosa *petals can be used in salads; pineapple sage has bright red flowers for many months; the flowers of common sage taste very similar to the leaves; elderflowers are traditionally made into cordial (see page 118) and wine.*

LAVENDER ICE-CREAM

In a saucepan put 8 washed and dried stems of English lavender with 600 mL thick cream and 1 small piece lemon rind. Heat until almost boiling, then stir in 160 g sugar until dissolved.

Strain through a fine sieve, then gradually pour onto 4 egg yolks, lightly whisked in a bowl. Return to the pan and stir over low heat until thick enough to coat the back of a spoon; do not boil. Pour into a chilled metal tray to cool. Freeze until frozen around the edge, but not in the centre.

In a food processor or bowl, beat until smooth. Freeze again and repeat this process twice more. Cover with greaseproof paper and freeze. **Serves 6–8.**

Sorrel

Also known as spinach dock and narrow-leaved dock, this bitter green looks similar to spinach, and, because of the presence of oxalic acid, has a lemony, slightly metallic flavour to it. For this reason, young, tender leaves and even sprouts are best eaten. It can be made into a soup, used in salads and is often served with eggs. Wrapping fish with it will keep the flesh moist and give it a slight tang. With its red veination, this species of sorrel makes a particularly attractive addition to the garden.

VITAL STATISTICS

Scientific name: *Rumex sanguineus.*
Family: Polygonaceae.
Climate: Most climates are suitable, but seed germinates best at 7–23°C.
Culture: Sorrel can often be found growing wild in pastures, and it is one of those 'wild greens' people will often forage for.
Colours: Bright green foliage and red veins.
Height: Grows to about 30 cm.
Planting time: Plant in spring in temperate areas and through winter in tropical regions.
Soil: Grow in moist soil with a pH of 5.5–7. It likes fertile ground.
Position: Grows best in partial shade.
Planting spacing: Sow the seed 3 cm deep, 30 cm apart.
Fertiliser: Add some well-composted manure or organic matter prior to sowing.
Pests/diseases: Caterpillars at times.
Propagation: Grow from seed.
Storage: Foliage can be stored frozen if blanched first.

Feature herb

As for the garden of mint, the very smell of it alone recovers and refreshes our spirits, as the taste stirs up our appetite for meat.

PLINY THE ELDER

Fruit

Autumn's selection is based on nuts and the firmer-fleshed fruit such as apples and pears, which store well. There are also some late harvests from tropical fruits available in temperate climates that will add interest to the fruit bowl and also delight your taste buds.

CLOCKWISE FROM TOP LEFT: *'Packham' is an excellent eating pear; 'Granny Smith' apples, an Australian variety, developing; when quince ripen they remain hard, but soften after cooking; as apples begin to ripen, make sure you stay alert to any signs of damage from codling moth larvae (see page 337).*

Pome fruit

Pome fruit are all members of the rose family and include nashi pears, apples, pears, quinces, medlars and loquats. If growing fruit yourself sounds appealing, but space is limited, consider espaliered fruit trees (see 'Winter', page 436) or a potted collection. Many trees have dwarf varieties that are suitable for containers (see 'Dwarf apples and stone fruit for pots', page 336).

Apples and pears grow best in temperate and cold temperate regions, and are seldom damaged by frosts. They are some of the hardiest and longest lived of all fruit trees.

The modern apple varieties have been developed from crab apples (*Malus* sp.), and there is now a great range of varieties available, including 'Cox's Orange Pippin', good for cold areas; 'Golden Delicious', which stores well and has good yield; 'Granny Smith', the most popular culinary variety, suitable for any climate; and 'Jonathan', which is popular commercially.

Apples make excellent home garden trees because they do not need considerable attention and have great keeping properties. At planting time, prune the leading shoots back to three buds. They do need cross-pollination, and should either be multigrafted or planted 10 m or closer to another suitable apple.

Pears (*Pyrus communis*) withstand more frost than stone or other fruits. Most varieties require cross-pollination, so check with your local garden centre. 'Beurre Bosc' is a good dessert pear, a regular and heavy cropper. 'Packham', an Australian variety, is a large pear, perfectly shaped and with excellent flavour. '20th Century', a nashi pear that originated in Japan, is a variety that combines the flavour and sweetness of a pear with the crispness of an apple.

Fruits of the loquat (*Eriobotrya japonica*) are yellow to orange and can be eaten fresh, stewed or preserved. They do well in subtropical to cool temperate areas and are useful because many varieties ripen over winter when there is a general lack of fresh fruit.

Quinces (*Cydonia oblonga*) grow on a deciduous tree that reaches about 4 m. The fruit tastes delicious once cooked, when it is miraculously transformed into a pink-fleshed, sweet-tasting sensation, perfect for jams, jellies and stews.

Pome fruits

1 'Corella' pear 2 '20th Century' China pear 3 'Rouge d'Anjou' pear 4 'Beurre Bosc' pear 5 'Nijiseiki'
China pear 6 'Shinsei' China pear 7 Unripe 'Purpurea' crab apples 8 'Kosui' China pear 9 'Splendour' apple
10 'Frosts Seedling' apple 11 'Smyrna' quince 12 'Coal' pear

13 'Aromatic' apple **14** 'Geeveston Fanny' apple **15** 'Canadian Pippin' apple **16** 'Bulmers Norman' apple **17** 'Starks Blushing Gold' apple **18** 'Winter Nervis' apple **19** 'Ya Li' China pear **20** 'Red Williams' pear **21** 'Tsu Li' China pear **22** 'Winter Banana' apple **23** 'Pink Lady' apple **24** 'McIntosh' apple **25** 'Cox's Orange Pippin' apple **26** 'Candian Spartan' apple **27** 'Earligold' apple **28** 'Twenty Ounce' apple

Persimmon

The persimmon is a handsome tree, with its picturesque trunk and glossy green leaves, which turn burnt orange and scarlet as the cold weather approaches. Many of the named cultivars have a delightful pendulous habit. Closely related to ebony, from which a piano's black keys are made, it also has superb qualities as a timber tree and is used to make precious objects in East Asia. The orange-skinned fruit has a unique texture and flavour.

VITAL STATISTICS

Scientific name: *Diospyros kaki*.

Family: Ebenaceae.

Climate: Subtropics to cool temperate zones.

Culture: The trees have a fragile root system, which should not be allowed to dry out during planting.

Colours: The flowers are small, greenish yellow and rather insignificant.

Height: Up to 13 m, normally half this in gardens.

Planting time: Winter.

Soil: Will tolerate moist conditions and heavy clay.

Position: Full sun for maximum leaf colour and cropping.

Planting spacing: 6 m apart from other trees.

Fertiliser: Dress with citrus fertiliser each winter.

Pests/diseases: Birds love the fruit. Fruit fly can damage the skin.

Propagation: Seed or grafted named varieties or suckers in winter.

Storage: Ripen fruit indoors once the skin has coloured, but the flesh is still firm. This protects it from birds. There are astringent varieties, which must be eaten when mushy, and non-astringent varieties, which can be eaten like an apple, so choose carefully to suit your taste.

Feature fruit

Dwarf apples and stone fruit for pots

With space for the productive garden diminishing in the average backyard, more people are looking for ways to grow fruit trees in a smaller, more efficient space. Dwarf apples are perfect for pots or tight spaces. The Ballerina® series, which includes 'Polka', 'Bolero' and 'Waltz', grows like a pole, upright to 2 m and with no significant side branches.

There are also standard cultivars—such as 'Jonathan', 'Delicious' and 'Granny Smith'—that have been grafted onto dwarfing rootstocks. 'M27' rootstock is best for pots. These trees will produce the same-sized branches and fruits but on a smaller tree, with the usual added bonus of crops after two to three years. Apples like a cold winter and calcium-rich soil. Apply a handful of dolomite each year, after pruning in winter. Most apples need other apple trees to pollinate them, but the cultivar 'Pinkabelle' is partially self-pollinating if you are really short on space.

PEST PATROL: CODLING MOTH

The codling moth is a small brown moth approximately 1 cm long. It can cause a significant amount of damage to apples, pears, crab apples, quinces, stone fruit and walnuts. The moth lays eggs on or near the fruit. Once hatched, the larvae chew their way into the fruit core, where they feed, producing webbing and droppings.

Once the larvae are fully fed (having ruined your fruit), they chew out a tunnel and move down the branches and trunk searching for a suitable place to pupate. During the warm weather, there may be up to three generations on the one tree.

At this time of the year, codling moths are pupating for their final cycle before winter. You can trap them now by tying a piece of hessian around the tree trunk, then checking this at regular intervals and destroying any of the 1 cm long pupae.

Maintaining good hygiene with your fruit trees—such as cleaning up any old fruit from the ground, avoiding leaving any rubbish or packing cases about where the larvae can hide, and spraying with a copper spray in winter—will all help control this serious pest. Spinosad is also registered for use over the fruiting period.

A dwarf apple tree espaliered as a space-saving measure makes an eye-catching feature.

Walnuts and pears you plant for your heirs.

OLD PROVERB

Peaches and nectarines—both *Prunus* species—require fewer chilling hours than apples, and there are even varieties that grow in the subtropics. In the 'Sunset Backyard Beauty' series there is a yellow-fleshed nectarine and a white-fleshed peach, which have very low chilling requirements and only grow to about 1 m. Both have lovely pink blossoms in spring. Gardeners in colder areas can try the 'Edward Valley Red', a yellow-fleshed peach with a red blush and a very sweet flavour.

ABOVE: *Apple guava fruit grow to about the same size as their namesake.*

ABOVE RIGHT: *The cherry guava is the apple guava's smaller cousin.*

RIGHT: *Pineapple guava leaves have a silver underside that shimmers in the breeze, and the trunk has a marvellous mottling to it.*

The guavas

Some delicious fruit ripen throughout autumn. The pineapple guava, or feijoa (*Acca sellowiana*), is a beautiful tree, not only because of its fabulous fruit but also because of its marble-patterned trunk and handsome foliage, which has a silver underside. The green-skinned oval fruits, about the size of a passionfruit, can be eaten fresh, juiced or cooked. They tolerate any position you can dish up, and any soil you plant them in.

The other guavas include apple guava (*Psidium guajava*) and cherry guava (*P. cattleianum*). They are no trouble to grow in the garden, and make an attractive evergreen tree to about 8 m, which has the added bonus of bearing sweet fruit that can be juiced, cooked or eaten raw.

POMEGRANATE BY ANOTHER NAME
Guavas originated in South America, and the name 'guava' comes from a South American Indian word. The botanical name *Psidium* is from the Greek word, *psidion*, for pomegranate. True pomegranate (*Punica granatum*) is one of the oldest trees in cultivation and its masses of seeds, in a sweet red pulp, look like jewels.

In a nutshell

Nuts evoke some of the magic of autumn. Images of squirrelling away reserves of food for winter come to mind, as do open fires, roasted chestnuts and hearty conversation.Some nuts need to be grown in a cold climate and take a long time to reach maturity. Included in this group are pistachios, walnuts, hazelnuts and chestnuts.

Others, such as almonds, require hot, dry summers and cool winters—a typical Mediterranean climate—and most (but not all, look for the Almond All-in-One®) need another almond type with which to cross-pollinate.

Some nuts are tropical or subtropical. Native to Australia, the macadamia has sweet and soft round, white kernels that mature in autumn and winter. The tropical almond (*Terminalia catappa*) can also be grown in coastal areas. It is an unusual-looking tree with a very wide, flat canopy that is much broader than it is tall. The almond-like fruits can be eaten roasted or raw. There is also a tropical chestnut or shaving brush tree (*Pachira aquatica*), and of course peanuts (*Arachis hypogaea*), which are not true nuts but actually legumes, can also be grown in warmer climes.

Some pine trees have edible nuts; the most noteworthy is *Pinus pinea*, from which pine nuts are harvested. The Australian native bunya-bunya pine (*Araucaria bidwillii*) is now being harvested commercially as bush tucker, but it has always been prized by Aboriginal Australians. Bunya-bunya pines have to be at least 15 years old to produce nuts; even then, the trees bear well only every second or third year, when each tree produces about 100 nuts.

Who will eat the kernel of the nut must break the shell.

OLD PROVERB

YDID YOU KNOW? Bunya nuts are about 30 cm across, about the size of a football, and weigh about 10 kg.

CLOCKWISE FROM TOP LEFT: *Almond fruit look like peaches, to which they are related; macadamia nuts are the most successful Australian food export; peanuts are underground nodules; chestnuts have attractive foliage as well as sweet nuts; these individual bunya nuts come from one giant cone; pistachios are great trees for arid areas.*

Vegetables

Autumn is the time to plant winter vegies. Choose a sunny spot and improve the soil, then plant carrots, beetroot, cabbages, cauliflower, broccoli, Brussels sprouts, onions and spinach.

A fruit is a vegetable with looks and money. Plus, if you let fruit rot, it turns into wine, something Brussels sprouts never do.

P.J. O'ROURKE

Brassicas for a winter harvest

Brussels sprouts, cabbages, cauliflower and broccoli are among the most notable members of the Brassica family, which also includes mustards, turnips, pak choi, calabrese, kale, kohlrabi and cress. These have one thing in common: they are basically cool-weather crops.

Cabbages tend to be overlooked by those of us who remember childhood meals accompanied by smelly boiled cabbage, but the Chinese and Eastern Europeans have used them extensively and creatively in their cuisines. These strong-growing mainstays of the winter kitchen garden are not fussy about

CLOCKWISE FROM TOP LEFT: *The least favourite vegetable of all time is the Brussels sprout; rich in vitamins, kale is said to lower your risk of cancer; cauliflower's white heart can these days be yellow, purple or orange; cabbage is extremely versatile, and pickling it (to make sauerkraut or kimchi) is a popular option.*

climate, and store well, whether fresh or pickled. The many varieties are suited to different climates and seasons, making them available year-round. The leaves are bluish, red or green with either smooth or crinkled textures.

Broccoli, like cauliflower, is actually a head of flowers that are eaten green, before the yellow petals show. Like Brussels sprouts, the central head can be picked, which forces side shoots that will also crop and continue your harvest. A purple form of broccoli makes a nice change from the usual green type. Cauliflower, too, is available in a number of different colours, including orange, yellow and purple.

BROCCOLI Before eating, soak broccoli heads in cold salted water to kill any hidden caterpillars.

The purple colour in this Sicilian broccoli contains anthocyanin, which is said to help prevent heart disease.

Celeriac

Although celeriac is closely related to celery, it's not the stalks that are eaten but the greatly swollen root. Don't be put off by the lumpy, brown and somewhat hairy look of the root; the wonderful flavour is well worth the effort of peeling it ready for consumption.

VITAL STATISTICS

Scientific name: *Apium graveolens* var. *rapaceum.*
Family: Apiaceae.
Climate: Cool-season vegetable that is quite cold-hardy.
Uses: Great for soups, salads and gratins.
Colours: Creamy white root and green celery-like leaves.
Height: Up to 50 cm.
Planting time: Sow seed in early autumn.
Soil: Plant in well-drained and friable soil with added organic matter.
Position: Full sun.
Planting spacing: Plant 40 cm apart.
Fertiliser: Pelletised animal manure every few weeks.
Harvest: After 20 weeks.
Propagation: From seed.

Feature vegetable

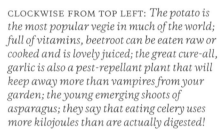

CLOCKWISE FROM TOP LEFT: *The potato is the most popular vegie in much of the world; full of vitamins, beetroot can be eaten raw or cooked and is lovely juiced; the great cure-all, garlic is also a pest-repellant plant that will keep away more than vampires from your garden; the young emerging shoots of asparagus; they say that eating celery uses more kilojoules than are actually digested!*

Going underground

You can grow many root vegetables—including carrots, beetroot, parsnips, celeriac, turnips and white or red radishes—from seed directly into your patch of earth. All are deliciously sweet when eaten fresh.

The potato

The most widely eaten vegetable in the Western world, the potato (*Solanum tuberosum*) is a tuber, a root modified as a starch storage vessel, which can be propagated from the 'eyes' of seed potatoes (see 'Winter', page 444), usually purchased in your local nursery as certified disease-free. For a similar flavour, try Jerusalem artichokes.

Although readily available in shops, spuds that are grown at home have a

flavour all their own. They can be harvested early to be eaten as 'chats' or sweet baby potatoes. Other interesting potatoes include 'Désirée' and 'Pink Eye', which both have pink skin; 'Purple Congo', which has purple or bluish skin; 'King Edward', which has light skin dappled with pink; and sweet potatoes.

Garlic

Some root vegetables are actually edible bulbs rather than tubers. These include garlic, spring onions, chives, onions, leeks and shallots, all members of the allium family. As a cultivated vegetable, the onion goes back so far that its origins are now uncertain—it may be native to Central Asia—and it seems probable that the Romans spread it through Europe; Roman soldiers ate garlic to keep their strength up.

For centuries garlic has been renowned as a remedy and infection preventative, as its sulphur content acts as a strong disinfectant. In the Middle

DID YOU KNOW? Garlic is also said to prevent leaf curl in peaches and ward off black spot on roses.

CLOCKWISE FROM TOP LEFT: *'Golden Nugget', 'Queensland Blue', ornamental gourds, 'Japanese' and 'Triamble'. Pumpkins come in a huge range of shapes, colours and sizes up to one 921 kg monster-grown in California in 2013—that was almost as big as a car.*

Ages it was hung outside the door, rather ineffectually, to stop the plague, but in the First World War sphagnum moss soaked in garlic juice was used as a dressing to heal gunshot wounds.

The longer garlic is cooked, the milder the flavour; also, the bigger the clove, the less intense the flavour. Reduce 'garlic breath' by eating parsley, basil, mint or thyme, or do as the Chinese do and chew cardamom pods.

Stems and leaves

Other vegetables can be covered with earth, but it's the stems and leaves that are eaten, not the roots. For example, you can improve the taste of asparagus, celery and chicory enormously by using a technique called 'earthing up' to blanch the stalks. Simply mound the soil around the plants as shoots emerge and the stalks will become elongated, white and tender. Asparagus won't be ready for full harvesting for five years, however, so you'll need to be patient.

Pumpkins and gourds

Rogue pumpkins have a habit of coming up all over the garden, courtesy of the compost heap. 'Queensland Blue' and 'Butternut', both oldies, are reliable fruiters. Tolerant of a wide range of soils, pumpkins and gourds respond well to added manure or compost. They do best in full sun and, if you plant flowers nearby, you'll encourage bees to help with pollination.

When you are buying plants, select the bushy varieties with fewer leaves that won't take over the garden. These include 'Golden Nugget', which is common in the shops, 'Baby Blue' and 'Butterbush'. They can even be grown in a large pot, or over an arch, a great idea for a balcony or courtyard garden. Allow the plants to die completely before harvesting your crop at the end of the growing season.

Gourds are extremely ornamental versions. Some are worth eating, but others are simply decorative.

Winter

Quiet. Chilly days, skeletal
leaves and bare branches. Cold
noses, rosy cheeks, chapped lips.
Cardigans and coats. Big plans.
Winter in the garden.

Overview of the season

These cooler months can be the best time of the year in the garden. There is time for pause and contemplation, drawing together events from the gardening year and making plans for the one to come.

Winter also gives you a chance to warm up with hard physical work; after all, there's plenty to do in the garden, and no excuse for hibernating. Tidy up, fix fences, and service equipment and tools, ready for the more demanding seasons to follow.

What winter lacks in colour it certainly makes up for with fragrance. Many of the finest perfumed plants— such as early jonquils, freesias, boronia, daphne and osmanthus—create their own little scented atmospheres at this time of year.

Temperatures are low enough to consider doing some serious work in the garden. It's a great opportunity to move plants that need rearranging, take control of the weeds and put any grand plans into action. Major projects—such as putting in ponds, gazebos, garden lighting and paving—can all be done with a minimal effect on anything that has to be shifted.

Mulching now will help contain the warmth which has built up in the soil over summer and autumn. It will also keep weeds at bay and save watering throughout summer. A thick blanket layer of leaf litter will return all those lost nutrients to the soil where they will benefit your garden. Either use old leaves as mulch or compost them into nutritious leaf mould. However, be cautious, because old mulch may now be harbouring fungal spores around roses and other disease-prone plants so replace this annually after pruning.

There is often a bit of wind around in winter so check that plant ties are secure but not cutting into trunks or branches. Although the days are cooler at this time of year, the wind can be as drying for plants as summer heat, so deep watering once a week will help replenish this moisture.

In cold zones

If you live in an area where snow and heavy frosts occur throughout winter, you may need to take extra precautions during late autumn and winter. Any frost-tender plants—such as geraniums, mint and chrysanthemums—should be stored over winter in a greenhouse or in boxes with a cover.

Even ponds may need some work. Store or keep floating aquatics in a frost-free spot, and remove, clean and dry pumps so that ice doesn't damage them. You may need to cover delicate new seedlings with a cloche or some other covering. In areas with heavy snowfall, bind conifers with twine to stop branches breaking and disfiguring formal shapes after heavy falls.

LEFT: *The bare dark stems of* Cornus *and the grey foliage of tree germander (*Teucrium fruticans) *can be trimmed into hedges and are very hardy, coping with frosts, poor soils and coastal conditions.*

Weatherwatch

If your plants die off suddenly in wet weather, you may have drainage problems. Installing drains will address these problems. Drains can either be subsurface, such as agricultural pipe, or surface drains, such as swales or gravel trenches.

Garden design and detail

As the weather starts to cool, take some time to consider your garden's design. Perhaps your garden lacks a focal point or needs some interest, especially during winter. It's fun to add your own stamp and personality with detailing.

Whether it's a piece of sculpture, a fountain or a seat for relaxation after a hard day's work, there are many non-essential but attractive features that can be added to the basic framework of your garden. Whatever feature you choose, remember to ensure it fits into its surroundings and requires minimum maintenance. Combine sympathetic materials, such as timber or stone, or pick up on the specific theme or style of your garden.

Garden furniture

A garden seat can bring great pleasure. From it you can relax, plan your next project, note the combinations of texture and colour that work well, and keep a garden diary with notes and ideas for next year.

Well-chosen garden furniture can provide an extra dimension to a small garden. In tight spaces it's unlikely that you'll have room for more than one seat, so siting that chair or bench needs careful consideration. Think about having banquet seating or a raised garden wall built with wide ledges for extra seating if you like entertaining.

Decide whether you want to sit in the sun or in the shade then use your seating as accent points—tucked into a corner, set against a wall or hedge, or sheltering under an arbour where you'll have some cover. Try and anchor furniture with background shrubbery and pots of trailing plants around their base.

To keep wooden furniture at its best, check it annually for white ants or wood rot and look after it with regular oiling.

That time of year thou mayst in me behold
When yellow leaves, or none, or few, do hang
Upon those boughs which shake against the cold,
Bare ruin'd choirs, where late the sweet birds sang.

WILLIAM SHAKESPEARE

What lies beneath your seating is also important but often forgotten. Try to position your garden furniture on a solid level surface of pavers, bricks or compacted gravel. Grass might look idyllic, but the charm will soon wear off after you've spent a few weekends lugging a heavy bench out of the mower's path, or have to remedy a muddy patch in front of it.

Select furniture that matches the style of your garden as well as your lifestyle. Wicker furniture might look great, for example, but if you don't have a verandah for weather protection it won't last. If the area is exposed, consider one of the polymer plastic lookalike weaves tailored for outside, or a faux bamboo that's actually metallic.

Materials

Timber has long been popular, with the classic teak bench remaining the benchmark by which others are measured. Not all timbers weather as well, and will probably need sanding back and oiling at least every few years. If your garden has a rustic, cottage feel to it, bush furniture made from rough-hewn logs would complement it well.

Iron and iron/timber combinations, such as the classic railway bench, last well, although the iron may need repainting or oiling every few years to keep it free from rust and cracking. Iron and glass furniture has become very popular, but if you're considering this option, ensure the glass is double-laminated and positioned in a sheltered part of the garden such as a courtyard.

One of the most durable of materials is stone or reconstituted stone. Its classic look is rarely out of place, it will never date and it lasts forever in all weathers. And always use a sun- and waterproof fabric for your soft furnishings—there are many UV-resistant products, but even oiled fabrics like oilskins can work. Garden furniture can be made from just about anything. In the right spot even a couple of planks of wood on brick bases are suitable; just use your imagination.

TOP: *Stone seats like these need some shade so that they don't overheat in summer and become too hot to sit on.*

ABOVE: *This Asian-style granite bench looks very much at home surrounded by bamboo.*

Sculpture and garden ornaments

Browse around any garden centre and you'll find figures of every size and description, ranging from gnomes painted in football team colours to stalking cats. The selection of statuary and ornaments varies so much it's worth shopping around: look in galleries as well as in shops specialising in garden artistry. Sometimes a good piece is hard to find, and you might have to wait until it finds you, or even make it yourself!

Whatever your choice, try and site it in a place that makes sense, such as at the end of a narrow path or nestled beside a tree. A focal point should draw your eye and entice you through the garden, personalising it. Be sure to secure garden features properly and plant around them so that they become part of the garden.

Origins

In the earliest gardens, ornamental features fulfilled a useful domestic role: sundials indicated the time of day; dovecotes housed pigeons which were eaten when fresh meat was in short supply; wellheads supplied water for drinking or bathing; and urns held funerary ashes.

Today, many garden features serve merely as a design element or focal point, but of course there is nothing to stop you from making use of them.

Adaptions

Objects of garden history, old farming equipment and even architectural details can all enjoy second lives as garden sculpture. Forcing pots for rhubarb, old ploughs, barrows and even chimney pots can add character and interest.

Make your own ornament

Creating your own garden art is easy. Stack pebbles on top of each other to form a tower or cairn, or make your own birdbath using terracotta pots and a large saucer or dish: just stack two or

LEFT: *Marking the entrance with pots makes a statement. The Italianate oversized urn adds grandeur and scale to this walkway, as well as creating a focal point.*

three pots of different sizes by inverting them on top of each other so that the largest is on the bottom. Top off the stack with the terracotta saucer or dish, but make sure you waterproof it with a silicone-based waterproofing agent before you fill it with water.

Installation art is very popular now, and can look great in the garden. It is simply a short-lived display, so it's perfect for adding a bit of seasonal fun. Hang strings of shells and driftwood on fishing line for a seaside garden, or 'plant' pink flamingoes for a touch of whimsy. Even painting stakes in a bright colour and using them en masse in your garden can look great.

In cooler months, too, consider adding a fire pit or brazier. It provides a natural hub for people to gather around, and if chosen well can be a lovely focal point even when not alight. Gas or timber, the ambience and warmth of outdoor heaters will entice most homebodies out of doors.

FINE DETAIL

Adding small finishing touches such as tap tops, wall plaques and plant stands can really make a garden, so keep your eye out for those small details that complete the picture.

The air is cold above the woods;
All silent is the earth and sky,
Except with his own lonely moods
The blackbird holds a colloquy.

RICHARD HENRY THORNE

CLOCKWISE FROM TOP: *This carved bust is made from limestone, which easily grows a full head of 'hair' out of moss; a finial, half smothered with blue potato vine, adds a stately effect to the garden; a tub of petunias brings a splash of colour closer to eye level.*

After hours

You've made the garden look great from the outside and now you're ready to withdraw to the comfort of your home, but have you remembered to link your outdoor rooms with your interior views? Examine your garden again. This time, look out the kitchen window, or through the dining room's French doors. Can you see inviting glimpses of nature from your lounge or family room?

If not, jot down a few ideas on how to create views, frame windows, or let the winter sun in. You may need to prune branches or remove excess plants. Winter is still a good time to move many shrubs, or for planning a major transplantation of any large deciduous plants (see page 327). Don't be nervous about moving things around. A garden should always change and be adaptable to the needs of its owners.

Another way to enjoy the best of the garden from inside your home is to install some exterior lighting and transform your garden from a black hole after dark to an extension of your indoor rooms. Diffuse outdoor lighting will allow you to enjoy the courtyard or the whole garden area at night—in the warmer months for outdoor living, and in winter as illuminated views. So use this dormant time of the year in the garden to lay wiring.

Lighting can either be decorative, such as uplighting in trees or wash lighting in a pond, or functional, lighting up driveways, steps and paths, making your home more secure.

LIGHT-EMITTING DIODES
LEDs are much better than using fairy lights because they don't use as much power or need their bulbs changed as often.

Lighting creates mood cheaply and simply. Extend your outdoor living into the evening with the soft glow of candles and lanterns.

Carefully placed lights will highlight any features in your garden, such as stonework, a statue or a wall plaque. Sometimes picking out small details can make all the difference.

The advent of low voltage and LED garden lighting in recent years has made the job safe and a lot of fun. First, select the areas that must be lit, such as paths and accessways, and then add some imaginative touches. Some light here for effect, a pool of colour there for impact, but don't overdo it. Less lighting always works better. Finally, always employ a licensed electrician to install an all-weather power point outdoors.

LIGHTING THE GARDEN

- Downlights are perfect for illuminating task spots, such as dining tables or steps, whereas uplights add ambience or accent, for example, highlighting tree trunks or statues and other features.
- Always light steps, hidden edges and bodies of water.
- Ensure lights are evenly spaced with light spread overlapping.
- Sensor lights are excellent security options.
- Avoid too many uplights, otherwise your garden will look like a miniature runway.

Starting from scratch

If you're gardening on a new block, don't try to landscape the entire area in one year. Rushed gardens seldom last.

Instead, sow grass seed to green up the area and prevent mud and dirt being tracked into your new home. Grass seed is cheap and lawns can be removed later as the garden takes shape.

The next step is to make a plan of the block on graph paper. Plot the essentials first: the clothesline, a paved area for entertaining and the barbecue, a playground if necessary, vegetable patch, compost area and garden shed. Plot the open lawns, pathways and garden beds. Look through magazines, books on garden design and open gardens for inspiration and create a 'source' book of ideas and palette of colours and materials.

Plan one or two large deciduous shade trees to allow the winter sun into your house and garden. These trees should be planted first, as shade is essential in hot summers for creating a microclimate in which the smaller plants can grow. Then tackle one small area at a time. This way you won't break your back or your budget.

In order to green a bare look, plant some fast growers. Marguerite daisies, geraniums and lavenders are ideal for filling up any sunny spot, and will be a mass of flowers for much of the warm weather. Wattles are great for instant shade, and provide a lovely spring show of yellow. Another useful tree is tree-in-a-hurry (*Virgilia capensis*). It has soft pink pea-shaped flowers throughout spring and summer. Plant slow-growing, longer-lived trees that can take the place of the fast growers when they die after about ten years. Try magnolias, maples, ash, camellias and blossom trees.

Taking the time to plan your garden carefully will pay off in the long term.

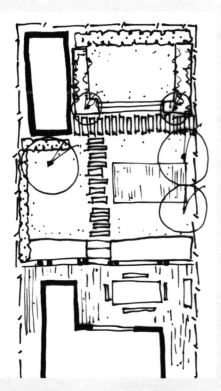

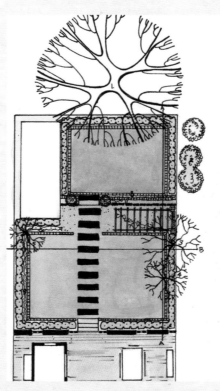

A rough concept sketch (far left) can be developed into a final garden plan (left).

Pruning

Winter is a busy time for pruning, so sharpen those tools. Roses, fruit trees, grapevines and many trees and shrubs should all be trimmed now. Perennials also need dead-heading and cleaning up. Many, such as cannas, should be cut right down to ground level.

🌿 PROTECTION
When pruning protect yourself by wearing gloves, long sleeves and glasses if possible, and always limber up with some stretches—before and after.

The object of pruning is to encourage growth—to create a bushy, vigorous, well-shaped plant. Pruning stimulates growth because the 'terminal bud'—the first shoot or leader—contains a chemical which inhibits growth below it. Light pruning removes this chemical control mechanism, resulting in bushier growth.

Flowering and/or fruiting can also improve as a result of pruning. The removal of old wood and letting in more sun encourages fruit set and flower.

Pruning tips

- Don't make the mistake of pruning back the entire garden. This can remove spring-flowering buds on banksia roses and shrubs such as viburnum, weigela and philadelphus, and on climbers such as wisteria.

- Magnolias, frangipani and jacarandas should never be cut back as pruning destroys their wonderful, natural shape and results in stress growth at awkward angles and a framework that can never be regained.

BELOW: *Bonsai, first developed by the Chinese, was refined by the Japanese.*

BELOW RIGHT: *The art of topiary dates back to ancient Roman times.*

- Be careful not to start winter pruning too early. In warm coastal areas you can start pruning in early winter, in mild temperatures wait until mid-winter and in cooler areas leave it until the end of winter. If in doubt, prune later rather than earlier.

- Removing up to a third of the growth is generally quite safe, but some plants can take considerably harsher treatment. The golden rule is to prune after the flowers have finished, though there are exceptions with some deciduous shrubs, or shrubs that are grown for fruit as well as flowers.

- Have clean, sharp tools. Make sure the cut is a clean one as tearing or bruising stems can result in infection, and slows down the callusing process.

- To protect against the spread of disease, wipe the blades with a cloth moistened in bleach or disinfectant before pruning the next plant.

- If you are going to use a wound dressing, make sure you apply it immediately after cutting. Rather than a tar concoction or a homemade brew, use a quality product such as Yates' Bacseal, which contains the fungicide tebuconazole and is also elastic, so it doesn't crack or peel.

- With shrubs, prune just above a healthy bud or buds if the shoots are opposite. Alternate shoots should be cut on an angle, while opposite buds should be cut straight, above the shoot.

- If you are trying to encourage bushy growth, you should 'tip prune'—trimming back by 10 cm or so, just enough to remove old flower heads and encourage branching.

- To rejuvenate a plant that has grown woody, you can cut it back hard (as with hibiscus and photinia), or prune back sections (for semi-hardwood perennials such as lavender and daisies) or prune back in stages, taking one third each year. This encourages growth lower down without cutting into old wood that is less likely to reshoot.

CLOCKWISE FROM FAR LEFT: *Box, pruned into cylinders, adds a monumental look to the garden; the rounded spheres of germander lend a contemporary feel to an otherwise traditional garden; espaliered fruit trees look marvellous even in winter.*

new growth is often more striking than older wood, and therefore has ornamental value. Typical candidates for this sort of pruning are cornus and willows.

- **Pollarding.** This technique is similar to coppicing, except that growth is cut back to a permanent framework. Plants that could be used include gums, willows, cornus, plane trees and crepe myrtle.

- **Topiary.** This is the technique of pruning plants into shapes such as balls, cones, spirals and animals. Suitable species include shrub honeysuckle, conifers and box. Standardising is a popular form of topiary. Climbers as well as shrubs can be grown up on a single stem, then shaped on top into a ball, or series of balls, or a weeping plant.

- **Bonsai.** This Japanese art of dwarfing plants involves regular pruning and cramping root growth. Theoretically, any plant can be treated this way.

- **Espalier.** Sometimes called 'fan-training', espalier is simply pruning plants flat against a frame or wall. Camellias, pyracantha, cotoneaster, fruit trees and roses are commonly used. (See page 437.)

- **Pleaching.** A popular device in garden design in the 16th and 17th centuries, pleaching is the art of creating a hedge on stilts. *Tilia* (European limes) are often used, although any tree with a bushy habit would be suitable. If you live in a warmer climate, you may like to try pleaching temperate plants such as coffee trees, which also withstand pruning. Start by removing the bottom two-thirds of growth to create a standard, then shorten lateral growth to encourage bushiness and remove the apical bud or 'top leader' once the desired height is reached.

BELOW: *Never prune below the ridge collar, which is like an airlock protecting healthy plant tissue; leave a short stub on the branch—it will soften with age.*

BELOW RIGHT: *Willow stems from coppicing can be woven into wicker or used in flower arrangements.*

Other pruning techniques

Some plants are trained into shapes and screens through pruning techniques such as coppicing, pollarding, topiary, bonsai, espalier, standardising and pleaching.

- **Coppicing.** This technique was developed in order to provide a constant and renewable supply of wood for cane work and firewood. Basically, plants are cut back regularly to near ground level, which encourages a mass of new growth. This

The garden shed

If you're serious about gardening, get serious about your tools, and they'll repay you with a lifetime's service. Now is the ideal time to sharpen your spade and secateurs as well as restore any cracked or splintered handles.

Buy the best quality tools you can afford, which doesn't necessarily mean the most expensive. Look for high-carbon steel with solid, well-balanced wooden handles. Stainless steel, which is alloyed with chromium and nickel, is an expensive but good rust-resistant option for those who occasionally leave tools out in the garden!

Store each tool neatly by tying a string loop through a hole in the handle and hanging it on a tool rack. You can either buy one especially or make your own by mounting an old rake head on the shed wall. Alternatively, keep sharp handtools clean and oiled in a bucket of sand mixed with oil.

Essential tools

🍂 **Round-nosed shovel.** This long-handled tool is ideal for heavy digging, moving materials and lifting.

🍂 **Secateurs.** These should always be parrot-beaked. This allows one blade to hold the stem while the other cuts cleanly. The cutting blade should face the plant so that a clean cut, not a bruised branch, is left behind.

🍂 **Square-nosed spade.** When it comes to excavating planting holes, this type of spade has no equal.

🍂 **Garden trowel.** This is the indispensable planting tool.

ABOVE LEFT: *Round-nosed shovel, leaf rake and flat-head soil rake (also called steel-tined rake).*

ABOVE: *Weeder, three-pronged cultivator, double-sided cultivator, secateurs and trowel.*

Sharpening and cleaning secateurs

1 Loosen the bolt with a spanner and remove the spring.

2 Take the secateurs apart and spray the parts with lubricant.

3 Sharpen the cutting or bevelled side of the blade on an oilstone. Make sure you rasp the blade away from you.

4 Soak the spring and the nut and bolt in a bowl of turpentine. Rub the spring with an abrasive pad. Then reassemble the secateurs.

Flat-head soil rake. The hard tines of this rake are useful for scarifying lawn and breaking up clods of earth, while the flat reverse is good for levelling the planting surface.

Leaf rake. These flexible tines can be made from metal, plastic or bamboo and are great for cleaning the lawn and gravel.

Cultivator. A handtool for weeding and cultivating small areas.

Mattock. Terrific for breaking up heavy ground as the weight of the head does most of the work.

Fork. The best tool for breaking up soil, turning sods and aerating compacted areas. It can even be used as a pitchfork!

Hedge shears. These will save your wrists if you have a lot of pruning to do, but note that they will leave a brown line on a cut leaf.

Wheelbarrow. The single wheelbarrow was first developed as a gardening tool in the Middle Ages, and has been invaluable ever since.

Knife. Great for trimming roots when re-potting, opening bags and all sorts of odd jobs.

Pruning saw. Don't ruin secateurs and loppers by using them to cut through oversized branches. This is the tool you should use.

Telescopic-handled loppers. Great for high-up branches that need trimming.

Hand rake. Good for clearing small areas for seed sowing and bulb planting.

DID YOU KNOW? The wheelbarrow was invented by the Chinese in about 200 AD. It was a fulcrum with two levers.

ABOVE LEFT: *Long-handled loppers, pruning saw and hedging shears.*
ABOVE RIGHT: *Always choose a wheelbarrow with pump-up tyres and comfortable handles.*

Restoring handlles

1 Gather together steel wool, a rag, a mixture of linseed oil and turpentine in an old jar, sanding block, fine- and medium-grade abrasive paper and the handle that needs restoring.

2 Sand back the spade handle with medium-grade abrasive paper and then clean it.

3 Dip the rag into the oil and turpentine mix. Rub the handle with the soaked rag, then leave it to dry overnight.

4 Lightly sand with fine-grade abrasive paper. Repeat the process if necessary. Finish by rubbing the handle with some steel wool.

Checklist

Jobs to do now

Annuals, perennials and bulbs

🍂 In windy winter weather you may need to stake any taller perennials such as foxgloves and delphiniums that are coming up for spring.

🍂 Cut back your chrysanthemums to about 15 cm to encourage strong new growth.

🍂 If you have bulbs planted and stored in a cool dark place, bring them out into the sun when the shoots are 3–5 cm tall.

🍂 Cut back impatiens and begonias in frost-free areas.

🍂 If you haven't already done so, lift and store the best dahlias. Discard inferior plants.

🍂 Divide perennials such as perennial asters, astilbe, achillea, lupin, cannas, Shasta daisy and polyanthus once their flowering has finished. Pull the rootball apart with your hands, or cut it up with a sharp spade or knife. Keep the divided clumps well watered until they're re-established.

🍂 Plant spring-flowering perennials with a handful of organic matter, such as mushroom compost, to ensure healthy spring growth.

Grasses, groundcovers and climbers

🍂 Remove winter grass.

🍂 Use bindii killer to control broad-leaved weeds in your lawn.

🍂 Trim lawn edges and re-mark garden beds where appropriate.

🍂 Apply 30 g iron sulphate diluted in 4 L of water to control moss in your lawn.

🍂 If ferns have become shabby, give them a haircut quite close to the crown at the end of winter, just as the new growth is about to start, and feed them with liquid fertiliser.

🍂 Prune ornamental grape back to its main branches.

🍂 Prune wisteria back to flowering stems and check for signs of borer or damaged wood.

Shrubs and trees

🍂 Encourage new blooms on bird of paradise plant by removing old flowers as they finish.

🍂 Tip-prune luculias after their autumn/winter flush.

🍂 Cut back geraniums and fuchsias in frost-free areas.

🍂 Remove about one third of the oldest shoots on flowering quince to make way for new canes immediately after flowering, otherwise the interior of the plant may become very congested.

🍂 Begin spraying azaleas for petal blight every fortnight from bud stage to full flower. This disease, which shows up as transparent blotches on the petals before destroying the flower, can be especially bad in damp weather. Remove affected flowers.

🍂 Continue giving New South Wales Christmas bush sulphate of iron for extra vivid flowers.

🍂 Prune hydrangeas by cutting back to the second pair of buds. Don't go too low as this can encourage leaf growth at the expense of flowers.

Add organic matter when planting spring-flowering perennials.

Winter is the season for pruning non-flowering growth from wisteria.

Deal with winter grass before the seeds spread.

Trim shrubs such as elaeagnus and plumbago to a manageable size.

Disbudding camellias now will ensure larger blooms later.

It's rose-pruning time. Always prune above the bud scar.

🌑 Feed camellias. Disbud camellias to ensure larger blooms.

🌑 Prune abelia, Chinese bellflowers, shrimp plant, elaeagnus, ceratostigma and plumbago.

🌑 If you want to manipulate the colour of your hydrangea flowers, start now by adding either bluing tonic (aluminium sulphate) for blue flowers or lime for pink flowers until late spring.

🌑 Prune, transplant and plant roses into well-prepared rich soil.

🌑 Spray scale-affected roses with white oil or lime sulphur.

🌑 Prune frost-hardy evergreen trees and shrubs if they have finished flowering.

🌑 Check gums and wattle trees for signs of borer.

🌑 Take hardwood cuttings from trees and shrubs. Choose healthy growth about the length and thickness of a pencil. Plants that can be treated this way include: *Aucuba japonica*, buddleia, dogwood, forsythia, mock orange, plane tree, poplar, currant and willow.

🌑 Replace mulch under roses. This not only replenishes nutrients but also removes any fungal spores.

Herbs, fruit and vegetables

🌑 In cold climates, you should lift mint and chives, then pot them and place them in a protected spot.

🌑 Fertilise citrus trees with citrus food and clean up any old fruit from the ground. Check for gall wasp infestations, and prune and burn affected parts. Spray with winter-spraying oil to protect against scale.

🌑 Prune peaches and nectarines by 50 per cent of the previous year's wood to stimulate new fruiting wood. Spray with Bordeaux® at bud swell to protect against leaf curl.

🌑 Check fruiting blossom trees for any signs of borer.

🌑 Thin apples and pears to form an open-centred shape.

🌑 Grapevines need hard pruning. Cut out most of last season's wood to leave short 'three bud' spurs at 20 cm intervals along the main arms of the older stems.

🌑 Spread cow or sheep manure around the drip line of fruit trees. This is where the canopy finishes and feeder roots are plentiful, and where most benefit is received. Avoid building up manure and soil against the trunk as this can cause collar rot.

🌑 Divide and plant rhubarb into rich soil. Rhubarb can be 'forced' by excluding light with straw or an upturned plastic bin.

🌑 Tie the outer leaves of cauliflower over the curd to prevent discolouring of the heads.

🌑 Lay out seed potatoes to encourage sprouting before you plant.

🌑 Harvest Brussels sprouts, silverbeet, cabbage, cauliflower and broccoli.

Plant now

Annuals, perennials and bulbs

🍂 Plant annual beds with new seedlings of Swan River daisy, Canterbury bells, linaria, statice, delphiniums and dianthus.

🍂 Flower seedlings such as lobelia and alyssum can all be planted out now. Protect frost-sensitive seedlings with hessian, fern fronds, glass covers or cloches.

🍂 Sow seeds or plant crowns of gerbera.

🍂 Tuberoses and waterlilies.

🍂 Liliums, hippeastrum, gladiolus, crinum, lily-of-the-valley and daylilies.

🍂 Plant spring-flowering perennials—such as tree peonies, Russell lupins, pelargoniums, penstemon, astilbe and phlox—together with a handful of organic matter to ensure healthy spring growth.

Grasses, groundcovers and climbers

🍂 Sow seeds of carpeting pinks and carnations (*Dianthus* sp.) in tropical and subtropical areas.

🍂 Divide ground-smothering perennials such as windflowers, erigeron and Shasta daisy.

🍂 Deciduous vines such as wisteria and ornamental grape.

Shrubs and trees

🍂 Deciduous shrubs—including viburnum, mock orange, may, weigela, hydrangea and lilac.

🍂 Deciduous trees not noted for their autumn displays—plane trees, poplar, elm, oak and willows—are best planted before bud break.

🍂 Select magnolias and other early flowering deciduous trees such as the Judas tree (*Cercis siliquastrum*), ornamental peach, cherry, pear and apple blossoms.

🍂 If you are after a showier, larger tree, why not plant the magnificent yulan (*Magnolia denudata*)? Its lemon-scented, goblet-shaped flowers are pure white and at their best from early winter through to mid-spring. After this, lettuce-green leaves appear, creating a light canopy of shade.

Herbs, fruit and vegetables

🍂 In cold areas plant mustard and cress.

🍂 Raspberries and other soft fruits are best planted in late autumn and winter when dormant. Cut the stems of raspberries back to about 30 cm to stimulate new shoots from the base.

🍂 Rhubarb is planted from crowns in winter. Their large ornamental leaves make them an attractive feature in the garden bed.

🍂 In tropical areas, plant beans, choko vines, Cape gooseberries, rosellas, okra and marrows.

🍂 Mediterranean shallots can be planted now in all but very cold climates. Unlike onions, they are grown from offsets, not seeds, which should be placed in a drill so that the tips are just protruding.

🍂 In tropical and temperate areas, plant asparagus crowns.

🍂 Buy seed potatoes and keep them in a cool, dark place for a few weeks so they sprout before planting time.

Cape gooseberry seeds can be raised now in tropical areas.

These chitting (sprouting) potatoes are ready to be cut up and planted.

CLOCKWISE FROM TOP LEFT: *Double-flowered helleborus; white-edged liriope (turf lily); bergenia colouring up from the cold; this prostrate Cootamundra wattle will be in full flower by mid-winter; star magnolia flowers in late winter; many viburnum have winter flowers; Stachyurus praecox blooms at the same time as helleborus; primrose jasmine.*

Flowering now

Annuals, perennials and bulbs

❧ Early annuals such as pansies, violas, stock and wallflowers.

❧ Perennials such as bergenia, polyanthus, primula, primroses, helleborus, pulmonaria, orchids, bromeliads and clivias.

❧ Bulbs such as early jonquils, 'Erlicheer' daffodils, snowdrops, early crocus, cyclamen, winter iris and freesias.

Grasses, groundcovers and climbers

❧ Grasses such as false grape hyacinth (*Liriope muscari*) and blue oat grass (*Helictotrichon sempervirens*), which has lovely silver leaves and seed heads that last all winter.

❧ Groundcovers such as sweet violets, and prostrate wattles and camellias.

❧ Climbers such as orange trumpet vine and false sarsaparilla.

❧ Climbers that are useful as ground-covers and look lush and green over winter: ornamental dwarf English ivies, Chinese star jasmine, evergreen Boston ivy and Guinea flower.

Shrubs and trees

❧ Euphorbia, poinsettia, reinwardtia, golden dollar bush and *Jasminum mesnyi*, heaths and ericas.

❧ Flowering deciduous shrubs such as japonica, *Jasminum nudiflorum* (winter jasmine), *Hamamelis mollis* (Chinese witch hazel), *Chimonanthus praecox* (wintersweet), *Lonicera fragrantissima* (winter honeysuckle), *Stachyurus praecox*, kerria and forsythia.

❧ Early blossom trees such as peach.

❧ Evergreen shrubs such as winter daphne and the early viburnums (e.g. *V. × bodnantense, V. farreri, V. tinus*).

❧ Magnolia trees and the shrub type (*M. stellata*).

❧ *Camellia japonica*.

❧ Natives such as wattles and many early boronias, bottlebrush and gums.

❧ Ericas, epacris, heaths and heathers.

Herbs, fruit and vegetables

❧ Cool-season vegetable crops such as broccoli, cabbage, cauliflower, carrots, lettuce, leeks, parsnips, silverbeet, spinach and broad beans.

❧ Citrus are in fruit.

Annuals, perennials and bulbs

Although this is a quiet time for colour in the flower garden, there are some exceptional beauties that can brighten winter beds. These include wallflowers, spurges, early bulbs, hellebores and primulas. But perhaps the best part about winter is planning for the warmer seasons ahead.

ABOVE: *Hellebores make a delightful splash of colour at a usually grey time.*

ABOVE RIGHT: *Grape hyacinths, forget-me-nots and daffodils herald spring in this late winter scene.*

🌿 **LEAF MINER** The only problem with growing cinerarias is the leaf miner, a tiny caterpillar that tunnels in the plant's leaves. A systemic insecticide is needed to control this pest; however, if your plants continue with vigorous growth they will tolerate an infestation.

Annuals

Don't suffer grey days and a winter whiteout each year. Instead, create a kaleidoscope of cheap and cheery annuals for brightening borders, window boxes and baskets.

The trick is to get your annuals in early enough so that they are flowering by the time winter comes around. Taller flowers such as snapdragons and wallflowers require four months from sowing to flowering, so you should plant them in late summer.

Other annuals don't take as long to reach 'adulthood': calendula, poppies and French marigolds flower after three months, while violas, pansies, linaria and nemesia take about ten weeks. It's possible to 'cheat', of course, by popping in established potted colour or larger seedlings that have already started flowering.

Favourite winter-flowering annuals

Annuals are great gap-fillers for covering bare spots left after perennials have died down and before bulbs emerge.

Cinerarias

These colourful daisy-like flowers come in singles and doubles and shades of blue, red, pink and white. Cinerarias (*Pericallis* × *hybrida*) flower well in full sun but they tend to become bleached and wilt easily. They are better grown in filtered shade where their bright colours have more impact. Use them as fillers between shrubs and let them brighten your winter garden.

Exciting news is that now there are a range of flowering perennial types called Senetti, which have a repeat-flowering nature, and will bloom from autumn to spring. Available in pink, blue, magenta and bicolour types, they are also suitable for indoor display when in bloom.

Stocks

For perfume in the garden over winter, stocks are without peer. Despite being closely related to Brussels sprouts, stocks have a delicious clove-like scent and are great picking flowers, provided the water is changed frequently. They tolerate temperatures as low as 4°C and prefer fertile, well-drained, ideally lime-rich soil. They need to be planted as seedlings in autumn each year and come in the most wonderful range of colours, including terracotta, mulberry, rose, magenta, clotted cream and white.

Primulas

Primulas are such good value in the flower garden. Sometimes called the fairy primrose, they will flower in sun or shade. Once you have them, they happily self-seed every year in pale pink, carmine, a lovely wine colour, ruby, lilac and pure white. Look out for some large hybrids and double-flowered varieties. (See also 'The primula family', page 366.)

Pansies and violas

Not just pretty faces, pansies are extremely versatile, and will grow happily in pots, baskets and borders. At one time there was a clear distinction between pansies, which had faces, and violas, which didn't. Now there's a lovely blend of both—some with kitten faces, some heavily patterned, and some in plain solid colours. All of them provide the garden with lovely colour for months, from winter to early summer. (See also 'Violets and violas', page 372.)

Poppies

The Iceland poppy (*Papaver nudicaule*) makes a wonderful addition to the garden. Not only does it look terrific in garden beds, it lasts well as a cut flower, making it one of the best value annuals to plant. It is available in mixes of reds, oranges, yellows and pinks, or in separate colours, and the delicate, silken, crepe-like blooms are held high on slender, downy stalks. Gallipoli (also

CLOCKWISE FROM TOP LEFT: *Fragrant white single stocks; mulberry-centred Shirley poppy; golden kitten-face pansies; fairy primrose.*

called Flanders) poppies (*P. rhoeas*) and Shirley poppies, which are derived from *P. rhoeas*, are brilliant survivors. They blend in well with a perennial border, although they may take as long as two years to flower, so you have to be patient. The Gallipoli poppy has a single scarlet flower with a black blotch; the Shirley poppy has either pink or white flowers. Both prefer cooler climates.

Snapdragons

Great value in the flower border, snapdragons produce flush after flush of flowers and last up to a year. They prefer full sunshine and grow well in the garden. For potted colour, try the dwarf varieties. Rust can be a problem over the warmer months, making winter a great time to have them in flower.

DID YOU KNOW? The dried latex of the opium poppy (*P. somniferum*) is made into a narcotic; its seed is used to flavour curries or decorate cakes and bread.

DID YOU KNOW? According to American superstition, it is unlucky to plant on Fridays.

Ranunculus come in many shades. Colour creates a mood, which can vary from season to season, year after year, to suit the fashion or feeling of the day.

COLOUR TIPS

- Outside, colour should be used to support the function and mood of the garden, with flower colour adding to the overall effect of the foliage, form and texture of shrubs, trees and groundcovers.
- Colour has a tremendous effect on mood. Use bright colours in lively environments, and softer, subtle tones in restful areas.
- Locate the strongest colours in the foreground, and allow the colours to become paler with distance. Too much strong colour at a distance foreshortens the space.
- Work with any surrounding colour schemes, including the house as well as the boundary and distant views.
- Grey foliage 'cools down' bright colours, and white flowers help contrasting colours blend more effectively.
- Colour changes, depending on the time of day and the intensity of sunlight. Pale colours that look soft and gentle in the morning and evening light can appear bleached and washed out during the day. Conversely, colours that work in the heat of the day can appear garish in softer light. Also remember that seasonal changes affect the strength of light.
- Colour attracts the viewer's attention. When you want something to stand out and be noticed, a loud splash of colour nearby will hold the eye.
- Select a range of colours that suits your home and personality, but try deviating from this range to allow contrast into your garden.
- Try working with foliage colour as the backbone of your garden and it will have interest all year-round. Darker foliage makes colours more pronounced.
- Large flowers are harder to blend successfully than smaller ones.

Colouring-in your garden

Historically, the most successful garden designers have used colour in the same way as artists, selecting from their palettes and blending each colour to create a harmony which results in a certain mood or effect. The result may be restful or flamboyant.

The three primary colours—red, blue and yellow—are the building blocks of all other colours. The three secondary colours—green, violet and orange—are mixtures of these. Together, the primary and secondary colours make up the colours of a rainbow. Shades or hues vary depending on the strength and intensity of each primary colour, while tone is a measure of the black and white component in each colour. Black, white and grey are inert colours: they don't change the colour, only the brightness.

The colour wheel can be divided into halves: the 'cool' colours of green, grey, blue and mauve, and the 'warm' colours such as yellow, red, orange and hot pink. Colours next to each other on the colour wheel, or nearby, are called harmonious colours, while colours opposite each other are called contrasting colours.

You can use this knowledge as a tool in garden design. For a vibrant garden full of vitality, use contrasting colours from opposite sides of the wheel—red and green, purple and yellow, blue and orange. Start with a cool colour as a base and add the hot colour as a highlight to intensify the effect of both colours. Alternatively, hues next to each other on the colour wheel harmonise. If you're trying to create a tranquil haven, then select complementary colours—such as pink and mauve—on the same side of the wheel. Gardens planted in one colour can also be very restful.

All gardening is landscape painting.

ALEXANDER POPE

Plant your own colour scheme

Red
- **Mood:** Passion; makes time seem longer; excellent for the creation of ideas
- **Plants:** Cinerarias, nemesia, pansies, polyanthus, poppies, snapdragons, strawflower, violas, wallflower

Orange
- **Mood:** Drama
- **Plants:** Calendula, French marigolds, pansies, poppies, snapdragons, strawflower, violas

Yellow
- **Mood:** Happiness
- **Plants:** Calendula, linaria, pansies, polyanthus, poppies, snapdragons, stocks, strawflower, violas, wallflower

Green
- **Mood:** Reduces nerves and helps concentration
- **Plants:** Bells of Ireland, mignonette, *Zinnia elegans* 'Envy'

Blue
- **Mood:** Blue is cooling, and makes weight seem lighter and time even shorter
- **Plants:** Cineraria, delphinium, forget-me-not, lobelia, love-in-a-mist, lupins, nemesia, pansies, statice, violas

Purple
- **Mood:** Intrigue, mystery, power
- **Plants:** Alyssum, cineraria, lobelia, love-in-a-mist, pansies, polyanthus, primula, stock

Pink
- **Mood:** Romance
- **Plants:** Alyssum, Canterbury bells, cinerarias, lobelia, pansies, polyanthus, poppies, primula, snapdragons, stocks

White
- **Mood:** Simplicity, peace, coolness
- **Plants:** Candytuft, cineraria, gypsophila, lobelia, nemesia, pansies, primula, snapdragons, stock, violas

Black
- **Mood:** Sombre, mournful
- **Plants:** Aquilegia, pansies, polyanthus, violas

CLOCKWISE FROM TOP LEFT: *Poppies come in a rainbow of colours; this yellow polyanthus is scented; the tall flower spires of lupins; pink pelargoniums often have deep maroon throats; pansies come in many colours, often with faces; a sweetly smelling viburnum in palest pink; the unmistakable bicolour blooms of cineraria; bells of Ireland is named for its emerald spires of bell-shaped flowers.*

DID YOU KNOW? The irritating hairs on German primula can cause an allergy, while other species may cause skin rashes. To be on the safe side, always wear gloves when handling them.

Cultivated since the 17th century, members of the Polyanthus Group (Primula × polyantha) come in a variety of shapes, colours and sizes.

The primula family

The primula family comes in many guises, known variously as primroses, cowslip, auricula, primula and polyanthus. They all form rosettes of lush leafy clumps, with tubular flowers that are flattened and face-like, or held on candelabra-like whorls. They like a moist, humus-rich soil and a dressing of lime. A spot under a deciduous tree is perfect for primulas: the winter sunshine promotes flowering and the canopy provides much needed summer shade and coolness.

Arguably the most popular primula of all is the annual fairy primula (see page 363). The stems reach up to 40 cm and are topped with umbels of musk-pink, lavender, white or rose flowers that can be doubles, but are usually single. The German primula (*Primula obconica*) is frequently grown as a pot plant, but is beautiful outdoors in shady, frost-free places. Colours include rose pink, apricot, red, blue, lilac and white.

Cowslip is the name given to a few species (*P. alpicola*, *P. florindae*, *P. sikkimensis* and *P. veris*) that all have yellow, perfumed blooms in summer. Candelabra primula (including *P. aurantiaca*, *P. beesiana*, *P. bulleyana* and *P. japonica*) are for cold climates only. They produce tiers of flowers up to 1 m high.

Strictly speaking, primroses (derived from *P. vulgaris*) have short flower stems. Polyanthus (*P. × polyantha*) are a cross between primroses and cowslips, and traditionally have flower heads borne on a single stem clear of the leaves. As these plants have been subject to intensive breeding, this distinction has been lost and the two fade into each other. They make great winter-flowering perennials.

CLOCKWISE FROM TOP LEFT: *A double rose-coloured polyanthus; Juliana's polyanthus; a ruffled-edged apricot type; an auricula type; Primula malacoides; P. pulverulenta; P obconica; and P. vulgaris.*

Their bright flowers, in red, orange, buttercup yellow, white, blue, lavender and terracotta, look wonderful in pots, or when planted in masses in the garden they give the effect of a colourful modernist painting.

Normally five-petalled, occasionally the odd primrose flower will have six petals. Once it was believed that such flowers brought you luck, and if you were in love they were a certain sign that your love was returned.

The soft petals, cheerful faces and wonderful colours of the primula family in their various forms make them an asset in any garden.

Wallflowers

Wallflowers earned their name by growing in cracks in walls or stonework. Both annual and perennial types tend to be extremely hardy plants, surviving in difficult positions and flowering at a time when little else is showing colour. They originally belonged to two genera, *Cheiranthus* and *Erysimum*, but now belong only to *Erysimum*. All like to be in well-drained positions and benefit from regular trimming to promote new compact growth and flowers.

The season starts in late autumn, when the winter wallflower (*E. × kewense*) begins to bloom. This is a dear shrub,

LEFT TO RIGHT: *Wallflower variety: Erysimum 'Bowles' Mauve' is a garden favourite; E. mutabile has a pretty lemon speckle through the flower heads; some annual wallflowers have beautiful rust shades but can vary through to butter cream.*

with apricot and mauve blended flowers that continue blossoming into spring.

The English wallflower (*E. cheiri*), which is sold as an annual but actually lasts a few years, is the next to bloom. Its fragrant, velvety flowers come in a range of autumn tones—from yellow, brown and cream to red, russet and orange.

Throughout spring the Siberian wallflower (*E. allionii*) makes a stunning display of apricot or brilliant orange-scented flowers. The variegated wallflower (*E. mutabile* 'Variegatum'), with its pinkish brown flowers in autumn and winter, has cream-striped leaves which make it useful for edges and contrast.

For paler tones, try the coast wallflower (*E. capitatum*), which has pale yellow flowers that fade to cream, and the fairy wallflower (*E. linifolium*) with its blue-grey leaves and soft white and mauve flowers that mature to deep pink.

All wallflowers make very good cut flowers ('Cheiranthus', the old genus name, means hand flower). They add scent and colour to the garden for most of the year and last well in a vase if the water is changed regularly.

Closely related are stocks (*Matthiola* sp.) with spicy clove-scented blooms. Although they generally need to be replaced each year, they are worth the effort for their array of colours: from white to apple blossom, peach, pink, lilac, lavender and lemon tones. They last well as a cut flower if the water is changed often.

Cleome

Cleome, or spider flower, is best known as a summer-flowering annual in white and pink shades that readily sets seed in the garden. This new hybrid, however, doesn't waste time seeding, and as a result can expend its energy on reflowering again and again, even through winter in warmer areas. It's sterile, too, so no dead-heading is needed.

VITAL STATISTICS

Scientific name: *Cleome* hybrid.
Family: Cleomaceae.
Climate: Suitable for growing in warm or cold climates.
Culture: Widely used as a cut flower.
Colour: Pinkish lilac with deep green foliage.
Height: Plants grow to 70 cm high.
Planting time: Plant from cutting-grown seedlings in spring.
Soil: Needs well-drained soil.
Position: Prefers full sun but tolerates part sun.
Watering: Take care that the soil does not become too wet or soggy.
Fertiliser: Apply a complete fertiliser once or twice during the growing season.
Pests/diseases: None.
Flowering time: All year in ideal conditions.
Pruning: Pruning and staking are not necessary.

Feature annual

Perennials

Winter is a busy time in the herbaceous border with lifting and dividing, remodelling and reworking jobs to be done.

Perennials—such as asters, astilbe, achillea, lupin, cannas and Shasta daisy—need lifting and dividing. To do this, simply pull the rootball apart with your hands, or cut it up with a sharp spade or knife. Keep the newly divided plants well watered until they are re-established. Other perennials flower in spring and need planting now, and these include oyster plant, foxgloves, penstemon and wallflowers.

Helleborus, the winter rose

Known by various names, including Christmas or Lenten rose, hellebores are valuable perennials because of their striking foliage and unusual flowers. The sometimes green, white or muted pink flowers are actually decorative, cup-shaped sepals. These can be delightfully spotted, throated or just pure colour. H. 'Winter Sunshine' is one of the more prolific flowerers and has creamy blooms that fade to soft pink. For purity, look for 'Ivory Prince', and for more intensity try the darker pink blooms of 'Penny Pink'. The foliage varies from species to species, and is deeply lobed or serrated, but it remains dark, glossy and handsome year-round.

Hellebores are great value planted under trees, where they like rich humus, moist soil and shade cast by overhead branches. They are, however, quite poisonous so no part of the plant should be eaten.

DID YOU KNOW? *Helleborus niger* is so named because of its black (Latin, 'niger') tap root. The flowers are actually white. The black-flowered helleborus is a cultivar called 'Queen of the Night'.

CLOCKWISE FROM TOP: Helleborus × hybridus 'Primrose Yellow Picotee'; H. × sternii 'Smokey Blue'; H. × hybridus 'Primrose Yellow'.

Helleborus

1 *Helleborus × hybridus* 'Primrose Yellow Picotee' 2 *H. × hybridus* 'Primrose Yellow' 3 *H. × hybridus* white blotched 4 *H. × sternii* 'Ashborne Silver' 5 *H. × hybridus* 'Picotee' 6 *H. × hybridus* double white 7 *H. foetidus* 'Gold Bullion' 8 *H. lividus*

9 *H. × hybridus* double rose pink **10** *H. × hybridus* purple black **11** *H. × hybridus* variegated form
12 *H. niger* **13** *H. × hybridus* double green purple bicolour **14** *H. × ballardiae* **15** *H. × hybridus* double
pale pink **16** *H. argutifolius*

ABOVE AND RIGHT:
The highly sought-
after cream clivia
sells for a pretty
penny but looks
divine; the more
common orange type.

Clivias

Clivias are versatile evergreen perennials from South Africa that look spectacular whether massed or as potted specimens. They love shade and do extremely well as underplantings to trees, or potted on a protected verandah. You can also bring them inside to enjoy these plants' striking blooms further, or use them as a cut flower.

Flowering from autumn through to late winter, clivias are mainly a soft apricot-orange, but there are also rare (and expensive) cultivars that flower burnt orange, apricot, peach, yellow and cream. The foliage itself is a handsome leathery green, which makes it an excellent border for drives and paths. There is also a variegated leaf form, though this, too, is quite rare.

Clivias enjoy an open, friable mix, and respond well to a spring application of organic fertiliser. Control snails with bait throughout the year, and watch out for mealy bugs in shade houses or patios. They also need protection from frosts and strong sun to prevent marking.

Propagation

The best way to propagate clivias is to divide an established clump down the middle with a spade. Ensure all divisions still have some roots before you plant them. You can also grow them from seed harvested from the seed pods, but they take years to reach flowering size.

Violets and violas

Violets are enchanting flowers: they evoke thoughts of fairies and elves dancing beneath ancient trees and hiding under giant toadstools. There are many species, which are popular in old-fashioned gardens and are currently enjoying a revival with enthusiasts.

Sweet violet (*Viola odorata*) is popular in posies because of its heavily scented, short-spurred flowers in winter and spring. This perennial grows to 10 cm from a rosette of heart-shaped leaves. There are many varieties, ranging from the dusty pink 'Rosea' and apricot-yellow 'Czar' to the deep violet 'Princess of Wales', but the most fragrant are known as Parma violets. These have mixed parentage and have shinier leaves and double flowers of mauve, white or violet. In the past it was used to treat respiratory disorders and is still used in the extraction of essential oil in the perfume industry.

Heartsease (*V. tricolor*) was known in Elizabethan England as love-in-idleness, and medieval herbalists used it in treating heart disease. It is also called 'Johnny-jump-up', because of its prolific self-seeding habit that has it popping up all over the garden. It carpets the ground around bulbs or shrubs and is not fussy, growing well in light to medium shade. Heartsease is one of the parents of the common garden pansy and the black and brown pansies known as 'All Black' and 'Irish Molly'.

Some violets have particularly attractive foliage. The purple-leafed wood violet (*V. riviniana* 'Purpurea') makes a decorative groundcover with leaves that are dark purple above and greyish pink underneath, with deep mauve flowers on short stems.

There is also a fern-like leafed violet, *V. dissecta*, which has the palest violet flowers in spring. The deciduous American species *V. sororia* 'Freckles' has a speckled surface like a bird's eggs and flowers in spring.

The Australian native species, ivy-leafed violet (*V. hederacea*), makes a

superb groundcover for sheltered positions, waterways and pond surrounds as well as a useful lawn substitute in shady areas. It has small, kidney-shaped leaves and white flowers with a mauve eye. It tolerates some sun, and spreads easily from the runners it produces, making it useful for topiary work as well. It blooms much of the year, and looks particularly good from winter until spring. Two particularly attractive cultivars of *V. hederacea* are 'Baby Blue', which has azure blue-coloured flowers, and 'Alba', which is pure white.

African violets

Native to East Africa, African violets (*Saintpaulia* sp.) are arguably the world's most popular flowering house plant, and were first successfully flowered outside their native habitat in 1893. They have a reputation for being granny plants—the sort of plant grandmothers grow on a sunny windowsill where they will flower reliably for months. There are even

societies where members can exchange leaf cuttings and ideas. Traditionally these plants were grown from leaf cuttings, and you can still grow them this way, but your local garden centre will have many beautiful potted specimens, which avoid the hassle and make a perfect gift.

African violets need lots of light in order to flower well plus year-round feeding to keep them healthy. They also benefit from wick-watering, which means water is absorbed by the plant as it's needed so overwatering is impossible! Stand each plant in a saucer of water, or better still, on a container filled with water to which special violet fertiliser drops have been added. Make a hole in the lid of the container and pass a cotton wick (venetian blind cord is good) from the pot, out through the drainage hole and into the water container beneath. More simply, just run the wick between the plant and a small container of water; see 'Wick watering' over the page.

LEFT TO RIGHT: *The sweet violet has dusky-pink flowers en masse in spring; self-seeding annual type 'Tinkerbelle' blooms for weeks from late winter; ivy-leafed violet makes an excellent lawn substitute.*

DID YOU KNOW? In William Shakespeare's play *A Midsummer Night's Dream*, the flower that is used to make Queen Titania fall in love with Bottom is love-in-idleness, or heartsease.

Yet mark'd I where the bolt of Cupid fell:
It fell upon a little western flower,
Before milk-white, now purple with love's wound,
And maidens call it love-in-idleness.

WILLIAM SHAKESPEARE

Propagation

African violets are easy to propagate, and using leaf cuttings is the simplest method (see below). Place the leaf stalk (petiole) into a peaty mix and keep it moist. New leaves will grow from the stalk, feeding off the original leaf until they develop roots. Once this happens, pot them into small pots and place them on a sunny windowsill. You'll soon have flowering-sized plants.

Miniatures

Exquisitely decorated, jewel-like cup-cakes, their tops adorned with bright icing and flowers, are the current big thing in food. The garden equivalent is a set of tiny pots, brimming with flowers and presented together to create a unique gift or display. To create your own, look for a set of pots that match your décor.

Plant them up with other stunning members of the Gesneriaceae, the family to which African violets belong. Familiar to some Australian gardeners are nodding violets (*Streptocarpus saxorum*) and Cape primroses (*S. × hybridus*). If treated with care, they'll flower for months, provided they are in a well-lit position away from direct sunlight. They don't like cold draughts, and flower best when temperatures are around 21°C.

Wick watering

1 Wrap a cotton wick around the rootball so that a length of wick is left at the bottom of the plant. Feed this end through one of the draining holes in the plastic pot and place the plant in the pot. **2** Put the plant and pot in a decorative container, then place the end of the wick in a small container of water.

Also members of the Gesneriaceae are gloxinias (*Sinningia* sp.), which are native to Mexico and South America as far south as Argentina. They have showy trumpet-like blooms and hairy leaves that look as if they've been covered in fine velvet. Some gloxinias are scented.

Members of both the *Streptocarpus* and *Sinningia* genera are frost-tender plants and need protection from cold conditions. Similarly, they like a

Propagating African violets

Dampen some peat moss.

Spread the peat moss in a seedling tray.

Pluck some leaves from an African violet and plant the petiole in the peat moss.

Keep moist till roots appear, then plant out.

draught-free, warm, sunny position, just like the African violet (again, the windowsill is ideal), and can also be propagated by leaf cuttings or division, as they form a small clump. Both methods will produce plants that are true to type (the same as their parent), whereas seeds could produce any colour as they may have been subjected to cross-pollination.

VERMICULITE

Vermiculite is a special type of expanded clay that is great for propagation as it maintains its dampness while still being light and airy. It is used in soilless media for vertical wall gardens, as a soil conditioner and top dressing to seeds when being raised.

Sometimes called Bolivian sunset, Sinningia sylvatica *has bright orange flowers that glow like embers. These plants love shade and will flower in late summer and autumn.*

Variegated thistle weed

This member of the daisy family is known for its stunning flowers and foliage. It is also the subject of close research scrutiny as a plant that may have important medicinal and pharmaceutical benefits.

VITAL STATISTICS

Scientific name: *Silybum marianum.*
Family: Asteraceae.
Climate: Will take frosts, and is very adaptable.
Culture: Will cope in dry conditions. Sometimes can be invasive, so check with your local council.
Colours: Purple thistle flowers and mid-green leaves with white venation.
Height: 0.5 m.
Planting time: Spring from seed.
Planting spacing: 0.5 m apart.
Soil: Well drained.
Position: Full sun.
Fertiliser: None needed
Pruning: After flowering.
Propagation: Propagate by seed. In some areas it can escape into bushland, so watch that it doesn't.

Feature perennial

Bromeliads

There are many different types of bromeliads, but the one most commonly grown is in fact the pineapple! Other types native to the tropical Americas and likely to be familiar to the average gardener belong to several different genera: *Neoregelia*, *Tillandsia* (air plants, which are found hanging from trees as Spanish moss), *Guzmania*, *Aechmea*, *Vriesea* and *Billbergia*.

The bromelaid family includes epiphytes, which attach themselves to living hosts such as trees; air plants, which take their water nutrients from mist; plants that grow on rocks; and others, such as the pineapple, that grow in the ground. This diversity means there's a bromeliad for any situation, including baskets, on old stumps or even en masse under trees, as they cope well with root competition from trees.

These plants come in all shapes and sizes, but perhaps the most striking of all is the giant bromeliad (*Alcantarea imperialis* 'Rubra'). It grows to over 1 m × 1 m, and has steel-blue leaves with reddish purple undersides.

CLOCKWISE FROM LEFT: *The giant bromeliad is well named; Neoregelia 'Aztec' has lovely red speckling; bromeliads with serrated foliage make safe homes for frogs.*

GROWING TIPS: BROMELIADS

- Bromeliads don't grow well in ordinary soil and need a special orchid mix that caters for their particular requirements. There are plenty of foods available on the market, but Campbell's Orchid Food (the yellow preparation) is probably the best.
- When a bromeliad has sent out 'pups' from the side, it can be divided up and propagated this way.
- You can re-pot at any time of year, but spring and early summer are best.
- Water plants regularly in hot months, and keep their central 'well' filled to act as a reservoir.

Neoregelia burle-marxii, *a native of Brazil, has a dramatic-looking purple 'well' at its centre.*

Plectranthus

Many gardeners are familiar with salvias and know them for their adaptability and reliable flowering. A genus that has just as much to offer, from the same plant family Lamiaceae, is the *Plectranthus*. They come in all shapes and sizes, from groundcover or trailing plants suitable for baskets and edging, right through to taller plants that can screen up to 2 m tall, like *P. barbatus*, which has exquisite blue flowers and a citrus scent to the leaves. They are mostly native to South Africa, though some are naturally found in Australia, growing successfully under trees, despite the root competition, with beauty and grace.

These plants are characterised by spires of flowers, which are usually in shades of blue, and felted foliage, which is often scented. Some have wonderful foliage, including *P. argentatus*, with its spectacular grey leaves. For spreading groundcover, try *P. forsteri*, which has many white-edged forms and white or blue flowers, depending on the type. The silvery leaves of *P. nicoletta*, which has violet flowers throughout the autumn months, are also particularly useful for garden contrast.

Increasingly popular are the more ornamental types, with coloured leaves, variegations in stripes and stunning flowers. Many plants have a unique 'well' in their centre, formed by overlapping leaf bases, which not only makes them drought-hardy but also popular with frogs. These plants can also be taken inside for weeks on end safely to be used as centrepieces.

Winter is the major bromeliad season, but they look great year-round because of their often striking foliage.

The famous Kirstenbosch Botanic Gardens in Cape Town is home to the newly developed *Plectranthus* hybrid 'Plepalila' (sold as 'Mona Lavender'), which has lilac-coloured blooms from late summer through to early winter and a deep burgundy underside to its leaves. Growing to just 80 cm tall, it's perfect for smaller gardens and pots.

Similar is *P. saccatus*, which has jacaranda-blue flowers and grows to about 1 m, and *P. ecklonii*, which has pink and white forms, too, and will grow to 1.5 m in height if allowed.

DID YOU KNOW? The pineapple was taken back to Europe on Columbus' second voyage. In its early days on the Continent, the pineapple became such a fashionable item that many architectural motifs were styled after it, and the rich kept specially heated houses, called pineapple houses, in order to grow them.

Plectranthus

1 *P. argentatus*   **2** *P. forsteri* 'Marginatus'   **3** *P. ecklonii* white form   **4** *P. ciliatus*

5 *P. ecklonii* pale pink form   **6** *P.* × 'Plepalila' ('Mona Lavender')   **7** *P. barbatus*   **8** *P. coleoides* 'Marginatus'
9 *P. suaveolens*

Bulbs

Bulbs, no matter what time of the year they flower, add a touch of surprise and magic to a garden. Their ephemeral nature makes them unique, so it's worth planting them even if it's only for a few weeks or months of their company.

Many early 'spring' bulbs actually begin to flower in winter. Some daffodils, jonquils, freesias, snowflakes and crocus are among the first to break through the soil.

Winter bulbs

Rare treats can appear through the winter cold, and remind us that spring is nearly there. Bulbs are particularly cheery, and none more so than the very first jonquils and *Narcissus* 'Erlicheer'. Not as tall, but incredibly charming, are the tiny *N. cyclamineus*, with their trumpets looking downwards and their petals pulled right back like they are being blown back in a storm. *Narcissus* 'Eye Spy' is also the essence of simplicity. Winter crocus, too, are particularly pretty, with many cultivars having candy stripes, and all revealing an early show that's worth planting under any tree!

Both snowdrops (*Galanthus* sp.) and snowflakes (*Leucojum* sp.) will also grow happily in the shade, and have such a purity to them with their white bells.

Then there is star of Bethlehem (*Ornithogalum sigmoideum*), with its white trumpets and black shiny centre, which also makes a pretty pot plant or less cold-hardy alternative. For lily-of-the-valley (see page 406), which is an all-time favourite for the perfumed garden, start planting bulbs in late May until the end of June into a moist, moderately rich soil. Add lots of leaf mould, and await your late winter and early spring scents of heaven to waft by.

ABOVE LEFT: Hippeastrum *'Apple Blossom' has pretty peach-toned trumpets.*

BELOW LEFT TO RIGHT: *Star of Bethlehem; the pleated snowdrop* (Galanthus plicatus); *Narcissus cyclamineus.*

Plant summer-flowering bulbs

Although it is too late to be planting spring-flowering bulbs, winter is the perfect time for planting many summer-flowering bulbs. Gloriosa lilies, Jacobean lilies, jockey's cap, pineapple lilies and spider flowers all fall into this category. Buying summer-flowering bulbs and perennials now while they are dormant means that they will establish easily and also cost less: after all, a brown scaly bulb or package of dried-up roots isn't as easy to sell as a luscious, fragrant lily. Keep an eye out for special nursery catalogues available at this time.

Hippeastrums

The large trumpet-shaped flowers of hippeastrums are a familiar sight in many established gardens. They are tremendously hardy and suit a wide range of positions, but prefer warmth and sunshine to cold zones, where they can be grown as an indoor plant. Hippeastrums are currently enjoying their moment in the sun. Their popularity has been steadily growing as more colours—from white to soft apple blossom, stripes and brick reds—have become available.

Hippeastrums are very successful container plants provided they are completely ignored over winter when the bulb is dormant—it can rot away if watered. Introduce them into your garden in autumn or winter: either buy them from nurseries or dig up and divide a clump donated by a friend. When planting, the neck of the hippeastrum bulb should protrude 15 cm or so above the soil level to help with heat exposure. Water after planting then leave it alone until leaves appear.

Red hot pokers

There are two different types of flowering *Kniphofia*: one flowers in winter and the other in summer (*K. praecox*). Native to South Africa, the winter-flowering 'Winter Cheer' is a rare bloom of garden 'heat' to enjoy on a cold and frosty morning, and it will also cope with summer drought and high temperatures, making it one of the toughest bulbs around. Other varieties worth hunting out include 'James Nottle'—its flowers are intense yellow torches that bloom from mid-winter through to early summer, and it grows to about 80 cm. At 1 m tall, 'Lime Glow' has, as its name suggests, torches with a green tinge, and 'Yellow Hammer', which starts as lime and develops more yellow as the colour moves up the torch. Plant bulbs out

DID YOU KNOW? The aloe is an excellent alternative to red hot pokers, especially in regions where red hot pokers can escape from gardens.

BIRDS AND FIRE Red hot pokers attract birds and are also fire retardants. They can become garden escapers in some regions, though, so take care to remove flowering stems as they fade.

LEFT TO RIGHT: *Now is the time to introduce colourful hippeastrums to your garden; winter-flowering red hot pokers add hot colours to the garden when they're needed.*

when dormant, usually autumn. As these are members of the Liliaceae family, care should be taken to ensure that they don't become garden escapees, so don't plant them in gardens that border reserves.

Cyclamen

Cyclamen, the aristocrat of flowering indoor plants, look their best in the winter months. Their elegant tulip-like blooms are available in a range of colours, from pure white through to cherry, lilac, fuchsia pink, musk, wine red and scarlet, both pure and bicoloured. The foliage is also a feature, with interesting markings of dark green, verdigris and silver.

There are two main species: *Cyclamen persicum* is the larger, florist's type; the other is *C. hederifolium* (or Neapolitan cyclamen), the most easily grown garden variety. This is a smaller species with daintier flowers, which look beautiful planted en masse under trees, in containers or in a rockery.

The soft pink flowers of cyclamen are very charming. Look out too for the striking pure silver leaf form.

Planting cyclamen seedlings

1. For each seedling, dig a hole large enough to accommodate the roots.

2. To release the seedlings, gently squeeze the bottom of each cell in the punnet.

3. Plant a seedling in the hole and backfill. Add some mulch around each plant.

4. Sprinkle snail bait.

Indoor plants

As the weather is colder, many people like to retreat inside where it is warmer. That doesn't mean you have to be without plants, however, as adding greenery makes indoor environments nicer to be in and better for you.

Air inside the home and workplace is polluted by fumes given off by electrical devices—such as computers, televisions, microwaves—and by chemically treated surfaces, paints and plastics. Apart from producing oxygen, plants absorb poisonous gases, especially those produced by plastic furniture and synthetic carpets.

The best thing you can do for your indoor environment is to bring a bit of the outdoors in. 'Plantscaping' your home need not be boring. There are many imaginative ways to decorate with plants.

How to choose an indoor plant

First, consider what function you want your indoor plant to perform. Ask yourself the following questions:

1 Should it feature flowers or foliage?

2 Should it stay small, grow tall, wide or narrow? For instance, choose small plants for a kitchen windowsill and tall ones with striking foliage for a large living area.

3 Should it be mobile? Sometimes smaller plants that can live outdoors in the shade for half the time make the best table-setting decorations.

Position

Few plants grow in the dark, so don't expect your house plants to perform miracles. Give them a little sunlight and as much daylight as possible. Avoid draughts, as nothing dries out a pot faster than a windy hallway or entrance area. Finally, indoor plants often have the odd flower when you first buy them, but remember that the nursery has grown the plants in perfect conditions, so be satisfied if you have happy, healthy leaves; flowers are a bonus.

Growing conditions

Will your plant have to endure heating in winter, poor light or air-conditioning?

Because there is no such thing as a naturally occurring indoor plant, we have to mimic outdoor conditions. Most indoor plants grow best in bright light. If you have a full-sun position inside, however, try to keep plants off the glass as it can really heat up and actually cause sunburn (dead, brown patches on leaves) or bleaching (whole leaf turns yellow or white). Cacti, succulents, croton, mother-in-law's tongue and ixora should be happy in such a spot, provided they are given regular drinks.

Hardy plants—such as madonna lilies, kentia palms, cissus, aspidistra, aglaonema, fatsia and philodendrons—will tolerate low levels of light, provided you don't let them get too wet. If the spot you have is really terrible, try rotating your plants every two to three weeks. Take them outside into a shady area, or let them stand in the rain.

TOP TO BOTTOM: *Chinese evergreen* (Aglaonema *'Silver King')*; Dracaena deremensis; *arrowhead vine* (Syngonium podophyllum*)*.

NEVER-SAY-DIE INDOOR PLANT

Most indoor plants suffer the most horrendous treatment. Often housed in dark rooms with air conditioning, poor ventilation and no natural light, they may be watered only by a cup of cold tea. If this is a description of your workplace, but you'd still prefer the real thing over an artificial plant, try a Chinese lucky plant (*Aglaonema* sp.). It has interesting mottled foliage and copes with just about anything. Or for flowers indoors, it's hard to go past the peace lily (*Spathiphyllum* sp.), which has white spoon-shaped blooms, while dragon trees (*Dracaena* sp.) make interesting indoor sculptural elements. Nurseries sell several varieties of syngonium, which are hardy, very attractive coloured-leaf plants. Although they rarely flower indoors, they are semi-climbing in habit and will also cascade from a hanging basket.

Spray water onto your indoor plants to get rid of sap-suckers, dirt and grime.

Tips for growing indoor plants

🍃 To keep your indoor plants thriving, wipe over the leaves with white oil or a tissue moistened with water to remove the dust and grime that clog up the breathing pores.

🍃 Quality potting mixes contain slow-release fertiliser and water crystals and will save you maintenance time. If you're using a cheaper mix, don't forget the plants are totally dependent on you for food, so give them some nine-month, slow-release granular fertiliser.

🍃 The best time to re-pot an indoor plant is when the plant will recover fastest, which is usually just after flowering, or at the beginning of spring. Vigorous plants will need re-potting every year, while slower plants such as rhapis palms will last for three to four years.

🍃 If the leaves on your indoor plant are getting smaller, appear to wilt soon after watering, or if roots appear on the surface, then your plant needs to be in a bigger pot.

🍃 Plants need feeding if their leaves start to yellow, show chlorosis (yellowing between the veins) or have different leaf sizes. Try a two-pronged approach to feeding by first using a slow-release fertiliser designed specifically for indoor plants in late winter. Second, apply a diluted liquid fertiliser every fortnight during the growing season. Good organic fertilisers can be applied to the soil and used as a foliage spray. Use foliar feeding at half strength, and apply it more frequently than you otherwise would.

Winter iris

The winter, or Algerian, iris provides a welcome spot of colour from late autumn to early spring. It comes in blue or white forms.

VITAL STATISTICS

Scientific name: *Iris unguicularis*.
Family: Iridaceae.
Plant/bulb type: They are rhizomes.
Climate: Warm and cold areas. Unsuitable for tropical regions.
Culture: Great for climate extremes, and needs little attention to look wonderful.
Height: 30–40 cm.
Planting time: Plant in autumn or winter.
Soil: Friable, and will cope with dry or wet soil.
Position: Grow in full sun to half-shade.
Planting depth and spacing: About 15 cm deep and 12–15 cm apart.
Watering: Start watering when growth appears and keep the soil slightly moist until the blooms brown off.
Fertiliser: Mulch annually with decayed manure.
Flowering time: Late autumn to early spring.
Pests/diseases: None.
After-flowering care: Trim off old leaves and flowers.

Feature bulb

Indoor plants need regular watering, especially during warm weather, or when you are applying liquid fertiliser. Don't, however, make the mistake of sitting plants in saucers. This may rot the roots, and should only be done if absolutely necessary, such as with African violets or ferns. Sit the pots on pebbles or stands to keep the roots free draining.

Water house plants thoroughly once a week rather than sprinkle them daily. They can even be taken outside for a hose down. The best way to tell if your indoor plants are dry is to use your finger. If the soil is dry at the second knuckle, then you need to water. If hot, dry air from heaters is a problem, try misting the leaves rather than watering the soil. An atomiser can also be handy in air-conditioned rooms throughout the summer.

The most common indoor plant pest is mealy bug, a fuzzy cotton wool-like insect, whose best method of control is to keep leaves clean, and spray or soak the rootball in a pesticide solution. Another problem pest is scale. These look like small raised lumps, and can be white or dark brown. Scale particularly affects palms, and can be treated by white oil.

Sometimes indoor plants can get red spider mite (two-spotted mite), a particularly difficult pest to control. Mites thrive in dry, dusty conditions, so regular spells outside and a good hosing will help prevent attack.

CREATING ATMOSPHERE Although the terrarium is a closed environment and will regulate its own watering needs, at first you may need to help establish the right moisture balance by removing the lid if the sides of the glass become foggy.

project

Plant a terrarium

For planting a terrarium, choose from miniature lilies, parlour palms, small-leafed madonna lilies, African violets and plants with contrasting foliage, such as hypoestes, nerve plant and peperomia.

1 Place a layer of charcoal (to help absorb wastes) on the bottom of a suitable vessel—anything with a sealable top can be used. Fit a cloth, such as some paper towel, to stop the potting mix from working its way into the charcoal layer.

2 Add a small amount of peat-based mix or African violet potting mix.

3 Gently plant your chosen greenery, firmly tamping down around the roots. Decorate the top with a layer or two of coloured pebbles or sphagnum moss.

4 Water in gently, washing down any dirty leaves. Replace the lid.

Grasses, groundcovers and climbers

Although winter is a fairly tranquil period for these cover-ups, ornamental grasses can be beautiful in their own right, with spent flower heads and winter silhouettes adding interest and form. The more traditional turf grass has virtually stopped growing and almost all climbers have slipped into a sleep now.

It is not spring 'til you can plant your foot upon twelve daisies.

ENGLISH PROVERB

Grasses

The cool weather of winter slows the growth of most turf grasses right down. This means you can raise your mower height, mow less frequently and stop fertilising until new growth starts at the end of winter and into spring.

While the grass has slowed, the weeds seem to show no mercy, and bindii, moss and dandelions all still grow. Dig these out by hand if there are only a few, or use a selective weedicide mixed with a few drops of dishwashing liquid (which helps the spray adhere to the leaves) if you are feeling overwhelmed by the task ahead.

For a bad case of winter grass, use one of these three methods: mow the weeds down, dig them out or spray as for bindii, moss and dandelions. Make sure you attend to the problem before the seeds drop and lie waiting for the next opportunity to attack.

If you are taking the opportunity to do any remodelling of your garden over winter, remember that lawn is slow to recover from heavy traffic at this time of year, and may need extra care to prepare it for spring growth.

Lightly fork over compacted areas, use a high-phosphorus lawn repair food and rope off the area if possible. If these remedies fail, transplant runners in spring from your healthy turf to grow over any bare patches.

Finally, make sure your lawn does not dehydrate. Even in winter, severe winds can be as desiccating as the hot sun in summer.

This mossy log has grass-like tufts of white hoop petticoat daffodils (Narcissus cantabricus), *which are yet to flower.*

Lawn flowers

Weeds aren't the only things that thrive in lawns, coping with repeated mowing and spreading easily. Lawn flowers—including buttered egg, dwarf pink clover, oxalis and lawn daisies—do too.

Buttered egg (*Lotus corniculatus*) and lawn daisy (*Bellis perennis*), the ancestor of the modern double form of English daisy, can both be bought as seed and sown over turf to create a romantic, whimsical effect. The single white flowers of the lawn daisy show during the cooler months before mowing starts.

Some hybrid oxalis make excellent groundcovers through lawn, as they flower in winter when the turf has all but stopped growing. One called 'Barber's Pole' (*Oxalis hirta*) has striped petals when in bud. Another, *O. purpurea*, has large flowers with yellow centres and deep green leaflets with purple undersides. Others have burgundy leaves which work well as a foliage contrast. A favourite is 'Hot Pink', guaranteed to brighten anyone's day when seen in flower en masse in a lawn.

The common clover can also be too easily dismissed as a weed, but don't forget it is terrific for improving soil fertility (see 'The Papilionaceae family', page 268), as it helps fix nitrogen into the soil and can look pretty and lush. Just remember not to run through it in bare feet, as bee stings could be a problem.

New Zealand flax grasses

The winter cold is great for bringing out the intense colour of many of these beautiful foliage plants (*Phormium* sp.), though of course they weren't always grown for ornamental purposes. In fact, until the last few decades, flax was grown commercially for its fibre and milled into ropes and cables until synthetics took over. Its botanical genus is *Phormium*, which is Greek for basket,

RIGHT: *New Zealand flax creates a focal point in the garden, adding texture, colour and form.*

LEFT: *Lawn daisies foretell spring.*

BELOW: Oxalis *will spread through a lawn, but some species, such as this one, are highly ornamental.*

Moss in a box

Winter is perfect weather for moss, which thrives in cooler temperatures. If you love the look of moss, plant a container with some groundcover and alpine plants that masquerade as moss—try scleranthus, sagina, pratia, mazus, thrift, fescue and pinks.

Any low container will do. Old boxes, fruit crates, limestone sinks and shallow troughs are ideal. Equip your container with adequate drainage and fill it with coarse, gritty potting mix for aeration and extra peat for moisture retention. Water in well.

and a vessel from which these fibres were also sometimes woven.

Native to swampy areas, flax is now used more as an architectural accent plant, with its dramatic silhouettes and interesting colour range creating interest year-round in the garden. Colours range from the common 'Atropurpureum', which is a solid brown, through to combinations of cream, red and pink like 'Cream Delight' and 'Tricolour', and red and pink forms like 'Firebird', 'Sunset' and 'Sundown'. There is also the golden-tinged 'Yellow Wave' and dwarf types like 'Jack Spratt'.

Mosses and fungi

The cool weather encourages moss to grow in the grass, lichens to cover flagging and fungi to emerge from rotting timbers. There are two ways of dealing with nature's fight-back: either celebrate it as a seasonal treasure or combat it with chemicals.

Providing the drainage is adequate, the warmer weather will kill off most mosses in your lawn so that you can afford to relax and take the time to look closely at these treasures and appreciate their beauty.

Many people have come to like moss so much that they go to any lengths to get it to grow on pots and statuary. To speed up the softening effect of mosses

and lichen on stonework or terracotta, smear on yoghurt, or paint over with sour milk. You'll soon have a lovely culture of moss and mould. Use this method to make composite concrete look like stone.

If you are despairing over paths slippery with moss, apply a bit of bleach with a stiff brush; this method will remove the moss without giving your paving the 'brand new' look you'll get with water blasting.

Some fungi and toadstools can be very colourful in their own right. Other fungi work in a symbiotic relationship with plant roots, and can improve plant growth. Many lawn seeds now come with fungal spore added to the seed and starter fertiliser, as it aids germination rates and significantly affects the success of the turf.

Machine maintenance

You should regularly clean your lawnmower, grass trimmer and garden mulcher. Sometimes this is as fast as cleaning the blades, changing the air filter and topping up the oil. Clean, sharp blades on grass-cutting equipment help stop the spread of weeds and diseases. Uneven, jagged cuts left by unsharpened blades create a scorch line, which is unattractive as well as stressful for your lawn. An annual overhaul of your machinery really does make a difference.

When letting steps grow a cover of moss, be careful to keep the tread clean so that accidents are avoided. The riser can look safely beautiful with its green covering.

Lawnmower maintenance

1 Remove the cover on the air filter and remove the old air filter. Once an air filter is clogged with dirt, it inhibits the air flow and your mower will simply stop.

2 Insert the new air filter by pushing it into place and replace the cover.

3 Remove the spark plug cover and using a spark plug socket, remove the spark plug.

4 Check to see if the point is dirty, and if so rub it with some fine sandpaper. Replace if necessary.

Miniature papyrus

Native to Africa and nearby islands such as Madagascar, this sedge has become particularly popular for growing in shady damp areas and giving ponds some grassy tufts, as it will quite easily grow in pots completely submerged. It looks great in clumps as a feature, and works well with Asian-themed gardens too.

VITAL STATISTICS

Scientific name: *Cyperus prolifer*.
Family: Cyperaceae.
Climate: Frost-free areas.
Colours: Grown for its green foliage in ponds and damp areas.
Height: 0.5–1 m.
Planting time: Any time of year.
Soil: Damp soil, boggy areas and in ponds. Do not plant more than 10 cm deep in water.
Position: Full sun in the morning or shade.
Fertiliser: Not necessary.
Propagation: Divide clumps in winter and plant about 10 cm apart for fast cover.

Feature grass

Mondo grass softens both the edges of this path and the stair risers.

Mondo grass

Perhaps the most popular grass of all is the Japanese mondo (*Ophiopogon* sp.). The common name 'grass' is actually a misnomer as it belongs to the lily family but has grassy foliage.

It is fantastic en masse and can be used effectively as a turf subsitute in the shade (especially the 'mini' cultivar) or as a border between beds and pathways. White, variegated, giant, dwarf and black cultivars make the long-lived mondo grass a very useful ornamental for foliage contrasts. Mondo lawns and long borders can be expensive to put in. Try and buy the smallest pots you can, as it clumps up quickly once planted.

Groundcovers

As winter brings out the worst in traditional grass, take
time to study nature's many alternatives.

After World War II, turf grass became
the most dominant element of the home
garden and alternative groundcovers
were ignored. Although most are not as
resistant to wear and tear, groundcovers
do provide flowers, fragrant foliage and
textural contrast.

Ferns

Ferns are one of the most ancient of
plant groups, reproducing themselves
not by flower and seed production but by
spore. They love cool, moist areas and
thrive in the shade. The detail in fern
fronds lifts these areas by introducing
rich texture. There is a great variation in
colour and pattern in fern fronds. Some
leaves have superb silver markings,
bronze new growth or lime young leaves,
while others glisten and shimmer.

Ferns can be evergreen or
herbaceous, dying back in winter, but
whatever the type, most can become
shabby at this time and need a close
prune back to the crown so that they
can regenerate themselves with fresh
spring growth. This is also the time to
divide up large clumps. Although many
ferns are sold as indoor plants, they grow
happily in a sheltered position outdoors
provided there is a reliable amount of
moisture and a rich mulch of leaf litter.

Australia is rich in its fern species,
which can be used effectively as understorey plants in a rainforest garden.
Many species, such as rasp ferns
(*Doodia* sp.) are even drought-tolerant.
Tree ferns (*Cyathea australis*, *C. cooperi*
and *Dicksonia* sp.) form tall, thin trunks
and are tolerant of full sun and frost.
Others, such as the bird's nest fern
(*Asplenium nidus*), make a great textural
contrast to finer foliage with their shiny
broad leaves.

Some native ferns, such as elkhorns
and staghorns, are epiphytic, growing
in trees. They feed off leaf mould
collected in the branches or, in the case
of the bird's nest fern, in the crown of
the plant itself.

ABOVE: *The national
emblem of New
Zealand is silver fern*
(Cyathea dealbata).

**DID YOU
KNOW?** *Dicksonia*,
the soft tree fern,
will still grow if you
cut the top off and
replant it.

BELOW: Dicksonia
antarctica *can grow
to 15 m in height
and will tolerate
low temperatures.*

ABOVE: *Elkhorns can be grown on boards,
stumps and tree trunks.*

1 Silver brake fern (*Pteris argyraea*) 2 Little club moss or spike moss (*Selaginella* sp.) 3 Bird's nest fern (*Asplenium nidus*, crested cv.) 4 Sword fern (*Nephrolepis* sp.) 5 Black-stem maidenhair (*Adiantum formosum*) 6 Bear's foot fern (*Polypodium glaucum*) 7 Mexican flowering fern (*Anemia phyllitidis*) 8 Bird's nest fern crosier (a crosier is the tip of a young fern frond that is bent into a hook shape) 9 Holly fern (*Cyrtomium falcatum*) 10 Button fern

Ferns

(*Pellaea rotundifolia*) **11** Hart's tongue fern (*Asplenium scolopendrium*) **12** Boston fern or sword fern (*Nephrolepis exaltata*) **13** Prickly rasp fern (*Doodia aspera*) **14** Common maidenhair (*Adiantum raddianum*) **15** Hen and chicken fern (*Asplenium bulbiferum* × *serratum* 'Island Beauty') **16** Ring fern (*Paesia scaberula*) **17** Canary Island hare's foot fern (*Davallia canariensis*) **18** Leather fern (*Rumohra adiantiformis*) **19** Brake fern (*Pteris quadriaurita*)

Aloe 'Always Red' throws up spears of blood red flowers throughout summer, autumn and winter.

Aloes

Most people know that aloe is a miracle medicine plant (*Aloe vera*), famous for its topical healing properties for burns and rashes. Sadly, the fame of this species has led to most of the other 400 or so species being overlooked, many of which are superb garden plants.

Equally at home in drought or periods of inundation, the aloe also has a huge range of flowers, shapes and sizes from which to choose. They are all typified by succulent leaves, but from there they diversify, with some growing only 30 cm tall and others reaching tree heights. In general, aloes are hardy, require no watering, and have virtually no pests or diseases. Their nectar-rich blooms encourage birds into the garden.

Chameleon plant

The chameleon plant has beautiful tricoloured foliage and looks good all year, but especially so in winter when the cold weather really seems to bring out its colour. The most common complaint about the chameleon plant is that it grows too easily and sometimes takes over. It does, however, cope with root competition from large trees and compete effectively with weeds on embankments, so it comes in handy for tricky positions.

VITAL STATISTICS

Scientific name: *Houttuynia cordata* 'Variegata'.
Family: Saururaceae.
Climate: Almost anything other than severe cold.
Culture: Around ponds and in the shade.
Colours: Foliage is a combination of green, yellow, red and pink.
Height: Up to 30 cm.
Planting time: Any.
Soil: Wet or free draining.
Position: Full sun or shade; the shade brings out the foliage colour better.
Planting spacing: 50 cm for a fast groundcover.
Fertiliser: Not needed.
Pests/diseases: None.
Propagation: Cutting.

Feature groundcover

Flower colours range from orange, apricot, red, white and cream through to yellow, pink and bicolours.

Zygocactus

Sometimes called Christmas or Thanksgiving cactus as it flowers at that time of the year in the northern hemisphere, *Schlumbergera truncata* is also known as zygocactus. In early winter these trailing beauties start to flower and make terrific trouble-free basket plants. They come in lovely corals, pinks, golds and crimsons; the temperature seems to affect the flower colour, resulting in gold flowers one year, then pink the next.

In their natural habitat, they grow from trees and between rocks in the rainforests of South America, where they are pollinated by hummingbirds. Grown 'in captivity', these exotic plants mostly prefer a morning sun, afternoon shade position, or sheltered from intense heat under a shade structure. To keep them looking good, feed with a balanced organic fertiliser such as liquid blood and bone every couple of months.

For something different, grow them in a strawberry pot, or pop them through the sides of a basket.

STRIKING ZYGOCACTUS
You can strike zygocactus from cuttings by simply sticking leaf sections into small pots filled with coarse sand and keeping them moist.

BELOW: *Two of the many hybrids of zygocactus.*

Climbers

Winter is a quiet time for flowering climbers. A few early displays can be found on Carolina jasmine, false sarsaparilla and orange trumpet vine, but most are dormant now and some have even shed their leaves.

This makes winter an especially good time to take control of some of the more unruly specimens which may have crept up into your eaves or swamped the neighbour's trees.

Climbers such as wisteria and grape vine are much easier to tackle after they have lost their leaves, but you need to pay special attention when pruning back wisteria. Leave flowering spurs, characterised by smaller lengths between buds, and remove unwanted leaf-producing growth, which will quickly get out of hand once the leaves and more tendrils arrive.

False sarsaparilla

Known variously as native wisteria, happy wanderer and false sarsaparilla, the Australian climber *Hardenbergia violacea* looks delightful throughout winter. The profusion of delicate chains of purple pea-like flowers against emerald green, gumtree-like leaves are a sight to behold in the bush or garden.

They make terrific groundcovers or climbers and come in purple, white, pink and bicoloured forms—all look great at this time of the year. There is also a shrub form called 'Mini-haha', and another, 'Little Boy Blue', which is a more vibrant, compact shrub. They

ABOVE: *False sarsaparilla's alternative name, happy wanderer, aptly describes its habit of sprawling through the bush.*

RIGHT: *Freesias offset the profusion of purple flowers on false sarsaparilla.*

A garden is a
      lovesome thing.
God wot!
Rose plot.
Fringed pool.
Fern'd grot.

T. E. BROWN

grow in full sun or semi-shade and benefit from light pruning after flowering to encourage bushiness and to stop pods forming.

Millettia

Also known as native or Australian wisteria, *Millettia megasperma* is a vigorous, glossy-leafed climber with showy sprays of purple pea flowers in summer and autumn. It likes moist, well-drained soil and a position with full sun or part shade, and can cope with light frost. Plant *Millettia* to attract seed-eating birds.

Attachment theory

Sometimes it's not possible to erect trellis or wiring to help climbers attach themselves. This is when plants with adventitious roots (that is, roots that grow from the stem) come into their own. For an easy cover over brickwork, creeping fig (*Ficus pumila*) is a great alternative to ivy (*Hedera* sp.), while Virginia creeper (*Parthenocissus quinquefolia*) and Boston ivy (*Parthenocissus tricuspidata*) are hard to beat for their autumn display and lushness over summer. *Campsis* will also develop roots along the stems if given

Clematis napaulensis

A more beautiful climber it would be hard to find. It looks like a cross between the most stunning passion flower and the most lovely of all clematis. Native to China and Nepal, *Clematis napaulensis* has the unusual habit of becoming deciduous in late summer, after which it re-grows foliage fresh for autumn and blooms throughout winter.

VITAL STATISTICS

Scientific name: *Clematis napaulensis*.
Family: Ranunculaceae.
Climate: Cool temperate to shade-house.
Culture: This climber needs a support or cradle of some sort, though can look delightful growing through shrubs.
Colours: The stunning purple and greenish white flowers have staminous bell-shaped blooms in winter and release a delicate perfume that hangs in the air.
Height: Grows to 2–3 m.
Planting time: Plant cuttings slightly deeper than most plants, as this encourages them to grow new shoots.
Soil: Moist, fertile, well-drained soil.
Position: Sun or semi-shade.
Planting spacing: 1.5 m apart.
Fertiliser: Apply a mulch of well-rotted garden compost around the base of the plant in early autumn.
Propagation: Purchase seed from online outlets.

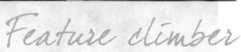

Feature climber

ABOVE: *Canary bellflower blooms in late winter and can be useful teamed with deciduous vines that are bare at this time of year.*

ABOVE RIGHT: Tropaeolum tricolor, *a relative of the nasturtium, has gorgeous orange and black flowers.*

help to climb, and the stunning summer flowers will make the extra work worthwhile. Some shrubs will also react this way when grown against a wall, *Euonymus* (spindle tree) being one of the easiest and hardiest examples. Monstera and Asiatic jasmine (*Trachelospermum asiaticum*) are both self-clinging climbers ideal for jazzing up a fence, and climbing hydrangea is great for a shady place.

Gone, not forgotten

Although there are many herbaceous plants—meaning that they die down and come back up again—there are not so many climbing ones in cultivation. It's a pity, because they can be very useful and provide 'instant colour' and interest. The most commonly grown is the coral vine (*Antigonon leptopus*), which has stunning flowers that attract bees and butterflies as well as the eye. Native to Mexico, its coral pink, heart-shaped flowers are borne en masse from early summer to mid-autumn.

Other herbaceous climbers, such as *Tropaeolum tricolor* and Canary bellflower (*Canarina canariensis*), are very useful because they burst into flower during winter, when lots of the garden is bare, and then die down for summer, leaving other plants to fill the colour void. The red-flowering *Tropaeolum* is in the same genus as nasturtium, but this one grows 3 m tall and has potato-like tubers that can be shared among friends who admire your plant. The Canary bellflower is a rare relative of campanula. Its orange-red blooms are about 5 cm long and appear from late winter to autumn, and are followed by edible fruits. Although it needs protection from frosts and is hard to find, it's worth the effort.

Worth trumpeting about

The family Bignoniaceae contains many plants with showy trumpet-shaped blooms. Orange trumpet vine (*Pyrostegia venusta*) is one member, with its lovely orange flowers creating a curtain of

tangerine, but it also contains other beautiful creepers such as herald's trumpet (*Beaumontia grandiflora*), which has perfumed white bells and enjoys

HOPS
Golden hops (*Humulus lupulus* 'Aureus') is a highly ornamental version of the plant used to flavour beer. It is herbaceous, too, dying down over winter. Golden hops loves sunshine, and will tolerate some shade, frost and most soils.

a subtropical climate. Useful shrubs such as the trumpet bush or Cape honeysuckle (*Tecoma* sp.) also belong to this family. These flower from late spring to late autumn, in either yellow or orange, and make a very good hedge in warm climates.

There are also some stunning trees that belong in this group. The trumpet tree (*Tabebuia* sp.), from the tropical Americas, has bell-shaped flowers in yellow, white, lilac and pink, and the famous jacaranda from South America flowers profusely in spring with purple flowers like foxgloves.

Orange trumpet vine looks spectacular trained onto tall supports so that the free-hanging flowers can be seen to their best advantage. Pergolas tend to hide the flowers as they sit on top and are only visible from above.

Shrubs and trees

Winter is the ideal planting time for almost all deciduous trees and shrubs. Their dormancy allows you to plant them with minimum disturbance. It also means you can save money by buying plants as bare-rooted stock, or move existing deciduous plants about the garden.

Mature elm trees line the entranceway to a large rural property. Crocus planted beneath the elms create a jewelled carpet in late winter.

The importance of evergreens, whether as hedging or privacy screens, becomes much more apparent in winter when many plants are bare. The tracery of unadorned branches creates a delightful cobweb against the sky, but looks much better against a solid green framework that screens your garden from the neighbour's windows.

Even when flowers are in short supply in the garden, remember the value of plants and trees with variegated leaves, attractive berries and interesting seed pods.

For coloured foliage, try the yellow tones of gold dust plant (*Aucuba japonica*) or euonymus, or the red tips of photinia. The shiny green leaves of *Camellia japonica* and holly are also great 'fillers', and the velvet-brown underside of Bull Bay magnolia (*Magnolia grandiflora*) are very popular with florists.

For unusually shaped leaves, don't forget palm fronds, ferns and strap leaves like flax (*Phormium* sp.) or bird of paradise (*Strelitzia* sp.), which look great in a vase. Crane flower (*S. reginae*) is a

CLOCKWISE FROM RIGHT: *The evergreen* Pseudopanax lessonii *'Cyril Watson' is an excellent choice for the shade; gold dust plant, in berry; the small flowers of* Fatsia japonica, *just about to open.*

clumping plant with stunning orange and violet-blue flowers in autumn and winter. The dark green leaves are paler and greyish underneath, with a prominent red vein. Various species of *Strelitzia* have interesting foliage, from reed-like (*S. parvifolia*) to spoon-shaped (*S. juncea*). The large banana-like *S. nicolai* has ice blue flowers.

The Araliaceae family

Some very useful evergreen shrubs and trees belong to the Araliaceae family, sometimes known as the ginseng or ivy family after its best known members.

The species after which the genus is named is *Aralia,* which includes *Aralia spinosa,* whose viciously sharp, spiny stems have earned it the common name, the devil's walking stick. There is also a lovely large shrub, sold as an indoor plant in most climates, called 'China Doll', which has delicate lacy foliage and white perfumed bell flowers. Also related is the false aralia (*Plerandra elegantissima*), which looks a bit like a marijuana plant.

The leaves of most of its members are often ivy shaped (palmate) and the flowers appear in clusters or umbels and are followed by fleshy fruit. Many are shade tolerant too, making them useful for gardening under tree canopies and so on. Umbrella trees are one such example, coping with indoor situations and heavy shade.

Many genera have beautifully variegated foliage, like the variegated *Fatsia japonica* 'Variegata' which is splashed with white markings that contrast well with its handsome green background. *Fatsia* plants are quite cool-hardy too, and add that tropical effect to even cold-climate gardens, provided they are not exposed to cold winds and are given some shelter.

One strange phenomenon has occurred in this plant family—an inter-generic hybrid. Just like crossing a horse with a donkey to get a mule, the rare crossing between *Hedera* (ivy) and *Fatsia* in this family resulted in *Fatshedera,* or tree ivy. It's characteristics mirror both parents, although it doesn't really climb.

Wintersweet should have place of honour among plants that will flower out of doors during winter months.

VITA SACKVILLE-WEST

RIGHT: *To bring flowering quince into early blossom for the home, simply place budding branches in a vase of tepid water.*

BELOW: *This collection of pretty spurges includes some with winter colour and others with flowers.*

Shrubs

You'd be forgiven for thinking that camellias are the only winter-flowering plants. Beautiful and popular as they are, there are many other plants that provide colour while most of the garden sleeps.

Many have red or yellow flowers, ideal for adding warmth and welcome to cold days. A popular source of winter colour are poinsettias, which light up winter skies with their fiery red bracts. There are also the lantanas, often overlooked due to their weedy cousins. The sterile dwarf forms, with aromatic leaves, come in a great colour range and flower non-stop year-round in temperate climates.

Sunny yellow from *Jasminum mesnyi*, the golden dollar bush, and later forsythia, brighten and scent the winter garden, as do other early blossoms such as those of kerria.

In China they call japonica or flowering quince (*Chaenomeles japonica*) the 'flower of a hundred days', and it is one of the most delightful blossoming deciduous shrubs for gardens today. You may recognise it from Japanese woodblock prints where it is often portrayed. The flowers are normally scarlet to deep crimson, although there are also more delicate tints of apple blossom and white available. Forming a tangled thicket of prickly branches, this big shrub is one of the easiest to grow in any non-tropical climate.

The spurges

The family Euphorbiaceae, known as the spurges, contains some extremely hardy plants, including two trees—the Chinese tallow tree and the Australian native bleeding heart. The entire family has a highly poisonous white milky sap—a skin irritant—which will ooze from broken stems.

The best known euphorbias are poinsettias, which with their bright

DISBUDDING CAMELLIAS

Camellias, mainly japonicas, tend to produce too many flower buds and cannot support them. This can cause the buds to drop and the flowers to fall prematurely. To disbud your camellias, remove excess buds, leaving only one or two buds at the end of each shoot. You may feel like a sadist, but doing this allows the plant to produce new growth as well as larger and longer-lasting blooms.

red leaf bracts make a showy winter display; the true flowers are held at the centre of each cluster and are actually small and yellowish green. Poinsettias have been popularised by the indoor plant industry, where they are grown in bulk for their Christmas colour.

Poinsettias grow into a rounded shrub with a short trunk and many ascending branches. They can be deciduous in cold areas, but are normally evergreen. Smaller growing cultivars include 'Annette Hegg', which reaches only 2.5 m, and 'Henrietta Ecke', which has large double-bracted flower heads. Cream, pink, salmon, speckled and marbled varieties are also popular as indoor colour.

To improve the life of cut poinsettias, go out just after dark in winter with a bucket of very hot water. Cut the stems and immediately plunge the lower part into the water. Hold them up for a few minutes. The sap is comparatively sluggish at that time of evening, and the heat seals off the cut to some degree.

A useful summer-flowering euphorbia, snow on the mountain (*Euphorbia marginata*), looks icy cold with its white marginated leaf and is a great foil for bright flowers. Some species have adapted to climatic extremes by developing succulent foliage. The crown of thorns (*E. milii*) flowers red or white in spring and summer, while Medusa's head (*E. caput-medusae*) has

white-fringed flowers upon its grotesque branches in spring or early summer.

Green-flowering varieties, known as spurge or milkweed (*E. characias* and *E. amygdaloides*), are popular in cottage and Mediterranean-style gardens. They tolerate drought and thrive in a well-drained, sunny position in any soil. Two cultivars—*E. amygdaloides* 'Purpurea', which has reddish purple leaves, and *E. characias* subsp. *wulfenii* 'Silver Song', which has brighter yellow bracts—are great garden specimens. 'Silver Song' is also a very attractive variegated cultivar with silver and white streaks and dainty flowers throughout winter and into spring, and only grows to 75 cm.

E. × *martinii* 'Rudolph' is a relatively new variety bred for its glowing red tips in winter. It brightens the gloomiest winter garden, and in spring the green blooms, each with a red 'eye', are also lovely. Growing 60 cm × 60 cm, its neat growth makes it ideal for both borders and pots. For year-round burgundy foliage, look for the hybrid cultivar called 'Blackbird' which has lime green flowers from winter to spring. It's extremely heat tolerant, and will stay compact to 40 cm and grow in semi-shade or full sun. The tricolour 'Ascot Rainbow' is another interesting foliage form with yellow, lime, red and pink streaks in the leaves and tonings in the flowers. It likes full sun and is happy even in very cold conditions.

LEFT TO RIGHT: Euphorbia 'Snow on the Mountain' is beautiful in the garden and lasts well as cut foliage; E. 'Ascot Rainbow' is an attractive form with a pink and gold variegated edge to its leaves; E. characias, or Mediterranean spurge, has many beautiful cultivars.

DID YOU KNOW? The corrosive white milky sap of petty spurge (*Euphorbia peplus*) has long been used by herbalists to treat warts and corns. It is now showing promise as a treatment for skin cancer.

One of the daintiest euphorbias is *E. leucocephala*, or snowflake bush. In late autumn and winter it is smothered in delicate white bracts that do in fact give the impression of snowflakes falling. Typically it grows 2–3 m tall by about the same width, and once established can cope with drought, although it doesn't like severe frosts. After flowering it will benefit from a prune back to save it from going 'leggy'. If you like the sound of this, but don't have the space, then consider *E. graminea* 'White Frost'. It grows to about 1 m tall, and almost year-round has delicate white flowers that look like whirly white butterflies. It's useful for semi-shade, too, though will happily grow in full sun.

Ericas and epacris, heaths and heathers

Winter is the time for heaths. This large group of shrubs is native to Europe and South Africa, although related plants such as the *Epacris* are native to Australia. These are very similar in appearance to the South African ericas, as both have small stemless leaves that are often spiky to touch.

Epacris sp. flowers look like tubular bells and so are known as native fuchsias, in full flower in the bush in winter. They are perfect for the rock garden and bloom well in containers, provided they are planted in sandy potting mix. Prune them back in spring after the flowers finally finish.

The coral heath (*E. microphylla*) is one of the smallest species, with tiny, heart-shaped pointed leaves, and neatly arranged white to pink flowers smothering its stems. It grows happily in damp spots and will take harsh windy conditions. The native fuchsia (*E. longiflora*) will grow happily in shade. Its brilliant red tubular flowers are tipped with white.

Heath (*Erica* sp.) has small needle-like leaves and bell-shaped tubular flowers in white, pink, violet, coral, crimson and bicolours. They prefer cool areas with low humidity and can succumb to root rot if soils are overly wet. They are short-lived, often only surviving three to five years, but are useful for winter colour and invaluable in cool temperate gardens.

Scotch heather (*Calluna vulgaris*) is famous for its purple flowers, but is also available in white and rose. Irish heather (*Daboecia cantabrica*) has larger flowers in the same colour range in summer.

All of these genera have very fine, hair-like roots which like a lime-free peaty soil, so the soil should never be allowed to dry out or become soggy.

Bridal heath (Erica bauera), *a South African native, will tolerate cold climates quite well.*

Winter in the perfumed garden

One of the most popular perfumed plants is daphne (*Daphne odora*), a much-beloved shrub and a must for the fragrant garden. From winter to early spring the pink or white flowers emit a scent that wafts far and wide.

Daphne has a reputation for being difficult to grow, but this can be overcome by providing adequate drainage and thick organic mulch each spring. It grows to about waist height and will flourish in a shaded corner. Most daphnes fare best in shade, though a new cultivar called 'Eternal Fragrance' is sun-tolerant and has a longer flowering period, so is definitely worth trying.

For something different, try a fabled blue daphne, called *D. genkwa*, which has lavender flowers on bare wood in late winter, then bronze-tinged new growth in spring. Daphne is also available in variegated leaf forms.

Boronias too have a reputation for being temperamental. The brown boronia (*Boronia megastigma*) and Australian native rose (*B. serrulata*) have very fragrant flowers. They are prone to suffer from root rot and phytophthora, dying suddenly when the drainage isn't ideal, so raise the garden beds and treat the soil before planting.

If these two plants sound too tricky, try mahonia. *Mahonia bealei* and *M. japonica* both have yellow flowers that smell like lily-of-the-valley in late winter. Winter honeysuckle (*Lonicera fragrantissima*) is near impossible to kill and has a delightful scent. It grows into a rambling shrub and needs an annual prune removing old canes to keep it from overtaking the garden.

Some of the deciduous viburnums have a delicious perfume, almost a mixture of carnation and gardenia. *Viburnum* × *burkwoodii*, *V. carlesii* and *V.* × *carlcephalum* all have clusters of fragrant white or pink flowers in winter.

Two other deciduous plants are known for their winter perfume. Winter-sweet (*Chimonanthus praecox*) has tiny

yellow flowers with a fragrance like jasmine and jonquils in mid-winter. It's easy to grow and flowers best in a sunny position. Chinese witch hazel (*Hamamelis mollis*) also has yellow flowers with a fragrance like jonquils.

CLOCKWISE FROM TOP LEFT: *Nepalese paper plant* (Daphne bholua)*;* Mahonia *sp.;* *Chinese witch hazel.*

Lily-of-the-valley lookalikes

If you love lily-of-the-valley (*Convallaria majalis*), then you should try some shrubs with similar flowers. Plants in the *Clethra*, *Pieris* and *Zenobia* genera are all known by the same common name, and have similarly lovely flowers.

Clethra arborea, or lily-of-the-valley tree, produces lovely white, scented flowers in late summer and grows in a similar way to the Irish strawberry tree (*Arbutus unedo*).

Lily-of-the-valley shrub, or *Pieris japonica*, is closely related to azaleas and enjoys a light friable soil with an acid pH and plenty of added leaf humus. Many pieris also have sensational red, pink or bronze young foliage—*P. formosa* var. *forrestii* is particularly good for its red new growth. Best planted in a protected position, all have sprays of white flowers with a delicate fragrance in late winter and spring.

An elegant lily-of-the-valley lookalike that rarely exceeds about 1 m, *Zenobia pulverulenta* produces lightly aniseed-scented white bell-shaped flowers at the ends of arching canes in early summer.

Golden oldies

Abelia is one of those tough-as-old-boots plants that you'll find growing in many gardens, simply because they never die. You could be forgiven for not planting it in newer gardens, because once upon a time it was so common it became a bit boring. If, however, you want a plant that flowers from spring to winter, can be trimmed, copes with cold, tolerates drought and also has some beautiful foliage forms, then perhaps this is one for you. It even attracts butterflies and

bees and will hold onto its rosy red calyxes, even when not in flower.

There are several species available, the most common of which is a hybrid known as *Abelia* × *grandiflora*, and a dwarf form named 'Nana', that only grows 1–2 m tall. Within this species there are some colourful cultivars including 'Frances Mason', which has marvellous golden leaves, 'Silver Anniversary', which has white edges, and 'Golden Anniversary', which has gold margins. The best new variety, however, is 'Kaleidoscope', which has variegated leaves that are combinations of dark green with, depending on the seasons, either lime green (spring), golden (summer), orange (autumn) or red (winter). It is smaller growing, too, getting up to 1 m tall and is much more compact than the original 'golden oldie'.

Other species worth hunting out include *A. schumannii*, which has lilac flowers in summer and autumn, and grows 2–3 m in height. It tends to be deciduous and a golden form, 'Saxon Gold', is also available.

Golden girls

Gold in the garden has the ability to cheer any dull winter day. Golden foliage is a great way of adding permanent lustre, but more ephemeral glimmers can also be a wonderful seasonal light. There is an array of winter 'Golden Girls' such as *Kerria* (both single and double), *Edgeworthia chrysantha* and *Forsythia*, which positively shimmer on bare stems. Then there are the evergreen *Berberis thunbergii* and *Azara celastrina*, which add permanence and colour, and *Reinwardtia indica* makes a very pretty addition to the winter garden, where it will reliably flower for three months. Another golden girl is the edible *Cornus mas*, which has golden fruits on display.

LILY-OF-THE-VALLEY
Many people covet the dainty white, sweet-smelling flowers of lily-of-the-valley. The plant is sold in autumn like a bulb as packaged pips: the swollen roots that will come to life in spring. Soak them in lukewarm water first, then plant them into a peaty, humus-rich soil. You can also grow them in pots, and force them to flower in winter early by planting them early.

DID YOU KNOW? The fragrance of flowers is thought to attract insects, birds and animals to pollinate the flowers. The fragrance is an essential oil that is released at different levels throughout the day or night, depending on the plant. Fragrance is more noticeable in a protected position because wind doesn't disperse the oil.

CLOCKWISE FROM ABOVE: *Golden-blooming plants in full flower:* Forsythia *sp.;* Berberis thunbergii; *a* Kerria *double; and* Edgeworthia chrysantha 'Grandiflora'.

Foliage plants

Creating a garden involves so much more than coaxing plants to survive. A truly successful garden is like painting a living picture, where seasons, shapes and forms all play a part in creating drama and ambience. Unlike flowers, foliage plants provide the garden with seasonal interest all year round, and this is especially important in winter when most flowers have long since faded.

Silver foliage

As the colour of silver is elusive, it is often used as a background for other, more brilliant colours. Many silver plants have a sheen that dazzles in the sunlight or is visible at night, while others have rich textures that create a tapestry among the other plants in the garden.

They are a wonderful buffer between colours, holding together a diverse palette (even hot tones) with their neutrality, or adding to the harmonious feel of a pastel garden. When silver and grey plants are planted in the border they create a sense of extended perspective.

Wonderful in a thematic garden or when they are used as accent plants,

silver foliage plants will highlight any dull corners in your garden, add light to a predominantly dark green garden bed and provide a feeling of freshness to well-established areas in your garden.

Some of the best silver foliage plants include shrubs such as lavender, teucrium, cotton lavender and *Correa alba*, all of which can be trimmed into shapes. There are some fabulous groundcovering plants, too, including *Lamium maculatum* 'White Nancy', *Dichondra argentea* 'Silver Falls' and *Brunnera* 'Jack Frost'—all cope with shade. Other great choices for difficult areas under large trees or shrubs include *Plectranthus argentatus* and *Tradescantia sillamontana*, a relative of the weed known as wandering Jew (*T. fluminensis*). As candidates for shady areas, it's also worth considering using species that are typically regarded as indoor plants. The aluminium plant (*Pilea cadierei*), for example, will grow quite happily outdoors in frost-free, shady areas.

More typically, however, silver plants are sun lovers. Borders of lamb's ears (*Stachys* sp.), 'Snow in Summer' and 'Garden Pinks' (*Dianthus* sp.) can often be found in cottage gardens, with clumps of *Lychnis* (including campion), popping up with brilliant red and pink flowers. Some salvias, too, have platinum foliage, such as *Stachys discolor*; one of the *Strobilanthes*, *S. gossypina* has pewter-like leaves with a felted appearance and golden underside—absolutely stunning!

Of all the silvers, however, perhaps the one best known is artemisia, named after the Greek goddess Artemis. Silver groundcover plants include varieties of gazanias, *Arctotis* and the sprawling *Helichrysum petiolare*, which also has a golden form. For silver grasses, *Lomandra* 'Silver Grace' is one tough cookie that can withstand temperatures from below 0°C to over 40°C, tolerate drought and cope with shade. *Dianella* 'Cassa Blue' has stunning steely blue leaves and blue flowers in spring—and it's as tough as steel! Anywhere and

CLOCKWISE FROM BELOW: *For shady places beneath trees, aluminium plant is a good choice in frost-free areas; wormwood has glimmering grey leaves that hedge well;* Strobilanthes gossypinus *shimmers silver and bronze, depending on the reflective light.*

everywhere, there's a chance to add some sheen and shine to your garden and make it gleam.

Variegated plants

The ornamental value of leaves—as distinct from the more obvious attraction of flowers—has long been recognised. Often neglected as a tool in creating tonal interest throughout the year, variegated foliage can lighten up dull corners, break up a solid mass of green foliage and even be a striking focal point.

The palette of variegated foliage ranges from the clear hues of smoky grey-greens through to acid yellows and milky whites and creams. There are also plants with purple, pink, orange and red markings. Leaves can have lighter-coloured edges, which highlight the leaf shape, or the reverse, which make them look lacy.

The range of variegated plants is increasing as breeders respond to the growing demand for multiple foliage effects in garden design. A sensible tip is not to place all your variegated plants together, or their special effect will be lost. Instead, use variegated foliage to highlight areas of importance around the garden and choose them with care. If you place a sun-loving species in too much shade, the foliage will tend to revert to green, while shade-dwellers in full sun scorch easily. Some plants will still throw back to their parentage, so simply trim these roguish portions out as you spot them.

For shady areas, variegations are particularly useful and many stalwarts include box, camellias, rhododendrons, hibiscus, ginger and even viburnum. The indoor section of your local nursery hosts a range of suitable subjects such as *Dieffenbachia*, *Aphelandra* and Chinese lucky plants, *Dracaena fragrans* 'Massangeana'. The variegated *Aucuba japonica* 'Variegata' and *Pseudopanax* 'Goldsplash' are also glimmering stars for shady corners.

Once out in the sunshine the choices open up enormously. There is a very pretty golden-leafed may bush called *Spiraea* 'Goldflame', which has lovely musk-pink coloured blooms in spring, and also golden forms of spring blossoming philadelphus (*P. coronarius* 'Aureus') and deutzia, so pretty with their yellow new growth and white blooms. Selecting from evergreens such as golden privet (the 'Lemon, Lime and Snippers' form is great) and the many forms of *Coprosma*—including golden euonymous and golden pittosporum—broadens your plants' range from coastal to mountain areas.

GREEN IS A COLOUR TOO! It's easy to overlook the value of green leaves in the garden. Some plants have fantastic foliage: try *Viburnum odoratissimum* 'Emerald Lustre', Bull Bay magnolia, loquat trees, *Camellia japonica*, evergreen laurel and gardenias. Although all these plants flower, they can also be grown solely for their glossy green leaves.

FAR LEFT: *This white-edged form of spindle bush* (Euonymus fortunei) *is tough, can be hedged and trimmed to shape, and is useful for foliage contrast.*

LEFT: *Yellow archangel* (Lamium galeobdolon) *is a wildflower in Europe where it grows under trees.*

Lophomyrtus 'Black Stallion'

Pittosporum 'Tom Thumb'

Loropetalum chinense
'Purpurea'

Breynia 'Iron Range'

Malus purpurea

Strobilanthes dyeranus

Purple foliage

Be adventurous and add some delicious plum and
burgundy shades to your garden. Use purple foliage
to gently warm silver-leafed plants and add lushness
to greens. Muted purple can intensify reds and warm
cool tones, and works well with bagged finishes.
Wine tones have a wonderful ability to harmonise
with anything; they even work well with various shades
of gold, lime and yellow.

Berberis thunbergii
'Atropurpurea'

RIGHT: *The deep purple of these canna lilies' leaves highlights the bright red flowers.*

FAR RIGHT: *This pink-edged cordyline takes on a stained-glass effect when the sun shines through it.*

Purple foliage

It's easy to add a splash of purple or burgundy to your garden. Some favourite taller plants with purple leaves include the ornamental plums (see page 106), and *Loropetalum* 'Plum Gorgeous' is a particularly handsome plant growing to 2–3 m in height with deep plum leaves and raspberry pink flowers in spring. *Cercis* 'Forest Pansy' has gorgeous heart-shaped purple leaves that colour orange in autumn and flower pink in late winter and early spring.

Purple beech (*Fagus sylvatica*) is a real treat for those with the space and a cool climate. A smaller tree, purple-leaf hazel (*Corylus maxima* 'Purpurea') is a good choice for not-so-big gardens in cool climates. For other diminutive purple touches, consider purple-leafed perennials like the *Dahlia* 'Bishop of Llandaff', *Canna* 'Tropicanna' and 'Purpurea', and the new azalea cultivars 'Plumtastic' and 'Shiraz'. Even purple weeping maples grafted onto short stems can work well.

If your climate is warmer, *Breynia* 'Iron Range' is a bold shrub growing to 3 m, with reddish purple leaves. The tricolour variegated form of *Breynia*, known as the confetti plant, is also an attractive warm-climate choice.

Cordylines come in a wonderful range of reds, pinks and purples, with even rarer varieties that have splashes of orange and creamy white through them. The most popular species are known as ti plants, or *Cordyline terminalis*, and they are native to New Zealand, Hawaii, Polynesia and South America. They generally prefer a shady position in the garden, but many of the darker purple types can withstand full sun. Once established, they are reasonably drought hardy, although they prefer a position with regular feeding, watering and bright light.

The other species commonly grown is *C. australis*, which in the 1970s was widely used in the pebble gardens popular at that time. New cultivars have increased the range and desirability of this species, and its tolerance to cold makes it an excellent choice for those in cool climates. A recent release, 'Red Fountain', is sensational, with deep burgundy foliage, and it also doesn't develop a trunk like the older cultivars. Then there are near-black forms such as 'Burgundy Spire', the yellow-and-red streaked 'Coffee and Cream', and the green-and-red 'Sundance'.

The Australian native cordyline, *C. stricta*, commonly called palm lily, can work well in rainforest gardens. Although it has lovely lilac sprays of flowers, as yet it is only available in a green-leafed form.

ADDING COLOUR Why not paint some stems to add colour? The old flowering stems on this *Miscanthus* have been sprayed with gold paint and left as a feature—an original, quirky and fun way of adding colour.

Roses

The most important winter job for roses is pruning. Winter is also the best time to combat many pests and diseases that can get out of hand in the warm weather if you leave them untreated now.

Pruning clears out the unwanted and dead branches and stimulates new, vigorous growth. This channels the energy of the rose into just a few main branches, instead of many smaller ones, and results in bigger flowers. Pruning also helps to keep roses to a desired shape and manageable size.

For pruning you'll need a sharp, clean pair of secateurs (parrot-beaked blades are best), a sturdy pair of gloves, old gardening clothes or an apron, and a pruning saw. Keep viral diseases in check by wiping the secateur blades with a cloth moistened with disinfectant or bleach after you prune each rose bush.

Pruning other rose types

Old-fashioned roses can be left unpruned, except for thinning and tidying. Train climbing roses to a horizontal position to increase flowering. Reduce good canes to half. On weeping roses, remove the oldest canes and shorten the longest canes to just above ground level.

How hard to prune

- **Hard pruning**. Cut stems back to only three or four buds. Hard pruning is recommended for newly planted roses or for rejuvenating neglected roses. It results in larger, but fewer, blooms.

- **Moderate pruning**. Cut stems back to half their length. This method is recommended for all established roses.

- **Light pruning**. Cut stems back to two thirds their length, so that the main stems are merely tipped. Use this method with very vigorous varieties. Light pruning generally results in a profusion of flowers.

Pruning rose bushes

1 A rose bush that is in desperate need of pruning. Note also that a replaceable mulch such as lucerne should be substituted for the pine bark. 2 This old cane should be removed. 3 Remove old growth with a pruning saw. 4 Remove the top two thirds of growth with sharpened loppers. 5 Prune to an outward-facing bud, and remove growth that is less than pencil thick. 6 Only relatively young wood, one or two years old, has been retained.

DID YOU KNOW? The scent of a rose comes from microscopic perfume glands on the petals.

HOW TO PRUNE MODERN SHRUB ROSES

- Remove any dead branches and thin, weak and spindly growth.
- Remove any old branches (they'll look dull and grey while new growth is red/green and shiny).
- Cut the stem off at the bud union. Remove any shoots (called 'suckers') growing from below the bud union.
- Remove any crossing and crowded branches to open the centre of the bush and allow good air circulation. Prune any branches that are thinner than the thickness of a pencil.
- Shorten the remaining branches by half and prune each one to a plump outward-facing bud. When making your cuts, cut on a 45-degree angle about 1 cm above an outward-facing bud (see step 5 in the sequence on the opposite page).

Planting bare-rooted roses

1 Prior to planting, soak your roses in lukewarm water for 12–24 hours.

2 Choose a site that has 4–6 hours of sun per day and well-drained soil.

3 Dig a hole large enough to easily fit the roots of the plants, and deep enough so that the bud union will be just above the soil level.

4 Before you backfill the hole, mix some rose food into the soil (follow the recommended dosage on the packet).

5 Trim off any broken roots or stems, then hold the plant in place (so the bud union will be at ground level) and backfill the hole. Tread the soil reasonably firmly and leave a basin at the base of the plant to help with watering.

6 Soak the soil with a few buckets of water.

Transplanting

Winter is also a good time for transplanting roses. Simply prune them back first, then dig up as much rootball as you can and re-plant, following the instructions above from step 2 onwards.

Gifts from Asia

The enchanted forests of Asia—where towering maples protect rhododendron and camellia bushes from harsh sun and cold, and leaf litter collects and forms a nutrient-rich layer of moist humus—contains much of what we plant in our gardens today.

And it was in these exotic places that magnolias, camellias, gardenias, rhododendrons, azaleas, hydrangeas and gordonias, just to name a few, originated.

Winter is flowering time for many of these beauties, with bare branches from the canopy above allowing the sun to awaken their blossoms.

Camellias

Sometimes referred to as 'queen of the winter flowers', the camellia grows happily in many parts of Australia. By planting the three main types—sasanquas, japonicas and reticulatas—you can enjoy their flowers from autumn to mid-spring, with the dainty flowers of *Camellia sasanqua* starting off the show.

PESTS If you have a problem with aphids and caterpillars because excessive spring feeding has resulted in soft, fleshy growth, try feeding your roses in winter with a rotted manure mulch, then feed them again in autumn to encourage late blooms. For the rest of the growing season, top up monthly with a liquid feed specifically formulated for roses.

DID YOU KNOW? Coco Chanel's favourite flower was the camellia. Not only was she known for having camellias throughout her apartment at 31 rue Cambon in Paris, they also found their way into her fashion and fine jewellery lines, and have become a motif of the fashion house.

CLOCKWISE FROM FAR LEFT: *Camellias are classified by flower shape. Featured here are the rose form double* C. sasanqua *'Early Pearly'; a formal double* C. japonica *'Roger Hall'; a white semi-double* C. japonica *'Ecclefield'; and a red Higo form* C. japonica *'Bokuhan' (also known as 'Tinsie').*

The most commonly grown type, *Camellia sinensis*, is actually not valued for its flowers. Rather, the leaves have boiling water poured over them to become the world's most consumed beverage—tea.

The sasanqua varieties can be recognised by their smaller, sharper leaves and open habit of growth. This feature, together with their long flowering period, makes them well suited for hedging.

Camellia japonica is the most popular of all the camellias, with thousands of named varieties dating back through the centuries, and a huge range of colours and forms in the flowers. The foliage, too, with its glossy texture and perfect shape, is probably superior. Some japonicas have remarkable foliage, such as the zigzag camellia (*C. japonica* 'Unryu'). This charming camellia, which has a curious zigzag branching pattern, originated in Japan. The name 'Unryu' means 'dragon in the clouds': to the Japanese the plant apparently looks like a dragon climbing up into the sky. The small, single flowers are crimson with deeper coloured veining.

Camellia reticulata is generally regarded as the aristocrat of the camellia family by virtue of its large flowers, on average around 20 cm in diameter. They are generally less hardy than the other species, and as such are often grafted onto vigorous rootstock or hybridised with *C. japonica* or *C. sasanqua*.

DID YOU KNOW? Botanists discovered *Camellia amplexicaulis* comparatively recently in Vietnam. Its very large leaves are glossy, but it is the crimson new growth that wows.

Grow camellias in large tubs for patio and courtyard gardens, or train them against walls and fences as espaliers (great for narrow beds). They are also ideal for shady gardens, although some varieties withstand full sunshine.

Camellias like a slightly acid soil that is rich in organic matter, and range in colour from the purest white through pinks and into purple and reds. They make great garden shrubs, pot specimens and even hedges, and have glossy green foliage that is attractive all year.

FISHTAIL CAMELLIA

A rarely seen variety is the fishtail camellia (*Camellia japonica* 'Kingyo-tsubaki'). The leaves of this camellia are split and twisted at the tips, so that each leaf resembles the tail of a goldfish. Although this plant is valued more for its foliage than anything else, it also has sweetly perfumed, rose-coloured flowers.

Camellia hybrids

If your garden has relatively low summer temperatures, try some of the camellia hybrids that cope better with the cold. Early in the 20th century, breeders crossed C. *japonica* with the western Chinese mountain species C. *saluenensis*; the resulting plants are some of the hardiest and most beautiful around. Known as C. × *williamsii* hybrids (after J. C. Williams who first crossed the two species), they include 'Donation', 'Tiptoe' and 'J. C. Williams'.

Miniature camellias

The small-leafed, small-flowered species camellias have a daintiness and attraction of their own. Many, such as C. *lutchuensis* and C. *fraterna*, are perfumed, while others, like C. *assimilis* and C. *tsaii*, have interesting foliage which adds to the garden's year-round interest. Miniature hybrids—such as 'Alpen Glo', 'Blondy', 'Gay Baby', 'Baby Bear', 'Tiny Princess', 'Fragrant Pink' and 'Snow Drop'—are extremely free-flowering and make a worthy addition to any garden.

Camellia lutchuensis starts flowering in winter and, like many camellias, makes an ideal tub plant. Its gentle weeping habit and tiny snowflake-like blooms make it particularly pretty for the winter garden. It also looks lovely grown as a standard. This miniature camellia flowers for months, and is sweetly perfumed. It also has attractive bronze growth.

The best position for miniature camellias is in a shaded, protected area.

Indian hawthorn

Despite the name, Indian hawthorn is native to southern China. It is a wonderfully useful shrub that can either be grown into a clipped hedge or used as an informal shrub in many gardens, coping with some frost and salt and the occasional hot spell or drought. 'Ballerina' is a very pretty dwarf form and 'Spring Rapture' has lovely perfumed flowers. The new growth on many cultivars comes in attractive bronze shades too.

VITAL STATISTICS

Scientific name: *Rhaphiolepis indica*.
Family: Rosaceae.
Climate: Very hardy; adapts to a range of climates.
Colours: White and pink.
Height: Plants grow 0.6–5 m tall depending on the variety.
Planting time: Ideally plant in autumn.
Soil: Tolerates a wide range of soil conditions.
Position: Shade to part sun.
Watering: Keep moist while establishing.
Fertiliser: Use a complete fertiliser applied annually in early spring.
Flowering time: Flowers autumn to winter.
Pruning: Trim any untidy foliage after flowering to keep the plant neat.

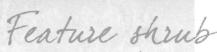

Feature shrub

ABOVE: *Winter lays bare the fascinatingly twisted branches of the Taiwan cherry tree* (Prunus campanulata).

RIGHT: *The gorgeous twin-shaped leaf of the maidenhair tree turns lime green before going golden and dropping.*

Trees

Trees make up the 'roof' of gardens, and become the dominant element of all landscapes, both in private gardens and public spaces.

They vary greatly from one climate to another, yet all have winter seasonality with something special to offer.

The outline of bare branches against a grey sky is one of the season's great pleasures. Equally delightful is the golden haze from early wattle trees, or the fiery red blooms of the African coral trees. It is also a time when other aspects of a tree—such as its form, bark and pods—can be appreciated without the floral confusion of spring.

Conifers

Cone-bearing plants, or conifers, come into their own in winter. These include some of the most ancient genera on the planet, some with lineage dating back 290 million years. They boast both the world's tallest tree, redwoods (115.7 m *Sequoia sempervirens*), and its oldest, a bristlecone pine (a 5000-year-old *Pinus longaeva*), in their number.

Another tree only known as a fossil for many years is the *Ginkgo biloba*. It was found in Japan outside a monastery back in 1690, and is common in this position as it is cherished for its longevity, with individual trees surviving for 1500 years. Commonly called the maidenhair tree, it has beautiful butter yellow leaves and edible fleshy nuts.

Many conifers are shrouded in mystery and mysticism. Yews, for example, are sometimes known as the protectors of death. Poisonous to stock, they have for many years been grown in churchyards, where domestic animals were not allowed to venture.

Tree of life, or *vitae arborvitae*, is the name given to many things, from religious notions to scientific names and parts of your brain. It is also the common name of *Thuja*, which are widely grown as ornamental trees, and used for hedges in the landscape. The timber is light, soft and aromatic, easily worked and resists decay, and has many insect-repelling qualities making it ideal for hope chests or glory boxes that repel moths and also for shingles for rooftops. The timber of western red cedar (*Thuja plicata*) is used for everything from guitar soundboards to saunas and beehives. Many *Thuja* species also have medicinal qualities, and oil of thuja tea has been used to prevent and treat a range of conditions, including scurvy, warts, ringworm and thrush.

Another great timber tree, which also has beautiful weeping foliage, is the rimu (*Dacrydium cupressinum*). A member of New Zealand's largest conifer family, the podocarps—a group that does not have woody cones but rather fleshy structures that attract birds—it can live for more than a thousand years.

The Kashmir cypress (*Cupressus cashmeriana*) is another stunning weeping tree, with grey lacy leaves that droop downwards like a decorative tablecloth. It makes a lovely feature in the garden and superb evergreen backdrop to lawns, with the branches sweeping the ground.

Conifers, though often trees, can also be groundcovers, grafted weeping plants, pot plants, hedges and even bonsai specimens. They have stood the test of time and are worth considering for a position in your garden.

Conifers can provide the perfect solution to a winter garden, with many, such as the Leyland cypress (× *Cupressocyparis leylandii*) terrific for hedges. Some are great accent plants, punctuating the air with their vertical spires (such as *Juniperus chinensis* 'Spartan'), while others, such as the shore juniper (*J. conferta*), make superb groundcovers, coping with a wide range of conditions.

Their foliage varies in colour from velvety green (like the Bhutan cypress) to the blue and grey of the Arizona cypress and blue spruce. Some are even apricot,

turning shades of reddish brown and russet in autumn and winter as the cold air intensifies—look out for *Thuja occidentalis* 'Rheingold' and *Cryptomeria japonica* 'Elegans'.

Deciduous conifers

The majority of conifers are evergreen, but a number of species are deciduous, dropping their foliage over winter. These include larch, metasequoia, taxodium, sequoia and ginkgo. Marvellous autumn colour and fresh new spring growth accompany many of these, making them seasonally interesting and allowing winter sun to come into your garden.

CLOCKWISE FROM LEFT: *Conifers add structure, colour and interest year-round:* Cupressus macrocarpa *'Greenstead Magnificent' (in foreground); western red cedar (*Thuja plicata*); the winter foliage colour of Japanese cedar (*Cryptomeria japonica*).

DID YOU KNOW? You can tell a fir (*Abies* sp.) from a spruce (*Picea* sp.) by looking at the needles and cones. Fir trees have blunt needles and cones that sit on top of the branches sitting upright, whereas spruce have sharp needles and cones that hang downwards.

ABOVE: *The fluffy red flowers of silk trees bloom through the summer.*

ABOVE CENTRE: *Pine cones decorate a larch tree.*

ABOVE RIGHT: *The fragrant flowers of* Viburnum odoratissimum *'Emerald Lustre'.*

Commonly known as dawn redwood or water fir, *Metasequoia glyptostroboides* loses its foliage in late winter, much like its American relative *Taxodium distichum* or bald cypress, so named because it's bare in winter. Famed for its longevity, some specimens are nearly 1700 years old, and the tree can also withstand being waterlogged. Its cousin, the Californian redwood (*Sequoia sempervirens*), can grow to more than 100 m in height and nearly 8 m in girth.

Across North America and Russia, larches (*Larix* sp.) have long been valued for their timber, which is resistant to rot and relatively free of knots, but these are beautiful garden trees if you have the space. Very cold-tolerant, their pine-like needles turn a rust brown before dropping in early winter.

Trees for paved areas

With the popularity of outdoor living and our increased awareness of sun damage these days, the demand for small, obedient trees that behave well in confined spaces has become greater.

Small deciduous trees that suit this situation include trident or Japanese maples, magnolias, the silk tree (*Albizia julibrissin*), South African daphne (*Dais cotinifolia*), flowering plums and crepe myrtles (*Lagerstroemia* sp.). Small evergreen trees that also fit the bill include gordonia, the Irish strawberry tree and port wine magnolias.

With age, some shrubs can also work as a small tree. Try *Camellia sasanqua*, *Viburnum odoratissimum* and murraya. For the double benefit of fruit and foliage, try citrus or stone fruit.

THE WOLLEMI PINE

In the 1990s a most exciting discovery was made by a bushwalker just 200 km from Sydney. The Wollemi pine (*Wollemia nobilis*), thought to be extinct and only seen previously in 200-million-year-old fossils, was still living in several deep gorges in the Blue Mountains region. The only species in the third living genus (*Wollemia*) of the conifer family Araucariaceae, it has features in common with the other living genera *Agathis*, of which kauri is one type, and *Araucaria*, which includes bunya pine, monkey puzzle tree and Norfolk Island pine. This discovery led to the eventual release of Wollemi pines as garden plants. In the wild they can grow 40 m tall, and have remarkable knobbly bark, though plants grown in cultivation are likely to grow only half that size—they can even be grown as an indoor plant.

Old houses often have old terracotta pipes full of hairline fractures that are vulnerable to attack by tree roots. PVC pipes are much safer around trees, as root hairs can't penetrate unless there are existing cracks. There is a belief that some trees 'search' for water and will crack pipes, but this is a bit misleading. Few trees do this, although obviously the larger the tree, the more extensive a root system it needs to support itself.

As a guide, remember that everything above-ground will be mirrored below-ground and slightly beyond. For that reason, avoid liquidambars, robinias, alders, willows, poplars, figs, umbrella trees, rubber trees and elms, unless you have ample space to accommodate their roots. Also remember that some trees can act as enormous soaks—one mature paperbark can soak up as much as 450 L of water on a hot summer's day!

Magnolias and michelias

The Magnoliaceae is one of the most ancient of flowering plant families. Two of its most widely grown members are magnolias and michelias.

Few flowering trees can rival the elegance of magnolias. Their great scented goblets are borne on bare grey branches, relieving the gloom of winter. These well-known late winter/early spring flowers include many varieties.

Most widely grown are the ones with goblet-shaped flowers. *Magnolia × soulangeana* varies in colour from almost white through to purple, and there is also a near-black form called 'Black Tulip', which has 12 cm long black goblet flowers, and 'Star Wars' and 'Felix' that have rosy pink blooms the size of a person's head! Two other unusual cultivars include 'Yellow Lantern' and 'Elizabeth', both of which have yellow flowers. *M. stellata* has star-like flowers and grows into a large shrub. The pure white yulan (*M. denudata*) is a favourite species, with its milky white, scented flowers.

Most magnolias grow to a mid-forest-tree size and look their best with shelter

ABOVE: Magnolia 'Star Wars' has huge flowers that are reddish in bud then open pink. It grows to about 4 m high with a similar spread.

LEFT: Star magnolia (M. stellata) is a smaller shrubby species that gets to about 2.5 m × 2.5 m.

CLOCKWISE FROM TOP: *Bull Bay magnolia has dinner-plate-sized flowers throughout summer;* Magnolia *'Elizabeth' has creamy lemon blooms through winter;* Michelia yunnanensis *makes a wonderful screening plant or small tree, growing to around 7 m.*

from taller trees and protection from hot westerly winds. Evergreen magnolias are becoming increasingly popular, and the most commonly available is the Bull Bay (*M. grandiflora*), which flowers in summer, has a lemon fragrance and will grow into a large park tree. Smaller evergreen cultivars to choose from include 'Little Gem', which grows to 5–10 m and has rich cinnamon undersides to its leaves, and 'Saint Mary', which has a wavy margin to the foliage and similar brown felted undersides.

Michelias are closely related to magnolias. Instead of using blooms in bright colours to attract pollinators, they rely on perfume and can throw their scent quite a distance to lure insects. Even one plant will become a loved part of your neighbourhood's 'scentscape' and will certainly lift your senses on those dreary winter days when summer seems an age away.

Like *Magnolia grandiflora*, michelias' glossy green leaves are so beautiful they are used in floristry, and many have a handsome velvet brown underside. But their recent popularity is due to their perfume, with scents varying from light lemon to port wine or orange blossom.

Most people have probably only heard of the port wine magnolia, but *Michelia figo* and its relatives and hybrids are becoming more widely grown as they adapt perfectly to temperate climates and acid soils. *M.* 'Fairy Magnolia' is a pretty pink, autumn-flowering type recently receiving accolades, and 'Bubbles' is a lovely large-flowered cross with *M. doltsopa* which is known for its spring scent and beauty. 'Coco' and 'Lady of the Night' both flower eight months of the year, have slightly larger white flowers tinged with pink as they age and a slightly bigger leaf.

One of the showiest of cultivars of *M. doltsopa* is called 'Silver Cloud'. During spring it has large white flowers that are heavily scented, and look like a cross between the Bull Bay and star magnolia. It grows to about 12 m × 6 m and has a bushy, pyramidal shape,

RIGHT: *Native to China,* Michelia maudiae *has pure white flowers with an enticing perfume. It is fairly slow growing and will only be about 4 m tall after ten years.*

FAR RIGHT: *The heady scent of port wine magnolia* (Michelia figo) *makes it a popular large shrub or hedge in the shade.*

making it ideal for average-sized gardens as either a specimen tree or a large screen.

For perfume alone, few could resist the divine fragrance of 'Pak-lan' (*M. × alba*). In summer the apple-green leaves and creamy white flowers, which have slender pointed petals and a light orange blossom perfume, make it heavenly for any garden. *M. longifolia*, or 'Buk-lan', is similar in habit.

The 'Cham-pak' (*M. champaca*) has a smallish (only about 3 cm) butterscotch yellow flower, but makes up for its size with the strength and reach of its heady scent. This species grows into a medium-sized tree, has glossy foliage and creates year-round shade.

Hard to come by, although well worth the effort to find, is *M. maudiae*. Another medium-sized tree, it has bluish green leaves and large (10 cm) fragrant white flowers in late winter and spring, similar to those of *M. doltsopa*.

If your garden doesn't have the space for a large tree, think about using *M. yunnanensis* 'Scented Pearl', which only grows 3–4 m tall and makes an excellent hedge or espaliered specimen. The foliage is comparatively small, and has chocolate-coloured felt-like hairs on the underside of the leaves. The white cup-like flowers are 5 cm wide and look very striking against the foliage's green and brown background.

Vireya rhododendrons

Vireya rhododendrons are stunning plants that tend to flower spasmodically throughout the year, including winter, when not much else is in bloom. Native to Australia, New Guinea, Malaysia, Borneo and areas around this tropical archipelago, they have glossy foliage, are often scented, and tend to be epiphytic—growing in the nooks of trees in leaf mould—though they grow well in pots and in freely drained areas in the ground. Their beautiful flowers range in colour from white, to cream, pink, yellow, red and orange.

DID YOU KNOW? The lovely white flowers of *Michelia alba* are best known as the essence in the perfume Chanel No. 5.

BELOW: *Vireya rhododendrons have stunning blooms that make long-lasting corsages and cut flowers.*

London plane tree

Betula nigra

Betula pendula

Silk floss tree

Acer negundo 'Flamingo'

Australian native cork tree

Arbutus glandulosa.

Bark

Bark is a tree's skin: a layer that protects the important cells beneath it. Luckily for gardeners, many trees have extraordinarily patterned, coloured and detailed bark that is so much more. From the flaky bark of paperbarks and the stunning silver and paper birches, to the spotted bark of the London plane and leopard trees, and on to the thorny 'hide' of the silk floss tree, bark shows an incredible beauty and variety.

Trees for winter structure

A garden without structure can lack gravitas, especially in winter when many plants become dormant or deciduous and reveal clearly any holes in the garden's design. Trees can help form the walls and roof of a garden, giving a space structure.

Their timber can also be used in beautiful built garden structures, such as arbours, seats, summer houses and pergolas, which remain as focal points year-round.

Willow

The willow (*Salix* sp.) is famous for travelling along water courses, as it loves damp areas and strikes so easily from pieces. There are many different species. Tortured willow has twisted stems, pussy willow has furry buds, golden willow has yellow stems and black willow dark stems. All make lovely cut stems for floristry, and can be made into garden furniture. Many can become weedy too, so check with your local council to make sure you are safe to plant them in your area.

Corkscrew hazel

The small genus *Corylus* contains some interesting plants. Some have attractive catkins, while others produce edible nuts (such as hazelnuts). There are also species that feature coloured leaves or extraordinary branches, some of which are used for making walking sticks. Filbert, as corkscrew hazel (*Corylus avellana* 'Contorta') is also known, has curiously twisted branches, not unlike tortured willow, as it is multi-branched in habit. The leaves colour golden yellow in autumn before they fall, and in winter the tree is draped in catkins like yellow lambs' tails. It is best suited to cool climates.

ABOVE: *Corkscrew hazel's contorted branches look magnificent during winter.*

ABOVE: *Willow can be woven into rustic furniture like these beautiful chairs.*

424

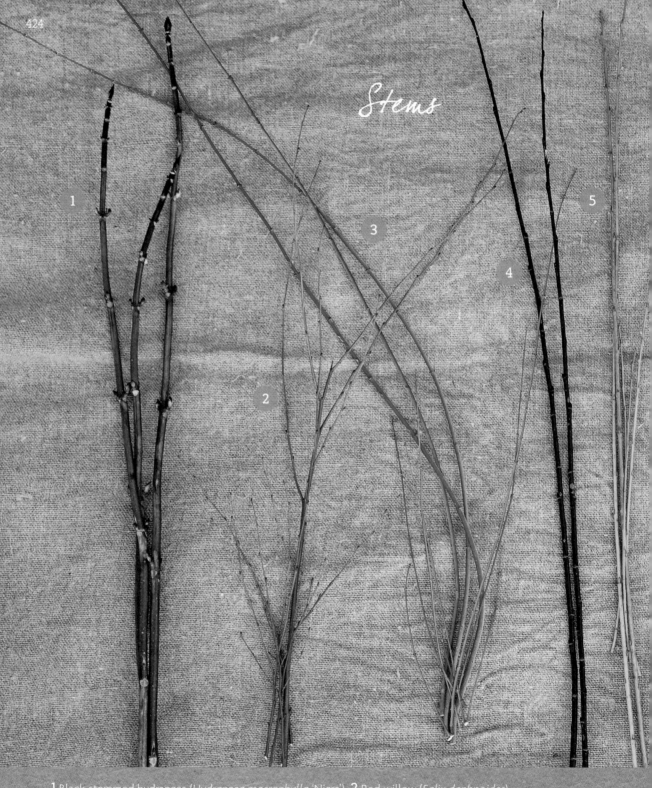

Stems

1 Black-stemmed hydrangea (*Hydrangea macrophylla* 'Nigra') **2** Red willow (*Salix daphnoides*)
3 *Acer palmatum* 'Sango Kaku' **4** Black willow (*Salix nigricans*) **5** Yellow-stemmed willow (*Salix* × *rubens*)

425

6 Beech (*Fagus* sp.) 7 Paperbark maple (*Acer griseum*) 8 Red-stemmed cornus (*Cornus alba* 'Siberica')
9 Yellow-stemmed cornus (*Cornus sericea* 'Flaviramea') 10 Liquidambar *(L. Styraciflua)*

project

A willow 'igloo'

This 'igloo', made from willow, grew in weeks and was fabulous fun to make. It's perfect for a child's cubby house, a folly, or modified into a series of arches for a tunnel. All you will need is the space and some willow cuttings. A simple metal framework of galvanised pipe makes this project easy, but this structure can also be made 'free form'.

1 Plant large cuttings of willow in a circular shape, to match the size of your metal frame, if using. Water and mulch the cuttings. They very quickly take root.

2 Attach the tops of each branch to the frame of galvanised pipe.

3 Weave the smaller branches in on themselves to form a basket-like structure that continues to grow.

DIY ROOTING LIQUID To make your own rooting liquid, take a few stems of willow and strike them in water. Pour the water from those cuttings onto anything else you are striking for extra-strong root growth.

Taking hardwood cuttings

1 Collect the materials needed for taking hardwood cuttings: wooden box, bucket of peat moss, secateurs and hardwood cuttings (these were taken from a willow in winter).
2 Spread an even layer of peat moss in the wooden box. 3 Cut pencil-sized lengths of willow to use as hardwood cuttings. Use the cutting blade of the secateurs to expose the cambium layer in the base of each hardwood cutting. 4 Place the cuttings in the box of peat moss for callousing. 5 Backfill with peat moss. Plant out when shoots appear.

Wattles

It would be hard to name a native plant that evokes more patriotism in Australians than the wattle (*Acacia* sp.). There are over 1200 species of wattle, all different and flowering at various times throughout the year. Wattles are actually widespread across the southern continents, with some species endemic to Africa, although most of those have thorns and are commonly referred to as mimosa bushes.

None are as lovely as the many Australian varieties that burst into glowing masses of golden blossom in winter and spring. It would be impossible to list all the species here, so the focus is on the most ornamental types for gardens. There are over 700 species of wattle indigenous to Australia and it is important to choose one from a similar climate to your own.

Proclaimed as Australia's National Floral Emblem in 1988, the golden wattle (*A. pycnantha*) represents the spirit and soul of Australians. Each year the wattle has its own day, 1 September, to celebrate its beauty. Found in every state, the golden wattle is indigenous to the dry inland districts, where it grows in shallow sandy soils and helps bind the topsoil. The large, fragrant ball-shaped golden flowers make this a truly magnificent sight in spring.

Prickly Moses (*A. ulicifolia*) is perfect for encouraging small birds into the garden. It reaches 2–3 m in height.

Mount Morgan wattle or Queensland silver wattle (*A. podalyriifolia*) has beautiful grey rounded leaves which make it a feature regardless of the season. It is quick-growing, to 6 m, and suitable for dry conditions with little or no topsoil. The ball-shaped, perfumed gold flowers appear in late winter, making it one of the first wattles in the season to flower.

Probably the best known of all wattles, the Cootamundra wattle (*A. baileyana*) has ferny grey foliage, which is sometimes tipped purple (var. 'Purpurea'). It grows to about 5 m in

ABOVE: *Wyalong wattle* (Acacia cardiophylla) *is a fast grower.*

LEFT: *Prickly Moses grows into a rounded shrub that can be hedged. Its prickly foliage shelters many small birds.*

WHAT'S IN A NAME?

It is said that *Acacia* became known as wattle because the thin branches were used to form the walls of the earliest colonial houses: they were woven together and then sealed with clay or mud. This form of construction was known in Europe as wattle and daub. Strangely, the plant often used in this wickerwork is called blackwattle, actually not an acacia at all but a *Callicoma*. Another theory is that the name 'wattle' came from the Aboriginal name for the plant—*wattah*. Whatever the background, there are lots of famous Australian aliases for wattles, including mulga, gidgee, blackwood and mimosa.

height, although there is a prostrate variety that grows to only about 0.5 m. The spectacular golden yellow flowers appear in winter. It thrives in most soils but does best in areas outside the tropics and subtropics.

The cedar wattle (*A. elata*) will quickly grow to a fine screening tree about 15 m tall. Its fern-like foliage is tipped coppery pink with new growth in spring, then it becomes smothered in soft lemon flowers in summer. Unlike most wattles, the cedar wattle is actually fairly long-lived.

The wattle best known to those living on the eastern seaboard is the Sydney golden wattle, or golden Sally (*A. longifolia*). It has golden yellow flowers very early in spring, grows to about 4.5 m and is extremely hardy, capable of thriving in pure sand with full salt exposure. There is a semi-prostrate variety, called 'Sophorae', which is handy for dune stabilisation.

A very unusual wattle is *A. leprosa* 'Scarlet Blaze', which, as the name hints, has red flowers. Also commonly known as cinnamon wattle, its crushed leaves do indeed smell like the spice. The 4–5 m tall shrub was discovered one spring in the 1990s by bushwalkers near Melbourne, when they noticed the balls of red, with stamens tipped in yellow.

Wattles have long been regarded as great plants to begin a garden. They grow quickly to stabilise the soil and give protection and screening while other, slower species of plants are growing. Of course, many will last only five years, by which time the garden will be fully established. Wattles are also able to come back quickly after bushfire; they also have nitrogen-fixing nodules on their roots which help build up the soil fertility, allowing other species to germinate and grow.

Weeping and dwarf wattles

There are now many groundcover wattles and dwarf varieties that may better suit most home gardens. Some particularly lovely forms of *A. cognata* are now available, such as 'Bower Beauty', which grows to 1 m tall by about the same width and has lovely fine foliage, a weeping habit and bronze new growth. 'Fettuccine' has wiggly leaves and a slightly smaller habit, and 'Limelight' grows to about 0.5 m tall. They all make lovely additions to the garden, and can be used as single specimens or massed.

River wattle (A. cognata) has a relaxed weeping habit and grows to about 5 m tall.

The Bush was grey
A week today
(Olive-green and brown and grey)
But now the spring has come my way
With blossom for the wattle.
It seems to be
A Fairy tree.
It dances to a melody.
And sings a little song to me
(The graceful, swaying wattle).

VERONICA MASON

Wattles

1 Green wattle (*Acacia decurrens*) **2** Sydney golden wattle (*A. longifolia*) **3** White sallow wattle (*A. floribunda*) **4** Fringed wattle (*A. fimbriata*) **5** Sunshine wattle (*A. terminalis*) **6** Cootamundra wattle (*A. baileyana*) **7** *A. cognata* 'Green Mist' **8** *A. iteaphylla* **9** *A. longifolia* subsp. *sophorae* **10** Zigzag wattle (*A. macradena*)

Wattles: Care and maintenance

- **Pruning.** Cut wattles back after each flush to promote vigorous new growth that is resistant to borers.

- **Planning.** Repeat planting so that as one wattle reaches the end of its lifetime, there is another well on the way.

DID YOU KNOW? During World War I, sprigs of wattle were sold by the Red Cross to raise funds for the war effort. Depots were set up in Sydney to receive wattle sent in from country areas. After the huge loss of life at Gallipoli, the Wattle League arranged for the planting of wattle trees near the graves of the Anzacs.

- **Feeding and watering.** Use an Australian native slow-release plant food once a year after flowering to promote healthy new growth. Water in dry periods, and always have the root zone covered in a thick layer of leaf litter.

- **Pests.** Borers, scale, caterpillars and galls can all attack wattles, although keeping the plant well watered and vigorous is your best means of control. Let the birds do the rest for you!

Forest pansy

This is a tree for all seasons with a beautiful shape, lovely pink blossoms in late winter/early spring, and stunning purple heart-shaped leaves that change to orange, red and yellow in autumn.

VITAL STATISTICS

Botanical name: *Cercis canadensis.*
Family: Fabaceae.
Climate: Adapts to many climates but may benefit from part shade in hot areas.
Culture: Perfect as a small tree or in groups to create woodlands and for foliage contrast.
Colours: Pink flowers on bare wood. Purple leaves in spring and autumn.
Height: 5–8 m.
Planting time: Autumn and winter are best, and doesn't like being transplanted.
Soil: Free-draining soil is a must and needs to be lime free.
Position: Full sun or light shade, shelter from cold wind.
Planting spacing: 6 m apart.
Fertiliser: Mulch with manure in spring with Australian native fertiliser.
Pests/diseases: Not usually.
Pruning: Can be pruned to keep as a shrub.
Propagation: Cuttings.

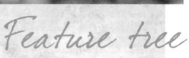
Feature tree

Hakeas

Closely related to grevilleas, though less often grown, are the incredibly tough hakeas. Many are extremely tolerant of drought, and they make great hedges and screens. The pin-cushion hakea (*Hakea laurina*) is a stunning Australian native plant that now can be found commonly in Italy and America, though it's not as popular at home as it should be. All this might change, however, with the release of 'Stockdale Sensation', which has even larger blooms. Another stunning cultivar to look out for is 'Burrendong Beauty', the hybrid cross of *H. myrtoides* and *H. petiolaris*.

Planting hakeas in your garden will also ensure you have birds, as the trees have nectar-rich blooms that attract various honeyeaters and, later, seeds that parrots enjoy. All hakeas benefit from regular pruning and excellent drainage, and the more sun they get, the more flowers you will have.

ABOVE LEFT: *Many hakeas have prickly leaves, but the needlebush (H. sericea) is particularly vicious.*

ABOVE: *Growing to 1.5 m, H. 'Burrendong Beauty' has spectacular ball flowers that bloom prolifically.*

One thorn of experience is worth a whole wilderness of warning.

JAMES RUSSELL LOWELL

Herbs, fruit and vegetables

The peace and calm of winter in the kitchen garden should be broken by some periods of hard work! Digging over the vegie patch, liming where appropriate and planting some cold-tolerant crops, such as lettuce and broad beans, is good exercise for gardeners.

Although most plants are hibernating, you can trick some of them, such as chicory and rhubarb, into early arrival by forcing them with covers. In late winter, to get a head start with warm-season herbs and vegies, raise seedlings in protected greenhouses and on sunny windowsills and plant them out after all chance of frost has passed. You can also purchase bare-rooted fruit trees and berry canes during their dormancy, saving money, and plant them out in winter. This gives them a chance to settle in before the growing season.

Herbs

Now that the winter cold has set in, many herbs have either died down or gone completely, and that's when the woody perennial herbs come into their own.

Rosemary, thyme, wormwood, bay laurel and some of the spices—such as cloves, nutmeg, cinnamon and cardamom— make fabulous additions to slow-cooked meals, and some can still be picked fresh from the garden. Indoor sowing of leafy herbs and salad greens can help germinate early crops, and if you live in a mild area you can raise seedlings in cold frames and cloches.

Tarragon and wormwood

The genus *Artemisia* contains lad's love, absinthe, wormwood and tarragon. All are noted for their pungent foliage, feathery leaves and medicinal or herbal uses. They are excellent plants for dry sunny sites, where they can be kept trimmed to retain a neat shape or hedge.

DIY INSECT REPELLANT Blend together ½ cup wormwood with 250 mL olive oil. Steep and strain through muslin. Add 10 drops of eucalyptus oil. Use an atomiser to spray.

Wormwood has lovely silver foliage and is a useful insect repellant.

Winter is the season for harvesting citrus fruit and for planting cool-weather crops such as potatoes and members of the Brassica family—cabbages, broccoli, cauliflower, Brussels sprouts and kohlrabi.

The most valued species is French tarragon (*A. dracunculus* var. *sativa*) which has a delicate anise taste that is useful for flavouring asparagus, fish, poultry, pickles and vinegars, and is sometimes used as a substitute for garlic. Don't buy the Russian tarragon (*A. dracunculus* var. *inodora*) by mistake as its leaves can taste slightly bitter and it tends to grow a bit wild.

Other species include lad's love (*A. abrotanum*), which acquired its name as an aphrodisiac and was sometimes called maid's ruin, and wormwood (*A. absinthium*), the chief ingredient in absinthe, an anise-tasting liqueur with a high alcoholic content. Roman wormwood (*A. pontica*) is also used to flavour vermouth. Some cultivars of wormwood are grown for their ornamental foliage and include *A. absinthium* 'Lambrook Silver', 'Powis Castle' and 'Lambrook Giant'.

All forms, including those used in alcoholic beverages, need to be consumed with extreme caution, as

FROST PROTECTION If you live in a cold area, protect frost-sensitive seedlings by inverting a glass jar over each one.

CITRUS CORDIAL

Consider making excess citrus into cordial. Remove rinds (taking care not to add the pith) of 3 fruits and simmer with 500 g of sugar and 600 mL of water for 10 minutes. Add the juice of the fruits and 15 g of citric acid, and strain and pour when slightly cooled into sterilised bottles. Add water to taste when serving. Keeps for months.

CINNAMON

This extraordinary spice is actually the bark of a cinnamon tree (shown below). Native to Sri Lanka, and grown throughout Asia for its flavour, and warm scent, it has been traded for millennia, and was used in ancient Egypt. The plants commercially grown are coppiced to make them multi-trunked, young and easily harvested. Two species are grown: *C. verum*, often called true cinnamon, is the Ceylonese (Sri Lankan) type; *C. aromaticum* is the Chinese cinnamon, also known as cassia.

Curry plant

Curry plant is often confused with curry leaf plant (*Murraya koenigii*), which is used to flavour curries. This species, however, is a small, low-growing grey-leafed bush with yellow daisy-like flowers and foliage that smells like curry. The leaves are normally used fresh as tender young shoots in salads, with savouries like eggs, and even with cream cheese. If used in cooking, the leaves should be removed before serving as they can impart a bitter flavour.

VITAL STATISTICS

Climate: *Helichrysum italicum.*
Family: Asteraceae.
Climate: Warm climate; will take light frosts.
Height: 0.5 m.
Planting time: Any time from containers.
Soil: Any well-drained soil.
Position: Full sun.
Planting spacing: About 1 m apart, unless using as a border, in which case every 50 cm.
Fertiliser: Blood and bone in spring.
Pests/diseases: None.
Propagation: Semi-hardwood heeled cuttings in late summer.
Storage: Best used fresh and only young shoots. Foliage can be dried for potpourri.

Feature herb

The nutmeg plant has a yellow fruit enclosing (once dried) two layers that are used as spice. The outer, net-like casing is mace, and the kernel is nutmeg.

they contain a cumulative poison that is dangerous to the nervous system and makes them extremely useful in discouraging mice, moths, worms and many other pests if dried and strewn.

Nutmeg

True nutmeg is *Myristica fragrans,* but there are a few other plants worth noting for their similar flavour or scent. The nutmeg flower (*Nigella sativa*), related to love-in-a-mist, has black seeds that are nutmeg scented and used to flavour cakes. Nutmeg bush (*Tetradenia riparia*) has nutmeg-scented leaves and pinkish flowers all through winter, making it an excellent shrub for the winter garden.

Cloves

Another interesting tree from the Malay-Indonesian archipelago is the lilly-pilly (*Syzygium aromaticum*). Cloves are the flower buds of this tree which, when picked as red buds, have a marvellous scent and are used to flavour curries and chai tea.

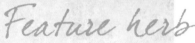

DID YOU KNOW? Curry is usually a blend of spices such as ground cumin, coriander, turmeric, cayenne pepper, ginger and mustard. Each cook might have their own special blend, but curry leaf plant (*Murraya koenigii*) tastes like a ready-made combination.

Fruit

It's good to grow your own fruit. One of life's little pleasures is the flavour of freshly picked fruit ... delicious, because it can fully ripen on the tree, not in a box on its way to the fruit shop or supermarket! Leftovers can be used for jams, jellies, chutney, relish, preserves and liqueurs.

Deciduous fruit trees

Winter is the best time for planting deciduous fruit trees. Depending on the climate, apples, pears, peaches, plums, nectarines and cherries are all easy to grow. A tree for all seasons, your deciduous fruit tree will give you delightful spring blossoms, shade you from hot summer sunshine, produce delicious fruit and then, once the leaves fall, will allow welcome winter sunshine into your garden.

Select a spot where there is space for your fruit tree to grow unhampered. Avoid planting close to walls or fences, unless you are going to espalier it.

Short of space?

In small gardens fruit trees can be trained against sunny house walls and fences. If you grow them this way you need to pay a little more attention to pruning in order to maximise the yield. Patterns include:

- Cordon, where a single stem is grown at an angle.

- Fan, where several branches fan out from one point on the trunk.

- Espalier, where the branches are trained horizontally from the trunk.

Even in the smallest garden you should be able to use one of these pruning methods to grow at least one, and possibly more.

The grace and elegance of this ornamental silver pear would add colour and texture to any garden.

If space is at a premium in your garden, you can also plant dwarf trees, such as miniature nectarines and peaches (sold as 'Nectazee' and 'Pictazee'), or totem cultivars such as 'Ballerina' apples, which are perfect for narrow areas, such as garden beds edging driveways and paths.

Fruit trees can also be bought in a 'multigrafted' form. This simply means that a few varieties have been budded on to the one plant. For example, you may find peaches, plums and nectarines or lemons, oranges and limes on the one tree. This looks great and saves space. If you have really tight parameters, grow a fruiting vine, such as a passionfruit or kiwifruit, plants which are usually grown on a fence or pergola.

Pruning an apple tree

1 Neglected for some years, this apple tree has put its energy into producing wood instead of fruit. **2** Leave fruiting spurs. **3** Cut back to fruiting spurs. **4** Remove excess wood. **5** Remove the stubs of old bad cuts. **6** Remove old pruning wounds just above the ridge collar. **7** Remove branches butting against one another. Thin out the centre of the tree to let in the sun and air.

DOLLAR SAVER
Those plants that are traditionally sold as 'bare-rooted' should be planted now while they are completely dormant (see page 438). They are usually a third of the price of potted plants.

Espaliered fruit trees

Espalier is the art of training trees to branch in formal patterns, usually along a wall or on a trellis. The technique of espalier first became popular several hundred years ago in the walled gardens of medieval Europe. Very few, if any, fruit trees could be grown in these gardens because of the limited space available. By placing the trees along the garden walls and training them to grow in two-dimensional form, however, trees were incorporated into the garden with little loss of available space.

Gardeners in the more northerly regions of Europe soon found another benefit in espalier. Where the climate was cool and the summer short, the warm sunny microclimate directly adjacent to a south-facing wall permitted fruit trees to crop in one season, a result that could not be achieved with freestanding trees. In the southern hemisphere, north-facing walls warm early in spring, collect heat throughout summer, and remain warm later into autumn.

A third benefit of growing fruit trees in an espalier form is that the open frame created by this method permits excellent light infiltration, with all parts of the tree exposed to direct sunlight.

This results in a higher level of flowering, greater fruit production, and better colour development on the fruit. In addition, picking fruit from an espaliered tree is a simple process because of the small stature of these trees.

If you want to espalier a fruit tree, start with an apple or pear. These trees bear fruit on long-lived spurs and are probably the best for beginners. Stone fruits such as plums and cherries can also be espaliered, but many bear fruit on the shoots of the previous season's growth. This means that renewal pruning is necessary to ensure a continuous crop.

Espalier design

There are a few basic designs used in espalier. A T-shaped design, a cordon (which looks like a Jewish menorah, pictured at right) or a fan are formal in style. The easiest design is probably an informal espalier where branches are not forced in any particular direction, but are simply trained along a wall. Apple trees are usually trained as T-shapes or cordons, while cherries or plums are renewal pruned in a fan or informal design.

The espaliered design of this apple tree looks like a menorah, an eight-branched candelabrum that is an emblem of Judaism.

STEPS TO BUILD AN ESPALIER FRAME

- Establish a frame to work from. String heavy wire (12 or 15 gauge) from eyebolts on the wall or fence to provide a frame. Three levels of wire are usually sufficient for starting an espalier. The bottom wire should be at least 0.5 m from the ground, with the remaining wires spaced from 0.5 m to 1 m apart. Sturdy posts can also anchor a freestanding trellis into the ground and wires can be fixed to them. The trellis must be strong enough to support what should become branches heavy with fruit.
- Plant the tree 15–20 cm from its support, ensuring that the graft union is at least 1 cm above ground level.
- Tie the selected branches to bamboo canes with budding tape; this keeps them absolutely straight. Over a few weeks, slowly lower the canes to the wire. Prune off any branches that are not part of the design.
- Rub off any flower buds. This permits the tree to direct its energy into productive growth until the espalier pattern is complete. No fruit should be allowed to develop until the framework growth is complete.
- Tie new growth to bamboo canes and lower two branches to the wire, leaving one branch vertical. The following spring, prune this vertical branch to the height of the next wire, where new shoots will form to repeat the pattern.
- Each year a new layer is formed, so that on a three-layered trellis, at least three years of growth are required to complete the effect, four years for four layers, and so on.

BROKEN CAN BE MENDED If you are bending a branch and it cracks, don't despair. A partially broken branch that is securely fastened to the frame will usually heal and grow normally.

Planting a bare-rooted tree

1 Dig a hole. **2** Take the rootball out of its protective covering. **3** Check that the roots are healthy. **4** Position the tree in the hole. **5** Backfill the soil around the tree. **6** Create a 'doughnut' ring around the plant to hold water. **7** Water it in. **8** The 'doughnut' retains the water and stops any run-off.

General tips on fruit growing

🌿 **UNDER WRAPS**
Make sure there is no delay before planting fruit trees as the bare roots will dry out very quickly. If you anticipate any delay, wrap the plants in damp hessian or heel them into the soil as a temporary measure.

🍂 All fruit needs full sunshine. If planted in shade or semi-shade, your tree will not yield well. It will lack vigour and be susceptible to disease and insect attack. Protect it from strong winds and it will grow better.

🍂 Gardeners in temperate climates are able to grow a large range of fruit trees—from citrus, apples, pears, stone fruit and berries to tropical delicacies and even nut trees.

🍂 Position is everything when it comes to fruit. Avoid planting in low-lying patches which will encourage root rot and collar rot, and improve drainage either by adding manure and gypsum to your soil or by mounding the soil to elevate the bed.

🍂 Regular water supply is important for ensuring good cropping. Water crystals, deep weekly watering during summer and a layer of compost as a mulch will all help to conserve moisture.

🍂 In warm-climate regions, select low-chill fruit varieties, which don't need cold night-time temperatures to set fruit. For example, instead of planting cherries, try tropical nectarine varieties.

CLOCKWISE FROM
TOP LEFT:
*Apple scab, a fungus
that spreads readily
in warm, showery
weather, may be
prevented by keeping
the ground under
your tree clean; these
citrus are affected by
the fungus melanose,
but the fruit is
usually edible; foliage
with peach leaf curl,
a fungus that will
weaken the whole
tree if left unchecked;
mosaic virus is
spread through plant
sap, so wash your
hands, disinfect
cutting tools and
spray for aphids.*

- Select plants that are self-fertile (that is, plants that don't need another variety with which to cross-pollinate).

- General maintenance includes feeding, watering, removal of weeds, pruning to shape, spraying when necessary and, of course, harvesting.

- Peaches and nectarines must be pruned regularly by half the previous year's wood in winter. This stimulates new fruiting wood.

- Apple trees and pear trees should be thinned in the centre to form an open vase shape. This lets in the sun and promotes heavy cropping.

- If growing a fruit tree on grass, leave a 1 m diameter circle of bare soil round the trunk. Dig a hole only slightly larger than the plant container before planting. Do not add any organic material.

- Watch out for critters that may spoil your fruit, such as fruit fly and codling moth. Take precautions early in the season so that your fruit remains edible until harvest.

Bush tucker: good enough to eat

In recent years bush tucker has become increasingly popular. Native spinach, mint, lemon pepper, bush tomatoes, lemon myrtle and native citrus are just a few of the delicacies on the menu at gourmet restaurants.

Aboriginal people have long used wattle seeds as a source of protein. These seeds have become more popular in mainstream gourmet cooking as an increasing number of people discover the delicious nutty flavour. Try wattle pavlova—it's a real treat!

For something really special, indulge yourself with a taste of quandong, also known as *bidjigal*, *gudi gudi* and other Aboriginal names, depending on the region. In the days of early European settlers, the quandong (*Santalum*

That which one eats as the fruit of his own labour, is properly called food.

PROVERB

acuminatum) was given the name 'wild' or 'desert' peach, though it is closer in taste to an apricot crossed with rhubarb, with a hint of cinnamon.

The quandong is an impressive tree, reaching 7 m in ideal conditions and having olive-like foliage and bright red globular fruit. Widespread in semi-arid and arid environments across the country, it makes an ideal crop in degraded soil areas, although it can be difficult to cultivate in the home garden. For best results, try planting it in a dry spot.

The quandong is actually a parasitic species and obtains its nutrients through the roots of nearby plants, particularly when they are young. For this reason they are often potted with lucerne or clover, which can act as a host plant. Grafting is currently used to obtain quality fruit.

Quandongs ripen from early to mid-spring. An average tree should harvest at least 2 kg of fresh fruit, although a mature specimen may yield up to 30 kg. They taste good with apples, nuts, figs, bananas and pears and also work well with mint, thyme, garlic, chilli and with 'warm' spices such as cardamom, cinnamon and nutmeg.

Often called wild peach, the quandong contains twice the vitamin C content of an orange.

Lemon-scented myrtle

If you love lemon fragrances, you cannot go past lemon-scented myrtle (*Backhousia citriodora*), which flowers in late summer when it becomes smothered in clusters of fluffy, creamy-yellow blooms.

Native to the rainforests of Queensland and New South Wales, it will grow in all but cold, frosty districts and the dry inland. Lemon-scented myrtle makes a great screening plant, growing to 10 m and retaining its branches right to the ground.

Plant it in sun to half shade, and for best results, remember to keep the soil moist through summer. These trees rarely have problems, and are a joy to smell after a hot day or rain, when the oils are released into the atmosphere.

NEW CULINARY PARTNERS

- Put quandongs in couscous or polenta to accompany kangaroo, beef or lamb.
- Quickly pan-fry some butterfly pork steaks with mint, quandong and chilli sauce.
- Macerate quandongs in sugar and liqueur and use them as an unusual centre for chocolates.
- Use quandong syrup over fruits, ice-cream and crepes.
- Lemon-scented myrtle is delicious in both teas and curries.

Citrus trees

Citrus are the most popular of home-grown fruits, and with good reason. A citrus is a year-round tree with bright winter fruits which are a delicious source of vitamin C. The smell of citrus in bloom is always magnificent in spring and the aromatic fragrance of its foliage in summer is welcome too. The range includes tangelos, oranges, lemons, kumquats, limes, mandarins, lemonades and the enormous fruit of the shaddock, a type of large grapefruit. Look for 'Thompson's Pink' grapefruit, which has pretty pink flesh; 'Kaffir' lime, great for Asian cooking (just add a few leaves to a green curry for authentic flavour); or the 'Australian Lime', perfect for a gin and tonic. For great picking fruit, 'Honey Murcott' mandarin has bright orange flesh that peels readily and tastes delicious. There are even Australian bush citrus.

All varieties of citrus do well in warm temperate climates. They are best planted in the warmer months of the year. The three points to consider before planting are sunlight, drainage and feeding. All citrus love heat and water, as long as it drains away. It is a good idea to plant your citrus tree on a mound, with lots of organic mulch to keep its surface roots cool and moist. Fertilise regularly.

Novelty citrus

Some citrus plants look nothing like the traditional oranges and lemons. Take *Citrus medica* var. *sarcodactylis*, more commonly known as the Buddha's hand. It's one of the most ancient citrus, and, rather than being round in shape, actually looks like it is a squid covered in peel with its strange finger-like protrusions. Inside, there is very little pulp; rather, it's the fragrant rind for which it's grown, and is commercially

CLOCKWISE FROM TOP LEFT: *Tangelos are a hybrid of mandarins and grapefruit; Nagami kumquats, also known as teardrop kumquats, have a sweet skin and sharp juice; blossoms of the 'Meyer' lemon.*

CITRUS CARE TIPS
- To produce good fruit reliably every year, all citrus trees need regular feeding and watering. You should feed your citrus in winter with a special citrus fertiliser. Make sure you water your tree first. Never apply powdered fertiliser to dry soil as it can burn the roots.
- Some citrus—limes and kumquats, in particular—grow well in pots. The best way to feed potted citrus plants is with controlled-release fertiliser because it is gentle and releases as it's needed.
- Watch for citrus leaf miner, a tiny insect that tunnels in the cuticle of the new leaf, causing deformity and hindering growth. Spray affected trees with white oil.
- Remove all grass and vegetation for a radius of at least 2 m around the tree trunk. Carefully cultivate the soil, avoiding any shallow roots, add the citrus fertiliser and mulch with cow manure, then water thoroughly.

AUSTRALIAN HERBS Native basil, parsley, peppermint, warrigal greens and lemon myrtle are just a few of the indigenous herbs available.

used to flavour specialty vodka and liqueurs, candied, and employed as an air freshener in religious ceremonies.

The Australian native finger lime (*Citrus australasica*) hangs like a small sausage in a fine foliaged bushy tree. Inside, the flesh is not segmented, but looks like tiny beads of caviar. It is used for garnishing desserts, oysters, canapés and salads. Fruits can be frozen for use later. It will grow well in the ground or in a large pot, and can reach 6 m in height. Frost-free conditions are needed and regular feeding like traditional citrus. Branches have thorns, so take care in picking.

Oranges and lemons say the bells of St Clement's

ENGLISH NURSERY RHYME

Cornelian cherry

Everybody loves cherries, but only a few have tried the cornelian cherry, which is actually a species of dogwood that flowers in late winter with golden blooms, then is followed by red cherry-like fruits in late summer and autumn. Its leaves give a beautiful autumnal display and its bark is also very attractive in winter.

VITAL STATISTICS

Botanical name: *Cornus mas.*
Family: Cornaceae.
Climate: Requires cool conditions to colour well and is frost-hardy.
Culture: Very adaptable to different soil types; it does not like drying out during summer.
Colours: Flowers yellow in late winter; red edible berries follow in late summer and autumn.
Height: Grows up to 5 m.
Planting time: Any time from pots.
Soil: Prefers acid soil and good drainage, although it does enjoy moist conditions. Prepare the soil before planting with organic matter and humus. Generous amounts of well-made compost will provide the plant with excellent nutrition.
Position: Full sun or semi-shade.
Planting spacing: About 5 m apart.
Fertiliser: Dress with compost or rotted manure each spring.
Pests/diseases: Birds love the fruit.
Propagation: Hardwood cuttings in winter.
Harvest and storage: Eat the fruit fresh or use for jam; the seeds can be dried and roasted into a coffee substitute.

Feature fruit

Vegetables

Winter conjures up images of warm pies and pasties, hot soups and baked potatoes.

The winter garden supplies all the essentials. Grow potatoes, carrots, turnips, mushrooms, cabbages, parsnips, cauliflower, artichokes, Brussels sprouts, celery, silverbeet, spinach, shallots, leeks and onions for hearty winter meals.

Winter can, however, sometimes look a little drab, so brighten up the vegie garden by selecting some vegetables that look the part as well as taste good, such as kohlrabi.

A potager

Luscious leafy vegetables such as cabbage, lettuce and spinach can be handsome plants, coming in a vast range of colours and textures. Blue-green, red or rich green cabbages, glossy green or reddish brown lettuces (try red oak leaf, radicchio or mignonette), ruby chard and purple kohlrabi are just a few that are perfect for dotting about flowers or for adding structure to formal displays. Even parsley planted en masse looks great as a border.

Many herbs and vegetables have beautiful flowers in their own right. Runner beans have scarlet flowers in profusion and climbing peas have pretty white flowers that are edible. Nasturtiums have vibrant red, orange and yellow flowers, while lavender, chamomile, chives and borage will pretty up any boring vegie patch.

It's the right time to be planting ornamental kale (*Brassica oleracea*, Acephala Group) for a spring display. Its bright pink and frilly green foliage makes it an interesting potted plant but it also brightens up a vegetable garden when it is used to make decorative patterns.

Grow kale in full sun, in a free-draining position, although you may need to occasionally dust with derris or diatomaceous earth to keep away the snails and cabbage moth caterpillars.

TOP: *Bramble fruit in winter before pruning.*

ABOVE: *A formal vegetable garden laid out in a cartwheel pattern.*

LEFT: *Box hedging is a popular choice for edging a potager.*

Mushroom kit

To make the mushroom kit, you'll need peat, lime, mushroom spore and a suitable container, such as an old wooden box lined with plastic.

Moisten the peat with a little water until it feels damp all over and releases some water when you squeeze it.

Thoroughly blend the peat and lime together. Spread the peat and lime to a depth of about 15 cm over the mushroom spore.

The fruiting bodies, or mushrooms, appear about 4 weeks later.

DID YOU KNOW? A truffle is a fungus that grows underground, under the shade of certain trees, especially pines and beech. They are normally sniffed out by specially trained dogs or pigs, and are an expensive commodity due to both their rarity and their exquisite perfume.

Mushrooms, toadstools and fungi

The fruiting bodies of fungi, mushrooms can be grown and harvested from kits throughout the year. Many types of mushroom are highly poisonous, so only experts should forage in the wild. A much safer bet is to plant your own. Fungal spore can be purchased for a whole range of varieties, with more of the exotic Asian types, such as shiitake and oyster, coming onto the market daily. All they need is a cool, dark place—such as a garden shed or cellar—in which to grow.

Forcing winter vegies and blanching

In the past, food shortages over winter led to some creative ways of manipulating plants so that they could either produce early or hold onto crops

Planting seed potatoes

Keep some seed potatoes until they sprout. This is called 'chitting' potato tubers and will give your plants a head start.

Using a spade or hoe, double dig a trench. Create a wide, flat-bottomed or V-shaped 15 cm trench with a trowel.

Cut the seed potatoes into pieces so that each piece contains an eye.

Plant the pieces of seed potato in the trench. Backfill the trench and water in.

Kale

Kale, an ancient form of cabbage, is getting lots of attention these days as people rediscover its wonderful health benefits. It's best when cooked, so make sure you lightly steam or boil it before munching it. Also known as borecole, from a Dutch word meaning 'farmer's cabbage', it is one of the most cold tolerant and interesting winter vegies. The most commonly grown cultivar is Tuscan kale ('Cavolo Nero').

VITAL STATISTICS

Botanical name: *Brassica oleracea*.
Family: Brassicaceae.
Climate: Any, but the leaves can become bitter in hot weather.
Colours: The usual colour is steel grey, but there are also red- and purple-leafed types and some with deeply divided or curly leaves.
Height: 0.5 m.
Planting time: Seed sown in autumn will be ready in winter, normally about ten weeks after sowing.
Soil: Most well-drained soils; add manure and lime a few weeks before planting time.
Position: Best in full sun.
Planting spacing: About 45 cm apart.
Fertiliser: Use a liquid fertiliser.
Pests/diseases: White cabbage moth and white butterfly.
Harvest: Pick leaves by hand from the outside in.
Propagation: Seeds sown in autumn.
Storage: The blanched leaves can be frozen.

Feature vegetable

for longer than normal. These methods include placing terracotta bell jars over rhubarb so that the plant has enough warmth to produce shoots early, or mounding up earth and straw over crops such as leeks and celery to sweeten them and protect them as the weather cools.

When this blanching technique was applied over winter to chicory in a Brussels cellar in the middle of the 19th century, the end result was 'witlof'. When upturned, the terracotta pots revealed that the roots had grown 'white leaves', which is the literal translation of the Flemish name.

PERPETUAL VEGETABLES

Most vegetables are annuals and need replacing each season. There are, however, a small number that live for many years, making them a useful addition to the garden for year-round production. Examples include perennial varieties of beans, beets and lettuce.

Better eat vegetables and fear no creditors, than eat duck and hide from them.

THE TALMUD

Index

Page numbers in *italics* refer to photographs.

Sincere thanks to my publisher Diana Hill (for her fortitude), Kay Scarlett (for her trust), Vivien Valk (for her vision) and Sue Hines (for her perseverance). Also, to Claire Grady, my first editor, for taking on a gardening title (and who learnt more about plants than I think she thought was possible), Melanie Ostell and John Mapps (for your precision) and lastly to Barbara McClenahan for seeing that the book finally reached the printing press.

Photographic credits

All photography by **Sue Stubbs** except for the following.

Alan Benson 94 t; 232 tl; 237 tl.
Joe Filshie 15 t; 33 tc; 46 b; 53 br; 66; 134 t; 137 b; 143 r; 226 bl; 235 tr; 243 t; 266 tl; 274 bl; 287 t; 288; 294 bl; 306 bl; 309 t; 331 tl; 352 b; 364; 365 1st row r, 2nd row l & r, 3rd row r, 4th row r; 383 rt, rc, rb; 406; 414 tl, tr, cl; 443 b; 251.
Denise Greig 317 b; 333 tr; 441 tr.
Ian Hofstetter 254 r.
Andrea Jones 67; 75; 113 bl; 148 b; 423 b.
Chris L Jones 137 cl; 329 tl; 339 tl, cl; 342 tc, tr.
Jason Lowe 434b.
André Martin 60 t; 137 cr.
Luis Martin 254 b.
Brian McInerney 254 tl; 255.
Natasha Milne 328; 339 br; 342 tl.
Murdoch Books Photo Library 22 lc; 24 lt; 208; 232 tr; 235 tl; 238 b; 256 b; 271 tl; 273 br; 287 bl; 329 b; 342 bl, br; 365 3d row l; 416 t.
Howard Rice 355 c.
Lorna Rose 38 b; 42; 44; 53 c; 56 t; 69; 79 t; 80 t; 81 b; 82 l; 83 l, rb; 91 t; 94 cr; 96 tl, tc; 97 tr; 108 tr; 110-2; 115 r; 122; 134 b; 144 t; 145 b; 147 t; 152; 154 lb; 158; 169 c; 170 cr; 176 bl; 184 r; 189; 192 bl; 196; 198 t; 199 tr, b; 201 tc, cl; 202; 207 t; 210 l; 220; 222 r; 223; 225 t; 228 r; 236 tl, bl, br; 247 b; 262 cl, cr, br; 267 b; 267 t, cl; 271 tr; 272; 274 t; 281 cl; 286 tl, cl, cr; 294 br; 296 tr; 306 t; 311 r; 312 t; 314 tl, cr; 316; 319; 326; 330 b; 333 tl, br; 337 t; 338 tl; 339 tr; 340 br; 354; 365 1st row l, 4th row l; 367 2nd row 1st & 3rd; 373 c; r; 380 t; 383 bl; 387 tr; 391 bl; 395 bl, br; 396 b; 399; 403 r; 404; 418 tl; 423 t; 427 t; 433 tl, tr; 437; 439-40; 441 tl, b; 443 c.
Shutterstock 178 r; 315 b.
Juliette Wade 140 b.
Mark Winwood 70 t; 293 b; 353 t.

Gardeners are an amazing, sharing folk, and my heartfelt thanks go to those who shared their gorgeous gardens. In particular, from Bundanoon, thanks to Thomas Andrew Baxter (Bromhall Rd), Cosette Morris (Fidelis St), Kerrie and Trevor Brown (Forwood Cres), and Laurel and Ron Hanes (Lorna Close), and many thanks to Sue Davidson from Bundanoon Garden Club. Thanks to Peter and Kate Gullett, for sharing their incredible property 'Lambrigg', truly one of the nations great treasures, with me, and also to Dinah Meagher, from Canberra Gardens for assisting me in finding a few of the garden locations in the ACT. Also, in the Southern Highlands, thanks to Les and Elaine Musgrave, Clearys Lane, Wildes Meadow (www.musgravebotanicalart.com) for welcoming me to their place and introducing Pat and Judy Bowley from 'Birchbeck', Wildes Meadow, who have assembled an incredible collection of cold-climate plants and generously opened their doors.

In Bathurst, the wonderful horticulturist Sarah Ryan not only allowed me to photograph at her nursery, Hillanddale (hillandalegardenandnursery.com), and garden twice, but also helped me gain access to 'Blackdown', formerly owned by Janet and Tim Storrier, and Dayle and June Bland's 'Limberlost'. Up in the Blue Mountains, thank you to John Egan of 'The Braes', Leura, for allowing us into the beautiful Paul Sorenson-designed heritage garden you care so much for. Also, to the Cottage Garden Club's Mike and Sue Perkins, of Quincy Cottage, Medlow Bath, for sharing your place.

In Sydney, Jeanne Villani (www.jeanne.villani.com) of 'Waterfall Cottage'; Edward and Nancy Shaw, Narla Rd, Bayview, both talented gardeners; and Deirdre Mowat, Albert St, Beecroft (www.igarden.com.au): many thanks for sharing your knowledge and gardens. Wendy McCready and Sue Nurse, thanks too for allowing me into you North Shore gardens.

At Victoria's Mt Macedon, sincere thanks go to the brilliant horticulturist Stephen Ryan of Dicksonia Rare Plants (www.stephenryan.com.au) and 'Tugurium', and his partner, botanical artist Craig Lidgerwood, for allowing me to stay, helping name so many rare treasures, and organising entry to 'Duneira' (www.duneira.com.au) and 'Alton', both in Mt Macedon.

In the Hunter Valley, particular thanks to Sandy and Phillip Redman, of 'Albion Farm' for sharing their slice of paradise at Woodville. My next-door neighbours, Margaret and Ken Atkins, thanks for lending me your lovely children to play at my farm and also thanks to my husband, Michael Bradford, for his support and care of our garden at 'The Top Place', Johns River.

Many nurseries also helped provide plants for the images in the book.

Thanks to Michael Dent from Aloe Aloe (www.aloe-aloe.com.au), Peter Leigh, from the *Helleborus* specialists The Post Office Farm Nursery (www.postofficefarmnursery.com.au), John Hunter from Herons Creek (for his stunning clivias), and Eden Gardens and Garden Centres (www.edengardens.com.au). Lastly, thanks to Crafty Shoes, Kendall (www.craftyshoes.com.au), for lending me the bokashi buckets.

The publisher would like to thank the following for allowing photography in their gardens: O Abbott, Huonville TAS; Mrs Dell Adam, Cheltenham NSW; 'Al-ru farm', One Tree Hill SA; Alstonville Tropical Fruit Research Station, Alstonville NSW; Arcadia Lily Ponds, Arcadia NSW; Arizona Cacti Nursery, Box Hill NSW; 'Ashcombe Maze', Shoreham VIC; Ashfield, Sandy Bay, Hobart TAS; Austral Watergardens, Cowan NSW; Australian Turf Research Institute; Australian Wildflower Producers Assoc, Morley WA; Australian Wildflower Show, Albany WA; Sarah Baker and John Spence, Leichhardt NSW; Bankstown Municipal Park, Bankstown NSW; Bay Street Nursery, Double Bay NSW; Bebeah; Virginia Berger, Canberra ACT; Trevor Birley, Pymble NSW; Gordon Boots, ACT; Bonnie Banks Iris Garden, Gravelly Beach TAS; Botanic Gardens, Coffs Harbour NSW; Brindley's Nurseries, Coffs Harbour NSW; Bringalbit, Sidonia VIC; Mr and Mrs Brooks, Castle Hill NSW; Jenny Brown, Avalon NSW; Don Burke, Southern Highlands NSW; 'Burnbank', Wagga Wagga NSW; Burrendong Arboretum, Mumbil NSW; 'Buskers End', Bowral NSW; Di Callaghan (design of pond), Sydney; Camellia Grove Nursery, St Ives NSW; Lindsay Campbell, 'The Sorn', TAS; Naomi Canning, Hobart TAS; Heather Cant, Burradoo NSW; Amanda Caulfield and Brad Jamieson, Hunters Hill NSW; F Cavenett; Ray, Myrtle and Ron Charter, members of Brisbane Organic Growers, Inc; 'Cherry Cottage', Mt Wilson NSW; Chinese Growers, Botany NSW; Ted Clapson, Camden NSW; Cloudehill, Olinda VIC; Cockington Green, Canberra ACT; John Coco, Vineyard NSW; Lynn Coddington, 'Wycombe', Armidale NSW; Common Scents Nursery, Dural NSW; Cooramilla Nursery, Brown's Creek NSW; Mr and Mrs Copes, Southern Highlands NSW; E Cossil and T Carlstrom, Frenchs Forest NSW; Barbara Cotles; Cowra Japanese Garden, Cowra NSW; K & P Cox, Thirlmere NSW; Craigie Lea, Leura NSW; Cranebrook Native Nursery, Cranebrook NSW; Dr G Cummins, Pymble NSW; 'Curry Flat', Nimmitabel NSW; Michelle Cutler and William Tocher, Tascott NSW; G & D Davey, Castlemaine VIC;

Davidson's Wholesale Nurseries, Galston NSW; Denbrovski's Garden, Ferntree TAS; Chris and Ruth Dimmock, Pennant Hills NSW; K and B Dobson, Berry NSW; Mr Duke, Clare SA; 'Dunedin', St Leonards TAS; Janet Dunlop, Orange NSW; Earthwise Permaculture Garden, Subiaco WA; Zeny Edwards, Turramurra NSW; 'Elmwood', Exeter NSW; Engalls Nursery, Epping NSW; Erina Fragrant Garden, Erina NSW; 'Eryldene', Gordon NSW; Fagan Park, Galston NSW; Johnnie Felds, Marulan NSW; Mrs Ailsa Ferguson, Killara NSW; Finches of Beechworth, VIC; Flagstaff Cottage, Bowral NSW; Flecker Botanic Garden, Cairns QLD; Floriade, Canberra ACT; 'Foxglove Spires', Tilba Tilba NSW; D D Franklin; Franklin Tea Gardens TAS; Jody and Lynton Frost-Foster, Tascott NSW; Peter Furner, Putney NSW; Fuschia Farm & Mt Tambourine Garden Centre, Eagle Heights QLD; 'Galapagos Farm', Bruny Island TAS; Garden World, Keysborough VIC; Gemas, Leura NSW; Gillespies Cottages, Yarrawonga VIC; K & M Goddard, St Ives NSW; Mr and Mrs Gray, Wahroonga NSW; Mr and Mrs Greene, Thornleigh NSW; Hahndorf Country Garden, Hahndorf SA; Julia Hancock, Erskineville NSW; Margaret Hanks; Harvey Garden, Gravelly Beach TAS; Don & Vicki Harrington, Balmain NSW; T & J Harris, Orange NSW; Mr and Mrs Heckenberg, Mosman NSW (Design: Marcia Hosking, Glebe NSW); 'Heronswood', Dromana VIC; Diana Hill and David Potter, Ashfield NSW; S Hill, Thornleigh NSW; 'Hillview', Exeter NSW; Kevin Hobbs, Sydney NSW; Merv and Olwyn Hodge, Loganview Nursery, Logan Reserve, QLD; E Hogbin, Mt Kuring-gai NSW; Jennie Holbbaum, Beecroft NSW; Howell Garden, Rosevears TAS; I and J Howie, Orange NSW; John Hunt, Kenthurst NSW; Ian Jewell, Glenreagh NSW; 'Kennerton Green', Mittagong NSW; Kewarra Beach Resort, Cairns QLD; 'Kiah Park', Jaspers Brush NSW; Graham & Doris King, Mt Hunter NSW; Kings Park and Botanic Garden, Perth WA; Kiwi Down Under Organic Fruit Farm, Bonville NSW; R & M Klaasen, Cairns QLD; Klerk's Nursery, Ingleside NSW; Kuring-gai Wildflower Garden, Kuring-gai NSW; Michael & Sharon Kvauka, Nambour QLD; Lambruk, Fryerstown VIC; Lawrences Plant Nursery, Mirboo North VIC; Colin and Linda Lawson, Putney NSW; Kirsten Lees and Mark Woodward, Riverview NSW; Levens Hall, Cumbria, United Kingdom; Mary Lidbetter, Berry NSW; 'Lindfield Park', Mt Irvine NSW; Linton Historic House; V Little, Chatswood NSW; 'Lorquon', Albury NSW; Charles and Lucy Lott, Myrtle Bank SA; Ree & Wilton Love, Tanah Merah QLD; Elizabeth Luke, Mosman NSW; Robert and Carmela Machin, Putney NSW; Angus and Alison McIntosh, Deakin ACT; Garth and Sandy McIntyre, Mt Eliza VIC; S Magoffin, Marrickville NSW; Jane Mander-Jones, Killara NSW; John Manents; C & R

Marquard Pannell, Willoughby NSW; Josie Martin; Phil Mathews, Port Douglas QLD; Menzies Nursery, Kenthurst NSW; Mercure Hotel, Heritage Park, Bowral NSW; 'Merrygarth', Mt Wilson NSW; Lorraine Meymouth, West Pennant Hills NSW; Ros Mitchell, Canberra ACT; 'Moidart', Bowral NSW; Helen Moody, St Ives NSW; Alice Morgan, Pymble NSW; Peggy & Bryce Mortlock, Cammeray NSW; 'Mossy Pines', Bermagui NSW; Mt Coot-tha Botanic Gardens, Brisbane QLD; Mt Tomah Botanic Gardens NSW; Mr & Mrs K Munro, Strathfield NSW; New Federation Daisies Colourwise Nursery; NSW Agriculture, Orange NSW; 'Nooroo', Mt Wilson; North Coast Regional Botanic Gardens, Coffs Harbour NSW; E Ommaney, St Ives NSW (Ross Garden Design); Orange Botanic Gardens, Orange NSW; Ruth Osborne, Beecroft NSW; Out of Town Nursery, Beechworth VIC; Noel Outerbridge, Alstonville NSW; Mr and Mrs Park, Canberra ACT; S Parker, Roseville NSW; Parkers Nursery, Turramurra NSW; Parterre Garden, Mosman NSW; Paula Pellegrini, Randwick NSW; Merrill and Kevin Pentergast, Ladysmith NSW; 'Peppertrees', Berry NSW; Permaculture Institute, Tyalgum NSW; 'Pinecrest', Leura NSW; 'Pinehills', Bathurst NSW; Plants of Tasmania Nursery, Ridgeway TAS; Pockets, Billinudgel NSW; J & S Porteous, Medlow Bath NSW; Qualturf, West Ryde NSW; Quatre Saisons Heritage Rose Garden, Glen Forrest WA; Judy Quigley, Stirling SA; I Rabb, Pennant Hills NSW; Radisson Royal Palms Resort, Port Douglas QLD; Rainbow Ridge Nursery, Dural NSW; Sue and Robert Read, Pennant Hills NSW; Red Cow Farm, Sutton Forest NSW; Gita and Gunther Rembel, Middle Dural NSW; Renaissance Herbs, Warnervale NSW; Retirement Village, Castle Hill NSW; J Robb, Pennant Hills NSW; Jill and Colin Roberts (ASGAP), TAS; 'Rose Cottage', Deviot TAS; Linda Ross, Kurrajong NSW; Ross Roses Nursery and Garden, Willunga SA; Janet and Lee Rowan, Newcastle NSW; Royal Botanic Gardens, Melbourne VIC; Royal Botanic Gardens, Sydney NSW; 'Runnymede', Newtown, Hobart TAS; Ruston's Roses, Renmark SA; Jan and Pirrie Sargent, Miallo QLD; Kay Scarlett, Cobbitty NSW; Dora Scott, Wahroonga NSW; Michele Shennen Garden Centre, Willoughby NSW; Maggie Shepherd, Canberra ACT; 'Shirley', Monaro NSW; Shoalmarra Quandong Farm, Tumby Bay SA; Sally and Mel Siddall, Morayfield QLD; 'Silky Oaks Lodge', Mossman QLD; Cliff Smith, Riverstone NSW; Diane Smith, Ranelagh TAS; Mrs Smith, Orange NSW; Gary Sobey, Skydancers Orchid and Butterfly Conservatorium, Harcourt VIC; Sorenson Garden; Derek and Karyn Sprod, Netherby SA; John Stowar, Mt Murray NSW; 'Strathrook', Orange NSW; Sue Swain, Bayview NSW; Swane's Nursery, Dural NSW; Sydney Wildflower Nursery, Marsden Park NSW; Mrs E Symonds, High Range NSW; Pat Taylor, Pymble NSW; The Flaxman, Croydon VIC; 'The Folly', Chewton, United Kingdom; The Garden in a Forest, Stanley VIC; The Hedgerow Roses, Tumbarumba NSW; The Lilian Fraser Garden, Pennant Hills NSW; 'The Orangerie', Stirling SA; The Rose Garden, Watervale SA; The Wildflower Farm, Somersby NSW; 'Thirty-Eight', Leura NSW; Douglas Thompson, Killara NSW; Anne Thomson Garden Advisory Service, St Ives NSW; D & B Thomson, Barkers Creek VIC; Murray Thomson, Woollahra NSW; Pam & Ross Thyer, Sydney NSW; 'Tintagel', Mittagong NSW; Tomar House, Rosevears TAS; A & R Tonkin, Orange NSW; Merv & Wendy Trimper, Myrtle Beach SA; Tropical Fruit World, Duranbah NSW; 'Vireya Vale', Mt Pleasant NSW; Jan Waddington, Kergunyah VIC; Wagga Wagga Botanic Gardens, Wagga Wagga NSW; West Brook, Mt Hunter NSW; B & R Wilkinson, Kingston TAS; 'Willows End', Killara NSW; Sandra Wilson, Epping NSW; 'Winterwood', Mt Tomah NSW; Wollongong Botanic Gardens, Wollongong, NSW; Woodlyn Nurseries, Five Ways VIC; 'Woodridge', Berrima NSW; Yabba Yabba, Blackheath NSW; S Yates, Erskineville NSW; Yellowrock Nursery, Yellowrock NSW; Yengo, Mt Wilson NSW.

Published in 2014 by Murdoch Books, an imprint of Allen & Unwin

Murdoch Books Australia
83 Alexander Street
Crows Nest NSW 2065
Phone: +61 (0)2 8425 0100
Fax: +61 (0)2 9906 2218
www.murdochbooks.com.au
info@murdochbooks.com.au

Murdoch Books UK
Erico House, 6th Floor
93-99 Upper Richmond Road
Putney, London SW15 2TG
Phone: +44 (0) 20 8785 5995
Fax: +44 (0) 20 8785 5985
www.murdochbooks.co.uk
info@murdochbooks.co.uk

For Corporate Orders & Custom Publishing contact Noel Hammond,
National Business Development Manager Murdoch Books Australia

Publisher: Diana Hill
Designers: Vivien Valk and Avril Makula
Cover Design: Vivien Valk
Project Editor: John Mapps
Editor: Melanie Ostell
Editorial Managers: Claire Grady and Barbara McClenahan
Production Manager: Mary Bjelobrk

A cataloguing-in-publication entry is available from the catalogue of the National Library of Australia
at www.nla.gov.au.

A catalogue record for this book is available from the British Library.

Colour reproduction by Splitting Image Colour Studio Pty Ltd, Clayton, Victoria

Printed by 1010 Printing International Limited, China